Standards-Based AI Innovation for the Learning Ecosystem

Frederic Andres
https://orcid.org/0000-0002-5003-7579
National Insitute of Informatics, Japan

Teeradaj Racharak
https://orcid.org/0000-0002-8823-2361
Japan Advanced Institute of Science and Technology, Japan

Gerlinde Weger
https://orcid.org/0000-0002-5126-2938
In-Sight Consulting, Canada

Andreas Pester
https://orcid.org/0000-0001-7278-7349
The British University in Egypt, Egypt

Chandrasekhar Anantaram
Indraprastha Institute of Information Technology, India

IGI Global
Scientific Publishing
Publishing Tomorrow's Research Today

Vice President of Editorial	Melissa Wagner
Director of Acquisitions	Mikaela Felty
Director of Book Development	Jocelynn Hessler
Production Manager	Mike Brehm
Cover Design	Jose Rosado

Published in the United States of America by
IGI Global Scientific Publishing
701 East Chocolate Avenue
Hershey, PA, 17033, USA
Tel: 717-533-8845 | Fax: 717-533-7115
Website: https://www.igi-global.com E-mail: cust@igi-global.com

Library of Congress Cataloging-in-Publication Data

Names: Andres, Frederic, 1962- editor
Title: Standards-based AI innovation for the learning ecosystem / [edited by] Frederic Andres, Teeradaj Racharak, Gerlinde Weger, Andreas Pester, Chandrasekhar Anantaram.
Description: Hershey, PA : IGI Global Scientific Publishing, [2026] | Includes bibliographical references and index. | Summary: "This book explores the transformative potential of standards in shaping AI-driven education and training"-- Provided by publisher.
Identifiers: LCCN 2025031504 (print) | LCCN 2025031505 (ebook) | ISBN 9798337322353 hardcover | ISBN 9798337322360 paperback | ISBN 9798337322377 ebook
Subjects: LCSH: Artificial intelligence--Educational applications | Educational technology--Standards
Classification: LCC LB1028.43 .S726 2026 (print) | LCC LB1028.43 (ebook)
LC record available at https://lccn.loc.gov/2025031504
LC ebook record available at https://lccn.loc.gov/2025031505

British Cataloguing in Publication Data
A Cataloguing in Publication record for this book is available from the British Library.

Table of Contents

Detailed Table of Contents

approaches focused on Developmental Capacity as key criteria of e-learning efficiency. Co-creation of e-courses involves multi-agent/sector/disciplinary interaction. Content-Structure Model allows managing, measuring and programming complex process of students cognitive and personality development in the very process of mastering academic subjects. It is described content-structure patterns of discipline matrix, student profile, e-course-unit-task structures, virtual laboratories and virtual reality laboratories new application.

Artificial Intelligence (AI) is changing the evaluation method to be more precise, versatile, and individualised in education. Regularized structures confirm that data accumulation, interpretation, and utilization utilizing AI in particular is moral, unopaque, and trustworthy as it becomes a part of education. Such frameworks, directed by such bodies as IEEE, ISO, and UNESCO, are aimed at equality, inclusiveness, and privacy. The AI-supported formative and summative assessment such as adaptive testing or predictive analytics identify the gaps in learning using real-time feedback to allow utilizing the knowledge of both students and teachers continuously. Learning media such as Coursera and Khan Academy are also dynamic and customized with the introduction of AI. These increasing concerns about ethical considerations of use, accessibility and interoperability of data to systems serves to keep AI systems up-to-date with educational aims, and provide fair and equitable AI-based assessment of all learners.

This chapter presents a pilot case study exploring the ethical, cultural, and pedagogical implications of AI integration in technical education, conducted at the IT department of TGM, a leading secondary vocational school in Vienna. Recognizing that AI in education constitutes not merely a technological shift but a broader socio-cultural transformation, the study applied a mixed-methods diagnostic approach, which was designed to capture complex social and ethical dimensions beyond technical literacy. Seven thematic patterns emerged from the data, informing pedagogical responses to promote ethical awareness and responsible AI use. Rigorous scientific oversight ensured a comprehensive and ethically grounded analysis. Conducted over a defined period in 2025, the project delivers the first comprehensive AI mindset and ethics diagnostic scan in Austrian vocational education and training (VET), offering a scalable framework for ethical AI integration in learning environments.

As education is influenced by AI, learners are required to conform to their directive. For the majority of learners with normal automated nervous systems, this is a great advantage because these systems are trained predominately for them. But the learners who are outliners and are neurodiverse? Neurodiversity comprises up to 30% of the population. Individuals with ADHD, Autism, Dyslexia, hyper-mobility and PTSS are often challenged with prescriptive systems. The IEEE has two tools to ensure neural diverse learners are considered: CertifAIEd Algorithmic Bias Criteria and the standard Algorithmic Bias Consideration considers system bias to maximize productive bias, intentionally. By acknowledging AI systems require specific biases, they can be calibrated to consider neural diverse stakeholders thus AI Learning systems can maximize their benefits to both normal neural and diverse neural stakeholders. This chapter will review the CertifAIEd Algorithmic Bias Criteria and the standard Algorithmic Bias Consideration to demonstrate how neurodiverse learners can be considered.

Artificial Intelligence (AI) is transforming education through adaptive platforms, intelligent tutoring, predictive analytics, and generative feedback, enabling personalization at scale. While these tools can enhance engagement, retention, and teaching efficiency, they also raise ethical, technical, and social concerns, including bias, privacy, and learner autonomy. This chapter explores how technical, ethical,

Foreword

In so many communities all over the world, suddenly, it seems, everyone is talking about Artificial Intelligence (AI). In most domains of human activity, AI has emerged very quickly as a systems disruptor while enabling new productivity not previously imagined. Common to these discussions are deeply human concerns with issues that span discerning fact from fiction, fake from authentic, real from unreal. A new digital divide is emerging between those fearing dystopian futures and those imagining techno-utopias. Issues of anxiety, mental health, and wellbeing; concerns for privacy and autonomy. Who and what can we trust? Together these issues and many more communicate a clear signal that AI is no longer just a sub-field of Computer Science. Technically, of course, it is. Or perhaps not? The rendering and deployment of intelligence into our social and economic infrastructures has consequences for public policy and for cross-disciplinary inquiry. The field of AI in Education is situated at this nexus, producing so many new possibilities. But also causing some pause – to reconcile with Education's core concern, the cultivation of human agency. What is the scope of this agency when we are outsourcing parts of it to the machine?

So how might a book about standards-based AI innovation add perspective or reassurance? For educators, *standards* are often synonymous with measurement and grading, stimulating thinking about achievement, rank, and quality. It is also a term that many educators often push back against. Standards-based approaches such as standardised testing and benchmarking are perceived as narrowing the curriculum, as limiting creativity and professional autonomy, as colliding with student-centric rhetoric advocating 'one size fits all', and introducing unnecessary pressure to the classroom. This book sits differently on the shelf because within it standards are framed as essential components to the systems and infrastructures that support everything we do. Such standards are technically precise, fit for purpose, and represent consensus of the stakeholders who put their attention to formulating them.

By emphasising the role of standards, this book has been conceived with a bigger picture in mind. By situating learning within an evolving ecosystem of history, of society and culture, of educational practices and evolving sensibilities, of technological capability, we can access a mix of perspectives that must be addressed. 'Safe, responsible, and ethical' has new resonance for the digital environment into the future. Read on and participate in the conversations that will follow.

Jon Mason
Charles Darwin University, Australia

Preface

Artificial Intelligence (AI) in the educational landscape is an active force reshaping how we learn, teach, and assess knowledge. Adaptive platforms, generative feedback systems, and predictive analytics now make it possible to personalize learning at a scale once unimaginable. At the same time, these advances bring new challenges involving questions of ethics, fairness, inclusivity, and the standards needed to guide responsible innovation.

Standards-Based AI Innovation for the Learning Ecosystem explores these opportunities and challenges through a comprehensive, multi-perspective lens. The central theme of this book is that well-formulated standards (such as ISO or IEEE standards) play a very crucial role in helping to build and roll out viable and trustworthy AI-powered educational systems. Such standards help formulate clear technical specifications and also give guiding principles that connect technology with educational values, cultural contexts, and human dignity. Without clear standards, AI systems risk amplifying inequities, embedding bias, or eroding trust. By following well-formulated standards the educational AI systems can expand access, ensure transparency, and create resilient learning ecosystems.

This book brings together scholars, practitioners, and innovators to address five key areas:

- Foundations of AI in Education – frameworks for ethical and pedagogical alignment.
- Ethics, Equity, and Human Factors – ensuring fair treatment for diverse learners, including neurodiverse populations.
- Personalized Learning Pathways – how AI can adapt to individual interests and needs while maintaining accountability.
- AI Literacy and Practical Applications – equipping educators and learners to work responsibly with AI-generated content.
- Future Directions – outlining international collaboration, policy priorities, and benchmarks for inclusive AI adoption.

This book is a forward-looking resource for educators, policymakers, researchers, and technology developers. Each chapter not only analyzes current practices but also points toward actionable strategies for shaping an AI-enabled future in education.

By framing innovation within a standards-based approach, this book calls for a global conversation on how we design AI for education—one that balances innovation with responsibility, creativity with fairness, and technology with human values. Our hope is that this first volume will serve as both a reference and an inspiration for those committed to building trustworthy, inclusive, and future-ready learning ecosystems.

Acknowledgment

We gratefully acknowledge Dr. Ghada Farouk Naiem Elsayed, Assistant Professor at the British University in Egypt (BUE), and Dr. Rosa María Gómez de Regil, Centre National de Documentation Pédagogique (CNDP, France) and Convenor of ISO/IEC JTC1/SC36/WG3 – Learner Information, for their thoughtful and constructive reviews, which significantly strengthened this chapter.

We also extend our sincere appreciation to Prof. Jon Mason, Associate Professor in Education in the Faculty of Arts & Society at Charles Darwin University (CDU), whose foreword and intellectual guidance helped inspire and shape the conceptual foundations of this book.

Chapter 1
Establishing the Cornerstones of Ethical AI in Education

Binod Kumar
https://orcid.org/0009-0002-9721-1367
Radha Govind University, India

Oindrilla Ghosh
https://orcid.org/0000-0001-9609-0781
Christ University, Bangalore, India

ABSTRACT

Establishing the cornerstones of ethical AI in education is essential for fostering an inclusive and equitable learning environment. Ethical AI can enhance personalization, improve access to resources, and empower educators with data-driven insights. Key principles include transparency, accountability, fairness, and privacy. Transparency ensures that AI algorithms are understandable and their decisions are explainable, allowing educators and students to trust the technology. Accountability involves clear guidelines on who is responsible for AI's actions and decisions. Fairness seeks to prevent biases that can adversely affect marginalized groups, ensuring equal opportunities for all students. Privacy is crucial to protect sensitive data and safeguard students' rights. Educators, policymakers, and technologists must collaborate to establish frameworks that prioritize these ethical foundations, promoting responsible AI integration. By embedding these cornerstones into the educational system, we can harness AI's potential while safeguarding the rights and dignity of all learners.

DOI: 10.4018/979-8-3373-2235-3.ch001

INTRODUCTION

The advent of Artificial Intelligence (AI) in education has ushered in transformative possibilities, redefining how teaching and learning processes are approached (Tinto, 2022). As educational institutions increasingly rely on AI technologies from adaptive learning systems and chatbots that provide academic support to tools that assess student performance ethical considerations have become paramount (Bhagat & Kim, 2020). Establishing the cornerstones of ethical AI in education is critical to ensure that these technologies serve all learners equitably, foster inclusive learning environments, and uphold the integrity of educational values (Barnard, 1997).

Ethical AI refers to the development and implementation of artificial intelligence systems that align with moral principles and social norms (Schwartz, 2020). In the context of education, ethical AI must prioritize transparency, accountability, fairness, and inclusivity. To achieve these principles, stakeholders including educators, policymakers, technologists, and students must engage in an ongoing dialogue about the implications and potential pitfalls of AI in educational settings. This involves not only acknowledging the benefits of AI technologies but also critically examining their limitations, potential biases, and the ethical dilemmas they may present.

The urgency of establishing ethical guidelines is underscored by various reports highlighting the risks associated with the misuse of AI in education (Bernard et al., 2009). These risks include privacy concerns related to data collection, algorithmic bias that can exacerbate existing inequalities, and the potential for AI to reinforce harmful stereotypes or misinform students (Martin & Bolliger, 2018). By focusing on the cornerstones of ethical AI, educators and technology developers can collaborate to create systems that enhance learning experiences while mitigating adverse outcomes (Nguyen et al., 2021).

Moreover, the establishment of ethical AI in education is not merely a matter of regulatory compliance; it serves a broader purpose of cultivating critical thinking and moral reasoning among students. As learners engage with AI-driven tools, they must be equipped to navigate the complexities of these technologies and understand the ethical dimensions inherent in AI systems (Fredricks et al., 2004). By integrating ethical considerations into AI development, educators can foster a generation of students who are not only tech-savvy but also socially responsible and ethically minded (Kuh, 2001).

The need for collaborative frameworks that emphasize responsible AI practices in education cannot be overstated (Dixson, 2015). Because AI technologies are dynamic and rapidly evolving, ongoing monitoring and assessment are crucial to ensure that ethical guidelines remain relevant and effective (Henrie et al., 2015). This entails fostering partnerships between educators, ethicists, and technologists, ensuring that diverse perspectives are included in the development of AI applications (Castelli &

Sarvary, 2021). Ultimately, the goal is to create an educational ecosystem where AI tools are used to empower, educate, and inspire students, rather than to alienate or disenfranchise them (Gemmel et al., 2020). By laying the groundwork for ethical AI, we can harness the power of technology to promote equitable access to quality education, thus shaping a brighter future for learners everywhere (Schwenck & Pryor, 2021).

HISTORICAL EVOLUTION

The historical evolution of AI in education traces back several decades, culminating in the contemporary landscape where ethical considerations are increasingly at the forefront (Bluemink & Järvelä, 2004). The journey began in the mid-20th century, around the 1950s, when scholars and computer scientists began to explore the possibilities of using machines for problem-solving and decision-making. Early examples included simple tutoring systems and programmed instruction that utilized rule-based methods to deliver educational content (Giesbers et al., 2013). Though rudimentary, these early efforts laid the groundwork for the later development of more sophisticated AI applications (Gemmel et al., 2020).

By the 1980s and 1990s, the field witnessed significant advancements with the emergence of cognitive tutors and intelligent tutoring systems, which incorporated elements of AI to adapt to individual learner needs (Jamieson, 2020). These systems aimed to provide personalized learning experiences, akin to one-on-one tutoring, and demonstrated promising results in improving student outcomes (Perets et al., 2020). However, this era also marked the first instances where concerns regarding data privacy and algorithmic bias began to surface, albeit in a nascent form (Singhal, 2020).

The late 1990s into the early 2000s saw the rise of the Internet and digital technology, accelerating the integration of AI into educational platforms (Van Heuvelen et al., 2020). With the advent of online learning management systems (LMS) and the explosion of educational content available online, the emphasis shifted toward leveraging AI for data-driven decision-making and analysis (Bhagat & Kim, 2020). However, this period also raised ethical questions about access to technology, as disparities in availability reflected broader societal inequalities (Swan & Ice, 2010). The lack of equitable access to digital tools often hampered efforts to democratize education through AI.

In the 2010s, with the rapid advancements in machine learning and natural language processing, AI technologies became more prevalent in everyday educational contexts (Bhagat & Kim, 2020). Comments-based systems like Google Classroom and adaptive learning platforms emerged, allowing for nuanced tracking of student progress and tailoring education to individual needs (Schwartz, 2020). However, ethical dilemmas regarding fairness and transparency emerged as algorithms began to influence educational pathways for countless students (Barnard, 1997). These concerns spurred the first discussions on the need for ethical frameworks surrounding the development and deployment of AI in educational settings.

The urgency of addressing these ethical concerns became undeniable, leading to the establishment of various organizations and initiatives dedicated to promoting ethical standards in AI. For instance, in 2019, the EU's High-Level Expert Group on Artificial Intelligence proposed ethical guidelines, emphasizing a human-centric approach to AI (Kumar et al., 2021). Similarly, academic institutions began incorporating discussions of AI ethics into their curricula, recognizing the importance of preparing future educators and technologists to navigate the complexities of AI responsibly (Martin & Bolliger, 2018).

As we move into the 2020s and beyond, the historical evolution of AI in education is characterized by a growing awareness of the profound ethical implications that accompany these technologies (Flener-Lovitt et al., 2020). The dialogue around ethical AI is now more nuanced and inclusive, encompassing a broader array of perspectives (Moore, 1989). It invites stakeholders from various disciplines education, technology, ethics, and policy to collaboratively establish guidelines that prioritize the welfare of learners (Ertl et al., 2006). This historical journey emphasizes that while AI holds significant potential for educational transformation, ensuring its ethical deployment remains an ongoing challenge demanding collective action and vigilance (Woodbury et al., 2022).

THEORETICAL FRAMEWORKS

The integration of artificial intelligence (AI) in education holds immense promise for enhancing learning experiences, personalizing instruction, and automating administrative tasks (Wise et al., 2012). However, the rapid adoption of AI technologies also raises significant ethical concerns that necessitate a robust framework for their responsible deployment in educational settings (Vonderwell & Zachariah, 2005). To effectively navigate these challenges, several theoretical frameworks can be employed, each serving to emphasize different aspects of ethical AI implementation (Myers et al., 2012).

Utilitarianism: This ethical theory, centered around the greatest happiness principle, evaluates actions based on their outcomes. In the context of AI in education, utilitarianism would advocate for AI applications that maximize the overall benefit to students and educators while minimizing harm (Chandler, 2016). For instance, an AI system designed to provide personalized learning paths could be assessed by examining its impact on student engagement and performance (Fung & Lam, 2020). However, utilitarian considerations must be balanced with potential negative repercussions, such as data privacy concerns or exacerbation of existing inequities (Moog & Spencer, 2008).

Deontological Ethics: Opposed to purely outcome-based reasoning, deontological ethics focuses on the morality of actions themselves, advocating for adherence to rules and principles (Woodbury et al., 2022). In the realm of educational AI, this framework emphasizes the importance of transparency, accountability, and consent in AI deployment. Educational institutions must establish guidelines that ensure AI systems are designed and operated with the respect for individual rights, such as the right to privacy and agency (Bernard et al., 2009). Implementing deontological principles can help safeguard against biases inherent in AI algorithms, thus promoting fair treatment for all students (Gillies, 2008).

Social Justice Framework: Addressing systemic inequalities is paramount in education, and employing a social justice framework ensures that AI technologies promote equity and inclusion (Bernard et al., 2004). This framework encourages stakeholders to critically evaluate who benefits from educational AI and who may be marginalized (Reschly & Christenson, 2022). For instance, when schools adopt AI-driven tools for assessment or resource allocation, it is essential to assess their impact on underrepresented or disadvantaged student groups (Garrison et al., 1999). Ensuring equitable access to AI resources can enhance educational outcomes and foster a more inclusive environment for learning (Richardson et al., 2012).

Virtue Ethics: This framework emphasizes the character and intentions of those deploying technology rather than focusing solely on rules or outcomes (Fiock, 2020). In education, fostering an ethical culture among educators, administrators, and AI developers can shape the development and use of AI systems (Eberlein et al., 2008). By encouraging virtues such as responsibility, empathy, and integrity, educational institutions can cultivate a mindset that values ethical considerations and prioritizes the well-being of all stakeholders involved (Tanner, 2013).

IMPACT OF ESTABLISHING ETHICAL CORNERSTONES

Implementing these theoretical frameworks in educational AI can yield several positive impacts (Van Heuvelen et al., 2020). First, ethical AI practices can foster trust between students, educators, and technology providers, creating an environment where AI is embraced as a supportive tool rather than a feared replacement (P. L. Smith & Dillon, 2009). Second, aligning AI applications with ethical guidelines can enhance the quality and fairness of educational experiences, ensuring that all students receive equitable opportunities for success (Dutton et al., 2019).

Moreover, promoting ethical AI can spur innovation, as institutions that prioritize responsible AI practices may attract partnerships with researchers and technology companies committed to social responsibility (Castelli & Sarvary, 2021). Ultimately, establishing ethical cornerstones in AI-driven education can mitigate risks while maximizing the transformative potential of technology for learning (Gherhe et al., 2021).

Thus, the journey towards ethical AI in education necessitates a comprehensive understanding of various theoretical frameworks and their implications (Van Dusen & Nissen, 2020). By applying these frameworks, educational institutions can navigate the complexities of technology integration, ensuring that AI serves as a catalyst for positive change rather than a source of division or harm (Li et al., 2022). The collective effort to establish ethical guidelines will not only enhance the learning experience but also pave the way for a more just and equitable educational landscape (Rodriguez et al., 2020).

USE OF AI AND ML

Artificial Intelligence (AI) and Machine Learning (ML) are increasingly playing pivotal roles in transforming educational landscapes. They offer versatile solutions that are capable of personalizing learning experiences while raising critical ethical considerations that must be addressed to ensure fairness and equity (Alzen et al., 2018).

AI and ML algorithms are being integrated into educational tools for tasks such as student assessment, personalized tutoring, and learning analytics. By analyzing vast amounts of data, these technologies can identify student learning patterns, predict performance outcomes, and suggest tailored educational resources (Moog & Spencer, 2008). For instance, platforms like intelligent tutoring systems adapt the complexity of their content based on the learner's performance, ensuring that material is neither too challenging nor too simplistic (Bernard et al., 2004).

However, the capabilities of AI and ML raise ethical dilemmas that educators, policymakers, and technology developers must navigate (Eberlein et al., 2008). One significant concern is data privacy. The efficacy of AI and ML relies on collecting and analyzing data about students, including their behaviors, performance, and even personal information (Fredricks et al., 2004). Educational institutions must implement robust data governance frameworks to protect students' privacy and comply with regulations like the Family Educational Rights and Privacy Act (FERPA) in the U.S. (Dixson, 2015). Ensuring that students' data is anonymized and securely stored is a foundational element in establishing ethical AI practices (Kuh, 2001).

Moreover, biases in algorithms pose considerable risks (Henrie et al., 2015). If the algorithms are trained on datasets that are not representative of diverse populations, they may inadvertently reinforce existing inequalities (Nguyen et al., 2021). For example, biased AI models could result in disproportionate disciplinary actions against certain student demographics or skew the academic support provided to particular groups. To mitigate this risk, educational institutions must prioritize diversity in training datasets and continually assess AI models for bias throughout their lifecycle (Bluemink & Järvelä, 2004).

Stakeholder collaboration also plays a crucial role in fostering ethical AI in education (Castelli & Sarvary, 2021). Engaging educators, parents, students, and technology developers in discussions about the impact of AI can lead to a more rounded understanding of its implications (Giesbers et al., 2013). Establishing ethical guidelines and best practices in development phases will foster greater transparency and trust (Wenzel, 2020). Additionally, incorporating ethics modules within the curriculum can raise awareness among students about the implications of AI and teach them to engage critically with technology (Schwenck & Pryor, 2021).

Lastly, fostering an ethical AI environment in education requires ongoing evaluation and adaptation (Bhagat & Kim, 2020). As technologies evolve, so will the ethical challenges connected to them (Schwartz, 2020). Continuous monitoring and assessment of AI tools will ensure that they adapt to changing societal norms and legal frameworks (Kumar et al., 2021). These evolving practices should also reflect cultural sensitivities and inclusiveness to cater to a diverse student population (Wester et al., 2021).

MORAL USE OF AI, BALANCING TECHNOLOGY AND THOUGHT

The moral use of artificial intelligence (AI) is a topic of increasing significance in an era where technology permeates every aspect of life (Ghosh & Kumar, 2025). While AI offers remarkable potential to enhance education, streamline processes, and solve complex problems, it is critical to address the ethical implications of its use, especially concerning the intellectual development of learners (Raker et al., 2021). As AI tools become readily available, there is a pressing need to ensure that their application promotes critical thinking, creativity, and independent problem-solving rather than replacing these essential cognitive skills with pre-packaged answers (Nguyen et al., 2021).

One of the most significant risks posed by the reliance on AI in educational contexts is the potential for learners to substitute their own thinking with AI-generated solutions (Schwenck & Pryor, 2021). When students consistently seek AI assistance for answers, they may inadvertently hinder their intellectual growth (Wester et al., 2021). The learning process involves grappling with challenges, making mistakes, and discovering solutions through inquiry and reflection (Fulfer et al., 2020). AI, particularly when it offers instant answers, can create an illusion of understanding, leading learners to misinterpret surface-level knowledge as deep comprehension (Fung & Lam, 2020).

Therefore, educators must actively block this unintended use of AI by integrating practices that foster critical engagement with technology (Gemmel et al., 2020). One essential strategy is to encourage students to compare their own solutions with those suggested by AI (Jamieson, 2020). This approach compels learners to remain intellectually engaged, prompting them to analyze differences, question the reasoning behind AI-generated answers, and ultimately refine their thought processes (Perets et al., 2020). Rather than viewing AI as a crutch, students should be taught to use it as a tool for critical reflection and enhancement of their cognitive abilities (Van Heuvelen et al., 2020).

To accomplish this, educational institutions can embed AI literacy into curricula, allowing learners to understand not only how to use AI tools effectively but also the ethical considerations surrounding their use (Wenzel, 2020). This includes discussions around algorithmic biases, the limitations of AI, and the importance of maintaining one's intellectual autonomy (Reiserer et al., 2023). Such discussions should emphasize that while AI can be a powerful ally in problem-solving, it should not supplant the critical thinking and creativity that are hallmarks of strong intellectual development (Tinto, 2022).

Moreover, it is crucial to cultivate an environment where questioning and skepticism are encouraged (Schwenck & Pryor, 2021). Students should feel empowered to critique AI outputs, fostering a mindset where they evaluate, improve, and creatively build upon AI-generated ideas (Casey et al., 2023). This not only helps to mitigate the risk of over-reliance on AI but also prepares learners to navigate a future where AI is increasingly prevalent in decision-making processes across various fields (Alzen et al., 2018).

Incorporating project-based learning and critical thinking exercises that specifically highlight the juxtaposition of human and AI problem-solving can also serve as effective educational strategies (Rodriguez et al., 2020). By engaging students in collaborative projects that require human ingenuity complemented by AI's analytical capabilities, educators can help learners appreciate the unique contributions of both human and machine intellects (Gherhe et al., 2021).

ROLE OF AR, VR, AND MR

Augmented Reality (AR), Virtual Reality (VR), and Mixed Reality (MR) represent innovative avenues for enhancing the immersive educational experience (Tinto, 2022). As these technologies reshape how education is delivered and experienced, they also present unique ethical challenges that must be addressed in conjunction with AI principles (Nguyen et al., 2021). The intersection of AR, VR, and MR with ethics in AI signifies a holistic approach to developing educational technologies that prioritize inclusivity, safety, and fairness (Castelli & Sarvary, 2021).

One of the key benefits of AR, VR, and MR in education is their ability to create experiential learning environments, fostering deeper engagement and understanding among students (Schwenck & Pryor, 2021). For instance, students can explore historical sites through VR or engage in science experiments virtually using AR applications (Wester et al., 2021), providing a hands-on approach to learning that is often not feasible within the constraints of traditional classrooms (Fulfer et al., 2020). However, ensuring that these technologies are accessible to all learners is a vital aspect of ethical education (Fung & Lam, 2020). This includes consideration for students with disabilities, language barriers, and varying socio-economic backgrounds (Gemmel et al., 2020).

The design of AR and VR experiences must prioritize inclusivity, actively avoiding biases in content creation (Jamieson, 2020). For instance, developers should ensure that virtual environments reflect diverse cultures, perspectives, and backgrounds, promoting a sense of belonging and respect for all learners (Perets et al., 2020). If not carefully managed, these experiences could reinforce stereotypes and the marginalization of certain groups (Van Heuvelen et al., 2020).

Data privacy and security are also critical elements (Casey et al., 2023). Both AR and VR applications can track student interactions, movements, and engagement levels, gathering extensive data that may include sensitive information (Shockley et al., 2021). Educational institutions must implement safeguards to protect this data, ensuring compliance with privacy laws and regulations. Transparent data handling practices can build trust with students and parents, illustrating a commitment to ethical standards.

Moreover, the potential for misuse of VR and AR technology raises ethical considerations as well. Inappropriate content or virtual experiences can negatively impact student learning and wellbeing (Tharayil et al., 2018). Educational institutions should establish clear guidelines for acceptable content, incorporating ethical considerations into curriculum development and content curation (Casey et al., 2023).

Furthermore, incorporating ethical principles into the development of AR and VR applications is crucial (Castelli & Sarvary, 2021). By involving educators, students, and ethicists in the design process, developers can ensure that their technologies serve broader educational goals and do not exploit or manipulate learners (Gherhe et al., 2021). This collaborative approach can lead to the establishment of ethical standards for the creation and implementation of these technologies in schools (Bowen & Cooper, 2022).

Finally, an important role for educational institutions is to promote digital literacy and critical thinking skills among students when engaging with AR, VR, and MR (Canning et al., 2019). Educating students about the implications of these technologies encourages them to navigate the complex landscape of digital media responsibly (Bhagat & Kim, 2020). Preparing students to critically analyze virtual experiences not only enhances their understanding of the content but also fosters a more ethically-minded generation that can engage responsibly with emerging technologies (Schwartz, 2020).

CHALLENGES

The integration of Artificial Intelligence (AI) in education presents numerous opportunities for enhancing learning outcomes, personalizing student experiences, and improving administrative efficiencies (Kumar et al., 2021). However, the establishment of ethical AI practices also faces a myriad of challenges that need to be addressed to ensure that technological advancements are equitable, responsible, and transparent (Barnard, 1997).

One of the primary challenges is data privacy and security. Educational institutions collect vast amounts of sensitive information, including personal data of students and staff. AI systems often rely on this data to function effectively, but the risk of data breaches raises significant ethical concerns. Entities involved in educating students must ensure that data is collected, stored, and processed with the utmost care (Moore, 1989), adhering to compliance regulations like the Family Educational Rights and Privacy Act (FERPA) in the U.S. Additionally, students may not fully understand the implications of their data usage, leading to a lack of informed consent.

Another major challenge is bias in AI algorithms (Martin & Bolliger, 2018). AI systems are only as good as the data they are trained on (Appleton et al., 2008). If historical data reflects social inequalities or biases whether related to race, gender, socioeconomic status, or other factors these biases can be perpetuated or even amplified by AI systems (DeMonbrun et al., 2017). For instance, an AI algorithm used for personalized learning may inadvertently disadvantage students from certain backgrounds if the training data is not representative (Furlong & Christenson, 2008). This necessitates comprehensive audits of training datasets and algorithms to identify and rectify biases, which is a resource-intensive and ongoing effort.

Equitability also poses a challenge. Not all educational institutions have equal access to advanced AI technologies, which can exacerbate existing disparities (Flener-Lovitt et al., 2020). While wealthy institutions may leverage AI to create tailored learning experiences for their students, underfunded schools may struggle to implement even basic technological resources (Raker et al., 2021). This digital divide could potentially widen educational inequities, necessitating policies and funding initiatives aimed at ensuring all students benefit from AI's capabilities (Van Heuvelen et al., 2020).

Finally, there lies a challenge in teacher training and professional development (Reschly & Christenson, 2022). For AI to be effectively integrated into educational practices, educators must be adequately prepared to utilize these technologies ethically and effectively (Dutton et al., 2019). There is a need for comprehensive training programs that not only cover the technical aspects of AI but also emphasize its ethical dimensions (Castelli & Sarvary, 2021). Educators must be empowered to critically assess AI tools to ensure they align with pedagogical goals and ethical standards (Gherhe et al., 2021).

GOVERNANCE

Governance is a crucial component in establishing ethical AI in education, as it provides the frameworks, policies, and guidelines necessary for responsible implementation (Van Dusen & Nissen, 2020). To navigate the complexities of integrating AI in educational settings, a robust governance structure is needed (Rodriguez et al., 2020), involving various stakeholders including educators, administrators, policymakers, technology developers, and students themselves (Li et al., 2022).

First and foremost, creating clear ethical guidelines is fundamental (Woodbury et al., 2022). Educational institutions must establish a set of principles governing AI use that prioritize students' rights, data privacy, and equity (Fung & Lam, 2020). This often involves developing frameworks that align with existing laws and regulations, such as FERPA or the General Data Protection Regulation (GDPR) (Flener-Lovitt et al., 2020). By involving multiple stakeholders in this process, educational institutions can ensure that diverse perspectives are considered, enhancing the guidelines' acceptance and relevance (Singhal, 2020).

Another key aspect of governance is establishing accountability mechanisms (Jayasundara et al., 2022). Educational institutions need clear policies about who is responsible for the outcomes of AI systems whether the AI developers, educators, or school administrators (Gherhe et al., 2021). This accountability should not only apply to the technology used but also extend to the pedagogy and graduate outcomes influenced by AI (Shockley et al., 2021). In cases where biases or harmful outcomes occur, protocols should detail how to address these issues and ensure reparative measures are in place (Casey et al., 2023).

Engagement with technology developers and vendors is equally important in governance (Castelli & Sarvary, 2021). Institutions must choose AI tools from providers committed to ethical practices, which means conducting rigorous evaluations of these technologies and their implications for educational equity (Canning et al., 2019. This can be facilitated through partnerships aimed at mutual learning and improvement, where educational institutions collaborate (Bowen & Cooper, 2022) with tech companies to ensure that products are designed with ethical considerations at their core (Bhagat & Kim, 2020).

Additionally, ongoing professional development is essential for educators (Barnard, 1997). Governance should include investments in training programs focused on ethics in AI technology, equipping teachers with the skills to critically assess the tools they use in classrooms (Bhagat & Kim, 2020). Educators must understand both the capabilities and the potential consequences of AI, enabling them to make informed choices about how these tools fit into their educational practices (Schwartz, 2020).

CASE STUDIES

Educational AI has seen remarkable real-world applications that illustrate its potential to transform learning environments. One prominent example is the use of AI-driven platforms like Duolingo, which utilizes natural language processing to personalize language learning (Castelli & Sarvary, 2021). The application adapts to individual learners' pace and proficiency by analyzing their responses and providing tailor-made lessons that enhance their strengths while addressing weaknesses (Myers et al., 2012). This adaptive learning approach not only fosters a more engaging experience but also significantly improves learning outcomes (Shockley et al., 2021).

Another notable case study is the integration of AI in the Khan Academy platform, which incorporates AI to deliver personalized learning experiences (Gemmel et al., 2020). Khan Academy's smart algorithms assess student performance on various topics, and based on this data, the platform creates customized learning pathways (Ghosh & Kumar, 2025). A study showed that students using the AI-powered features achieved higher retention rates in mathematics, demonstrating the effectiveness of personalized learning driven by AI (Selco & Habbak, 2021).

Moreover, the use of AI in educational assessment systems, such as Gradescope, underscores how technology can streamline administrative processes while enhancing feedback quality (Flener-Lovitt et al., 2020). Gradescope uses machine learning to assist in grading assignments across diverse formats, providing instant feedback to students and freeing up valuable time for educators to focus on instruction (Fiock, 2020). This real-world implementation exemplifies how AI can reduce administrative burdens while maintaining educational integrity (Perets et al., 2020).

IMPLEMENTATION OF REGULATORY FRAMEWORKS

The implementation of regulatory frameworks aimed at establishing ethical AI in education is a multifaceted endeavor (Barnard, 1997) that requires careful consideration of diverse stakeholder interests, technological capabilities, and ethical imperatives. As institutions increasingly integrate AI technologies into their operations, a rigorous regulatory approach becomes essential to mitigate risks (Fredricks et al., 2004) and ensure that AI applications benefit all educational stakeholders, including students, teachers, and administrators.

Stakeholder Engagement

A key initial step in the implementation of regulatory frameworks is stakeholder engagement (Swan & Ice, 2010). This involves a collaborative approach involving educators, students, technology developers, policymakers, and legal experts (Furlong & Christenson, 2008). Workshops, focus groups, and public forums can help gather diverse perspectives, ensuring that the frameworks reflect the needs and values of all those affected by AI use in education. Involving stakeholders fosters a sense of ownership and accountability, crucial for successful compliance (Vonderwell & Zachariah, 2005).

Establishing Clear Guidelines and Standards

Once stakeholder inputs are gathered, the next step is to establish clear guidelines and standards that dictate how AI can be ethically utilized in educational settings (Myers et al., 2012). This could involve creating a comprehensive set of principles that align with broader ethical mandates, such as transparency, fairness, accountability, and privacy. For example, standards could ensure that AI algorithms used for grading or student assessment are explainable and bias-free, allowing educators to understand how decisions are made (Chandler, 2016).

Regulatory Compliance and Monitoring

Implementing regulatory frameworks also necessitates creating mechanisms for compliance and monitoring (Moog & Spencer, 2008). This would involve the development of audit processes to evaluate the efficacy of AI systems regularly (Garrison et al., 1999). Institutions might be required to submit reports on AI system performance, detailing how they align with ethical standards (Richardson et al., 2012). Additionally, independent bodies could be established to oversee compliance and investigate violations, ensuring that schools and universities remain accountable for their AI deployments (Woodbury et al., 2022).

Training and Education Programs

Education on the ethical use of AI is critical for all stakeholders involved (Eberlein et al., 2008). Professional development programs tailored for educators and administrative staff can enhance their understanding of how AI technologies work and the ethical implications of their usage (Schwenck & Pryor, 2021). Furthermore, curricula for students can include modules that promote digital literacy and responsible AI usage, fostering a culture of ethical awareness from an early age (Selco & Habbak, 2021).

Legal and Policy Frameworks

Legal frameworks must be established to provide protections for individuals and organizations involved in AI in education (Gemmel et al., 2020). This includes policies that safeguard student data privacy under regulations like FERPA in the United States or GDPR in Europe, ensuring that AI systems are compliant with data protection laws (Jayasundara et al., 2022). Innovative legal measures that respond to emerging technologies can help mitigate potential risks while empowering educational institutions to leverage AI responsibly (Bowen & Cooper, 2022).

Pilot Programs and Iterative Development

To refine regulatory frameworks, pilot programs utilizing AI in education can be rolled out under controlled conditions (Allen & Seaman, 2016). This would help institutions understand the real-world implications of AI applications before implementing them on a larger scale (Bernard et al., 2009). Feedback from these pilot programs can inform ongoing adjustments to regulations and standards, creating a living document that evolves alongside technological advancements (Kumar et al., 2021).

ETHICAL USE OF AI BY STUDENTS

The ethical use of artificial intelligence (AI) by students is paramount in fostering a responsible learning environment (Jamieson, 2020). As students increasingly rely on AI-driven tools for research, analysis, and problem-solving, the potential for misuse amplifies (Fulfer et al., 2020). Ethical considerations must guide students in navigating these advanced technologies, ensuring that their usage enhances rather than undermines their educational integrity and personal development (Kumar et al., 2021).

First and foremost, students should prioritize academic honesty (Reiserer et al., 2023). Utilizing AI to gain insights, improve writing, or generate content can be beneficial; however, it is crucial to differentiate between assistance and outright plagiarism (Selco & Habbak, 2021). Proper attribution and understanding AI-generated content's origin are essential to uphold ethical academic standards (Bowen & Cooper, 2022). Students must also critically evaluate AI outputs, recognizing that these models can sometimes perpetuate biases or misinformation (Casey et al., 2023). Engaging with AI should not replace critical thinking but should complement and enhance students' analytical skills (Martin & Bolliger, 2018).

Additionally, students should be aware of the privacy implications when integrating AI tools into their studies (Fung & Lam, 2020). Many applications collect personal data, and students must understand the terms and conditions associated with these technologies (Woodbury et al., 2022). Practicing digital literacy, knowing how to use AI responsibly and understanding the consequences of sharing personal information can prevent potential risks (Rodriguez et al., 2020).

Finally, collaboration with peers and instructors is vital when using AI for educational purposes (Li et al., 2022). Sharing insights gained from AI resources fosters a culture of mutual learning and respect (Van Dusen & Nissen, 2020). By openly discussing AI's advantages and limitations, students can collectively build a more informed academic community (Gherhe et al., 2021).

RECENT DEVELOPMENTS IN EDUCATIONAL AI

Recent developments in educational AI are paving the way for innovative learning experiences that cater to the needs of diverse learners (Dutton et al., 2019). For instance, OpenAI's ChatGPT and similar conversational AI tools are being increasingly utilized in classrooms (Castelli & Sarvary, 2021). These AI-driven platforms can facilitate tutoring sessions, answering students' queries in real-time and providing explanations for complex topics (Reschly & Christenson, 2022). By doing so, they serve as on-demand resources that support individualized learning at any time, extending beyond traditional classroom hours (Van Heuvelen et al., 2020).

Another significant advancement is the introduction of AI-powered analytics tools that assess student engagement and performance in real-time (Raker et al., 2021). Tools such as Civitas Learning enable educators to identify at-risk students by analyzing data from various sources like attendance, grades, and engagement metrics (Nguyen et al., 2021). This data-driven approach empowers educators to intervene early and provide targeted support, ensuring that no learner is left behind (Schwenck & Pryor, 2021).

Furthermore, the rise of AI in virtual and augmented reality applications has transformed experiential learning (Wester et al., 2021). Companies like zSpace are integrating AI with AR/VR to create immersive environments where students can engage in interactive simulations (Fulfer et al., 2020). Such experiences enhance understanding and retention of complex subjects, such as biology and engineering, by allowing learners to visualize and manipulate concepts in a hands-on manner (Fung & Lam, 2020).

Lastly, the COVID-19 pandemic accelerated the adoption of AI tools for remote learning, leading to the development of platforms that integrate AI for various instructional methods (Gemmel et al., 2020). Innovations like AI-powered learning management systems are now enabling personalized education at scale, enhancing the way educators deliver content and students interact with learning materials (Jamieson, 2020).

CONCLUSION

The advent of artificial intelligence (AI) in education has the potential to revolutionize teaching and learning processes, delivering personalized experiences and improving administrative efficiency (Selco & Habbak, 2021). However, the excitement surrounding AI capabilities is tempered by growing concerns regarding ethical implications, including bias, transparency, privacy, and accountability (Reiserer et al., 2023). As educational institutions navigate this complex landscape, establishing robust cornerstones of ethical AI becomes imperative for fostering a responsible and equitable learning environment (Bowen & Cooper, 2022).

As AI systems become increasingly integrated into educational practices ranging from adaptive learning technologies and predictive analytics (Casey et al., 2023) to automated grading there is a pressing need to ensure that these systems are designed and deployed ethically. Ethical AI in education must prioritize inclusivity and equity, catering to the diverse needs of students while avoiding the perpetuation of existing inequalities (Kumar et al., 2021). The implementation of ethical guidelines can help protect students from discriminatory practices and ensure that all learners benefit from technological advancements (Martin & Bolliger, 2018).

Additionally, fostering a culture of ethical literacy within educational institutions is vital (Dutton et al., 2019). Training educators, administrators, and students to understand the ethical implications of AI empowers them to make informed decisions regarding its use (Reschly & Christenson, 2022). Incorporating discussions about the ethical dimensions of technology into the curriculum cultivates a responsible mindset among students, preparing them to navigate an AI-driven future (Van Heuvelen et al., 2020).

Recommendations for Inclusion in a Provisional Ethical Code for the Use of AI in Education

Transparency and Disclosure: Students and educators should transparently disclose their use of AI tools in assignments and projects (Perets et al., 2020). When submitting work that has been influenced or generated by AI, there should be an explicit statement acknowledging the AI assistance (Van Heuvelen et al., 2020). This principle upholds academic honesty and sets a precedent for responsible disclosure (Wenzel, 2020).

Data Privacy and Protection: All AI applications utilized in an educational context must comply with data privacy regulations (Reiserer et al., 2023). Institutions should ensure that students are informed about how their data is collected, used, and stored (Tinto, 2022). Clear guidelines should be established on best practices for maintaining privacy when employing AI tools (Schwenck & Pryor, 2021).

Critical Engagement: Students should be encouraged to critically engage with AI-generated content rather than accept it at face value (Casey et al., 2023). Educational institutions should emphasize digital literacy, teaching students to analyze and verify the accuracy and reliability of AI outputs, fostering a culture of skepticism and inquiry (Alzen et al., 2018).

Equity and Access: The ethical code should advocate for equitable access to AI resources (Rodriguez et al., 2020). Schools should strive to ensure that all students have the opportunity to engage with AI tools without financial or technological barriers (Gherhe et al., 2021). Recognizing disparities in access will help maintain a level playing field in education (Castelli & Sarvary, 2021).

Accountability and Responsibility: All users of AI, including students and faculty, should understand their responsibility to use these tools ethically (Shockley et al., 2021). The code should outline the consequences of misuse and provide a framework for accountability, encouraging self-regulation among the educational community (Gemmel et al., 2020).

Interdisciplinary Collaboration: Institutions should promote interdisciplinary collaboration in developing AI tools and resources (Selco & Habbak, 2021). Engaging students from various fields can lead to a more robust understanding of AI's implications, fostering diverse perspectives on ethical concerns and innovative solutions to challenges (Reiserer et al., 2023).

Suggestions

Framework Development: Establish a clear ethical framework for AI applications within educational contexts (Raker et al., 2021). This framework should align with existing ethical norms in education, encompass principles such as fairness, accountability, transparency, and respect for students' privacy (Nguyen et al., 2021). Collaboration among educators, ethicists, technologists, and policymakers is vital to create a cohesive structure guiding AI development and deployment (Schwenck & Pryor, 2021).

Stakeholder Engagement: Engage all stakeholders in the educational ecosystem students, parents, teachers, school administrators, and technology developers (Wester et al., 2021). Their insights will be invaluable for understanding diverse perspectives and concerns regarding AI technologies (Fulfer et al., 2020). Conducting surveys, focus groups, and public forums can facilitate dialogue, ensuring the ethical framework resonates with the values and expectations of all involved parties (Fung & Lam, 2020).

Bias Mitigation: Prioritize the identification and mitigation of biases in AI algorithms used in educational settings. Research indicates that AI systems can perpetuate existing social inequalities if not carefully designed (Gemmel et al., 2020). Regular audits and evaluations should be instituted to assess algorithmic fairness, ensuring that AI tools do not disadvantage particular groups of students (Jamieson, 2020). Continuous monitoring and iterative improvements should be in place to adapt to emerging biases as educational contexts evolve (Perets et al., 2020).

Data Privacy and Security: Establish robust data protection measures to safeguard students' personal information (Van Heuvelen et al., 2020). This includes transparent data handling processes and informed consent for data usage. Educational institutions must comply with legislation like GDPR in Europe or FERPA in the United States (Wenzel, 2020), ensuring ethical standards are upheld in data collection, storage, and processing. Additionally, implementing technologies like data anonymization can help mitigate risks associated with potential data breaches (Reiserer et al., 2023).

AI Literacy: Promote AI literacy for both educators and students (Tinto, 2022). Understanding how AI works, its capabilities, and potential pitfalls will empower educators to use these tools responsibly and disclose limitations to students (Schwenck & Pryor, 2021). Educational institutions should consider incorporating AI ethics into their curriculums, cultivating students' critical thinking about technology's role in society (Casey et al., 2023).

Evaluation Metrics: Develop and apply evaluation metrics to assess the effectiveness and ethical implications of AI tools in education (Alzen et al., 2018). These metrics should encompass not only academic performance but also social and emotional aspects of learning (Rodriguez et al., 2020). By enabling educators to gauge the broader impacts of AI on the student experience, they can adjust their strategies to promote positive outcomes (Gherhe et al., 2021).

Multidisciplinary Research: Foster collaborative research initiatives that unite experts from various fields education, computer science, philosophy, psychology, and sociology to explore the multifaceted impacts of AI on education. By drawing on diverse expertise, researchers can address ethical dilemmas effectively and propose comprehensive solutions to complex challenges posed by AI adoption in educational contexts (Castelli & Sarvary, 2021).

Policy Advocacy: Advocate for clear policies at institutional, local, state, and national levels that address the ethical use of AI in education (Myers et al., 2012). Policymakers should work closely with educators and technologists to establish guidelines that protect against potential harms while enabling innovation (Shockley et al., 2021). These policies should be flexible to adapt to technological advancements (Gemmel et al., 2020).

Future Research Directions

Longitudinal Studies: Investigate the long-term effects of AI integration on student learning outcomes and psychosocial development (Selco & Habbak, 2021). This research can provide insights into the sustainability of AI applications in educational settings, examining their influence on critical thinking, creativity, and interpersonal skills over time.

Cross-Cultural Studies: Conduct research that examines the ethical implications of AI in diverse educational contexts globally (Flener-Lovitt et al., 2020). By comparing how different cultures and educational systems adopt AI technologies, scholars can identify best practices and potential pitfalls that extend beyond a single cultural context.

AI in Special Education: Explore the specific implications of AI technologies in special education settings (Fiock, 2020). Research should focus on how AI can be tailored to support individualized learning plans, address accessibility issues, and foster inclusive environments for students with disabilities.

Ethics in AI Development: Delve into the ethical implications of AI model design, focusing on the values integrated into algorithmic decision-making processes (Perets et al., 2020). This research can illuminate the ethical trade-offs inherent in various AI applications, helping to inform developers about responsible design practices.

Impact of AI on Teacher Roles: Investigate how AI technologies are reshaping teachers' roles, responsibilities, and relationships with students (Jamieson, 2020). This research should assess the balance between human and AI contributions in the classroom and the potential impacts on teacher job satisfaction and professional identity.

Ethical AI Training for Educators: Develop effective training programs for educators on the ethical use of AI in teaching and learning (Fulfer et al., 2020). Research can focus on best practices for delivering this training, measuring its effectiveness, and assessing educators' preparedness to navigate ethical dilemmas that may arise from AI use.

Adaptive Learning Systems: Study the ethical considerations in the deployment of adaptive learning systems powered by AI (Kumar et al., 2021). Research could explore how these systems can personalize education while balancing student autonomy and the risks of over-reliance on technology. Evaluating their efficacy and ethical implications will be vital for responsible implementation.

Community and Parental Involvement: Investigate how to engage parents and communities in conversations about AI in education (Reiserer et al., 2023). Understanding community perspectives can help shape effective policies and ensure that AI tools are developed and utilized in ways that reflect societal values and priorities. By focusing on these suggestions and future research directions, educators and stakeholders can ensure that AI technologies are leveraged ethically and responsibly, creating an educational environment that is equitable, inclusive, and conducive to holistic learning experiences.

REFERENCES

Alzen, J. L., Langdon, L. S., & Otero, V. K. (2018). A logistic regression investigation of the relationship between the Learning Assistant model and failure rates in introductory STEM courses. *International Journal of STEM Education*, *5*(1), 56. DOI: 10.1186/s40594-018-0152-1 PMID: 30631745

Appleton, J. J., Christenson, S. L., & Furlong, M. J. (2008). Student engagement with school: Critical conceptual and methodological issues of the construct. *Psychology in the Schools*, *45*, 369–386. DOI: 10.1002/pits.20303

Barnard, J. (1997). The World Wide Web and Higher Education: The Promise of Virtual Universities and Online Libraries. 37(3), 30–35. DOI:https://dl.acm.org/doi/10.5555/282065.282072

Bernard, R. M., Abrami, P. C., Borokhovski, E., Wade, C. A., Tamim, R. M., Surkes, M. A., & Bethel, E. C. (2009). A Meta-Analysis of Three Types of Interaction Treatments in Distance Education. *Review of Educational Research*, *79*(3), 1243–1289.

Bernard, R. M., Abrami, P. C., Lou, Y., Borokhovski, E., Wade, A., Wozney, L., Wallet, P. A., Fiset, M., & Huang, B. (2004). How Does Distance Education Compare With Classroom Instruction? A Meta-Analysis of the Empirical Literature. *Review of Educational Research*, *74*(3), 379–439. DOI: 10.3102/00346543074003379

Bhagat, S., & Kim, D. J. (2020). Higher Education Amidst COVID-19: Challenges and Silver Lining. *Information Systems Management*, *37*(4), 366–371. DOI: 10.1080/10580530.2020.1824040

Bluemink, J., & Järvelä, S. (2004). Face-to-face encounters as contextual support for Web-based discussions in a teacher education course. *The Internet and Higher Education*, *7*(3), 199–215.

Bowen, R. S., & Cooper, M. M. (2022). Grading on a Curve as a Systemic Issue of Equity in Chemistry Education. *Journal of Chemical Education*, *99*(1), 185–194.

Canning, E. A., Muenks, K., Green, D. J., & Murphy, M. C. (2019). STEM faculty who believe ability is fixed have larger racial achievement gaps and inspire less student motivation in their classes. *Science Advances*, *5*(2), eaau4734. Advance online publication. DOI: 10.1126/sciadv.aau4734 PMID: 30793027

Casey, J. R., Russell, A., & Courey, A. J. (2023). Participation in high-structure general chemistry course increases student sense of belonging and persistence to organic chemistry. *Journal of Chemical Education*, *100*(8), 2860–2872. DOI: 10.1021/acs.jchemed.2c01253 PMID: 37577453

Castelli, F. R., & Sarvary, M. A. (2021). Why students do not turn on their video cameras during online classes and an equitable and inclusive plan to encourage them to do so. *Ecology and Evolution*, *11*(8), 3565–3576. DOI: 10.1002/ece3.7123 PMID: 33898009

Chandler, K. (2016). Using Breakout Rooms in Synchronous Online Tutorials. *Journal of Perspectives in Applied Academic Practice*, *4*(3). Advance online publication. DOI: 10.14297/jpaap.v4i3.216

DeMonbrun, M., Finelli, C. J., Prince, M., Shekhar, P., Henderon, C., & Waters, C. (2017). Creating an Instrument to Measure Student Response to Instructional Practices. *Journal of Engineering Education*, *106*, 273–298. DOI: 10.1002/jee.20162

Dixson, M. D. (2015). Measuring Student Engagement in the Online Course: The Online Student Engagement Scale (OSE). *Online Learning : the Official Journal of the Online Learning Consortium*, *19*(4). Advance online publication. DOI: 10.24059/olj.v19i4.561

Dutton, J., Dutton, M., & Perry, J. (2019). How do online students differ from lecture students? *Online Learning : the Official Journal of the Online Learning Consortium*, *6*(1). Advance online publication. DOI: 10.24059/olj.v6i1.1869

Eberlein, T., Kampmeier, J., Minderhout, V., Moog, R. S., Platt, T., Varma-Nelson, P., & White, H. B. (2008). Pedagogies of engagement in science: A comparison of PBL, POGIL, and PLTL. *Biochemistry and Molecular Biology Education*, *36*(4), 262–273. DOI: 10.1002/bmb.20204 PMID: 19381266

Ertl, B., Fischer, F., & Mandl, H. (2006). Conceptual and socio-cognitive support for collaborative learning in videoconferencing environments. *Computers & Education*, *47*(3), 298–315. DOI: 10.1016/j.compedu.2004.11.001

Fiock, H. (2020). Designing a Community of Inquiry in Online Courses. *International Review of Research in Open and Distance Learning*, *21*(1), 134–152. DOI: 10.19173/irrodl.v20i5.3985

Flener-Lovitt, C., Bailey, K., & Han, R. (2020). Using Structured Teams to Develop Social Presence in Asynchronous Chemistry Courses. *Journal of Chemical Education*, *97*(9), 2519–2525. DOI: 10.1021/acs.jchemed.0c00765

Fredricks, J. A., Blumenfeld, P. C., & Paris, A. H. (2004). School Engagement: Potential of the Concept, State of the Evidence. *Review of Educational Research*, *74*(1), 59–109. DOI: 10.3102/00346543074001059

Fulfer, K. D., Wachter, E., Muzyka, J. L., Demoranville, L. T., Fieberg, J. E., Haile, J. D., Scott, D., Song, Y., Workman, J. M., & Young, K. J. (2020). #StayCentred: Maintaining Personal Education at Centre College During COVID-19. *Journal of Chemical Education, 97*(9), 2783–2787. DOI: 10.1021/acs.jchemed.0c00726

Fung, F. M., & Lam, Y. (2020). How COVID-19 Disrupted Our "Flipped" Freshman Organic Chemistry Course: Insights Gained from Singapore. *Journal of Chemical Education, 97*(9), 2573–2580. DOI: 10.1021/acs.jchemed.0c00590

Furlong, M. J., & Christenson, S. L. (2008). Engaging students with school and academics: A relevant construct for all students. *Psychology in the Schools, 45*, 365–368. DOI: 10.1002/pits.20302

Garrison, D. R., Anderson, T., & Archer, W. (1999). Critical Inquiry in a Text-Based Environment: Computer Conferencing in Higher Education. *The Internet and Higher Education, 2*(2–3), 87–105. DOI: 10.1016/S1096-7516(00)00016-6

Gemmel, P. M., Goetz, M. K., James, N. M., Jesse, K. A., & Ratliff, B. J. (2020). Collaborative Learning in Chemistry: Impact of COVID-19. *Journal of Chemical Education, 97*(9), 2899–2904. DOI: 10.1021/acs.jchemed.0c00713

Gherhe , V., imon, S., & Para, I. (2021). Analysing Students' Reasons for Keeping Their Webcams on or off during Online Classes. *Sustainability, 13*(6), 3203. DOI: 10.3390/su13063203

. Ghosh, O & Kumar, B. (2025). *The impact of remote experimentation on student engagement.* Revolutionizing Education With Remote Experimentation and Learning Analytics. 523-544.

Giesbers, B., Rienties, B., Tempelaar, D., & Gijselaers, W. (2013). Investigating the relations between motivation, tool use, participation, and performance in an e-learning course using web-videoconferencing. *Computers in Human Behavior, 29*(1), 285–292. DOI: 10.1016/j.chb.2012.09.005

Gillies, D. (2008). Student perspectives on videoconferencing in teacher education at a distance. *Distance Education, 29*(1), 107–118. DOI: 10.1080/01587910802004878

Henrie, C. R., Halverson, L. R., & Graham, C. R. (2015). Measuring student engagement in technology-mediated learning: A review. *Computers & Education, 90*, 36–53. DOI: 10.1016/j.compedu.2015.09.005

Jamieson, M. V. (2020). Keeping a Learning Community and Academic Integrity Intact after a Mid-Term Shift to Online Learning in Chemical Engineering Design During the COVID-19 Pandemic. *Journal of Chemical Education, 97*(9), 2768–2772. DOI: 10.1021/acs.jchemed.0c00785

Jayasundara, J. M. P. V. K., Gilbert, T., Kersten, S., & Meng, L. (2022). How UK HE STEM Students Were Motivated to Switch Their Cameras on: A Study of the Development of Compassionate Communications in Task-focused Online Group Meetings. *Education Sciences*, *12*(5), 317. DOI: 10.3390/educsci12050317

Kuh, G. D. (2001). Assessing What Really Matters to Student Learning Inside The National Survey of Student Engagement. *Change: The Magazine of Higher Learning*, *33*(3), 10–17. DOI: 10.1080/00091380109601795

Kumar, P., Saxena, C., & Baber, H. (2021). Learner-content interaction in e-learning- the moderating role of perceived harm of COVID-19 in assessing the satisfaction of learners. *Smart Learning Environments*, *8*. Advance online publication. DOI: 10.1186/s40561-021- 00149-8 PMID: 40477398

Li, N., Romera Rodriguez, G., Xu, Y., Bhatt, P., Nguyen, H. A., Serpi, A., Tsai, C., & Carroll, J. M. (2022). *Picturing One's Self: Camera Use in Zoom Classes during the COVID-19 Pandemic*. Proceedings of the Ninth ACM Conference on Learning @ Scale, 151–162. DOI:https://doi.org/DOI: 10.1145/3491140.3528284

Martin, F., & Bolliger, D. U. (2018). Engagement Matters: Student Perceptions on the Importance of Engagement Strategies in the Online Learning Environment. *Online Learning : the Official Journal of the Online Learning Consortium*, *22*(1). Advance online publication. DOI: 10.24059/olj.v22i1.1092

Moore, M. G. (1989). Editorial: Three types of interaction. *American Journal of Distance Education*, *3*(2), 1–7. DOI: 10.1080/08923648909526659

Myers, T., Monypenny, R., & Trevathan, J. (2012). Overcoming the glassy-eyed nod: An application of process-oriented guided inquiry learning techniques in information technology. *Journal of Learning Design*, *5*(1), 12–22. DOI: 10.5204/jld.v5i1.97

Nguyen, K. A., Borrego, M., Finelli, C. J., DeMonbrun, M., Crockett, C., Tharayil, S., Shekhar, P., Waters, C., & Rosenberg, R. (2021). Instructor strategies to aid implementation of active learning: A systematic literature review. *International Journal of STEM Education*, *8*, 9. DOI: 10.1186/s40594-021-00270-7

Perets, E. A., Chabeda, D., Gong, A. Z., Huang, X., Fung, T. S., Ng, K. Y., Bathgate, M., & Yan, E. C. Y. (2020). Impact of the Emergency Transition to Remote Teaching on Student Engagement in a Non-STEM Undergraduate Chemistry Course in the Time of COVID-19. *Journal of Chemical Education*, *97*(9), 2439–2447. DOI: 10.1021/acs.jchemed.0c00879

(2008). POGIL: An Overview. InMoog, R. S., & Spencer, J. N. (Eds.), *Process Oriented Guided Inquiry Learning (POGIL)*. American Chemical Society., DOI: 10.1021/bk-2008-0994

Raker, J. R., Dood, A. J., Srinivasan, S., & Murphy, K. L. (2021). Pedagogies of engagement use in postsecondary chemistry education in the United States: Results from a national survey. *Chemistry Education Research and Practice*, *22*(1), 30–42. DOI: 10.1039/D0RP00125B

Reiserer, M., Ertl, B., & Mandl, H. (2023). Fostering Collaborative Knowledge Construction in Desktop Video-conferencing. Effects of Content Schemes and Cooperation Scripts in Peer Teaching Settings. In G. Stahl, Computer Support for Collaborative Learning (1st ed., pp. 379–388). *Routledge*. DOI:https://doi.org/DOI: 10.4324/9781315045467-55

Reschly, A. L., & Christenson, S. L. (Eds.). (2022). *Handbook of Research on Student Engagement*. Springer International Publishing., DOI: 10.1007/978-3-031-07853-8

Richardson, J. C., Arbaugh, J. B., Cleveland-Innes, M., Ice, P., Swan, K. P., & Garrison, D. R. (2012). Using the Community of Inquiry Framework to Inform Effective Instructional Design. In Moller, L., & Huett, J. (Eds.), *The Next Generation of Distance Education* (pp. 97–125)., DOI: 10.1007/978-1-4614-1785-9_7

Rodriguez, J.-M. G., Hunter, K. H., Scharlott, L. J., & Becker, N. M. (2020). A Review of Research on Process Oriented Guided Inquiry Learning: Implications for Research and Practice. *Journal of Chemical Education*, *97*(10), 3506–3520. DOI: 10.1021/acs.jchemed.0c00355

Schwartz, H. (2020). *Remote Learning Is Here to Stay: Results from the First American School District Panel Survey*. RAND Corporation., DOI: 10.7249/RRA956-1

Schwenck, C. M., & Pryor, J. D. (2021). Student perspectives on camera usage to engage and connect in foundational education classes: It's time to turn your cameras on. *International Journal of Educational Research Open*, *2*, 100079. DOI: 10.1016/j.ijedro.2021.100079

Selco, J. I., & Habbak, M. (2021). STEM Students' Perceptions on Emergency Online Learning during the COVID-19 Pandemic: Challenges and Successes. *Education Sciences*, *11*(12), 799. DOI: 10.3390/educsci11120799

Shockley, K. M., Gabriel, A. S., Robertson, D., Rosen, C. C., Chawla, N., Ganster, M. L., & Ezerins, M. E. (2021). The fatiguing effects of camera use in virtual meetings: A within-person field experiment. *The Journal of Applied Psychology*, *106*(8), 1137–1155. DOI: 10.1037/apl0000948 PMID: 34423999

Singhal, M. K. (2020). Facilitating Virtual Medicinal Chemistry Active Learning Assignments Using Advanced Zoom Features during COVID-19 Campus Closure. *Journal of Chemical Education, 97*(9), 2711–2714. DOI: 10.1021/acs.jchemed.0c00675

. Smith, P. L., & Dillon, C. L. (2009). *Comparing distance learning and classroom learning: Conceptual considerations.* 13(2), 6–23. DOI:https://doi.org/DOI: 10.1080/08923649909527020

Swan, K., & Ice, P. (2010). The community of inquiry framework ten years later: Introduction to the special issue. *The Internet and Higher Education, 13*(1–2), 1–4. DOI: 10.1016/j.iheduc.2009.11.003

Tanner, K. D. (2013). Structure Matters: Twenty-One Teaching Strategies to Promote Student Engagement and Cultivate Classroom Equity. *CBE Life Sciences Education, 12*(3), 322–331. DOI: 10.1187/cbe.13-06-0115 PMID: 24006379

Tharayil, S., Borrego, M., Prince, M., Nguyen, K. A., Shekhar, P., Finelli, C. J., & Waters, C. (2018). Strategies to mitigate student resistance to active learning. *International Journal of STEM Education, 5*, 7. DOI: 10.1186/s40594-018-0102-y PMID: 30631697

Tinto, V. (2022). Exploring the Character of Student Persistence in Higher Education: The Impact of Perception, Motivation, and Engagement. In Reschly, A. L., & Christenson, S. L. (Eds.), *Handbook of Research on Student Engagement.* Springer International Publishing., DOI: 10.1007/978-3-031-07853-8

Van Dusen, B., & Nissen, J. (2020). Associations between learning assistants, passing introductory physics, and equity: A quantitative critical race theory investigation. *Physical Review. Physics Education Research, 16*(1), 010117. DOI: 10.1103/PhysRevPhysEducRes.16.010117

Van Heuvelen, K. M., Daub, G. W., & Ryswyk, H. V. (2020). Emergency Remote Instruction during the COVID-19 Pandemic Reshapes Collaborative Learning in General Chemistry. *Journal of Chemical Education, 97*(9), 2884–2888. DOI: 10.1021/acs.jchemed.0c00691

Vonderwell, S., & Zachariah, S. (2005). Factors that Influence Participation In Online Learning. *Journal of Research on Technology in Education, 38*(2), 213–230. DOI: 10.1080/15391523.2005.10782457

Wenzel, T. (2020). Collaborative Group Learning in Remotely Taught Analytical Chemistry Courses. *Journal of Chemical Education, 97*(9), 2715–2718. DOI: 10.1021/acs.jchemed.0c00520

. Wester, E. R., Walsh, L. L., Arango-Caro, S., & Callis-Duehl, K. L. (2021). Student Engagement Declines in STEM Undergraduates during COVID-19–Driven Remote Learning. *Journal of Microbiology & Biology Education*, 22(1), ev22i1.2385. DOI:https://doi.org/DOI: 10.1128/jmbe.v22i1.2385

Wise, A. F., Saghafian, M., & Padmanabhan, P. (2012). Towards more precise design guidance: Specifying and testing the functions of assigned student roles in online discussions. *Educational Technology Research and Development*, *60*(1), 55–82. DOI: 10.1007/s11423-011-9212-7

Woodbury, J., Arneson, J. B., & Offerdahl, E. G. (2022). Adapting Team-Based Learning for an Online Biochemistry Course. *Journal of Chemical Education*, *99*(8), 2964–2971. DOI: 10.1021/acs.jchemed.2c00259

Chapter 2
Standardization Without Losing Diversity and Blocking Innovations

Tetyana Sergeyeva
https://orcid.org/0000-0002-0481-316X
National Technical University "Kharkiv Polytechnic Institute", Ukraine

Sergiy Bronin
https://orcid.org/0000-0003-3094-0450
Vilnius University, Lithuania

ABSTRACT

Exponential development of technologies changes educational paradigm introducing new generation LMS standards. An innovative Eco-Humanistic Technology of Self-Development aimed at human-environment synergetic interaction causing their co-development is proposed for synergizing human intelligence and AI within e-learning. Interaction presents system-forming factor based on holistic understanding of environment as natural-social-techno spheres and student as bio-socio-creative being. Innovative e-learning integrates student-orientated and subject-orientated approaches focused on Developmental Capacity as key criteria of e-learning efficiency. Co-creation of e-courses involves multi-agent/sector/disciplinary interaction. Content-Structure Model allows managing, measuring and programming complex process of students cognitive and personality development in the very process of mastering academic subjects. It is described content-structure patterns of discipline matrix, student profile, e-course-unit-task structures, virtual laboratories and virtual reality laboratories new application.

DOI: 10.4018/979-8-3373-2235-3.ch002

INTRODUCTION

The exponential development of technologies has not only redefined the boundaries of possibilities in educational environment, but also introduced tools that radically change the way knowledge is transmitted, acquired and assessed, essentially changing the paradigm of education itself. With increased potential comes responsibility. Changing landscape of education creates new problems that must be addressed from the start, rather than "living through the troubles as they come," since the speed, scope, scale and impact of AI are so great that problems will multiply proportionally and the loss of control will become irreversible.

Traditionally, this problem has been addressed through the introduction of standards as a basis for trust, interoperability, and accountability to ensure the reliability and ethics of AI-Powered Education. But how to preserve uniqueness and diversity as conditions for quality education that ensures survival in the face of uncertainty? The default assumption is that standardized AI solutions can improve the learning and teaching process. It is proposed to align innovations with global standards through the use of standardized frameworks in the development, deployment, and management of AI solutions aimed at meaningful and sustainable learning achievements (ISO, 2022), (UNESCO, 2021), (UNESCO, 2023), (UNESCO, 2023), (UNESCO, 2025), (GDPR.eu, n.d.), (U.S. Department of Education, n.d.). At the same time, educators, administrators, policymakers, and AI developers should be inspired to use standards as a tool for creating efficient and responsible educational ecosystems.

The practice of real teaching demonstrates a low probability of inspiring truly creative teachers, focused on innovation and continuous improvement of their teaching skills, with standards. A contradiction arises. Creative inventive individuals, by definition, are not standards, but the interaction of diversities is a prerequisite for synergetic development (Sergeyeva et al., 2023). How can we reconcile the innovative, creative and standardized?

This is possible if we focus on how living systems do it, which are characterized by an ambivalent desire for preservation and development. It is precisely this that is the driving force of development, which occurs in the process of balancing needs-resources-conditions, working as a perpetual motion machine of development, generating new non-equilibrium states in the balancing process itself, triggering the need to continue the development process (Sergeyeva et al., 2023). The strategic sense is development itself, the condition (in our case) is standardization, and the learning/development environment is the resource that must be brought into a state of equilibrium with needs and conditions.

The time of technologies exponential development is a time of uncertainty and at the same time of new opportunities. The answer to the challenges of the time can be raising the bar of standards - establishing the standards of the next generation.

How will they differ from today's? If to put it simply, today a standard is a goal and freedom in the way to achieve it. This approach, with all its attractiveness, allows for the measurement of a standard based on a formal feature of presence, which does not reflect the essence of the standard - the measurement of quality. There is a divergence of form and content, as in generative intelligence, with the average statistical approach, when original, innovative, creative solutions do not fall under the Gauss curve. Diversity is leveled out as a prerequisite for synergetic development - interaction of differences.

To prevent this from happening and to prevent a discrepancy between form and content when measuring the standard, it is necessary to introduce a measurement of the means to achieve the standards, i.e. to answer the question HOW? (to open the "black box"). Why is HOW so important? It determines whether society will receive a "mechanic" who is able to repeat the actions of a master, tailored to a specific situation, or a thinking "agent of change" who, having revealed the sense and principle of actions, is able to find a solution in any situation. The answer to the question HOW? also affects the moral component, so as not to fall into the Machiavellian trap, when "all means are good to achieve the goal."

But here it turns out that the answer to the question HOW tramples freedom in education, although it is precisely behind this screen that imitations and formal schemes are hidden. Then we need to answer the questions: "Freedom from what?", "From quality?", "From responsibility?" This is a bottleneck not only in education. At the same time, there is an opinion that it is possible to find HOW by answering the question "WHY", i.e. by transferring it to the sense level. That is, if we raise the standard to the level of meaning (introduce sense dimension), then the standard will be able to reflect not only the goal "WHAT?", but also the meaning of "WHY?", which, in essence, determines the way to achieve it "HOW?". Then education will remain free and safe.

The next generation educational standard should become multidimensional, answering the questions: "WHAT?" - "HOW?" - "WHY?". For the time of uncertainty, the sense dimension has a universal standard "Developmental Capacity", which implicitly includes the necessary set of competencies. It not only does not limit diversity, innovation, creativity, but also enhances them. But for its implementation, a new generation methodology is needed that develops students at the level of existential sense of development. Such a methodology, embodied in technology, exists. This is the Eco-Humanistic Technology of Self-Development (EHTSD), which focuses on the universal sense of development, through modeling in the conditions of learning natural conditions of synergetic human-environment, leading to their co-development. EHTSD sets the direction/principles, and not strict rules that limit freedom, and leaves the right to choose as a condition for diversity and innovation.

The proposed chapter considers the possibilities of introducing standards without losing diversity and innovation as conditions for development. It consistently answers the questions:

Where are we now? – Section 1 analyzes the current state of educational standardization in the context of the integration of educational technologies and AI. Criticism of current practices is presented and key problems are formulated: (1) the danger of excessive educational standardization; (2) contradictions between standardization – diversity and innovation; (3) shortcomings of existing LMS models; (4) risks of applying outdated pedagogical models to advanced technologies.

Where do we want to be? – 1) Section 2 analyzes trends that may change educational standards in the next 5-10 years: (1) possible transition to sense-oriented education, (2) integration of AI without loss of diversity, (3) personalization of learning in real time, (4) content-structural modeling, (5) multi-agent/sectoral/disciplinary co-creation.

How can we get there? – Section 3 presents the Eco-Humanistic Technology of Self-Development (EHTSD) as an innovative perspective of a holistic system solution for integrating AI into education without losing the humanistic core, resolving the dilemmas of standardization and diversity. EHTSD unfolds through the "concept – model – structure – algorithms" of e-learning. The structural and content matrix of the e-course – learner profile – patterns of the e-course, units, tasks are presented.

1. STATE OF THE ART: THE MAIN CHALLENGES IN AI-ENHANCED EDUCATION IN THE CONTEXT OF STANDARDS

The section analyzes the current state of standardization in the context of the integration of educational technologies and AI in education. It introduces the historical development of learning management systems (LMS) and pedagogical models/types of e-learning, with a critique of current practices. The section formulates key issues, such as: (1) the dangers of excessive educational standardization, creating tensions with diversity and innovation, especially through the lens of the integration of AI and digital technologies, which amplify this tension; (2) the contradictions between standardization and creativity in education are identified, especially in learning environments enhanced by AI. It is explained how standardized approaches can suppress diversity, especially in teacher autonomy and learner individuality; (3) the shortcomings of existing LMS models are highlighted, their rigidity, including limitations in interaction, personalization and impact on development; (4) the existing pedagogical approaches and the risks of applying outdated pedagogical models to advanced technologies are analyzed. A mismatch between technical capabilities and pedagogical understanding is observed. It is emphasized that technological integration without pedagogical transformation perpetuates outdated paradigms of learning in new formats. In conclusion, an innovative structural and content model of e-education based on the eco-humanistic approach embodied in EHSDT, based on scientific work and empirical observations, is proposed to solve the problems.

1.1 Pros and Cons of Existing LMS

Technological development will change educational standards. To determine trends, it is necessary to analyze the state of the issue. AI integration is taking place under existing e-education. To understand the phenomenon, it is necessary to trace the history of its origin. E-learning is carried out through Learning Management Systems (LMS), the concept of which arose directly from e-learning (Hashemi-Pour, 2024), as a software application for the administration, documentation, tracking, reporting, automation and delivery of educational courses, curricula, materials or training and development programs. LMS made it possible to present customized content, track progress and use feedback mechanisms as an efficient tool for improving the skills and knowledge of learners. Thanks to LMS, students got access to all their educational (graded and ungraded) activities on one platform. Companies began to actively use LMS for general training, certification, compliance, onboarding, customer training and sales courses. LMS has become a comprehensive solution that meets the requirements of the e-learning environment.

There are a number of LMS and platforms for various educational purposes, including Blackboard, Brightspace by D2L, Canvas, Docebo, EducateMe, FutureLearn, Google Classroom, iversity, Khan Academy, LinkedIn Learning, LMS365, Microsoft LMS, Moodle, OpenLearning, OneNote, Sakai, Schoology, SkillShare and TalentLMS, Treehouse, Udemy, which have their own advantages and disadvantages. A comparative analysis of the most popular LMS showed the following (Fig. 1).

Figure 1. Pros and Cons of LMS

COMPARISON OF LEARNING MANAGEMENT SYSTEMS

LMS	Google Classroom (Papas, 2015)	Microsoft LMS (Leskovar, 2024)	Moodle (Porfenovich, n.d.)	BlackBoard (Brandt, 2023)	Canvas (Raymond, 2024)
NOTES	Integrated with Google Drive, Google Docs, & Google Forms it is a cloud-based LMS that is free for educational institutions to use	integrated with Microsoft Teams and the Office 365 suite of tools, such as Word, Excel, Outlook, and PowerPoint	is one of the most popular and widely used open source LMS, with over 396 million users in 239 countries and territories	widely used by both higher education institutions and the business world for employee training	used by leading universities around the world (Oxford and Ivy League)
PROS	it is a convenient platform for setting up virtual classrooms, and it makes it easy to create and manage assignments, grade students, and collaborate with them	provides seamless and easy synchronization & sharing between the LMS platform and the Microsoft tools that are already widely used. LMS365 is an AI-powered system built directly into Microsoft Office 365, including Microsoft Teams.	is used to manage, deliver, and measure online learning. The Open LMS app is a free, feature-rich option for all Moodle™ sites! With local Open LMS apps, you can access courses directly from your existing device, downloading content for offline access. The Moodle LMS source code as a platform allows anyone to download the software for free and customize it. Moodle is constantly evolving, and there is no other LMS that is as responsive to users.	to support the needs, goals, and challenges of each student, Blackboard includes integrated accessibility tools, supports competency-based programs, and has an intuitive, inclusive interface that works across all devices, making it easy to access learning content anytime, anywhere. One of the key benefits of Blackboard is that knowledge sources can be reused across systems or across problem areas, significantly reducing the development time for new projects.	a modern, easy-to-use, cloud-based LMS that connects teachers, students, and course content across online course sites to deliver high-quality, inclusive digital teaching and learning experiences. It is intuitive, scalable, and able to grow with the needs of the university. Canvas includes several features to facilitate online communication between teachers and students. Consolidation around a common platform for all public higher education institutions makes it easier for students to take courses cross-segment. Canvas LMS is 100% free for students if the university uses Canvas or through a free (non-university affiliated) account.
CONS	It lacks important features like built-in gradebooks, comprehensive student analytics, and course building modules. It does not allow to create pages or structured syllabi. It is more of an on-line assistant than a full-fledged learning management solution	higher initial cost and longer development time; technical expertise required to maintain; risk of over-customization	has advanced features and provides a comprehensive, customizable experience, can feel complex, heavy, and unintuitive, especially when developing multiple programs or delivering training to a larger number of students. It also has hosting issues. As more users and courses are added, the system may become less responsive, which can impact student performance and learning outcomes.	Blackboard has limitations in delivering content and grading student assignments due to its inability to handle large file sizes. It is limited in tracking student activity, offering only last login without detailed activity tracking. It cannot effectively manage grades and exams.	to unlock premium features, you must pay to upgrade to Canva Pro to create professional designs and content. Canvas software can top out at $140,000. The average cost of Canvas software is around $36,000 per year. Canvas LMS is limited in that it has fewer customization options than other LMSs. There may also be issues with latency and functionality, especially when a large number of users are accessing the platform at the same time

The number and diversity of LMSs used by all universities and organizations focused on the development of their HR demonstrates the confident transition of education to e-learning, the benefits of which are no longer in doubt after the pandemic and in the situation of military conflicts. E-learning has essentially changed the way we learn, making it more convenient, flexible, personalized and accessible than ever. With the advent of online platforms, students and professionals can learn anytime and anywhere. Since e-learning gives students full control over their own learning, students can work independently and flexibly at their own pace, receive a wider variety of courses, improve time management skills, and self-discipline. With the help of LMSs, higher education institutions can give teachers the opportunity to improve their practice and traditional teaching methods, become more flexible in their response to student needs. Those responsible for organizing the educational process can more effectively manage such elements as registration and access, calendars, communication, surveys, tests, certifications and notifications. Various studies have shown that learners learn five times more in online courses using multimedia content than in traditional face-to-face courses. Although a comprehensive study by Fisher involving 72,000 university students in 433 subjects found more modest results, online students tended to achieve slightly lower academic results than their in-class counterparts (Fischer et al., 2020). The discrepancy in the data can be explained by the significant advances that e-learning has made in the last 5 years.

But despite all the advantages, e-learning has not become a panacea. Many problems, such as maintaining engagement and discipline, remain, and new ones specific to e-education have been added. An analysis of the Pros and Cons of existing LMS revealed the following: outdated LMS models; lack of a holistic systems approach and system integration; underestimation of the role of educational and cognitive activity and teacher agency; rigidity, including limitations in interaction, personalization and impact on development; alienation of students;institutional resistance to change; gaps in the integration of ethical considerations; contradictions between personalization, diversity, innovation, creativity and standardization and.

Common disadvantages include:

1) For developers and teachers – difficulty in getting all the desired features; difficulty teaching practical subjects; ensuring that the content is relevant; time and resources to create initial educational content; time to learn how to use the platform; resistance to change (Srinivas, 2023);
2) For students – adapting to new learning styles; time management, maintaining motivation; distractions; lack of clear instructions or expectations; failure to receive timely feedback; lack of direct contact with peers and with the teacher; feeling isolated/lack of social interaction; too much time spent in front of a computer/phone or other mobile device; barriers to learning (disabilities/special needs). Of these, the most common problem with e-learning is student engagement, which is difficult for students to connect with course materials, stay focused and motivated without the physical presence of a teacher (Gherhe et al., 2021).

Considering all the advantages and disadvantages, the choice between e-learning and classroom learning depends on individual preferences, goals and circumstances. E-learning offers flexibility, personalized learning and access to resources, makes education more equitable, while classroom learning provides personal interaction, immediate feedback and a structured environment.

It should be noted that all the advantages of e-learning can be negated by outdated traditional approaches to learning. As the saying goes, "you can't pour new wine into old wineskins", they will break. Unfortunately, many teachers prefer not to leave their comfort zone and only imitate the use of e-learning technologies, continuing the unchanged focus on transfer learning based on the passive transfer of knowledge and concepts from teacher to student, only not in the classroom, but on the platform. Since the LMS concept as a basis for e-learning came out of the real practice of traditional education, characteristic disadvantages have penetrated into it through the irrational use of new opportunities: limited engagement; lack of connection with the real world; lack of personalization; contrasts between memorization and understanding; rigidity, boredom, and an overemphasis on grades.

Efficient e-learning is achieved through solutions that are interesting, relevant, and personalized. Efficient e-learning design takes into account current learner trends and dives into the needs and habits of end users. Hands-on activities should allow learners to reflect on learning, analyze and synthesize it, and apply it to real-life problems. As a solution, it is proposed to raise the bar of standardization to the level of introducing a universal Developmental Capacity standard, which is relevant to the current situation of uncertainty and synergistically integrates the cognitive and personality development of the student (subject-centered and student-centered learning). Such integration is possible within the framework of Eco-Humanistic Technology of Self-Development (EHTSD), which represents the next generation of LMS.

1.2 Types of Learning That Existing E-Courses are Based on

Educational standards determine the efficiency of learning based on the results determined by learning activities. The question arises: is e-education capable of making a qualitative shift solely by integrating AI into existing LMS? Unlikely. To understand this, let's compare the different types of learning that modern e-courses are based on. As a criterion, we use the type of learning activity (LA), which, as is known, determines the developmental effect (Fig. 2).

1.3. Political and Regulatory Context

It is necessary to take into account that standards are influenced by national or international education policies, data privacy laws and AI regulations that shape the development and implementation of educational technologies. Global policy frameworks have been established, such as the UNESCO Guidelines on AI in Education (UNESCO, 2021, 2023, 2023 & 2025), GDPR (GDPR.eu, n.d.) or FERPA (U.S. Department of Education, n.d.), which influence both innovation and standardization.

Figure 2. E-courses in the context of learning activity

ELECTRONIC COURSES

E-courses	Short description	Pros	Cons
Simulate **traditional learning** (Santilli et al., 2025)	knowledge is transferred directly from the teacher to the student in the form of ready-made lecture texts with questions for comprehension and intermediate/final multiple-choice tests	the subject system is not destroyed	dependence on teacher pedagogical skills/individual cognitive-sense/ meaning structure (ICSS) embodied in the structural-content model of the subject that determines the learning efficiency; load on involuntary memory; theory – practice gap
Simulate **programmed learning** (Sadykov et al., 2023)	based on a sample according to the stimulus-response principle, which requires repetition until complete matching with the sample is achieved (trial and error principle). A more advanced option, when a student solves problems until she/he understands the solution principle (statistical approach)	skill formation based on automation (achievement of unconscious knowledge)	craft training, a formalized approach within the behaviorist model, which does not work in a situation of uncertainty, since the choice of a solution is strictly linked to a specific situation and a reward stimulus
Model **metacognitive approach** (Rasmussen et al., 2018)	a solution principle is introduced and the student is asked to solve problems according to the principle. A more advanced option is when the student is asked to derive the solutionprinciple her/himself, answering the teacher's questions (the Socratic method)	solving problems in a situation of uncertainty	a shortage of teachers who are able to clearly derive the structure and content of the subject from its system-forming essence
Simulate **problem-based learning (PBL)** (Simanjuntak et al., 2021)	which uses complex real-world problems as a means to facilitate students' learning of concepts and principles rather than directly presen-ting facts and concepts. In contrast to the transfer mode of traditional teaching, the transactional mode is used, which relies on independent problem solving, collaboration, and engagement in authentic learning environments; and the transformative mode, which values the wholeness of the learner, the way he or she connects with himself or herself	simulation of practical application of knowledge with a focus on real situations	risk of losing the systemic view of the subject, built around its system-forming essence
Model **synthesis of metacognitive & problem-based approaches** (Downing et al., 2009)	the student has mastered the solution principle and is offered various situations in which she/he must find a solution in accordance with the principle. A more advanced option, when the student has mastered various solution principles and is offered complex situations in which the student must first determine the sequence of principles and then solve the problems	flexible and creative solutions in accordance with the situation	limited individual solutions, lack of synergistic solutions
Simulate **team project work** (Tsimhoni et al., 2005)	students independently solve project problems in a joint group project activity based on an initially defined function in the team ("ideally balanced team") in the shared leadership mode. A more advanced option – the learning environment simulates multi-agent / sectoral / disciplinary co-creation	team interaction affects social skills and emotional growth, the so-called hidden type of learning / curriculum / program is activated – lessons that are learned but are not intended to be openly taught, such as norms, values, including friend-ship, honesty, fairness, ethnic relations and cultural differences and beliefs transmitted in the social environment of the team. In many cases, this occurs as a result of social interactions and expectations. Invisible learning occurs through infor-mal, unofficial and random experiences, not through for-mal training. Learning alone and in a group through individual and shared experience.	often in teams where the same integrated assessment is given to all participants for the overall result, "para-sitic" team members appear who receive an undeserved assess-ment, unequal to their contribution due to the lack of clear assess-ment criteria and the lack of management experience of student team leaders
Simulate **situations of creation and co-creation of innovative solutions** (Antoniou et al., 2023)	students are asked to create a program for solving a problem themselves (for example, not to check it themselves, but to write a program for checking the correctness of the solution according to the principle "an engineer should be moderately lazy")	innovative solutions obtained as a result of the synergetic interaction of diversities	a shortage of teachers capable of ensuring multi-agent/sectoral/disciplinary co-creation

However, unfortunately, government-run ratings or quality assurance systems that ensure standardization, especially in non-Western contexts, are often focused on formal features, behind which quality is lost. They do not take into account how this or that indicator is achieved. The main thing is to prove its presence, but whether it is imitated or actually implements and brings the expected results is outside the scope of the assessment. Here is the "black box" of education, justified by the freedom of choice. Only the level of implementation of the standard determines what is inside this "black box" - a truly thinking, developing subject/agent of co-development or a crammer who has memorized the material before the exam without understanding its internal connections and interdependencies; a craftsman, imitating operations constrained within the framework of a specific situation or a creator capable of creating something new in any situation based on the principles she/he has mastered.

2. NEXT GENERATION LMS

The exponential development of technologies has necessitated a change in the educational paradigm and, as a consequence, educational standards. The section analyzes the educational trends that are already observed today, which are likely to change educational standards in the next 5-10 years. New trends arise at the intersection of standardization, innovation and diversity in AI-driven education. They are considered as responses to current deficits and opportunities for a more equitable and efficient change in the future of education.

The trends are presented as a transition to education focused on: (1) sense of mutual development (development focused on meanings); (2) the integration of AI into education without losing the humanistic core; (3) new functions of the next generation LMS, such as AI integration, structural and content modeling of student development, real-time personalization with AI support, adaptive content (Micro-courses), multi-agent/sectoral/disciplinary co-creation (Virtual Laboratories, Virtual Reality Laboratories, team learning).

The section examines the reasons for the slowdown in LMS development (2.1) and the characteristics of the next generation LMS (2.2), which Focus on Developmental Capacity (DC) (2.2.1); E-learning, centered on the learner (2.3.2); Multiagent/sector/disciplinary co-creation (2.3.3). The section also describes Methodology for creating a new generation LMS (2.4) including Strategic focus on the ultimate goal (2.4.1); Modeling the development process (2.4.2); Technologization of the high DC process (2.4.3.); Features of next generation education (2.5).

Exponential development of technologies radically changes the existential environment of a person, and as a consequence, her/his capabilities, needs, consciousness and behavior (Agell et al., 2024). In this regard, an unprecedented challenge and at the same time opportunities appear for the e-education system, which, unfortunately, lags behind the pace of development of society, although it is called upon to outpace it, developing agents of positive change. Universities have powerful potential, since they unite under their roof a multi-agent/sectoral/disciplinary human resource (Arnold et al., 2021). However, the traditional paradigm of education fetters education, not allowing it to reach a qualitatively new level (Nugent et al., 2023). This is also true for educational standards established within the traditional paradigm, which have fallen behind the times and are slowing down the transition to a new level of quality. To make the necessary transition, it is necessary to determine the reasons for the slowdown.

2.1 Reasons for the Slowdown in LMS Development

The rapid development of technologies required a quick response to emerging challenges and opportunities. It is not surprising that the most suitable agents of change at this point were technical experts. This logically explains the observed one-sidedness of innovations, which have tilted towards the technologization of education without changing the educational paradigm, the essence of which is learning activity (LA). LA is a complex system of interaction between a student and the learning environment, directly related to human consciousness and requiring deep scientific knowledge (Podolskiy, 2012), which, unfortunately, practitioners in the field of technology do not possess. Therefore, most modern electronic courses are reduced exclusively to the operational level (multiple choice tests, filling in gaps, establishing order, etc.) or the presentation of traditional material from lectures, textbooks, test questions, drawings and tables in a more convenient, accessible electronic form of presentations, without changing anything in the essence of the learning activity that determines the developmental potential of learning.

Undoubtedly, e-learning facilitated control and repetition for automation of skills, but could not qualitatively increase the developmental capacity (DC) of disciplines, since it remained subject-centered, and not student-centered, without changing, in essence, the educational activity aimed at the formation of the Individual Sense-Cognitive Structure of the student (ICSS) based on subject activity (Clarindo et al., 2020). For this, the LMS developers did not have enough competence, knowledge of the laws of the functioning consciousness (memory and thinking) of a person, which is the subject of pedagogical and developmental psychology. This can also become an obstacle to the qualitative integration of AI technologies into existing e-education.

At the same time, a formal focus on competencies and skills without understanding the deep processes and principles of their formation is akin to a purely statistical approach to teaching generative AI ("black box"), which gives rise to the problem of Singularity. It is not surprising, since modern e-learning, which has its roots in programmed learning, like AI learning, is organized according to the behaviorist type of "stimulus-response" through the "trial and error" mode characteristic of primates, imitation of ready-made models and frequent repetition of successful solutions. Here the question arises, what kind of specialists does the World need? Craftsmen (Gromyko, 2020) who repeat the actions of the master, obedient executors of someone else's will, for whom it is enough to create a situation to get the desired reaction / action, or those who develop the world, making events to happen and are able to find a solution in any situation based not only on a systemic understanding of the principles of the solution, but also its meaning, sense both personal and environmental (Epstein, 2021 & Tank, n.d.).

Modern LMS are already capable of ensuring the development of the sense-cognitive structure of the craft type of consciousness (Brinck, 2024), and the emergence of new technologies instills hope for a change in the educational paradigm, ensuring the development of system scientific thinking in synergy with the technologies of general-symbolic-generative intelligence (Jean, 2024, Jacobson et al., 2024 & Shah, 2022), based on an understanding of their system-forming essence.

2.2 Characteristics of the Next Generation LMS

AI technologies can provide a qualitative leap in the development of e-education of a new level due to multi-agent/sectoral/disciplinary co-creation. This requires interdisciplinary interaction, and the technological potential that has emerged in connection with the development of AI allows us to create the functionality of a next-generation platform capable of supporting such co-creation of innovative e-courses as an efficient environment with high developmental capacity based on the patterns of cognitive and personality development of students corresponding to professional-social-existential sense/meanings (Sergeyeva et al., 2022).

The new platform should ensure the creation of a content-structure model of the discipline as a developmental environment centered on interaction with the student based on the synergy of human and artificial (symbolic and generative) intelligence, providing scientifically based cognitive and personal development of students as agents of change in conditions of uncertainty. Achieving such an ambitious goal requires e-education to be able to develop in synergy with technical progress, without losing already achieved level of development of students as a living system in interaction with the existential environment. An innovative next generation platform can become a testing ground/prototype of e-education, ensuring the synergy of natural, technical sciences, SSH and advanced technologies.

2.3 The Concept of the Next Generation LMS

It is strategically focused on: 1) sustainable development (social – economic – ecological) of the existential environment; 2) human well-being; 3) inclusiveness, presented in the educational context as: a) focus on developmental capacity (DC); b) centering on the learner; c) multi-agent / sectoral / disciplinary co-creation. Let's consider each strategic orientation in more detail:

2.3.1 Focus on Developmental Capacity (DC)

Existential efficiency is determined by the DC that a person, community or process is able to provide. DC is a key unit of measuring efficiency in politics, economics, education, science and everyday life. Ensuring a high level of DC requires a scientific understanding of the essence of the developmental process, which is provided by the EHTSD, reflecting the civilizational need for synergetic human-environment interaction, where the environment is presented in a broad sense, as existential, natural, social and virtual, and human is a "system of systems" integrating eco-socio-techno spheres. In the process of synergetic interaction, co-development occurs. The driving force is the ambivalent desire of human to preserve and develop through the balance of sense-resources-conditions. To ensure DC (primarily in science and education), a global shift in the scientific and educational paradigm is required.

2.3.2 E-Learning, Centered on the Learner

It occurs through hers/his cognitive-personality development of a given target profile. The initial strategic focus on the ideal balanced profile of a modern graduate as a development agent allows organizing the entire e-learning process into an optimal system, where the result of the previous action becomes a way to implement the next one. This is the profile of a professionally – socially – emotionally competent, efficient – moral – harmonious, globally thinking and locally acting agent of society sustainable development and a subject of self-development.

2.3.3 Multiagent/Sector/Disciplinary Co-Creation

Expert knowledge implies not only knowledge of the discipline, but also an understanding of its essence as a system-forming factor and the ability to derive all phenomena of the subject from this abstract essence. It is this sense representation that underlies pedagogical skills, since "who thinks clearly, expresses clearly." Unfortunately, few "subject specialists" have such competence. But this is not enough. The necessary knowledge may go beyond the "core" of the discipline being studied. In this case, even a fairly developed set of competencies becomes insufficient. There is a need for multi-agent/industry/disciplinary interaction that is capable of creating a synergistic effect due to the interaction of differences and purposefully increasing DC by an order of magnitude due to innovative technology of co-creation of experts in the field of educational activities, developers of IT courses and teachers with expert knowledge in disciplines.

2.4 Methodology for Creating a New Generation LMS

2.4.1 Strategic Focus on the Ultimate Goal

The strategic goal of e-learning is the synergetic cognitive-personality development of the student based on interaction with the learning environment, determining the DC of the e-course within the framework of a given target profile. The graduate's target profile sets the initial strategic orientation in the context of the modern labor market, which optimizes the development process, preventing non-targeted actions. Development is implemented within the framework of educational activities organized as a system of tasks aimed at developing practical, scientific, social, emotional intelligence based on the development of theoretical, hypothetical, critical, economic, environmental, mathematical, etc. thinking. In order to avoid the well-known problem of the "bag of virtues", it is better to limit the list to the framework of specific goals of the discipline in the context of a given paradigm, where the future agent of positive change implements the sustainability, well-being and inclusiveness of the existential environment through her/his professional activities.

2.4.2 Modeling the Development Process

Simulation of the natural developmental process allows modeling the synergetic human-environment interaction causing co-development in the conditions of learning, which activates the natural mechanisms of human development in its entirety. This approach allows restoring the natural connection between theory and practice, since it initially activates the personal sense/meanings of development in the conditions of learning with an orientation towards existential needs. Training is fueled by the energy of real needs with the learner's awareness of its sense - an assessment of the possibility of realizing this sense in the existing conditions - choosing an adequate way to realize the sense - implementing activities to realize the sense - automation of successful actions, transformation and integration into resources. This process is described in more detail in the next section, dedicated to the Eco-Humanistic Technology of Self-Development.

2.4.3 Technologization of the High DC Process

AI allows to respond to new challenges not only by increasing the speed, volume, scaling and impact of information, but also by implementing the most complex concepts in technology based on a system understanding of the essence and modeling of the developmental process itself. The optimal system of a subject (Camilo, 2021) is derived from its essence as a system-forming factor, which, like a drop of water after rain, reflects the entire world (in our case it is a discipline. This approach allows not only to solve the main problem of presenting a course in digital format, but also to qualitatively solve the problem of its calculation without losing its DC. The system-forming factor is the connection (expressed in weights) between functions, which allows to ensure the isomorphism of artificial and human intelligence models to determine their similarities and differences in order to organize their synergetic interaction and, as a result, mutual development. The subject can be designed as a Sense-Cognitive Structure, presented in the form of a Content-Structure Pattern, both of the target discipline and the learner, where the content is structured and the structure is meaningful. This allows comparing patterns to determine their diversity as a prerequisite for synergetic interaction and similarities to identify a common system-forming factor. The identified "gaps" reflect the zones and dynamics of development that can be tracked and measured in correlation with the methods and techniques used, which allows not only to adjust and optimize the development process, but also to use it for scientific research as an experiment conducted in natural learning conditions, where the dependent variable will be the efficiency of learning, and the independent variable will be the learning strategy used.

2.5 Features of Next Generation Education

The integration of AI into the learning environment is changing the very paradigm of education, which is capable of providing training that meets not only the needs and opportunities of today, but also dynamically develops at the pace of society's development, or better yet, gets ahead of it. Let's define what features such education should have and what needs to be changed for this? Education should be: 1) human-centered; 2) practice-oriented; 3) integrating advanced technologies; 4) transparent / explainable; 5) integrating quality teaching; 6) manageable: a) measurable, b) providing constant feedback; 7) capable of development in the context of: a) technological trends, b) institutional and c) educational needs; 8) scalable; 9) multi-agent/sectoral/disciplinary; 10) cross-cultural; 11) focused on universal values; 12) safe.

The solution to provide such education is not easy, but it is possible. The task is solved within the framework of the Eco-Humanistic Technology of Self-Development (EHSDT) (Sergeyeva, 2009) that is described in the next section.

3. INNOVATIVE ECO-HUMANISTIC TECHNOLOGY OF SELF-DEVELOPMENT (EHTSD)

The section presents the Eco-Humanistic Technology of Self-Development (EHTSD) as an innovative perspective that distinguishes it from traditional models in educational technologies by offering a holistic systemic solution to one of the main contemporary problems of education. It is a model for integrating AI into education without losing the humanistic core. It provides a structured, theory-based approach to solving the dilemma of standardization and diversity. It considers WHERE EHTSD is located in relation to existing educational paradigms or taxonomies of learning and HOW it resolves the contradiction between scalable standardization and individualized innovation. The structure of the section allows to gradually deploy EHTSD through its concept - model - structure - algorithm of e-learning. For concretization, the content-structure matrix of the e-course – the profile of the student – the patterns of the e-course, unit, and assignment are presented.

3.1."What is EHTSD?"

The issues that arise require elaboration through a strong conceptual framing based on a deep understanding of the structural and philosophical problems of educational innovation. It is possible to overcome the shortcomings of the above approaches on the basis of a deep system understanding of the nature and principles of organizing efficient Educational Activity (EA), which, as the most advanced scientific theory, has received a second wind in connection with the development of advanced technologies.

EHTSD is original, comprehensive, systems-based approach to student development that integrates AI, cognitive science, systems theory, and education. EHTSD, which has undergone a long-term formative experiment under the conditions of natural university education, has received scientifically substantiated confirmation of the principles of organizing educational activities based on the laws of human memory and thinking functioning (Sergeyeva, 2014). Since the proposed approach is based on a scientific understanding of the synergistic relationship between human consciousness and behavior, it is not only promising in terms of co-creation of interdisciplinary solutions, but also significantly facilitates AI integration into the implementation of human solutions of high complexity and scale. EHTSD reveals the prospect of synergy between natural and artificial (generative and symbolic) intelligence. Within its framework, the Individual Sens-Cognitive Structure (ICSS) of the student is formed, reflecting the objects of the academic discipline and the connections between them in the context of certain conditions, reflected in the connections of the student's neural network. This entry point into learning ensures the synergy of natural and artificial intelligence due to a single system-forming basis – neural network connections formed as a result of interaction with the environment (existential/virtual/linguistic). The common basis allows for smooth integration of human learning as a living system and artificial (symbolic and generative) intelligence technologies.

EHTSD is based on understanding development as a process of human-environment synergetic interaction. Within this interaction there is an exchange of needs and services that are realized via mechanisms and patterns of interaction causing human-environment co-development. All this system process is reflected in the Figure 3.

Figure 3. Human-Environment Interaction

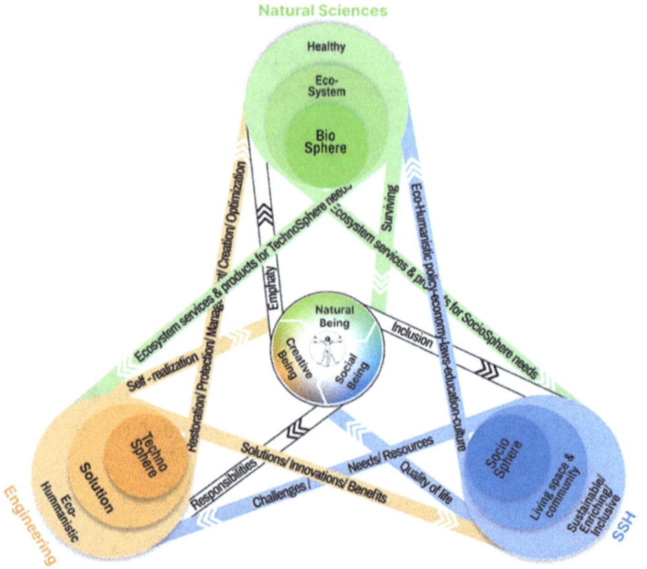

EHTSD allows creating a simulation of the natural development process, modeling the interaction of learner – developmental environment, causing co-development of both the learner and the environment. Development is presented as a cyclic process in the format of "Developmental circle" (event – sense – capacity – activity choice – activity realization – activity automation – event), including: 1) a learning event - 2) the learner's awareness of its sense - 3) an assessment of the possibility of realizing this sense in the existing conditions - 4) choosing an adequate way to realize the sense - 5) implementing activities to realize the sense - 6) automation of successful actions, transformation and integration into resources - 7) a new event (Fig. 4a). Going through these stages, the student climbs the "ladder of competence" from the stage of "unconscious ignorance" through "conscious ignorance" and "conscious competence" to "unconscious competence", i.e. automated skill and ability, achieving the transformation of acquired resources into personal abilities and qualities.

The "Developmental circle" is served by 4 mechanisms (Fig. 4b): 1) the basic Mechanism of consciousness- behavior interaction, where the subject of interaction (S) simultaneously carries out actions in the internal (A^{in}) and external (A^{ex}) plane. Due to the isomorphism of external and internal structures of activity and the principle of positive feedback, the process of mutual development is controlled by external/internal goals (O^{ex}/O^{in}) and conditions (E^{ex}/E^{in}) that determine the mutual human-environment co-development; 2) the mechanism of driving forces of development, based on the ambivalent desire for preservation and development, satisfied through the process of balancing senses/meanings – resources – conditions, continuously restoring nonequilibrium states; 3) the mechanism of developmental capacity, determined by the range of cognitive-sense orientation to the senses of survival – quality of life – the sense of life; 4) the mechanism of development optimization through the initial definition of a strategic goal that organizes actions into a system, where the result of the previous action becomes the means of implementing the next one. Graduate profile as an agent of change is a strategic orientation.

Figure 4. Development Circle

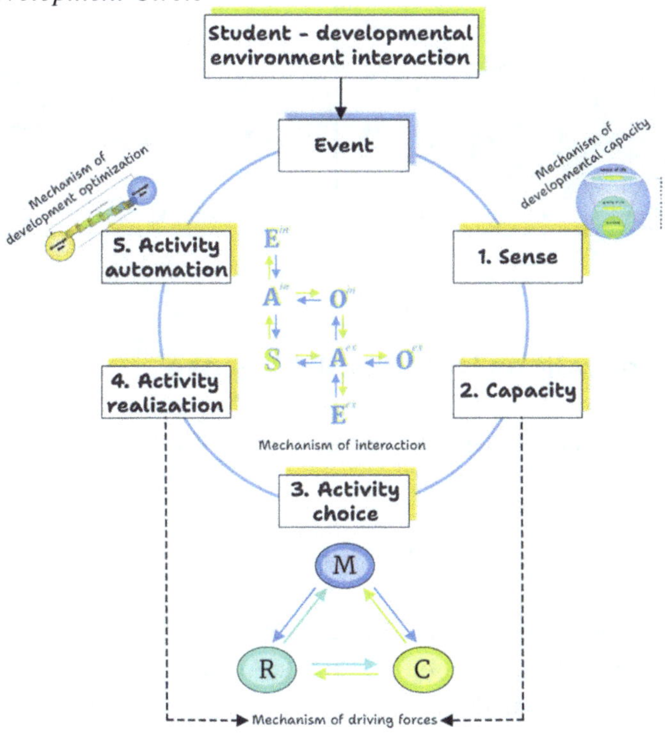

Mechanisms 2 and 4 are universal and coincide with such key deep learning algorithms as backpropagation and gradient descent proposed by Geoffrey Hinton (Gotesman, 2018). The common system-forming factor of both artificial neural networks and the individual sense-cognitive scheme (ICSS) are the connections between neurons/functions expressed in weights, which allows for the isomorphism of the content- structure patterns of artificial and human intelligence, to determine their similarities and diversities in order to organize their synergetic interaction and mutual development. The process and result of development are presented in the format of the content-structural patterns of the learner (ICSS network and content-structure profile) and discipline (Content-Structure Matrix).

Figure 5. Mechanisms

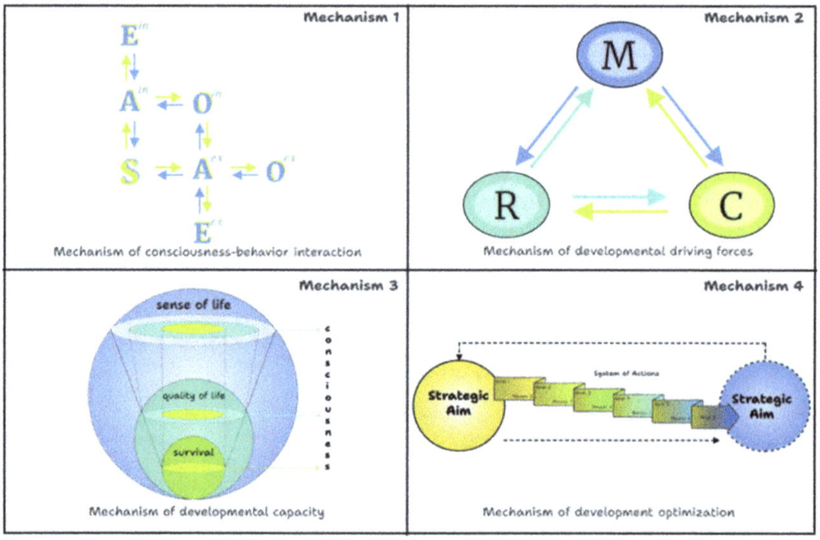

3.2. What Innovations Does EHSD Propose

In addition to the modelling natural process of Human-Environment co-development described above the EHSD propose the following innovations:

3.2.1 System-Forming Factor of the E-Learning Process.

In education the system-forming factor is presented by student-learning environment interaction (Sergeyeva et al., 2022). All the regularities of educational activity can be derived from this system-forming entity. In this case, the educational environment is understood in a broad sense, not only as being developed, but also as developmental environment, including natural-social-technological/creative speres (relevant to areas of knowledge or a multidisciplinary environment). The learner is understood as a living system-of-systems integrating natural-social-creative being, which is simultaneously the subject and the object of mutual development (Sergeyeva et al., 2024).

"Why is it Important?"

Without a systemic understanding of the holistic process, the complex multi-agent process of modern education disintegrates into many problems that are difficult to control. Efficient target management requires understanding the essence of the process, from which all resulting phenomena can be derived without losing the connection between them. Connections determine the sense/meaning of actions. As a result, the entire process can be optimally managed through the system-forming factor, as a single point of control, rather than solving previously solved problems each time as new ones (Freitas et al., 2022).

"How Does it Work?"

How to define the system-forming factor? EHTSD, aimed at developing system thinking as a metacognitive basis for cognition, is based on the scientific principle of deriving the essence of an object by tracing the history of its origin with the subsequent derivation of all objects from this essence, which allows to preserve connections, and therefore solve any problems in a situation of uncertainty by restoring connections, but not ready-made samples.

"Where is it Applied?"

From the point of view of the developmental effect, it does not matter whether the interaction occurs with a real or virtual environment, in both cases the development of the cognitive-sense structure of the learner, reflected in the connections of the neural network, takes place, and the virtual environment can be even more efficient in speed, volume, scaling and impact.

3.2.2 Technology of Superimposing Cognitive-Sense Structures

Educational standards must be measurable. EHTSD provides a universal "Technology of Superimposing Profiles" (Sergeyeva et al., 2021), as sense-cognitive structures which open up the possibility of multi-agent-multimodal-multidisciplinary use, including multidimensional assessment.

"Why is it Important?"

The technology allows: a) to combine a set of data into a single integrated system and present it in a visually convenient and understandable format for multi-agent users, regardless of their specialty or level of education; b) to translate a set of data into generalized indices (as a system of numbers used to compare values changing in accordance with each other or a fixed standard) by transforming the pixels of the real zone; c) to measure the efficiency of each indicator separately and their interaction as a whole, determining the synergistic effect; d) to compare different systems due to the isomorphism of the profile structure and make decisions both on processes and on people (i.e. rating, making choices, selecting teams, planning, etc.); e) to reflect individual and collective vision in the format of ideal-real-synergetic profiles.

"How Does it Work?"

It is an automated tool performing measurements based on data input automatically or manually.

"Where is it applied?"

It is applied for determining: 1) development needs or development zone (the gap between the ideal and real profiles); 2) a strategic goal (measured within the identified development zone); 3) the time required to meet/achieve needs/goals; 4) dynamics for monitoring success; 5) a synergistic effect.

3.2.3 Structural-content pattern of LMS within the framework of EHTSD

EHTSD is systematically presented as a concept-model-structure-algorithm, which allows it to be used as an Instructional Design methodology within the LMS, aimed at creating high-quality e-courses in accordance with accepted standards. LMS. within the framework of EHTSD is presented in the form of an original content-structure model, in which the structure is meaningful, and the content is structured (Herlo, 2024). EHTSD anticipates next-generation LMS features such as: 1) structure-based content modeling of student development; 2) AI-enabled real-time personalization; 3) adaptive content; 4) multi-agent/sector/disciplinary co-creation.

"Why is it Important?"

Objects and connections of the model can be easily converted into numbers and presented in a universal format of isomorphic structures/profiles, which can be compared in different contexts based on the original Technology of Superimposing Profiles as cognitive-sense structures (see above). Such a structure, expressed in numbers, is easily transformed into a solution profile, which, in fact, is a universal tool for measuring the efficiency of learning at all stages and allows for continuous monitoring of its progress in real time, visualizing its dynamics.

"How Does it Work?"

Digital representation enables the Eco-Humanistic concept to be embodied in technology that significantly increases the quality (speed-accuracy-capacity) and productivity of learning activities by allowing for the ability to alternate parallel task execution and team interaction, where diversities create a synergistic effect. Unprecedented scaling is possible, increasing the scale of impact by an order of magnitude.

"Where is it Applied?"

The model is built from the system-forming essence of training, allowing to manage, measure and program complex processes of students cognitive and personality development in the process of mastering academic subjects up to new generation multi-agent/sector/disciplinary projects.

4. STRUCTURAL AND CONTENT PATTERNS, TECHNIQUES AND LMS TOOLS

EHTSD, presented as a system of "concept - model - structure - algorithm" allows to purposefully manage the process of cognitive and personality development of students through a content-structure model consisting of content-structure patterns, in which the content is structured, and the structure is meaningful. This approach opens up the possibility of implementing a multidimensional measurement of the standards, answering the questions: WHAT? HOW? WHY? LMS implementing automated Instructional Design based on EHTSD through a systematic selection of content-structure patterns of the e-course - units - tasks, allows creating e-courses in the contexts of the standards and at the same time the individual needs of the learner. Here, student-centered and subject-centered learning work in synergy. And if we use a metaphor, the content-structure patterns organize students activity similar to a canvas on which each learner embroiders the picture or ornament that corresponds to her/his meanings-needs-skills. With this approach, standards do not hinder the development of individuality, diversity, innovation and creativity.

This section considers: 4.1. EHTSD content-structure model including matrix of the discipline (4.1.1), ICSS of the learner (4.1.2); profile of the learner (4.1.3); 4.2. Content-structure model measurement including measurement of Content-structure patterns (4.2.1); Real and ideal profiles (4.2.2); ICSS, individual profiles and content-structure patterns of different disciplines and students (4.2.3); Links between components of the learning/developmental environment. (4.2.4); 4.3. Content-structure pattern of the e-course including Metacognitive module (4.3.1); Practical module (4.3.2); Self-management and self-assessment module (4.3.3.); Support and communication system module and the Supplementary materials module (4.3.4); 4.4. Content-structure pattern of the unit; 4.5. Content-structure pattern of the task.

4.1. EHTSD Content-Structure Model

EHTSD content-structure model includes matrix of the discipline, ICSS and profile of the learner described below

4.1.1. Content-Structure Matrix of the Discipline

It reflects the target knowledge, abilities, skills and qualities specified by the curriculum in the context of the ideal graduate profile in correlation with the tasks united by the general topic of the course unit. The matrix performs the functions of: 1) a navigator, providing a transition from an individual program to a specific task on the platform; 2) assessment and reflection of success in the format of a graph of the success of the task completion and an individual profile of the development of the student's cognitive resources.

The structure of the pattern is universal and, as a rule, does not depend on the course. The content-structure matrix includes: code and/or name of the module; code and name of the topic; task code; link for direct transition to the task; an assessment zone, where the efficiency of task completion is calculated based on data on the ideal and actual speed, completeness and accuracy of the solution, which are automatically calculated as the tasks are completed. The result of each task is reflected in the efficiency graph; a zone of connection of tasks with the competencies/skills of the graduate profile. As the tasks are completed, a profile of cognitive and personality development is formed. Color markers indicate: a) the recommended level of task elaboration: deep study, viewing, searching; b) task categories: examination practice; theoretical material; practical material.

The following algorithm of educational actions is proposed within the framework of the course pattern: 1) familiarize yourself with the modules and topics of the course that need to be worked out to achieve the adopted goal/realization of personal meaning; 2) complete the tasks sequentially, each task in accordance with the color markers of the recommended level of elaboration; 3) go to a specific task by code and link; 4) complete the task in accordance with its conditions; 5) upon completion of work with the module tasks, familiarize yourself with the results reflected in the success graph and return to the tasks whose efficiency is below 0.7. Analyze the cause of errors and re-complete the tasks marked in red. Access to the next module opens only upon achieving efficiency of at least 0.7 for all tasks; 7) as a result of successful completion of the module tasks, familiarize yourself with the achieved level of cognitive and personal development reflected in the personal profile; 8) proceed to the next module, repeating the proposed algorithm.

4.1.2. Content-Structure ICSS of the Learner

It reflects cognitive and personality development in terms of mastered functions reflected in the connections of the subject being studied. They determine the efficiency of solving professional-social-existential problems that ensure the development and integration of personal sense-skills-qualities. ICSS models the learner's neural network, in which activated neurons reflect functions/features (in our case, acquired competence within a given topic), and connections between activated neurons (expressed in weights). Neurons reflect objects, and connections – meanings/sense. A graphical representation of the network allows to superimpose an ideal network on a real one and determine the learner's developmental zone. Moreover, superimposition is also possible in text format. Measuring the dynamics and efficiency of development allows to determine the efficiency of the learning strategies used, and measuring the efficiency of problem solving in conjunction with the development of personal characteristics allows to build an individual cognitive-personality profile.

4.1.3. Content-Structure Profile of the Learner

Figure 5 reflects the Content-Structure Matrix – Neuronet Profile – Content-Structure Profile transition. To determine the DC of both living and man–made systems, an innovative universal tool is used – a multifunctional content-structure profile. It visualizes, defines and measures the current state, efficiency, dynamics and development zones reflecting the DC in the context of a given goal of both an individual (a system of systems interacting with eco-socio-techno spheres) or an alliance (multiagent/industry/disciplinary), and a process (policy, education, science, production, business, art and culture, presented in the format of paradigms, strategies, methodologies, curricula/courses/tasks, specific events/meetings/sessions/trainings/classes/lessons, etc.). The tool models/simulates the work of neural networks in which the activation of neurons and the connections between them form content structure patterns, where the content is structured and the structure is meaningful. The neural network is transformed into a content-structure profile, which has a circular configuration along which points are located, corresponding to neurons/characteristics/properties/features (F) of an individual/ alliance/process, corresponding to a given goal. These points are activated by internal (meanings/sense) or external (conditions) stimuli, causing the development of a Feature, which is measured by a Vector directed radially from the center to the activated point on the circle. The length of the Vector corresponds to the current level of development of a specific Feature and is calculated according to the methodology corresponding to the goal. The connection of the endpoints of the Vectors visualizes the real Profile of an individual/alliance/process, revealing a structurally significant pattern that can be measured in pixels, and its DC is calculated by multiplying weights of Features of activated neurons by Vectors of connections.

The weight is calculated by the number of connections that the Features are capable of activating. Such connections are defined by the chords connecting the Features indicated on the circle. This allows calculating DC taking into account the synergistic effect produced by the interaction of Features, through correlation and factor analysis.

Figure 6. Content-Structure Patterns Transformations

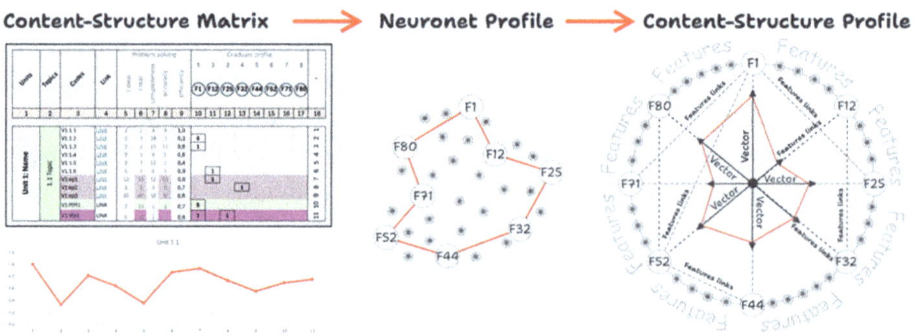

4.2. Content-Structure Model Measurement

The technology of superimposing cognitive-sense structures allows comparing patterns in order to determine similarities (find a system-forming factor), diversities (determine the possibility of synergetic interaction), developmental zones (define the goal and development strategy), as well as to measure and calculate.

4.2.1. Content-Structure Patterns

Content-structure patterns reflect discipline and the learner. The content-structure pattern of the discipline determines its complexity and Developmental Capacity (DC). DC measurement format: correspondence of tasks to the features (F), relevant target competencies and sense-abilities-qualities that make up the graduate's profile (measuring course congruence); problem solving efficiency; efficiency graph; ICSS complexity; cognitive and personality development profile; comparison of the developmental efficiency of learners. The content-structure pattern of the learner determines zones, dynamics, complexity and efficiency of personality development. Measurement format: ICSS complexity in terms of the number of functions and the weight of connections in the network (competence and experience); solution efficiency according to the speed-completeness-accuracy criteria; 3) problem solving efficiency graph within the course unit.

4.2.2. Real and Ideal Profiles

Real and ideal profiles reflect student and platform/curriculum/e-course/course unit/lesson. Profiles of the student determine: development zones (gaps between ideal and real indicators), dynamics (rate of change), capabilities and efficiency (data on the beam) in the context of a given goal. Measurement format: 1) cognitive development profile – indicators of problem-solving efficiency according to the speed-completeness-accuracy criteria in the context of the discipline topic; 2) personality development profile – indicators of the development of professional-social-existential sense-competencies-qualities in the context of the change agent's personal profile. Profiles of the platform / work program / course / course unit / lesson determine development zones (gaps between ideal and real indicators), dynamics (rate of change), capacity (data on the beam) in the context of a given goal. Measurement format: 1) to evaluate the DC of a platform, course, program, lecture or class, measurements of the assessment results by experts, teachers, students, practitioners, stakeholders are used, followed by comparison and identification of similarities, differences and communication blind spots to develop a strategy for synergistic co-creation; 2) course unit: prompt assessment of the results of assignments/tasks completed by students and teachers (Grade); 3) course: measurement of the DC of a discipline based on statistics obtained from the course unit format.

4.2.3. ICSS, Individual Profiles and Content-Structure Patterns of Different Disciplines and Students

They are aimed at comparing the DC of disciplines and for integrating the competitive factor into learning. Measurement format: to determine the most efficient courses and assignments in terms of DC, statistical data on the number of students and the gradation of development of cognitive and personal sense/abilities/qualities are used. The listed universal possibilities open up a number of innovative applications: 1) Profiles of cognitive and personality development reflect and measure the target and actual level, zone, dynamics and efficiency of development. The profile rays (like STEN scales) plot data on the efficiency of training and personality development obtained from the content-structure patterns of the course; 2) The area of the current profile measured in pixels reflects the level, and the area between the real and ideal profiles reflects the development zone. The obtained data can be used for self-assessment by students, for generalization by developers, for course improvement by teachers and for statistics by the administration and stakeholders; 3) The proposed tool can ensure multi-agent/industry/disciplinary co-creation, since the isomorphism of structures allows comparing various content-structure patterns and determining their efficiency and DC, reducing them to a single coordinate system; 4) Comparison of patterns allows to initially determine both the DC of a specific person, team, association, alliance, and the entire policy, science, education, economics, business, service, culture, etc.; 5) The method of superimposing profiles allows to quickly select and develop optimally balanced teams/associations/structures; 6) Depending on the set goal, the profile can be both general and differential, reflecting the personality/association/process both as a whole and in parts, highlighting target patterns without losing the integrity of the structure.

4.2.4. Links Between Components of the Learning/Developmental Environment

Links allow for a consistent/step-by-step transfer of data from one format to another to customize a course/program and then determine the dynamics and efficiency of mastering a subject using the method of superimposing cognitive-sense structures (real to ideal). The following sequence is followed: 1) assessment of task completion; 2) content-structure Matrix of the discipline; 3) ICSS of the student in the format of a neural network profile; 4) content=structure profile of the student's cognitive and personality development.

4.3. Content-Structure Patterns of the E-Course

The content-structure pattern of the e-course includes: Course code – Course title – Course objective – Metacognitive module (Starter test – Individual development program – Introductory interactive lecture and Video presentation of the course – Work plan – Questions for self-assessment) – Practical module (Motivational – Executive – Generalizing – Integrating blocks) – Self-management and self-assessment module – Support and communication system module – Supplementary materials module.

Let's consider the elements of the pattern in more detail. The Code and Course Title set the coordinates and allow the learner to identify the course and enter it via a link;

4.3.1. Metacognitive Module

Awareness of actions is based on the metacognitive approach (Hornby et al., 2022), which provides knowledge about the process of cognition, about the subject and about oneself. It allows to autonomously manage the e-learning process and is formed as a result of answers to 3 questions: "Where am I now?", "Where do I want to be?", "How can I get there?" To answer these questions, the following are provided:

The Course Objective allows the learner to answer the 1st question of the "Developmental Circle" regarding the sense of the development event "Do I want?" and creates a strategic orientation in the course content to determine its compliance with expectations;

Entry test. The initial testing allows the student to answer the "Where am I now?" and 2nd question of the "Development Circle" about their own capabilities "Can I?" and determine the development zone based on identifying the gap between the individual and ideal profiles (graduate/course);

Interactive content-structure curriculum. The individual program is built on the basis of the identified gap in the structural and content pattern of the discipline in the interactive content-structure curriculum format;

Metacognitive lecture. An introductory video lecture and presentation of the e-course create a metacognitive focus in the course and answer the questions WHAT? WHY? HOW? to familiarize with the structure, content, methods and tools of work; The work plan is presented in the form of tasks indicating the method of their processing and slide numbers as sources of information; Generalization in the form of questions for self-monitoring (key points to remember) and an algorithm to transfer the acquired knowledge into practice.

The metacognitive approach is provided systematically not only in the metacognitive module, but also throughout the entire e-course. Each task contains a metacognitive block that provides operational instructions and examples of completing tasks. If the instructions and examples are insufficient, there is an option to follow a link to a tutorial in the micro-lecture format, which is activated directly from the e-course tasks as needed, when problems arise. In essence, a series of tutorials are slides/video clips from metacognitive lectures united by a problem, structured around a task and supplemented with infographics to provide self-sufficient content for promptly solving problems that arise.

4.3.2. Practical Module

All further actions of the learners are aimed at practice, which becomes a conscious process of optimal work of memory and thinking (Zinchenko et al., 2011), since the ICSS of the learners is formed without unnecessary objects and connections (see Mechanism 4: "Strategic Orientation"). Practice in the e-learning mode includes tasks corresponding to the stages of the " Developmental Circle", which are set by the program, and the results are processed by the program. The main criterion is the DC of the learning activity. Overcoming the technical limitations of the platform (multiple choice operations, filling in gaps, comparison, selection, etc.) is possible through combining operations into logical algorithms of developing learning activities by introducing formats, the structure of which sets these algorithms. The content-structure pattern of practical module includes: Code – Title – Topic – Goal – Motivational – Executive – Generalizing – Integrating levels.

Let us consider each of them separately:

The motivational level, corresponding to the first two stages of the developmental circle and answering questions about the level of "Where am I now?", the sense of "Do I want?" and the possibility of "Can I?" satisfy personal senses in the current conditions. Here the DC mechanism is activated (Mechanism 3: "Breadth of cognitive-sense orientation") and hypothetical thinking is developed. That is, the motivational block reveals the personal sense of mastering the module (Why? For what? Important? Not important?); the zone of individual development (cognitive and personal level of development of one's own resources) and develops hypothetical thinking, fitting problems into an existential context.

The executive level corresponding to the 3th and 4th stages of the "Developmental Circle" related to the selection and implementation of actions, as well as the Basic Mechanism 1 "Connection of External and Internal Activity" and Mechanism 2 "Driving Forces of Development" (each discipline has its own set of balancing mechanisms). The level presents a set of practical tasks in the coordinates of the module and is implemented through solving problems/tasks, both individually and in a group, as co-creation of solutions. Tasks can be presented in a variety of formats, from texts, questions, interactive tasks to games linking to metacognitive module, tutorials, micro-lectures, thesaurus and supplementary materials.

The generalizing level is a generalization expressed in the structure of the ICSS, reflected in the individual neural network and integrated into the cognitive resources of the individual. Corresponds to the beginning of stage 5 of the "Developmental Circle". Generalization can be carried out in the format of a drawing, infographics, presentation, report, essay, critical review, article with links to the relevant textbook, samples, auxiliary material and formats.

The Integrating level – transfer of acquired competencies into real practice at stage 5 of the "Developmental Circle": repetition-automation and integration of successful operations into individual resources in the form of skills, abilities and qualities. An efficient tool for transferring knowledge into practice is the interactive "Learning Diary", reflecting the acquired knowledge and competencies in cognitive-sense-emotional contexts and transforming the educational/developmental material of the module into an individual professional, social and existential context. To develop reflection, it is proposed to personalize the acquired knowledge, projecting it onto a real-life situation in the essay format. "Individual diary" is also a tool for developing reflection by summarizing the acquired experience in a format that combines multiple choice with an essay. The learner determines: 1) key learning moments useful for personal efficiency; 2) reflection of acquired knowledge by answering the questions: "What have I learned about myself, the environment, resources?"; 3) assessment of the current state of the issue in the context of everyday life in the relevance of the acquired knowledge; 4) development zone: of one's personality, environment, resources; 5) cognitive, emotional and practical assessment, determining subsequent actions based on the generalization: "My thoughts"; "My feelings"; "My actions".

Integration of acquired knowledge into practice can be carried out in the project work mode (possibly in a virtual laboratory), aimed at multi-agent/sectoral/disciplinary co-creation.

4.3.3. Self-Management and Self-Assessment Module

Self-management of e-learning implies self-monitoring and self-assessment of success throughout the entire learning process. A whole system has been developed for this purpose. It includes: 1) an individual learning success graph, which is built automatically based on the results of each task, calculated based on the parameters of speed, completeness, accuracy of solutions and displayed in the Progress Bar (PB); 2) an individual profile of progress towards the final goal, which is built automatically based on the results of the e-course in accordance with its goals; 3) self-assessment of activity in the format of assessment matrix using "color palette" method; 4) operational self-monitoring of success based on control questions with keys/answer samples).

4.3.4. Support and Communication System Module and the Supplementary Materials Module

To support e-learning, there is a Tutor System, which includes: 1) e-tutor – an online learning program on the platform and micro-courses; 2) self-tutor – independent activity according to a given algorithm; 3) personal-tutor – teacher-consultant; 4) expert-tutor – expert on request; 5) social-tutor – partners in social networks for sharing experience; 6) partner-tutor – ranging from peer-to-peer activities (which is becoming a trend) to interacting with each other on forums and events.

The communication system operates in five modes: 1) Automatic – instruction letters, reminders, assignment and test results; 2) Correspondence – communication with the teacher; 3) Video conference – communication with the teacher; 4) Forums on the platform – exchange of opinions and assistance with quality control in the "report a bug" section; 5) FAQ on the platform – answers to typical questions.

User-friendly interface. To create a comfortable learning environment, each task is formulated in such a way that the student understands the meaning of their actions, capabilities, resources and can promptly ask for help to constantly monitor their progress. Help can be obtained in the form of instructions and solutions or examples, up to a detailed description of actions in text and video formats. To determine the mode, duration and frequency of work, a table is provided that allows to calculate an individual weekly workload. Speed of completion is determined by success: each task is completed until an efficiency indicator of 0.7 is reached. The supplementary materials module includes a Glossary, a List of Abbreviations, Links to resources – literature used and necessary for study. Links to supplementary materials are provided in each course assignment as needed. Figure 6 and Figure 7 shows the content-structure pattern of the discipline as it is presented to students in a metacognitive lecture or as a whole.

Figure 7. Content-structure pattern of the discipline presented to students in a metacognitive lecture

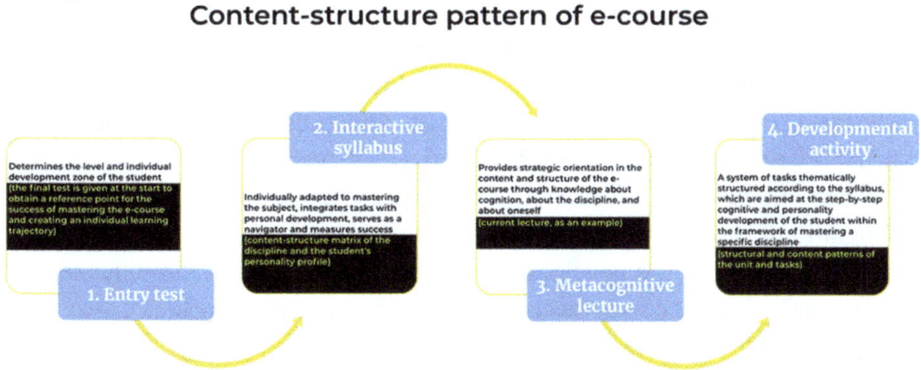

Figure 8. Content-structure patterns of the discipline as a whole

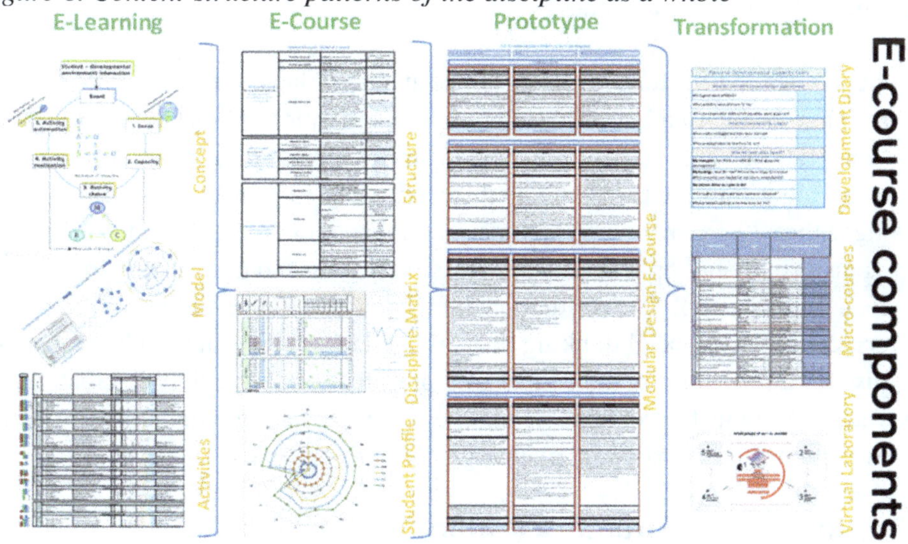

4.4. The Content-Structure Pattern of the Unit

The content-structure pattern of the unit corresponds to the topic of the syllabus and consists of tasks, according to the stage, goal and type of educational activity. The system-forming basis is developmental activity in the context of the topic of the academic discipline being mastered. The activity is divided into stages of competence development. Below is an example of a unit pattern typical for activity that develops student thinking within a lecture course.

1) Orientation/Perception - determines the personal content and resources for mastering the material based on hypothetical thinking, which is developed through the tasks: "Assumption": by the title of the topic, formulate a hypothesis about what is being discussed; "Content": analyze what is known about the problem; "Terminology": list of terms that may be needed.
2) Cognition/Comprehension - aimed at information processing of the material, which determines the development of analytical thinking through the tasks: "Review": check the hypothesis regarding the topic and key ideas; "Analysis": highlight and define key terms, compile a thesaurus; "Search": summarize the content of paragraphs in the form of questions in the context of the hypothesis about the known.

If necessary, practical tasks of "multiple choice", "establishing correspondence/sequence", "filling in" are added;

3) Generalization/Systematization – aimed at integrating information into personal resources, which leads to the development of systemic thinking through the tasks: "Integration": summarize information in the format of annotation according to an algorithm; "Criticism": analyze critically information according to an algorithm; "Visualization": summarize information in a graphical form.
4) Transformation/Application – aimed at evaluating and transferring the learned material in an application situation, which leads to the development of logical-critical-creative-social thinking through the tasks: "Presentation": present and discuss information in the format of a presentation; "Creativity": create innovative solutions to problems within the topic; "Planning": transform problems into opportunities based on planning subsequent actions.

4.5. The Content-Structure Pattern of the Task

The task pattern includes: 1) task code, 2) task type, 3) task condition, 4) tutorial indicating the goal, DC, instructions for completing (What to do?) and assessing (How to assess) the task, supporting materials, the learning material Zone (new subject knowledge in text format lecture/statistic/additional/critical review, etc. As the task progresses, the information is transformed into content-structure, which integrates into the IKSS) and the activity Zone (in the format of content-structure patterns that are filled in independently or from the proposed options using selection/matching/ordering).

5. NEXT GENERATION LMS FOR CO-CREATION OF SYNERGISTIC SOLUTIONS

5.1 Virtual Laboratories (VL)

E-learning uses virtual laboratories (VL), which are essentially interactive online scientific simulations that place students in real-world scenarios where they must apply their knowledge to solve real-world problems. VL is a learning/training/experimental environment that is either remote or has no immediate physical reality and serves a variety of functions such as education, research, and modeling.

Experimental VLs enable experimental activities to be carried out in the learning process itself, using interactive digital simulations of actions that would typically occur in a real laboratory setting. Students grasp concepts by performing experiments online. VLs mimic tools, equipment, tests, and procedures used in chemistry, biochemistry, physics, biology, and other disciplines. Scientific VLs (Online Simulated Labs) offer the experimental steps of a scientific experiment on-screen or interactively. Simulations are digital presentations used to show how something works. Educational VLs allow for the assessment and rating of student performance based on objective testing of student actions and skills against criteria for assessing real-world work tasks and outcomes. VLs have their pros and cons. Namely:

Pros. Academic research in specific fields of study shows that VL simulations have a tremendous positive impact on learning because they are supported by the personal experiences of students and teachers. Pros include enhanced learning opportunities such as: use case – simulations; skill refinement; access to new learning experiences and equipment; opportunity to repeat experiments; stimulation of interest and engagement; challenge to use critical thinking skills; distance learning and flexibility; resource optimization, cost efficiency and sustainability; 24/7 availability (a student can access virtual labs anywhere, anytime, at any pace, of any type, both online and offline); data security and protection; scalability.

Cons. While VLs provide unique opportunities for interactive and self-paced learning, they also pose challenges related to technical requirements, curriculum integration, and potential reduction of hands-on experience. One negative effect of VLs is that they reduce direct interactions between students, as well as between students and teachers, given that most of the communication between them takes place online. While scientific VLs are well suited for exploring and understanding unobservable phenomena, when used as the sole form of instruction in online science labs, they do not provide holistic/compelling learning experience.

As an alternative to VLs that overcomes these shortcomings, EHTSD offers an innovative approach that is fundamentally different from the limited use of VLs in the traditional learning paradigm. It is not just an experimental activity, but a co-creation of synergistic solutions. EHTSD enables the integration of multi-agent/sectoral/disciplinary practice-oriented learning into e-learning, based on project work aimed at co-creation of synergistic solutions. The proposed technology models the cognitive, communicative and regulatory functions of human consciousness, embodied in AI-Powered Educational Tools. Synergy is provided by the original technology of profile overlay, reflecting the individual vision of ideal and real transformations and the integrated multi-agent synergetic vision with the identification of congruence-contradictions-gaps, indicating readiness for implementation or the need for search. The advantage of this technology is its unprecedented speed, capacity, impact and scalability. The resulting synergetic profile provides strategic orientation. At the same time, the unique contribution of each participant is not lost, which creates diversity as a condition for synergetic development. Moreover, in the process of co-creation as a purposeful activity, thanks to the basic development mechanism, consciousness and behavior of students, awareness of human-environment interdependence, as a result, self-identification with the decisions made are developed.

It is presented an example of VL simulation for co-creating natural based solutions within New European Bauhaus coordinates (NBS^{NEB}) aimed at sustainable transformation of urban space (Fig. 8). The process is supported by intelligent tools: 1. Atlas of Interactive Dynamic Smart Maps as a virtual polygon; 2. Self-Developing NBS^{NEB} OmniBase; 3. NBS^{NEB} Synergetic Profile as Ideal-Real-Synergetic Solutions Integrator; 4. NBS^{NEB} Multi-scale Evaluation; 5. NBS^{NEB} Multi-stage transformation as Interactive Sequential Tasks Continuum. Content-structure model reflects cognitive-communicative-regulatory functions of human consciousness, which allows organizing the process of multi-agent co-creation based on the laws of synergy of human consciousness and behavior, creating the basis for their development, as well as self-identification with the decisions made and taking responsibility for them. The technology allows managing, measuring and scaling the process of co-creation impact.

5.2. Virtual Reality Labs (VRL)

It is necessary to distinguish between VL and VRL, which is a special room whose purpose is to allow users to interact with things and go through a scenario they see in a virtual environment using virtual reality technology. VRLs have a wide range of applications (electronics and communications; computer science and engineering). They can also be used for research: 1) in the field of education, to observe and record the behavior and learning strategies of users as they study educational content using this environment; 2) for gamification in virtual labs for language learning. Enhanced engagement: By incorporating game elements such as interactive challenges, exciting storylines and visually appealing graphics, gamification captures the attention of learners and keeps them engaged for a longer time. This sustained engagement leads to deeper learning and better retention of language skills; 3) for co-creation – Reality Labs brings together a world-class team of researchers, developers and engineers to create the future of communication in virtual and augmented reality.

Figure 9. Co-creation process

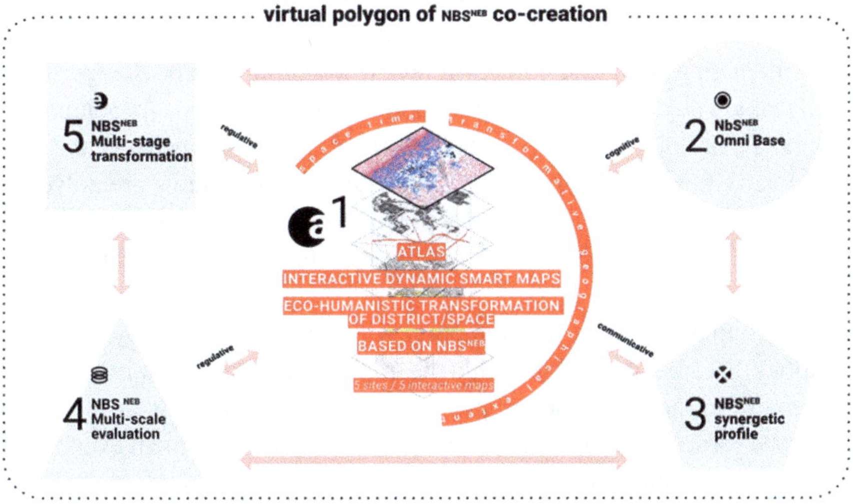

EHTSD proposes to integrate an educational component into VRL to increase its DC (Developmental Capacity) and expand the range of application (Sergeyeva et al., 2023). This requires: 1) creating VR as a developmental ecosystem taking into account the laws of personality development; 2) involving not only figurative but also abstract thinking to expand the way VR is described through abstract schemes in addition to images; 3) introducing a moral dimension to assessing the possible impact of VR on the mind and body of users, as well as on the real world.

EHTSD provides modeling of a digital learning environment based on the internal laws of human development, allowing to optimize the entire learning process. The built-in educational component provides a virtual learning environment with a developmental potential that significantly exceeds the simulated reality.

Unlike the situational approach, the process is modeled in its existential integrity. It is based on the idea of human development as a living system self-developing in interaction with the outside world as a developmental environment. In the process of balancing current needs, personal capabilities and environmental conditions, a synergistic development of all three components occurs. As a result, not only cognitive and personality development is optimized, but also the awareness of the interdependence and mutual development of oneself and the environment occurs. The innovative eco-humanistic model is focused on the development of existential, social and career meta-senses of a person through synergetic interaction with the environment, causing the development of competencies. The efficiency of the approach is confirmed by the results of a long-term developmental experiment. The concept, structure, strategy, mechanisms and tools of innovative e-learning courses are presented.

The educational component is integrated through the organization of VR as an ecosystem based on the patterns of cognitive and personality development of a person interacting with VR content relevant to the target knowledge through a system of tasks. The conditions of interaction determine the tasks/problems that the user solves. Their solution determines both internal (consciousness) and external (behavior) activities, which are linked synergistically. Problems are solved in the context of the final goal, the achievement of which occurs in the process of transition of intermediate actions from the status of the current goal to the status of means to achieve the subsequent goal.

The developmental effect of interaction with VR is enhanced by the following opportunities that are unavailable within the framework of traditional and e-learning: 1) involvement in the development process is enhanced not only at the cognitive, but also at the sense and emotional levels; 2) the set of development events expands almost indefinitely, their scope can be limited only by imagination; 3) access to resources that support development is practically unlimited; 4) EHTSD allows for a conscious choice of an environment that best suits the user's sense, goals, and needs based on the determination of the complexity of the individual cognitive-sense structure and the individual competency profile of the user. This allows for the creation of a self-developing structured database of capabilities and content of the VR ecosystem development environments.

VRL can integrate into education such types of learning activities (LA) that were not only previously unachievable, but were not considered in principle, since they were attributed to the level of consciousness (imagination, creativity), and not activity. Technological progress has made it possible to exteriorize consciousness and embody it in observable real actions in real time. This is invaluable material for scientific research and pedagogical influence. Of the many innovations, we will summarize and highlight the main ones:

1. A radical change in the efficiency of student development occurs through the presence effect. A common social space with avatars, where the user is represented by a name, image (Sergeyeva et al., 2023), a customizable avatar that can move, talk and / or perform animation actions, interactions with virtual objects increases awareness of actions not only due to the personal participation of stu-

dents in solving the problem, but also due to the ability to track the success of their actions from the inside. This creates a unique opportunity to significantly improve the development of reflection, acquiring metacognitive knowledge about oneself directly in the process of action and feeling the consequences, and not analysis "after."

2. A constantly updating "world" in which avatars can live and interact sets various conditions of the developing environment with which the student interacts. This is a whole multitude of worlds: 1) a virtual world that reproduces the limitations of space and imperfections of the real world; 2) a specially created world that is provided to the user for a specific game or time-sensitive event; 3) ideal VR, where each user shares one virtual world, where property is saved between sessions. And if this is a meaningful/substantive change in conditions (and not another "shooter"), it works to develop the ability to transfer knowledge into practice and, as a result, automate actions that integrate into internal resources in the form of abilities and qualities. Moreover, from a psychological point of view, it does not matter whether it is a real or virtual world. The main thing is the actions and their adequacy. Moreover, the unique opportunity to renew the world creates conditions for the development of students as agents of change.
3. Co-creation of the developing environment with which the student interacts not only develops the students' creative abilities, but also helps to individualize the environment, as well as create new tools for assessing the efficiency of training. The interaction of differences provides a synergistic effect of development. Although this does not lie on the surface, this is possible due to the creation of content of one's own materiality, which is an advantage for both users who will be able to form their virtual world at will, and for VR creators who will not have to spend a lot of time and effort to create each individual virtual object from a sketch. Relatively simple building blocks can produce network effects and allow for a wide variety of objects to be created in the world.

The integration of VR into the EHTSD is mutually beneficial, since it not only increases the Developmental Capacity (DC) of the EHTSD, but also enriches VR with mechanisms that ensure the synergy of natural and artificial intelligence. Thus, the integration of "Mechanism 1" introduces a conscious subject of development into the problem-solving process based on the interaction of its internal (consciousness) and external (behavior) activities, synergistically interconnected by internal and external goals and conditions. This implies the need for a moral measurement of one's own actions (means of achieving a goal), since their method, through feedback loops, influences not only external, but also internal goals and conditions. The integration of "Mechanism 2" into the VR ecosystem allows not only to purposefully develop the sense and resources of the user by developing the environment, but also to involve users in the development of an existing or creation of a new reality. The integration of "Mechanism 3" into the VR ecosystem allows one to initially determine the cognitive capacity of the user based on the level of sense orientation and offer a development environment commensurate with sense. Another entry point is also possible, when a sense orientation is initially introduced into the ecosystem, ensuring the development of the user's sense as a condition for the efficiency of cognitive development. The integration of "Mechanism 4" into the VR ecosystem enhances the developing effect of VR, ensuring awareness and consistency of the user's actions, and, as a result, their involuntary memorization.

All this involves the user as a proactive entity, capable of consciously managing the process of once own development in synergy with the development of VR. The initial sense and cognitive orientations reinforce each other, providing a synergistic effect due to the focus on the existential sense of mutual development in interaction with the environment. The technological capacity of the ecosystem significantly enhances the developing effect of VR.

6. FROM THEORY TO PRACTICE: APPLYING EHTSD IN REAL EDUCATIONAL SETTINGS

EHTSD is successfully implemented in the practice of real university education, which, while maintaining standardization, allows for freedom of choice, diversity, innovation and creativity. Below are real examples and results of experimental learning, based on measurable indicators of success, demonstrating the practical impact of EHTSD.

6.1. EHTSD Learning Experiment

It has been experimentally proven that EHTSD embodied in technology in the format of a content-structure model can be efficiently implemented in a real educational context. A number of studies conducted in the conditions of natural university education have shown high efficiency of students cognitive and personality development in the very process of mastering a specific subject. The following were compared: Control group - K, which received traditional teaching of the target subject through the transfer of ready-made knowledge, and 4 experimental groups (E1, E2, E3, E4), in which the target professional competence was developed through solving exclusively professional problems (E1), problems including a social context (E2); problems including an existential context of self-development (E3); problems including professional - social - existential contexts. The main strategy was to balance sense-resources-conditions. The following were measured: efficiency of problem solving; complexity of an individual sense-cognitive structure; sense: professional-social-existential; abilities: decision-making-communication-self-development; qualities: objectivvity-proactivity-autonomy-responsibility-flexibility-creativity-empathy. of EHTSD demonstrated not only the highest indicators of developmental efficiency at the sense, cognitive and activity levels, but also a synergistic effect, due to which the learning outcomes significantly exceeded the expected ones (Fig. 9). At the same time, the training followed all accepted educational standards.

Table 1. Training experiment results under conditions of natural university education

GROUPS	INDICATORS	COGNITIVE DEVELOPMENT					PERSONALITY DEVELOPMENT												
			problem solving				*sense*			*abilities*			*qualities*						
		SKS complexity	velocity	accuracy	completeness	efficiency	professional	social	existential	decision-making	synergetic interaction	Self-development	objectivity	proactivity	autonomy	responsibility	creativity	flexibility	empathy
		SKS	**Dsp**	**Dac**	**Dcm**	**ERZ**	**Spr**	**Ssc**	**Sek**	**Cpr**	**Cvz**	**Csm**	**Mre**	**Mpa**	**Mav**	**Mot**	**Mkr**	**Mgb**	**Mtm**
K	Ks	0.37	0.72	0.36	0.73	0.35	0.29	0.43	0.41	0.38	0.37	0.36	0.37	0.34	0.34	0.35	0.35	0.34	0.34
	Kr	0.49	0.74	0.38	0.75	0.38	0.40	0.39	0.38	0.38	0.38	0.40	0.49	0.37	0.36	0.37	0.36	0.35	0.34
	ΔK	0.12	0.02	0.02	0.02	0.03	0.11	0.04	0.03	0.00	0.01	0.04	0.12	0.03	0.02	0.02	0.01	0.01	0.00
E1	E1s	0.37	0.81	0.36	0.83	0.35	0.32	0.43	0.42	0.40	0.38	0.38	0.42	0.32	0.37	0.37	0.37	0.33	0.36
	E1r	0.62	0.83	0.54	0.85	0.53	0.53	0.47	0.46	0.45	0.45	0.53	0.62	0.52	0.58	0.36	0.36	0.35	0.34
	ΔE1	0.25	0.02	0.18	0.02	0.18	0.21	0.04	0.04	0.05	0.07	0.15	0.20	0.20	0.21	0.01	0.01	0.02	0.02
E2	E2s	0.37	0.84	0.33	0.86	0.34	0.32	0.43	0.42	0.39	0.39	0.38	0.39	0.37	0.37	0.35	0.38	0.38	0.33
	E2r	0.64	0.88	0.50	0.90	0.51	0.52	0.55	0.53	0.51	0.56	0.52	0.64	0.62	0.35	0.37	0.50	0.50	0.51
	ΔE2	0.27	0.04	0.17	0.04	0.17	0.20	0.12	0.11	0.12	0.17	0.14	0.25	0.25	0.02	0.02	0.12	0.12	0.18
E3	E3s	0.37	0.91	0.35	0.93	0.35	0.31	0.43	0.42	0.39	0.38	0.37	0.35	0.39	0.38	0.36	0.34	0.37	0.37
	E3r	0.62	0.93	0.50	0.95	0.53	0.62	0.54	0.53	0.53	0.51	0.62	0.62	0.65	0.63	0.54	0.47	0.39	0.39
	ΔE3	0.25	0.02	0.15	0.02	0.18	0.31	0.11	0.11	0.14	0.13	0.25	0.27	0.26	0.25	0.18	0.13	0.02	0.02
E4	E4s	0.37	0.94	0.35	0.96	0.35	0.32	0.43	0.42	0.39	0.39	0.38	0.41	0.36	0.33	0.38	0.35	0.34	0.35
	E4r	0.79	0.98	0.65	0.99	0.69	0.69	0.67	0.65	0.64	0.65	0.69	0.79	0.70	0.67	0.58	0.62	0.57	0.55
	ΔE4	0.42	0.04	0.30	0.03	0.34	0.37	0.24	0.23	0.25	0.26	0.31	0.38	0.34	0.34	0.20	0.27	0.23	0.20

6.2 EHTSD for Automated Instructional Design

Also provided is an original implementation of EHTSD in e-education, as a tool for automated design of e-courses, based on the structural and content models of EHTSD, in which educational standards and student-centered learning not only coexist, but also interact synergistically. It can be said that the individual learning trajectory, and as a result, diversity, are integrated into the standard through EHTSD.

With the development of AI-enhanced learning, EHSDT has not only retained its efficiency, but has also opened up new possibilities. Namely, it has been implemented in the e-educational environment. Based on it, an interactive e-curriculum has been developed as an Automated Instructional Design (AID) tool for e-courses.

AID has opened up the possibility of creating an interactive e-course database for universities, in which they can invest and from which they can extract ready-made e-courses or their templates that meet high quality standards based on their comparison according to needs.

The teacher-developer of the e-course, selecting the set and sequence of content-structure components of the e-course, its units/topics and task patterns/templates, forms the e-curriculum. From it, by the link from each task, the developer gets to the template of a typical task on the platform and, guided by the tutorial, fills it with subject content. Content-structure patterns of the e-course-unit-task ensure a high standard of quality, without limiting the freedom of choice and leveling differences/ individuality. This became possible due to the modeling of the natural mechanism of self-development, where everyone carries out actions in the context of their personal needs, based on their individual resources and taking into account the available conditions. Moreover, the student can manage this entire process himself based on the possibility of measuring both her/his cognitive development (automated calculation of the efficiency of problem solving in terms of speed-completeness-accuracy of the solution) and personality development (operational reflection of the efficiency, zone and dynamics of development in the format of a personal profile). With this approach, standards do not limit creativity, freedom of choice and diversity.

It is important to note that, based on the principles, algorithms, tools, structures and templates developed on the basis of EHSDT, any teacher can create or improve an existing course that combines subject-centered and student-centered approaches, and the student can build an individual learning path in accordance with their needs, goals, conditions and resources. At the same time, high standards of education are observed, focused on the synergetic interaction of the student with the developmental environment (educational, real, virtual).

Thus, the feasibility of both needs-based and standards-based learning has been proven. Institutional readiness is also critical for adoption. Experience shows that if the solution does not require additional costs and does not conflict with accepted standards, which is the case with EHSDT, then there are no problems. Since EHSDT is embodied in technology as an "implementation toolkit", the usual procedure of its introduction into the curricula is sufficient to obtain a next-generation learning management system. That is, the roadmap, the stages, the stakeholders, and the expected results are defined. One thing remains - the will to act.

6.3. Problems and Considerations for Implementing EHTSD

Implementing EHTSD may encounter limitations, barriers to adoption, or risks. These may include:

Resistance of teachers to AI. There are teachers who do not want to leave their comfort zone and continue to use time-tested approaches. This barrier can be overcome by introducing a teacher rating by students, clearly demonstrating an assessment of the quality of the subject taught by them, including in the context of students' expectations regarding the use of innovative technologies. The level of a teacher as a user of technologies cannot be lower than the level of the students they teach. In addition, EHTSD, embodied in technology, significantly facilitates the creation of a high-quality e-course by an ordinary teacher by selecting relevant templates in accordance with needs, which are then filled with subject content. The only difference is that a content-structure pattern is initially set for filling;

Institutional inertia, which is often explained by the rigidity of administrative bureaucratic mechanisms. Overcoming this barrier is possible through the standards, the implementation of which is mandatory for the accreditation of a university. The introduction of innovative technology into curricula becomes a law for implementation, which, in theory, should overcome institutional inertia and force action in a given direction.

Dependence on proprietary technology platforms is a barrier that is overcome through Instructional Design, which allows using the necessary combination of existing platform resources, and in their absence, solving the problem with plugins.

Technical barriers have not yet been encountered within the framework of the EHTSD, since the technology is based on structures and algorithms easily implemented within the usual technical capabilities of the university.

Evaluation difficulties are not typical for the EHTSD, since complex evaluation and measurements are integrated into the technology itself. Moreover, evaluation tools allow measuring both the cognitive and personality development of a student, determining the level, zone and dynamics of development in a format understandable to both the student managing her/his own development, and the teacher to improve the methodology; or controlling agents to check the quality and efficiency of training.

Unclear return on investment in e-learning. Overcoming this barrier is possible due to the high Developmental Capacity of EHTSD, which significantly exceeds the profitability of cumbersome systems, the development of which requires significant investments. In essence, EHTSD saves money on Instructional Design, which is presented as a technology in the format of an interactive curriculum, with the help of which any teacher can create a high-quality e-course by selecting patterns of, its units/topics and tasks in accordance with the needs.

6.4. Human Perspectives: Engagement, Agency, and Resistance

EHTSD may be of interest to both academic and professional audiences interested in innovation, policy, and practice.

The adoption of innovative models depends on the perspectives of key stakeholders. The target audience for studying educational standardization, innovation, and diversity in the context of new technologies can be divided into four groups: 1) policy and organizational decision makers (higher education policymakers and administrators, institutional administrators); 2) developers (educational researchers and theorists, curriculum designers and educational technology developers, graduate students in education or educational technology); 3) users (students and practicing educators studying AI integration); 4) evaluators (accreditation bodies, parents and community groups).

The decision-making group is interested in standards as a means of control, measurement and comparison of results for the purpose of forming the developmental policy in terms of specific decisions; the developers group needs standards as a framework for their activities; the users group needs standards as a visible strategic goal, which allows forming its own path to it; for evaluators, standards are criteria according to which the assessment of efficiency and success is carried out.

The problems of all groups are mainly connected with the convenience of using standards and their relevance to target needs. Resistance is generated by the natural ambivalent desire for preservation and development, which is resolved by balancing needs-resources-conditions. If this balance is achieved, then there are no problems with adoption. If this is a problem, then there is a need to develop the "lagging" component.

For the decision-making group, EHTSD provides generalized statistical data differentiated by types of target groups and their needs, which is important for making adequate decisions. For the development group, EHTSD provides a concept, a structural and content model, patterns, algorithms, tools and specific templates, which significantly facilitates development. For the user group, EHTSD solves not only the problem of professional but also personality development in the very process of mastering a specific subject. It allows a student to build a personal learning trajectory depending on his needs and manage the process of her/his own development based on measuring its success, and the teacher to track this trajectory and promptly adjust it, adjusting the available resources to the needs. For the evaluators group, EHTSD provides specific criteria and tools that allow determining the efficiency, dynamics and problems of training. Thus, almost all target groups benefit from using EHTSD. In fact, familiarization with these benefits can form the basis of the stakeholder involvement strategy. Moreover, EHTSD offers technologies of multi-agent-sector-disciplinary co-creation in the format of a virtual laboratory. If there is interest from the parties, this technology can be implemented in solving real problems by target groups.

EHTSD by its very nature "hears" the voices of students, as it models the real existential conditions of their development. The strategic orientation in the format of the graduate profile implicitly contains human and social dimensions, such as motivation, agency and resistance. The student-centered approach, which provides the student with a choice in accordance with his/her needs and capabilities, shows respect for the self-identity and personality of the student. And the results are not long in coming. The greatest advantage of EHTSD is not just efficient cognitive and personality development in the context of the demands of the modern labor market and social environment. It is the invariably emerging desire in students to develop further, based on the understanding of the existential sense of development as an endless process. The main result is the emergence of the Developmental Capacity of students, which becomes a key personality resource in the era of uncertainty caused by the exponential development of technologies.

6.5. Ethical Considerations in AI-Based Standardization.

Ethical and equality-related issues such as algorithmic bias, inequality of access, and data privacy are key areas in the discussions of AI standardization. We believe that in the context of the Eco-Humanistic approach ethical and equality-related risks are mitigated by the possibility to independently shape a personal learning trajectory in accordance with personality sense and individual resources under current situation. Here, equal conditions are realized for everyone. As for the social consequences, the EHTSD is initially strategically oriented towards the graduate's profile as an agent of positive change in society, as an existential environment, based on the synergetic human-environment interaction causing co-development. The system-forming essence of the approach is synergetic interaction based on the interconnection and interdependence of one's own well-being on the environment, which is a condition for the realization of personality sense.

7. CHALLENGES OF AI INTEGRATION INTO E-EDUCATION AND THE RESPONSE OF EHTSD

In conclusion, let us return to the challenges of AI integration into modern education in correlation with the possibilities of EHTSD. The matrix reflects the qualities that e-education should have; the challenges that arise in this regard, and how they are met within EHTSD (Fig. 10).

CONCLUSION: IT IS TIME TO RAISE THE BAR

Exponential development of technologies changes the existential environment, and as a consequence, human behavior and consciousness. There are dramatic changes in all spheres of life. The boundaries and possibilities of the educational environment are expanding, radically changing the way knowledge is transmitted, acquired and assessed. Unfortunately, education lags behind the pace of technologies development and loses its role as provider of agents of changes. It is required a change in the paradigm of education, which is capable of developing in synergy with advanced technologies without loosing its fundamental values and achievements that have stood the test of time, but multiplying them through new opportunities. Such synergy can become the basis for standardized frameworks in new paradigm coordinates.

For strategic orientation on the way to new standards it is necessary to understand new type of education features in order to determine its needs and possibilities. The systems analysis identified the following coordinates: 1) human-centered; 2) practice-oriented; 3) integrating advanced technologies; 4) transparent/explainable; 5) integrating quality teaching; 6) manageable (measurable and providing continuous feedback); 7) capable of development in pace of technological trends, institutional and educational needs; 8) scalable; 9) multi-agent/sectoral/disciplinary; 10) cross-cultural; 11) focused on universal values; 12) safe.

Figure 10. Next generation e-education

NEXT GENERATION E-EDUCATION

	Challenges	EHTSD answer
1	**Human-centered**	**Human-centered**
	adaptive algorithms for developing individual learning experiences	formation of an individual cognitive-sense structure (ICSS)
2	**Practice-oriented**	**Practice-oriented**
	adaptive learning methods/programs for real-time skill development/improvement based on AI	skill automation mechanism (5th stage of the self-development circle)
3	**Advanced technologies-integrated**	**Advanced technologies-integrated**
	smooth integration and ease of use of AI based on standards of synergistic interaction between AI tools, LMS and other educational systems	structure-content model of EHTSD
4	**Transparent and explainable**	**Transparent and explainable**
	tools, methods and standards that ensure transparency, explainability, interpretation and understanding of AI-based systems by users (user agency) to build trust among students, teachers, parents, and increase developer accountability	metacognitive approach
5	**Quality teaching-integrated**	**Quality teaching-integrated**
	train trainers/administrators to effectively use and understand standards-based AI-driven tools for adoption, operational readiness and smooth implementation in AI-enhanced environments	involving teachers in co-creation of solutions, their self-identification with the decisions made and responsibility for the implementation of decisions
6	**Managed**	**Managed**
	measurable: standards for continuous assessment and skills gap analysis	Profile Overlay Technology (POT)
	continuous feedback: improving feedback loops and results with data-driven AI tools	Progress Bar and Profile Overlay Technology (POT)
7	**Capable of self-development** in accordance with the economic and social needs of society	**Capable of self-development** in accordance with the economic and social needs of society
	building a learning ecosystem taking into account future trends and based on AI standards for education evolving new technological advances	self-developing system based on strategic cognitive-sense orientation towards the development of the ICSS
	developing AI tools in line with institutional needs without compromising quality	principles and structure-content model of EHTSD
	standards for monitoring the performance (+safety and ethical compliance) of AI to continuously improve AI systems based on user feedback and methods for fine-tuning AI models as educational needs evolve	Graduate Profile
8	**Scalable**	**Scalable**
	frameworks for building high-performance, standards-based AI applications for reliable scalable AI	principles and structure-content model of EHTSD
9	**Multiagent/sectoral/disciplinary**	**Multiagent/sectoral/disciplinary**
	standards for group and peer learning in collaborative learning environments using AI/ GenAI, balancing collaboration and personalization, including data privacy	multi-agent / sectoral / disciplinary synergistic co-creation leading to mutual development without loss of individuality – interaction of diversities as a condition for synergy
10	**Cross-cultural**	**Cross-cultural**
	standards that support cross-cultural (culturally inclusive) multilingual education based on adaptation methods and AI tools that overcome language barriers to meet different needs	orientation towards universal existential senses
11	**Focused on universal human values**	**Focused on universal human values**
	standards and practices to ensure fairness and equality in AI models based on the evaluation of AI tools to prevent the reinforcement of stereotypes/ discrimination/bias	interaction of diversities as a condition for synergy – Profiles
12	**Safe**	**Safe**
	identifying potential risks and standards to protect learners from unintended consequences of AI in education, mitigating and avoiding plagiarism by encouraging individual thinking in GenAI	orientation towards personal sense, existential sense of self-development

To implement such education, new technological opportunities for synergetic interaction of human and artificial (symbolic and generative) intelligence have emerged. They not only invest in the availability, pace, volume, scaling and impact of education, but also allow significant improvement of its quality by technologizing efficient multi-agent/sectoral/ disciplinary synergetic interaction and co-creation.

At the same time, problems that carry the risk of losing control are proportionally multiplied along with the opportunities. It is needed to prevent possible negative consequences of AI integration before they become irreversible.

One way to prevent risks is to introduce standards as a basis for trust, interaction, and accountability to ensure the reliability and ethics of AI-Powered Education. It is proposed to align innovations with global standards through the use of standardized frameworks in the development, deployment, and management of AI based solutions aimed at meaningful and sustainable learning. It is assumed that standardized AI solutions can improve the learning and teaching process. Here the question arises, how to preserve uniqueness and diversity as conditions for quality education that ensures survival in the face of uncertainty? What should standard frameworks be like so that with obvious new advantages, we do not lose the already achieved level of quality education, which provided such Developmental Capacity (DC) that made the emergence of advanced technologies possible? After all, they were created by those who received education within the existing education system.

We propose an original approach, to create standardized frameworks, not from scratch, but using time-tested standards in synergy of the best educational models with new technologies. In other words, to embody the best educational models in advanced technologies, without losing their diversity, developmental capacity and quality standards. Is it possible?

We believe that it is possible if we focus on how living systems do it, which are characterized by an ambivalent desire for preservation and development. It is the driving force of development, which occurs in the process of balancing needs-resources-conditions, working as a perpetuum mobile of development, generating new non-equilibrium states in the balancing process itself, triggering the need to continue the developmental process. In our case the strategic sense/need is development itself, the condition is standardization, and the developmental environment is the resource that must balance with needs and conditions.

This universal mechanism is based on a deep scientific understanding of the process of self-development of living systems, which has been tested by a long-term formative experiment and subsequent many years of practice in the conditions of natural university education. As a result, Eco-Humanistic approach, concept, model embodied in the Technology of Self-Development (EHTSD) appeared reflecting the civilizational need for human-existential environment synergetic interaction causing their co-development. In the EHTSD the environment is presented in a broad sense, as a natural, social and virtual one, and human as a "system of systems" integrating eco-socio-techno spheres. It is notable that the EHTSD fully corresponds to the New European Scientific and Educational Paradigm standing on 3 pillars: 1) sustainable development (socio-economic-ecological); 2) human well-being; 3) inclusiveness. In the educational context it is reflected as strategic focus: 1) sustainability – on developmental capacity (DC); 2) well-being – on human/student-centered education; 3) inclusiveness – on multi-agent/sector/disciplinary co-creation.

Developmental process modeled by EHTSD comes through 7 stages of the developmental circle (event – meaning – opportunity – choice – action – automation – event), served by 4 mechanisms (synergy of consciousness and behavior, driving forces, capacity and optimization of self-development). It is noteworthy that the mechanisms of driving forces and optimization are universal and coincide with the key mechanisms of AI (backpropagation and gradient descent). EHTSD modeling allows to present self-development in the process of human-environment interaction in the format content-structure pattern of both discipline and student, where the content is structured and the structure is meaningful. Such a representation: 1) provides a single system of coordinates for both discipline and student in the context of labor market needs; 2) allows to compare both cognitive-sense structures, 3) highlights development zones, 4) measures the dynamics and success of learning in cognitive, personality, social, professional and existential dimensions; 5) unifies the process, ensuring a high Developmental Capacity based on scientifically substantiated schemes for disciplines regardless of their specificity; 6) creates conditions for the integration of human intelligence and AI (symbolic and generative).

The proposed approach allows to qualitatively solve the problem of curriculum calculations without losing its Developmental Capacity, by deriving the subject (all its phenomena) from its essence as a system-forming factor. It is the connection between the functions (expressed in weights), allowing to ensure isomorphism of the models of artificial and human intelligence, to determine their similarities and diversities, to organize their synergetic interaction and co-development.

Student-centeredness is reflected in the strategic focus on the cognitive-personality development of target profile. The ideal profile of a graduate as agent of development reflects professionally-socially-emotionally competent, efficient-moral-harmonious, globally thinking, locally acting agent of society sustainable development and a subject of self-development.

Thus, EHTSD can set standardized frameworks within the new paradigm, since it provides: 1) transparent and explainable principles for organizing efficient educational activities based on a deep scientific understanding of their patterns and mechanisms; 2) synergy of human and artificial intelligence, and, as a consequence, synergy of AI-Powered Education and high-quality, time-tested education, without losing creativity and diversity as a condition for synergistic development; 3) high DC of innovative courses due to synergy of natural process of self-development and new opportunities that allow modeling and, as a consequence, technologizing creating previously unavailable opportunities for its management, measurement, scaling, impact at a speed and in volumes inaccessible to traditional education.

Standards describe educational goals, i.e., what students should have learned by the end of a course, level or period of study. Standards are not prescriptive: they define what to study, but they do not dictate HOW to teach it. This is a bottleneck, because HOW the standards are achieved will determine the quality of education in essence. Unfortunately, in accreditation, quality assessment is often carried out according to the formal features of the presence of benchmarks, and not the path to them, which determines quality. Will the standards become strict rules limiting individuality, diversity, creativity and innovation, or a strategic orientation indicating the path to the final goal, which everyone can choose depending on personality needs, individual resources and available conditions. HOW concerns methodology determining the principles that translate sense into efficient solutions, strategies and practices. Standards set the bar and, possibly, raise it. We consider that it is time to raise the bar.

Let us explain why. Exponential development of technologies forces us to live in a situation of uncertainty, since social and educational systems cannot withstand the given pace. In such a period, it is important to set a standard of education that would allow not only to survive, but also to live qualitatively and meaningfully in dynamic conditions of uncertainty. We believe that such a universal standard can be Developmental Capacity, which implicitly contains the necessary set of competencies, abilities and qualities. This is the standard that can be implemented in modern innovative education, which synergistically unites not replacing, but complementing human intelligence with artificial one.

The Original Eco-Humanistic Technology of Self-Development (EHSDT), modeling the natural conditions of human-environment co-development, demonstrates HOW to follow this universal standard without losing diversity, creativity and innovation. The concept of human-environment co-development, embodied in technology and presented in the format of content-structure models, in which the structure is meaningful and the content is structured, allows programming, managing, measuring, scaling the process of learning corresponding a given quality standard. In all likelihood, the future of education is in such models.

REFERENCES

Agell, N., & Prat-i-Pubill, Q. (2024, February). AI: Technological Revolution or Existential Threat? Retrieved from https://dobetter.esade.edu/en/artificial-intelligence-technological-revolution-existential-threat-AI

Arnold, A., Cafer, A., Green, J., Haines, S., Mann, G., & Rosenthal, M. (2021). Perspective: Promoting and fostering multidisciplinary research in universities. *Research Policy*, *50*(9), 104334. DOI: 10.1016/j.respol.2021.104334

Brinck, I. (2024). Craft thinking: A relational approach to making and design. In *Craft and Design Practice from an Embodied Perspective*. Routledge.

Camilo, M. G. (2021). The Elkonin-Davidov System: A Grove of Developmental Teaching Theory. *Revista Científica Multidisciplinar Núcleo Do Conhecimento*, *06*(06), 142–158.

Clarindo, C. B. da S., Miller, S., & Kohle, É. C. (2020). Learning Activity as a Means of Developing Theoretical Thinking Capacities. *Frontiers in Psychology*, *11*. Advance online publication. DOI: 10.3389/fpsyg.2020.603753 PMID: 33381070

Epstein, D. (2021). *Range: Why Generalists Triumph in a Specialized World*. Riverhead Books.

Fischer, C., Xu, D., Rodriguez, F., Denaro, K., & Warschauer, M. (2020). Effects of course modality in summer session: Enrollment patterns and student performance in face-to-face and online classes. *The Internet and Higher Education*, *45*, 100710. DOI: 10.1016/j.iheduc.2019.100710

Freitas, D., & Damazio, A. (2022). Conceptual thinking of fractions: the Davydovian mode of teaching organization. *Educ. Pesqui., São Paulo,* 48, e236913. Retrieved from https://www.scielo.br/j/ep/a/dGVVjR4FMSxRVKzZWXHhJnf/?format=pdf&lang=en

GDPR.eu. (n.d.). General Data Protection Regulation (GDPR) compliance guidelines. Retrieved from https://gdpr.eu

Gherhe , V., Stoian, C. E., Fărca iu, M. A., & Stanici, M. (2021). E-Learning vs. Face-To-Face Learning: Analyzing Students' Preferences and Behaviors. *Sustainability*, *13*(88), 4381. DOI: 10.3390/su13084381

Gotesman, R. (2018, May). Learning Backpropagation from Geoffrey Hinton. *TDS Archive*. Retrieved from https://medium.com/data-science/learning-backpropagation-from-geoffrey-hinton-619027613f0

Gromyko, Y. V. (2020). Vasiliy Davydov: The Founder of Activity Practice in Education. *Psychological Science and Education*, *25*(5), 5–18. DOI: 10.17759/pse.2020250501

Hashemi-Pour, C. (2024, October). What Is a Learning Management System (LMS)? *Search CIO*. Retrieved from https://www.techtarget.com/searchcio/definition/learning-management-system

Herlo, S. (2024, March). What Is Structured Content and How Do You Create It? Retrieved from https://www.rws.com/content-management/blog/what-is-structured-content/

Hornby, G., & Greaves, D. (2022). Metacognitive Strategies. In Hornby, G., & Greaves, D. (Eds.), *Essential Evidence-Based Teaching Strategies: Ensuring Optimal Academic Achievement for Students* (pp. 95–104)., DOI: 10.1007/978-3-030-96229-6_7

ISO. (2022). ISO/IEC 23053:2022(en) Framework for Artificial Intelligence (AI) Systems Using Machine Learning (ML). Retrieved from https://www.iso.org/obp/ui/en/#iso:std:iso-iec:23053:ed-1:v1:en

Jacobson, M. J., & Xue, Y. (2024). *Integrating Symbolic Reasoning into Neural Generative Models for Design Generation*. (arXiv:2310.09383). doi:/arXiv.2310.09383DOI: 10.48550

Jean, P. (pj). (2024, June). When To Use Symbolic And Generative AI. *Forbes*. Retrieved from https://www.forbes.com/councils/forbestechcouncil/2024/06/05/when-to-use-symbolic-and-generative-ai/

Nugent, A., Carroll, A., Lodge, J. M., Matthews, K. E., MacMahon, S., & Sah, P. (2023). A qualitative exploration of expert perspectives on applying the science of learning to higher education. *Frontiers in Education*, *8*. Advance online publication. DOI: 10.3389/feduc.2023.1233651

Podolskiy, A. (2012). Activity Theories of Learning. In Seel, N. M. (Ed.), *Encyclopedia of the Sciences of Learning* (pp. 83–85)., DOI: 10.1007/978-1-4419-1428-6_310

Sergeyeva, T. (2009). *Eco-Humanistic Self-Development: Monograph*. Kh. Blok., ISBN 966-961188-2-7.

Sergeyeva, T. (2014). Training course 'Eco-Humanistic Technology of Self-Development'. Retrieved from https://old.karazin.ua/docs/work/slavic_summer_2014_2_2.pdf

Sergeyeva, T., Bronin, S., & Glazar, T. (2023, November). Technology for Synergistic Solutions Co-Creation Based on Multi-Agents' Diversities Interaction. In Anisimov, A., Snytyuk, V., Chris, A., Pester, A., Mallet, F., Tanaka, H., Krak, I., Henke, K., Nikitchenko, M., Chertov, O., Marchenko, O., Bozóki, S., Tsyganok, V., & Vovk, V. (Eds.), *Selected Papers of the X International Scientific Conference "Information Technology and Implementation" (IT&I-2023)* (pp. 462–470). Conference Proceedings., Retrieved from https://ceur-ws.org/Vol-3624/#Short_7.pdf

Sergeyeva, T., Bronin, S., Glazar, T., & Degleria, V. (2023, May). Creating Digitized Tools for Supporting Multidisciplinary and Multi-Actor Solutions Based on Eco-Humanistic Model. *2023 IEEE International Conference on Smart Information Systems and Technologies (SIST)*, 251–256. doi:DOI: 10.1109/SIST58284.2023.10223539

Sergeyeva, T., Bronin, S., Glazar, T., & Njoo, J. (2022, December). E-learning Research within New European Paradigm. In Anisimov, A., Snytyuk, V., Chris, A., Pester, A., Mallet, F., Tanaka, H., Krak, I., Henke, K., Nikitchenko, M., Chertov, O., Marchenko, O., Bozóki, S., Tsyganok, V., & Vovk, V. (Eds.), *Selected Papers of the IX International Scientific Conference "Information Technology and Implementation" (IT&I-2022)* (pp. 137–147). Conference Proceedings., Retrieved from https://ceur-ws.org/Vol-3347/#Paper_12.pdf

Sergeyeva, T., Bronin, S., & Turlakova, N. (2022, April). Multidisciplinary Dimension of E-Learning in the Innovative Eco-System of a Modern University. *2022 International Conference on Smart Information Systems and Technologies (SIST)*, 1–8. doi:DOI: 10.1109/SIST54437.2022.9945768

Sergeyeva, T., Bronin, S., Turlakova, N., & Iamnytskyi, S. (2023). Integrating Educational Components into the Metaverse. In Guralnick, D., Auer, M. E., & Poce, A. (Eds.), *Innovative Approaches to Technology-Enhanced Learning for the Workplace and Higher Education* (pp. 412–425)., DOI: 10.1007/978-3-031-21569-8_39

Sergeyeva, T., Festeu, D., Bronin, S., & Turlakova, N. (2021, December). Student – Training Environment Interaction: Soft Skills Development within E-learning. In Anisimov, A., Snytyuk, V., Chris, A., Pester, A., Mallet, F., Tanaka, H., Krak, I., Henke, K., Nikitchenko, M., Chertov, O., Marchenko, O., Bozóki, S., Tsyganok, V., & Vovk, V. (Eds.), *Selected Papers of the VIII International Scientific Conference "Information Technology and Implementation" (IT&I-2021)* (pp. 290–298). Conference Proceedings., Retrieved from https://ceur-ws.org/Vol-3132/#Short_10.pdf

Shah, W. (2022). *Hybrid AI Models: Combining Symbolic Reasoning and Deep Learning for Enhanced Decision-Making*. doi:DOI: 10.13140/RG.2.2.11493.61920

Srinivas, N. (2023). ISSUES AND CHALLENGES OF E-LEANING TOWARDS HIGHER EDUCATION. *IJCRT - International Journal of Creative Research Thoughts (IJCRT)*. Retrieved from https://ijcrt.org/viewfull.php?&p_id=IJCRT2311300

Tank, A. (n.d.). Why the world needs deep generalists, not specialists | The Jotform Blog. *Jotform*. Retrieved from https://www.jotform.com/blog/the-world-needs-polymaths/

UNESCO, Fengchun, M., Holmes, W., Ronghuai, H., & Zhang, H. (2021). AI and education: Guidance for policy-makers(45 p.). https://doi.org/DOI: 10.54675/PCSP7350

UNESCO. (2023). Guidance for generative AI in education and research. https://www.unesco.org/en/articles/guidance-generative-ai-education-and-research

UNESCO. (2023). AI competency framework for students. https://www.unesco.org/en/articles/ai-competency-framework-students?hub=32618

UNESCO. (2025). AI competency framework for teachers. https://www.unesco.org/en/articles/ai-competency-framework-teachers?hub=32618

U.S. Department of Education. (n.d.). FERPA: Family Educational Rights and Privacy Act. Retrieved from https://studentprivacy.ed.gov/ferpa

Zinchenko, P. I., & Sereda, G. K. (2011). Involuntary Memory and Classroom Instruction. *Journal of Russian & East European Psychology*, *49*(1), 17–30. DOI: 10.2753/RPO1061-0405490101

Chapter 3
AI Standards for Data-Informed Assessment and Evaluation

R. Velmurugan
https://orcid.org/0000-0002-7925-9757
Karpagam Academy of Higher Education, Coimbatore, India

J. Sudarvel
https://orcid.org/0000-0001-6656-1992
Karpagam Academy of Higher Education, Coimbatore, India

R. Bhuvaneswari
https://orcid.org/0009-0003-9396-6129
Dr. Mahalingam College of Engineering and Technology, Pollachi, India

Ravi Thirumalaisamy
https://orcid.org/0000-0002-5954-5940
Modern College of Business and Science, Oman

ABSTRACT

Artificial Intelligence (AI) is changing the evaluation method to be more precise, versatile, and individualised in education. Regularized structures confirm that data accumulation, interpretation, and utilization utilizing AI in particular is moral, unopaque, and trustworthy as it becomes a part of education. Such frameworks, directed by such bodies as IEEE, ISO, and UNESCO, are aimed at equality, inclusiveness, and privacy. The AI-supported formative and summative assessment such as adaptive testing or predictive analytics identify the gaps in learning using real-time feedback to allow utilizing the knowledge of both students and teachers continuously. Learning media such as Coursera and Khan Academy are also dy-

DOI: 10.4018/979-8-3373-2235-3.ch003

namic and customized with the introduction of AI. These increasing concerns about ethical considerations of use, accessibility and interoperability of data to systems serves to keep AI systems up-to-date with educational aims, and provide fair and equitable AI-based assessment of all learners.

INTRODUCTION

Artificial Intelligence (AI) is reshaping educational assessment by introducing new paradigms of precision, personalization, and real-time feedback. As digital learning environments proliferate, AI technologies are increasingly embedded in assessment systems to analyze learner behavior, predict performance, and deliver adaptive feedback. These innovations mark a significant departure from traditional assessment models, which often rely on static, standardized testing. Instead, AI enables dynamic, formative assessment practices that respond to individual learner needs and promote deeper engagement with content (Zawacki-Richter et al., 2019).

The historical evolution of AI in education began with early rule-based systems and intelligent tutoring platforms, but recent advances in machine learning, natural language processing, and neural networks have dramatically expanded its capabilities. AI-powered assessment tools now include automated essay scoring, speech recognition for language learning, and predictive analytics for identifying at-risk students (Chen et al., 2020). These systems are not merely evaluative; they are increasingly diagnostic and prescriptive, offering insights into cognitive processes and learning trajectories that were previously inaccessible through conventional methods.

Several conceptual frameworks have emerged to guide the integration of AI into educational assessment. One influential model is the "Assessment as Learning" framework, which positions learners as active agents in the assessment process. AI supports this model by enabling continuous feedback loops and personalized learning pathways (Luckin, 2020). Similarly, the "Learning Analytics Framework" emphasizes the use of data to inform instructional decisions and improve learning outcomes. AI enhances this approach by automating data collection and analysis, thereby reducing the burden on educators and increasing the scalability of personalized assessment (Ifenthaler & Yau, 2020).

The benefits of AI in assessment are multifaceted. First, AI enhances precision by analyzing large volumes of learner data to detect subtle patterns and misconceptions. For example, AI-driven platforms can identify common errors in mathematical reasoning or writing structure, allowing for targeted remediation (Holmes et al., 2022). Second, AI supports personalization by adapting assessment tasks to individual learner profiles. This includes adjusting difficulty levels, content formats, and feedback styles based on learner preferences and performance history (Khosravi et al., 2022). Third, AI enables real-time feedback, which is critical for formative assessment and iterative learning. Immediate feedback helps learners correct errors, reflect on their understanding, and build metacognitive skills (Wang et al., 2023).

However, the implementation of AI in educational assessment raises several ethical, technical, and pedagogical concerns. Ethically, there are growing concerns about data privacy, algorithmic bias, and the transparency of AI decision-making processes. For instance, biased training data can lead to unfair assessments, particularly for students from marginalized backgrounds (Williamson & Eynon, 2020). Technically, ensuring the validity and reliability of AI-generated assessments remains a challenge. While AI can efficiently score essays or analyze clickstream data, it may struggle to evaluate complex constructs such as creativity, empathy, or critical thinking (Baker & Hawn, 2021). Pedagogically, there is a risk that AI tools may reinforce reductive models of learning if they prioritize quantifiable metrics over holistic understanding. Educators must therefore critically assess the pedagogical alignment of AI systems and ensure that they support meaningful learning outcomes.

Recent scholarship also emphasizes the importance of human-AI collaboration in assessment. Rather than replacing educators, AI should augment their capabilities by providing actionable insights and supporting differentiated instruction. The concept of "human-in-the-loop" AI underscores the need for educators to interpret and contextualize AI-generated data, ensuring that assessment remains responsive to individual learner needs and classroom dynamics (Holmes et al., 2022). Moreover, explainable AI (XAI) is gaining traction as a means to enhance transparency and trust in AI systems. XAI tools aim to make algorithmic decisions interpretable to educators and learners, thereby fostering accountability and ethical use (Gunning et al., 2023).

Looking ahead, the future of AI in educational assessment lies in developing hybrid models that integrate human judgment with machine intelligence. These models can leverage the strengths of AI—speed, scalability, and pattern recognition—while preserving the empathy, contextual awareness, and ethical reasoning that educators bring to the assessment process. Interdisciplinary collaboration among educators, technologists, ethicists, and policymakers will be essential to design robust governance frameworks that guide the responsible use of AI in education (Zawacki-Richter & Jung, 2023).

Thus, AI holds transformative potential for educational assessment by enabling more precise, personalized, and responsive evaluation methods. However, its implementation must be guided by thoughtful consideration of ethical, technical, and pedagogical dimensions. By situating AI within established educational frameworks and fostering collaborative innovation, stakeholders can harness its capabilities to support equitable and effective learning experiences. This chapter explores these dimensions in depth, offering a comprehensive analysis of the historical evolution, conceptual foundations, practical benefits, and future directions of AI in assessment and evaluation.

HISTORICAL EVOLUTION

The journey of Artificial Intelligence (AI) in education has been marked by significant technological and pedagogical milestones. It began in the 1980s with rule-based tutoring systems—early attempts to replicate human instruction through programmed logic and decision trees. These systems, such as the Intelligent Tutoring System (ITS), were designed to guide learners through structured problem-solving tasks, offering feedback based on predefined rules (Woolf, 2010). While limited in adaptability, they laid the groundwork for more sophisticated AI applications by demonstrating the potential of computer-mediated instruction.

The early 2000s witnessed a paradigm shift with the emergence of machine learning (ML) and natural language processing (NLP), which enabled AI systems to learn from data and interpret human language with increasing accuracy. These advancements allowed educational technologies to move beyond rigid rule-based frameworks toward more flexible, data-driven models. For instance, NLP facilitated the development of automated essay scoring systems and intelligent dialogue agents capable of understanding and responding to student queries in natural language (Chen et al., 2020). Machine learning, meanwhile, empowered systems to detect patterns in learner behavior, predict performance, and personalize content delivery—ushering in a new era of adaptive learning.

Today, AI is deeply embedded in both formative and summative assessment practices, with platforms like Coursera, Khan Academy, and Duolingo exemplifying its integration into mainstream education. These platforms employ AI to tailor learning experiences based on user interactions, assess progress in real time, and recommend personalized learning paths. Coursera, for example, uses AI to analyze learner engagement and quiz performance to suggest targeted content and interventions (Khosravi et al., 2022). Khan Academy's mastery-based learning model leverages AI to adjust the difficulty and sequencing of tasks, ensuring that learners build foundational skills before progressing (Wang et al., 2023).

The integration of AI into assessment is particularly transformative in the realm of formative evaluation. Unlike summative assessments, which typically occur at the end of a learning cycle, formative assessments are ongoing and designed to inform instruction and support learning as it unfolds. AI enhances formative assessment by providing immediate feedback, identifying misconceptions, and enabling iterative learning. For instance, AI-driven writing assistants can offer real-time suggestions on grammar, coherence, and argumentation, helping students refine their work before submission (Holmes et al., 2022). Similarly, adaptive quizzes can adjust in difficulty based on student responses, maintaining an optimal challenge level and promoting sustained engagement.

In summative assessment, AI contributes to efficiency and scalability. Automated grading systems can evaluate large volumes of student work—such as multiple-choice tests, short answers, and even essays—with consistency and speed. While concerns remain about the validity of AI in assessing complex cognitive skills, recent advances in explainable AI (XAI) are addressing these limitations by making algorithmic decisions more transparent and interpretable (Gunning et al., 2023). This is particularly important in high-stakes contexts, where fairness, accountability, and trust are paramount.

The pedagogical implications of AI-driven assessment are profound. By enabling continuous, personalized feedback, AI shifts the focus from performance to learning. It supports the development of metacognitive skills, encourages self-regulated learning, and fosters a growth mindset. Moreover, AI can help educators identify learning gaps and tailor instruction to meet diverse student needs. This aligns with inclusive education frameworks such as Universal Design for Learning (UDL), which advocate for flexible assessment methods that accommodate varied learner profiles (Rose et al., 2020).

However, the integration of AI into educational assessment also raises critical ethical and technical challenges. Data privacy is a major concern, particularly as AI systems collect and analyze sensitive learner information. Algorithmic bias—stemming from skewed training data or flawed model design—can lead to unfair assessments and perpetuate educational inequalities (Williamson & Eynon, 2020). Additionally, the over-reliance on AI may risk dehumanizing the learning process, reducing complex educational interactions to quantifiable metrics. Scholars emphasize the importance of maintaining a "human-in-the-loop" approach, where educators interpret AI-generated insights and contextualize them within broader pedagogical goals (Holmes et al., 2022).

Looking forward, the future of AI in educational assessment lies in hybrid models that combine the strengths of machine intelligence with human judgment. These models can leverage AI's scalability and precision while preserving the empathy, creativity, and ethical reasoning that educators bring to the learning environment. Interdisciplinary collaboration among technologists, educators, ethicists, and policymakers will be essential to develop robust frameworks that guide the responsible use of AI in education (Zawacki-Richter & Jung, 2023).

Thus, the evolution of AI in education—from rule-based tutoring systems to adaptive assessment platforms—reflects a broader shift toward learner-centered, data-informed pedagogy. Platforms like Coursera and Khan Academy illustrate how AI can support both formative and summative assessment, enhancing personalization, engagement, and learning outcomes. Yet, as AI continues to reshape educational practices, its implementation must be guided by ethical, technical, and pedagogical considerations to ensure that it serves all learners equitably and effectively.

LITERATURE REVIEW

Artificial Intelligence (AI) has emerged as a transformative force in education, offering tools that enhance precision, personalization, and inclusivity. Scholars such as Holstein et al. (2020) and Slavin (2022) argue that AI can democratize learning by adapting to diverse learner needs, identifying gaps in understanding, and providing timely feedback. These capabilities are particularly valuable in large-scale educational environments, where human instructors may struggle to offer individualized support. However, alongside its promise, AI introduces complex ethical challenges—particularly around bias, data privacy, and algorithmic transparency—that must be addressed to ensure equitable outcomes.

AI's potential to foster inclusivity lies in its ability to personalize learning experiences. Adaptive learning platforms, powered by AI, can tailor content to students' prior knowledge, learning pace, and preferences, thereby supporting differentiated instruction (Khosravi et al., 2022). This is especially beneficial for students with disabilities, language barriers, or non-traditional learning trajectories. For instance, Wang et al. (2023) demonstrate how AI-driven feedback systems can scaffold learning for students with cognitive impairments by offering multimodal support and real-time guidance. Similarly, Holmes et al. (2022) emphasize that AI can reduce achievement gaps by identifying struggling learners early and recommending targeted interventions.

Yet, the same systems that enable personalization can also perpetuate inequities if not carefully designed. Algorithmic bias—often rooted in skewed training data or opaque model architectures—can result in unfair assessments or exclusionary recommendations (Baker & Hawn, 2021). For example, Williamson and Eynon (2020) caution that predictive analytics used to flag "at-risk" students may inadvertently reinforce stereotypes or penalize students from marginalized backgrounds. These concerns are echoed by Zawacki-Richter and Jung (2023), who argue that without transparent governance, AI systems risk becoming instruments of surveillance rather than empowerment.

To mitigate these risks, scholars advocate for the development of ethical frameworks that prioritize transparency, accountability, and human oversight. Gunning et al. (2023) highlight the importance of explainable AI (XAI), which seeks to make algorithmic decisions interpretable to educators and learners. XAI not only fosters trust but also enables critical scrutiny of AI outputs, ensuring that decisions are pedagogically sound and ethically defensible. Ifenthaler and Yau (2020) propose a layered model of ethical AI integration, emphasizing stakeholder involvement, iterative evaluation, and contextual sensitivity.

Moreover, the ethical deployment of AI in education requires robust data governance. As AI systems rely heavily on learner data, issues of consent, ownership, and privacy become paramount. Chen et al. (2020) stress the need for clear data policies that inform users about how their information is collected, processed, and used. In the absence of such policies, students may be exposed to risks of data misuse or unauthorized profiling. Slade and Prinsloo (2022) argue for a rights-based approach to educational data, where learners are empowered to control their digital identities and challenge algorithmic decisions.

The pedagogical implications of ethical AI are equally significant. AI should not merely automate assessment or content delivery; it must support meaningful learning experiences. Luckin (2020) emphasizes the role of AI as a co-participant in learning, capable of fostering curiosity, reflection, and metacognition. However, this requires careful alignment between AI capabilities and instructional goals. Without such alignment, there is a risk that AI tools may prioritize efficiency over depth, reducing learning to a series of quantifiable metrics (Holmes et al., 2022).

Interdisciplinary collaboration is essential to navigate these complexities. Educators, technologists, ethicists, and policymakers must work together to design AI systems that are both innovative and inclusive. Rose et al. (2020) advocate for integrating Universal Design for Learning (UDL) principles into AI development, ensuring that tools accommodate diverse learner needs from the outset. Similarly, Kizilcec et al. (2021) call for participatory design approaches, where students and teachers contribute to the development and evaluation of AI tools.

Recent empirical studies underscore the importance of trust in AI adoption. Wang and Tsai (2021) found that students' willingness to engage with AI-driven learning platforms is strongly influenced by their perceptions of fairness and transparency. This suggests that technical excellence alone is insufficient; ethical design and clear communication are critical to fostering acceptance and sustained use. Holmes et al. (2022) reinforce this point by arguing that trust must be earned through consistent, accountable practices—not assumed through technological sophistication.

Thus, while AI offers powerful tools for enhancing inclusivity and precision in education, its implementation must be guided by ethical standards and transparent frameworks. Scholars across disciplines emphasize the need for human-centered design, participatory governance, and ongoing evaluation to ensure that AI serves all learners equitably. As educational institutions increasingly adopt AI technologies, the challenge lies not in resisting innovation, but in shaping it responsibly. By foregrounding ethics, inclusivity, and trust, stakeholders can harness AI's potential to create more just and effective learning environments.

METHODOLOGY

This chapter adopts a qualitative synthesis approach to explore the evolving landscape of AI-driven assessment in education. By integrating peer-reviewed research, global policy frameworks, and illustrative case studies, it aims to provide a multidimensional understanding of current practices, challenges, and future opportunities. The synthesis draws on scholarly literature published between 2019 and 2024, alongside guidelines from international organizations such as UNESCO, IEEE, and ISO, ensuring both academic rigor and global relevance.

Peer-reviewed studies offer critical insights into how AI technologies are reshaping assessment practices. Recent research highlights the shift from static, summative evaluations to dynamic, formative assessments powered by machine learning, natural language processing, and predictive analytics (Chen et al., 2020; Holmes et al., 2022). These technologies enable real-time feedback, adaptive testing, and personalized learning pathways, contributing to more inclusive and responsive educational environments. However, scholars also caution against over-reliance on algorithmic systems, emphasizing the need for human oversight, pedagogical alignment, and ethical safeguards (Williamson & Eynon, 2020; Baker & Hawn, 2021).

Global frameworks provide normative guidance for the ethical and equitable implementation of AI in education. UNESCO's 2021 Recommendation on the Ethics of Artificial Intelligence emphasizes principles such as transparency, accountability, and non-discrimination. IEEE's P7000 series and ISO/IEC JTC 1 standards further elaborate on technical protocols for AI deployment, including data governance, algorithmic fairness, and interoperability. These frameworks serve as foundational references for policymakers, educators, and developers seeking to align AI tools with human rights and educational values (UNESCO, 2021; IEEE, 2020; ISO, 2022).

Case studies from diverse educational contexts—ranging from adaptive learning platforms in higher education to AI-supported formative feedback in K–12 classrooms—illustrate both the promise and complexity of implementation. Platforms like Coursera and Khan Academy demonstrate scalable models of AI integration, while localized initiatives in India, South Africa, and Brazil reveal challenges related to infrastructure, digital literacy, and cultural adaptation (Zawacki-Richter & Jung, 2023; Wang et al., 2023).

By synthesizing these sources, the chapter not only maps the current terrain of AI-driven assessment but also identifies strategic directions for future research and practice. It advocates for interdisciplinary collaboration, inclusive design, and robust evaluation mechanisms to ensure that AI serves as a tool for educational equity, not exclusion.

RESEARCH OBJECTIVES

- Examine the role of AI standards in educational assessments.
- Explore the ethical and governance frameworks supporting AI integration.
- Identify challenges and propose strategies for inclusive and effective implementation.

THEORETICAL FRAMEWORKS AND FOUNDATIONS

Grounded in constructivist learning theory and data-informed decision-making, contemporary AI frameworks in education are designed to foster deeper, more personalized learning experiences. Constructivism emphasizes learner agency, active engagement, and the co-construction of knowledge—principles that align well with AI's capacity to deliver adaptive feedback loops tailored to individual progress. By analyzing learner interactions, performance trends, and behavioral cues, AI systems can dynamically adjust instructional content, pacing, and assessment formats to meet diverse needs (Khosravi et al., 2022; Holmes et al., 2022). This evidence-based personalization not only enhances academic outcomes but also supports motivation and self-regulated learning. Importantly, these frameworks are increasingly shaped by ethical imperatives, including transparency in algorithmic decision-making, fairness in data representation, and accountability in system design (UNESCO, 2021; IEEE, 2020). As AI becomes more embedded in educational ecosystems, its alignment with pedagogical values and ethical standards is essential to ensure that innovation serves equity, inclusion, and meaningful learning.

IMPORTANCE AND GOVERNANCE

Artificial Intelligence (AI) standards play a critical role in ensuring that educational assessments are unbiased, reliable, and pedagogically aligned. As AI systems increasingly influence how learners are evaluated, the need for robust, transparent, and ethical frameworks has become paramount. Standards help define the technical and ethical boundaries within which AI assessment tools operate, ensuring that they support—not undermine—educational goals. These standards address key concerns such as algorithmic transparency, data integrity, and fairness in decision-making processes (Holmes et al., 2022; Khosravi et al., 2022).

Governance by international organizations such as UNESCO, IEEE, and ISO has been instrumental in shaping these protocols. UNESCO's *Recommendation on the Ethics of Artificial Intelligence* (2021) outlines principles of human dignity, non-discrimination, and inclusive access, emphasizing that AI in education must be designed to promote equity and learner empowerment. IEEE's P7000 series, particularly P7001 (Transparency of Autonomous Systems) and P7003 (Algorithmic Bias Considerations), provides operational guidance for ethical AI development, including safeguards against discriminatory outcomes and opaque decision-making (IEEE, 2020). These standards are increasingly referenced by educational technology developers and institutions seeking to align their AI systems with global ethical norms.

Compliance with regional data protection regulations, such as the General Data Protection Regulation (GDPR), further reinforces the importance of ethical data use. GDPR mandates informed consent, data minimization, and the right to explanation—principles that are especially relevant in AI-driven assessment environments where learner data is continuously collected and analyzed (Slade & Prinsloo, 2022). Without adherence to such regulations, AI systems risk violating privacy rights and eroding trust among learners and educators.

Recent scholarship underscores the need for harmonizing technical standards with pedagogical values. Williamson and Eynon (2020) argue that AI governance must be grounded in educational ethics, not just computational logic. Zawacki-Richter and Jung (2023) highlight the importance of cross-cultural validation, noting that standards must be adaptable to diverse educational contexts and responsive to local needs.

In sum, AI standards and governance frameworks are essential for ensuring that assessment technologies are not only technically sound but also ethically responsible and educationally meaningful. As AI continues to evolve, these protocols must remain dynamic, inclusive, and collaboratively developed to safeguard the integrity of learning environments worldwide.

ADVANTAGES

Artificial Intelligence (AI) is revolutionizing educational assessment by enabling real-time, personalized feedback, enhancing grading objectivity, supporting predictive analytics for early intervention, and offering scalable solutions across diverse learning contexts. Real-time feedback mechanisms, powered by AI, allow learners to receive immediate insights into their performance, promoting self-regulated learning and deeper engagement. These systems analyze learner inputs—such as written responses, problem-solving steps, or interaction patterns—and deliver tailored feedback that adapts to individual needs (Wang et al., 2023; Holmes et al.,

2022). This dynamic responsiveness aligns with formative assessment principles and supports continuous improvement.

AI also contributes to enhanced objectivity in grading by minimizing human bias and ensuring consistency across large cohorts. Automated scoring systems, particularly those using natural language processing and machine learning, have demonstrated reliability in evaluating essays, short answers, and even spoken responses (Chen et al., 2020; Khosravi et al., 2022). While human judgment remains essential for nuanced evaluation, AI can complement educators by handling routine assessments and flagging anomalies for review.

Predictive analytics is another powerful application of AI in assessment. By analyzing historical performance data, engagement metrics, and behavioral indicators, AI systems can identify students at risk of underperforming or disengaging. These insights enable timely interventions, such as personalized tutoring or curriculum adjustments, which can significantly improve retention and achievement (Slade & Prinsloo, 2022; Kizilcec et al., 2021). Importantly, predictive models must be designed with ethical safeguards to avoid reinforcing stereotypes or penalizing vulnerable learners.

Scalability is a defining strength of AI in education. Platforms like Coursera, Khan Academy, and Duolingo demonstrate how AI can deliver personalized assessment experiences to millions of learners across geographies, languages, and educational systems. Zawacki-Richter and Jung (2023) emphasize that scalable AI solutions must be culturally adaptable and inclusive, ensuring relevance in varied pedagogical contexts. UNESCO (2021) and IEEE (2020) further advocate for standards that promote equitable access and ethical deployment of AI tools globally.

In sum, AI-driven assessment systems offer transformative potential when designed with pedagogical alignment, ethical integrity, and contextual sensitivity. Their ability to personalize feedback, enhance grading fairness, anticipate learner needs, and scale across diverse environments positions them as vital tools for the future of inclusive and effective education.

CHALLENGES

Despite the growing promise of AI in educational assessment, its implementation is fraught with challenges that demand careful scrutiny. One of the most pressing concerns is algorithmic bias, which can perpetuate existing inequities in education. Biases embedded in training data or model design may result in unfair evaluations, particularly for students from marginalized communities (Baker & Hawn, 2021). For example, predictive analytics used to identify "at-risk" learners may inadvertently reinforce stereotypes or penalize those who deviate from dominant learning patterns

(Williamson & Eynon, 2020). Addressing these inequities requires transparent model development, diverse datasets, and continuous auditing to ensure fairness.

Equally critical are data privacy and security risks. AI systems rely heavily on personal and behavioral data to generate insights, raising concerns about consent, surveillance, and misuse. Slade and Prinsloo (2022) advocate for a rights-based approach to educational data, emphasizing learner agency and ethical data stewardship. Compliance with regulations such as the General Data Protection Regulation (GDPR) is essential, but many institutions lack the infrastructure or expertise to implement robust safeguards (UNESCO, 2021).

Resistance to adoption among educators also poses a significant barrier. Many teachers express skepticism about the pedagogical value of AI tools, citing concerns over transparency, reliability, and loss of professional autonomy (Holstein et al., 2020). Professional development and participatory design approaches—where educators are involved in shaping AI systems—can help build trust and foster meaningful integration (Kizilcec et al., 2021).

Finally, integration with legacy systems remains a technical and logistical challenge. Many educational institutions operate on outdated infrastructure that is incompatible with modern AI platforms. This leads to fragmented data ecosystems, limited interoperability, and increased implementation costs (Zawacki-Richter & Jung, 2023). Strategic planning, modular system design, and cross-sector collaboration are needed to bridge these gaps and ensure scalable, sustainable adoption.

In sum, while AI offers transformative potential for educational assessment, its success depends on addressing algorithmic bias, safeguarding data privacy, engaging educators, and modernizing infrastructure. These challenges must be met with interdisciplinary collaboration, ethical governance, and context-sensitive strategies to ensure that AI serves as a tool for equity and innovation in education.

ETHICAL CONSIDERATIONS

Ethics frameworks in AI-driven educational assessment are increasingly recognized as essential for safeguarding fairness, inclusivity, and accountability. As AI systems become more embedded in evaluating learner performance, the potential for unintended consequences—such as algorithmic bias, opaque decision-making, and data misuse—necessitates robust ethical oversight. Frameworks developed by global organizations like UNESCO (2021), IEEE (2020), and ISO (2022) emphasize that AI must uphold human dignity, promote equitable access, and remain transparent in its operations. These principles are not merely aspirational; they serve as actionable guidelines for developers, educators, and policymakers.

Continuous auditing is a cornerstone of ethical AI governance. It involves regularly evaluating algorithms for bias, accuracy, and relevance to ensure that assessment outcomes remain valid and just (Baker & Hawn, 2021). Stakeholder transparency—where learners, educators, and administrators are informed about how AI systems function and how decisions are made—fosters trust and empowers users to engage critically with technology (Slade & Prinsloo, 2022). Moreover, adherence to privacy regulations such as the General Data Protection Regulation (GDPR) ensures that personal data is collected, stored, and used responsibly, with informed consent and clear boundaries.

Recent scholarship underscores that ethical frameworks must be context-sensitive and participatory. Kizilcec et al. (2021) advocate for co-design approaches that involve educators and learners in shaping AI tools, ensuring relevance and responsiveness. Ultimately, ethics in AI assessment is not a static checklist but a dynamic, evolving commitment to equity, transparency, and learner empowerment across diverse educational landscapes.

BUILDING RESPONSIBLE AI ECOSYSTEMS FOR EDUCATIONAL ASSESSMENT

1. Examining the Role of AI Standards in Educational Assessments

The integration of Artificial Intelligence (AI) into educational assessment has prompted the development of formal standards to ensure consistency, reliability, and ethical alignment across diverse learning environments. AI standards serve as foundational tools that guide the design, deployment, and evaluation of intelligent assessment systems. Organizations such as the International Organization for Standardization (ISO), the Institute of Electrical and Electronics Engineers (IEEE), and UNESCO have taken the lead in establishing global benchmarks that address technical interoperability, data governance, and ethical safeguards. For instance, ISO/IEC JTC 1/SC 42 outlines a comprehensive framework for AI systems, including standards for algorithmic transparency, risk management, and performance evaluation (ISO, 2022). These standards are particularly relevant in educational contexts, where assessment outcomes can influence learner trajectories, institutional accountability, and policy decisions.

IEEE's P7000 series, especially P7001 and P7003, provides ethical design protocols for autonomous systems, emphasizing human agency, data privacy, and algorithmic fairness (IEEE, 2020). These standards are increasingly being adopted by educational technology developers to ensure that AI-driven assessment tools do not inadvertently reinforce bias or compromise learner autonomy. UNESCO's 2021 Recommendation on the Ethics of Artificial Intelligence further complements these efforts by promoting inclusive, rights-based approaches to AI in education. It calls for transparent decision-making, equitable access, and participatory governance, all of which are critical in the context of high-stakes assessments.

Recent scholarship underscores the importance of aligning AI standards with pedagogical goals. Holmes et al. (2022) argue that technical standards must be interpreted through an educational lens to ensure that AI systems support meaningful learning rather than merely automate evaluation. Similarly, Khosravi et al. (2022) highlight the need for adaptive assessment systems to comply with both technical and instructional standards, ensuring that personalization does not come at the cost of validity or fairness. The challenge lies in operationalizing these standards across diverse educational settings, particularly in low-resource contexts where infrastructure and expertise may be limited.

In sum, AI standards play a pivotal role in shaping the future of educational assessment. They provide a shared vocabulary and set of expectations that enable stakeholders—educators, developers, policymakers, and learners—to collaborate effectively. As AI continues to evolve, these standards must remain dynamic, inclusive, and pedagogically grounded to ensure that assessment systems are not only technically robust but also educationally transformative.

2. Exploring Ethical and Governance Frameworks Supporting AI Integration

The ethical integration of AI into educational assessment demands robust governance frameworks that address issues of transparency, accountability, and equity. As AI systems increasingly influence learner evaluation, feedback, and progression, the stakes for ethical oversight grow correspondingly higher. Governance frameworks must ensure that AI tools are designed and deployed in ways that respect learner rights, mitigate bias, and promote inclusive educational outcomes. UNESCO's 2021 Recommendation on the Ethics of Artificial Intelligence provides a foundational blueprint, emphasizing human dignity, non-discrimination, and participatory governance. It advocates for the involvement of educators, learners, and communities in shaping AI policies, thereby fostering trust and contextual relevance.

IEEE's P7000 series complements this by offering operational guidelines for ethical AI design, including protocols for algorithmic transparency (P7001), data privacy (P7002), and bias mitigation (P7003) (IEEE, 2020). These standards are particularly critical in educational assessment, where opaque algorithms can lead to unfair evaluations or reinforce systemic inequalities. Williamson and Eynon (2020) caution against the unchecked use of predictive analytics in education, noting that such tools can inadvertently stigmatize learners or reduce complex learning processes to reductive metrics. To counter this, governance frameworks must incorporate mechanisms for human oversight, explainability, and continuous evaluation.

Recent scholarship also emphasizes the importance of contextual sensitivity in ethical governance. Slade and Prinsloo (2022) propose a rights-based approach to educational data, advocating for learner agency and informed consent. Holmes et al. (2022) argue that ethical governance must be embedded within institutional cultures, not treated as an external compliance requirement. This includes training educators to interpret AI outputs critically and empowering learners to question algorithmic decisions. Kizilcec et al. (2021) further highlight the role of participatory design in fostering ethical AI, suggesting that co-creation with users enhances relevance and accountability.

Moreover, ethical governance must address the global diversity of educational contexts. Zawacki-Richter and Jung (2023) stress the need for culturally responsive frameworks that accommodate linguistic, pedagogical, and infrastructural differences. Without such sensitivity, AI systems risk imposing homogenized models of assessment that may not align with local values or practices. Governance frameworks must therefore be flexible, inclusive, and iterative, allowing for adaptation and feedback across diverse settings.

Thus, ethical and governance frameworks are essential for the responsible integration of AI in educational assessment. They provide the scaffolding for trust, fairness, and inclusivity, ensuring that technological innovation serves pedagogical and societal goals. As AI continues to reshape education, these frameworks must evolve in tandem, guided by interdisciplinary collaboration and a commitment to human-centered design.

3. Identifying Challenges and Proposing Strategies for Inclusive and Effective Implementation

Despite the transformative potential of AI in educational assessment, its implementation is fraught with challenges that must be addressed to ensure inclusivity and effectiveness. One of the most pressing concerns is algorithmic bias, which can arise from skewed training data or flawed model design. Such bias can lead to inaccurate assessments, disproportionately affecting learners from marginalized communities (Baker & Hawn, 2021). Addressing this requires rigorous validation protocols, diverse datasets, and continuous monitoring to detect and correct disparities.

Another challenge is the digital divide, which limits access to AI-powered assessment tools in low-resource settings. Infrastructure gaps, limited connectivity, and lack of digital literacy can hinder equitable implementation, exacerbating existing educational inequalities (Wang et al., 2023). Strategies to overcome this include investing in scalable, low-bandwidth solutions, offering multilingual interfaces, and providing training for educators and learners. UNESCO (2021) emphasizes the importance of inclusive design, advocating for tools that accommodate diverse learner needs and contexts.

Ethical concerns also pose significant barriers. Learners may be unaware of how their data is used, or may lack the agency to challenge algorithmic decisions. Slade and Prinsloo (2022) argue for transparent data policies and learner empowerment, suggesting that ethical literacy should be integrated into curricula. Participatory design approaches, as proposed by Kizilcec et al. (2021), can also enhance inclusivity by involving users in the development and evaluation of AI tools.

Pedagogical alignment is another critical issue. AI systems must support—not supplant—educational goals. Holmes et al. (2022) caution against using AI merely for efficiency, advocating instead for tools that foster reflection, metacognition, and deeper learning. Educators must be trained to interpret AI outputs meaningfully and integrate them into instructional strategies. Cross-cultural validation is also essential, as assessment models developed in one context may not translate effectively to another (Zawacki-Richter & Jung, 2023).

To implement AI inclusively and effectively, a multi-pronged strategy is needed. This includes developing ethical standards, investing in infrastructure, fostering digital literacy, and promoting interdisciplinary collaboration. Policy frameworks must be flexible and responsive, allowing for local adaptation and continuous feedback. Moreover, implementation should be guided by principles of equity, transparency, and learner empowerment.

In summary, while AI offers powerful tools for educational assessment, its benefits will only be realized through thoughtful, inclusive, and context-sensitive implementation. By addressing challenges proactively and embracing collaborative design, stakeholders can ensure that AI serves as a catalyst for equitable and transformative learning.

FOSTERING COLLABORATION

Effective integration of Artificial Intelligence (AI) into educational assessment requires sustained collaboration among educators, policymakers, and technologists. This tri-sector partnership is essential to ensure that AI tools are pedagogically aligned, ethically grounded, and contextually relevant. Educators bring domain expertise and classroom insight, policymakers provide regulatory and strategic direction, and technologists contribute the technical infrastructure and innovation needed to operationalize AI systems. Holmes et al. (2022) emphasize that without meaningful collaboration, AI risks becoming a top-down imposition rather than a transformative educational tool. Participatory design approaches, as advocated by Kizilcec et al. (2021), allow stakeholders to co-create AI systems that reflect diverse learning needs and institutional goals.

Open-source platforms play a pivotal role in democratizing access to AI-driven assessment tools. By making algorithms, datasets, and development frameworks publicly available, open-source initiatives reduce barriers to entry for low-resource institutions and foster transparency in system design (Chen et al., 2020). These platforms also encourage innovation through community-driven contributions, enabling localized adaptations and continuous improvement. For example, adaptive learning systems built on open-source architectures can be tailored to regional curricula, languages, and pedagogical models, enhancing relevance and equity (Khosravi et al., 2022).

Shared global standards further support equitable implementation by providing a common framework for ethical and technical compliance. UNESCO's (2021) Recommendation on the Ethics of Artificial Intelligence and IEEE's P7000 series offer guidelines on algorithmic fairness, data privacy, and human oversight. These standards help harmonize practices across jurisdictions, ensuring that AI tools uphold principles of inclusivity and accountability regardless of geographic or economic context. Zawacki-Richter and Jung (2023) argue that global standards must remain flexible and culturally responsive, allowing for adaptation while maintaining core ethical commitments.

Ultimately, collaboration, openness, and standardization are interdependent pillars of responsible AI integration in education. When educators, policymakers, and technologists work together—guided by shared values and transparent tools—they can build AI systems that not only enhance learning outcomes but also reduce systemic inequalities. This collaborative ecosystem is vital for ensuring that AI serves as a catalyst for inclusive, scalable, and pedagogically meaningful assessment practices.

IMPLEMENTATION OF REGULATORY FRAMEWORKS

Responsible deployment of Artificial Intelligence (AI) in educational assessment is increasingly guided by international standards that promote accessibility, privacy, and ethical integrity. Among the most influential are the Web Content Accessibility Guidelines (WCAG) and the General Data Protection Regulation (GDPR), both of which provide foundational principles for designing inclusive and secure AI systems. WCAG, developed by the World Wide Web Consortium (W3C), outlines technical criteria to ensure digital platforms are accessible to learners with disabilities, including those with visual, auditory, cognitive, and motor impairments. When applied to AI-driven assessment tools, WCAG ensures that feedback interfaces, adaptive testing environments, and learning dashboards are usable by all learners, regardless of ability (Holmes et al., 2022; UNESCO, 2021).

GDPR, enacted by the European Union, sets rigorous standards for data privacy and protection. It mandates informed consent, data minimization, and the right to explanation—principles that are particularly relevant in AI systems that collect and analyze sensitive learner data. Institutions that align with GDPR not only safeguard personal information but also foster trust among students and educators by ensuring transparency in how data is used (Slade & Prinsloo, 2022). GDPR's emphasis on accountability and user control complements broader ethical frameworks such as IEEE's P7000 series, which advocate for algorithmic fairness and human oversight in autonomous systems (IEEE, 2020).

Adopting these international guidelines enables educational institutions to create assessment environments that are not only technologically advanced but also socially responsible. Zawacki-Richter and Jung (2023) argue that compliance with global standards enhances institutional credibility and facilitates cross-border collaboration in digital education. Moreover, open adherence to WCAG and GDPR supports equity by reducing barriers for marginalized learners and protecting vulnerable populations from data exploitation.

Recent scholarship also emphasizes the importance of integrating these standards into the design phase of AI tools, rather than retrofitting them post-deployment. Kizilcec et al. (2021) advocate for participatory design approaches that involve diverse stakeholders in shaping ethical and accessible AI systems. By embedding accessibility and privacy considerations from the outset, institutions can ensure that AI-driven assessments are not only effective but also inclusive, secure, and transparent.

CONCLUSION

Artificial Intelligence (AI)-driven assessment holds transformative potential for education, offering unprecedented opportunities for personalization, efficiency, and inclusivity. By leveraging machine learning, natural language processing, and predictive analytics, AI systems can tailor assessments to individual learner profiles, provide real-time feedback, and identify learning gaps with remarkable precision (Khosravi et al., 2022; Wang et al., 2023). These capabilities support differentiated instruction, foster learner autonomy, and reduce reliance on one-size-fits-all evaluation models. Moreover, AI can enhance efficiency by automating grading, streamlining administrative tasks, and enabling scalable assessment solutions across diverse educational contexts (Chen et al., 2020). For learners in remote or underserved regions, AI-powered platforms offer access to adaptive assessments that would otherwise be unavailable, contributing to more equitable learning environments (Zawacki-Richter & Jung, 2023).

However, realizing the full benefits of AI-driven assessment requires more than technological innovation—it demands robust governance, ethical oversight, and global collaboration. Governance frameworks must ensure that AI tools are aligned with educational values, respect learner rights, and operate transparently. UNESCO's *Recommendation on the Ethics of Artificial Intelligence* (2021) emphasizes principles such as human dignity, non-discrimination, and participatory governance, which are essential for building trust in AI systems. Similarly, IEEE's P7000 series provides operational standards for ethical AI design, including protocols for algorithmic transparency, bias mitigation, and data privacy (IEEE, 2020). These frameworks offer a foundation for institutions to implement AI responsibly, but they must be adapted to local contexts and continuously updated to reflect emerging challenges.

Ethical oversight is particularly critical in addressing concerns around algorithmic bias, data misuse, and opaque decision-making. Studies have shown that AI systems trained on biased datasets can produce inequitable outcomes, disproportionately affecting marginalized learners (Baker & Hawn, 2021; Williamson & Eynon, 2020). To mitigate these risks, institutions must implement continuous auditing, involve diverse stakeholders in system design, and ensure that learners have agency over their data. Slade and Prinsloo (2022) advocate for a rights-based approach to educational data ethics, emphasizing transparency, informed consent, and learner empowerment.

Global collaboration is also essential for scaling AI-driven assessment ethically and effectively. Open-source platforms and shared standards can democratize access to AI tools, enabling institutions in low-resource settings to benefit from cutting-edge technologies without prohibitive costs (Holmes et al., 2022). Collaborative efforts across countries and sectors can foster innovation while ensuring that AI systems reflect diverse pedagogical traditions and cultural values. Kizilcec et al. (2021) highlight the importance of participatory design in creating AI tools that are contextually relevant and socially responsive.

In conclusion, while AI-driven assessment offers transformative possibilities, its success hinges on a triad of governance, ethics, and collaboration. By embedding these principles into the design and deployment of AI systems, educational institutions can harness technology to support inclusive, efficient, and learner-centered assessment practices.

SUGGESTIONS

To ensure the responsible and effective integration of AI in educational assessment, institutions must adopt a comprehensive strategy that includes educator training, algorithmic auditing, open-source development, and alignment with pedagogical frameworks. Building AI literacy among educators is foundational. Teachers are not only end-users of AI systems but also interpreters of the insights these tools generate. Without adequate training, educators may struggle to integrate AI meaningfully into their practice or may mistrust its outputs. Professional development programs should focus on demystifying AI technologies, fostering critical engagement, and equipping educators to make informed decisions about data-driven instruction and assessment.

Equally important is the regular auditing of algorithms to ensure fairness and mitigate bias. AI systems trained on narrow or unrepresentative datasets can produce skewed results, disproportionately impacting learners from underrepresented groups. Continuous evaluation of algorithmic performance—through bias detection protocols, stakeholder feedback, and transparent reporting—helps maintain the validity and equity of AI-driven assessments. Ethical standards and data governance policies must be embedded into institutional practices to support this process.

Open-source development offers a powerful avenue for democratizing access to AI tools. By making codebases and datasets publicly available, open-source platforms enable customization, foster transparency, and reduce dependency on proprietary systems. This is particularly beneficial for institutions in low-resource settings, which may lack the financial or technical capacity to adopt commercial AI solutions. Community-driven development also encourages innovation and responsiveness to local educational needs.

Finally, AI deployment must be guided by evidence-based pedagogical frameworks. Technology should enhance—not replace—core educational principles such as formative feedback, learner agency, and metacognitive development. AI systems must be designed to support instructional goals, align with curriculum standards, and respect the diversity of learning contexts. Participatory design approaches, involving educators and learners in the development process, can ensure that AI tools are pedagogically coherent and socially responsive. Taken together, these strategies form a blueprint for inclusive, ethical, and effective AI integration in education. By investing in human capacity, safeguarding algorithmic integrity, promoting open access, and grounding technology in sound pedagogy, institutions can harness AI to advance equitable and transformative assessment practices.

SCOPE FOR FUTURE RESEARCH

Recent advancements in AI-driven assessment have prompted a shift toward multimodal systems that incorporate affective computing to capture a broader spectrum of learner engagement. These systems analyze facial expressions, voice tone, and physiological signals to infer emotional states, enabling more responsive and empathetic feedback mechanisms (D'Mello et al., 2020; Bosch et al., 2021). By integrating cognitive and affective data, educators can better understand learner motivation, frustration, and confidence—factors often overlooked in traditional assessments.

Simultaneously, longitudinal studies are beginning to reveal how AI influences learning equity over time. Research by Kizilcec et al. (2021) and Slade & Prinsloo (2022) highlights both the potential and pitfalls of AI in addressing disparities. While adaptive platforms can personalize learning for underserved populations, algorithmic bias and unequal access to digital infrastructure may exacerbate existing inequities if left unchecked.

To navigate these tensions, policy frameworks must balance technological innovation with ethical accountability. UNESCO (2021), IEEE (2020), and ISO (2022) have proposed guidelines emphasizing transparency, data privacy, and human oversight. These frameworks advocate for inclusive design and participatory governance, ensuring that AI tools align with educational values and human rights.

Finally, cross-cultural validation of AI assessment models is essential to ensure global applicability. Studies by Zawacki-Richter & Jung (2023) and Wang et al. (2023) underscore the importance of contextual sensitivity, revealing how cultural norms, language diversity, and pedagogical traditions influence the effectiveness and acceptance of AI systems across regions. Together, these dimensions form a critical foundation for equitable, ethical, and culturally responsive AI in education.

REFERENCES

Baker, R., & Hawn, A. (2021). Algorithmic bias in education: Challenges and solutions. *Educational Technology Research and Development*, *69*(3), 123–138. DOI: 10.1007/s11423-021-09993-7

Bosch, N., D'Mello, S., & Baker, R. (2021). Detecting student affect from multimodal data. *IEEE Transactions on Affective Computing*, *12*(2), 280–293. DOI: 10.1109/TAFFC.2018.2878658

Chen, L., Chen, P., & Lin, Z. (2020). Artificial intelligence in education: A review. *IEEE Access : Practical Innovations, Open Solutions*, *8*, 75264–75278. DOI: 10.1109/ACCESS.2020.2988510

D'Mello, S. K., Bosch, N., & Baker, R. S. (2020). Affective computing in education: From detection to adaptation. *User Modeling and User-Adapted Interaction*, *30*(1), 1–34. DOI: 10.1007/s11257-019-09222-0

Gunning, D., Stefik, M., & Choi, J.. (2023). XAI: Explainable artificial intelligence for education. *AI Magazine*, *44*(1), 15–28. DOI: 10.1007/s43684-023-00039-9

Holmes, W., Bialik, M., & Fadel, C. (2022). *Artificial intelligence in education: Promises and implications for teaching and learning*. Center for Curriculum Redesign.

Holstein, K., McLaren, B. M., & Aleven, V. (2020). Designing for complementarity: Teacher and AI support for student learning. *International Journal of Artificial Intelligence in Education*, *30*(1), 1–28. DOI: 10.1007/s40593-019-00186-0

IEEE. (2020). *Ethically aligned design: A vision for prioritizing human well-being with autonomous and intelligent systems*. IEEE Standards Association.

Ifenthaler, D., & Yau, J. Y.-K. (2020). Utilising learning analytics for study success: Reflections on current empirical findings. *Technology. Knowledge and Learning*, *25*(3), 545–559. DOI: 10.1007/s10758-019-09416-3

ISO. (2022). *ISO/IEC JTC 1/SC 42 Artificial Intelligence – Overview and Standards*. International Organization for Standardization.

Khosravi, H., Kitto, K., & Knight, S. (2022). Adaptive learning analytics: A review of AI-driven personalization in education. *British Journal of Educational Technology*, *53*(4), 1012–1030. DOI: 10.1111/bjet.13294

Kizilcec, R. F., Lee, H., & Reich, J. (2021). Participatory design for equitable AI in education. *Computers & Education*, *170*, 104225. DOI: 10.1016/j.compedu.2021.104225

Luckin, R. (2020). *Machine learning and human intelligence: The future of education for the 21st century*. UCL Press., DOI: 10.14324/111.9781787358760

Rose, D. H., Gravel, J. W., & Domings, Y. (2020). *Universal design for learning: Theory and practice*. CAST Publishing.

Slade, S., & Prinsloo, P. (2022). Educational data ethics in the age of AI. *British Journal of Educational Technology*, *53*(2), 234–248. DOI: 10.1111/bjet.13191

Slavin, R. E. (2022). AI and equity in education: Opportunities and risks. *Journal of Educational Change*, *23*(1), 1–15. DOI: 10.1007/s10833-021-09424-1

UNESCO. (2021). *Recommendation on the ethics of artificial intelligence*. United Nations Educational, Scientific and Cultural Organization. https://unesdoc.unesco.org/ark:/48223/pf0000381137

Wang, M., & Tsai, C.-C. (2021). Students' trust in AI tutors: A study of perceptions and engagement. *Journal of Educational Technology & Society*, *24*(3), 45–58. https://www.j-ets.net/ETS/journals/24_3/4.pdf

Wang, Y., Liu, S., & Zhang, H. (2023). Real-time feedback in AI-supported learning environments: A meta-analysis. *Computers & Education*, *193*, 104663. DOI: 10.1016/j.compedu.2023.104663

Williamson, B., & Eynon, R. (2020). Historical threads, missing links, and future directions in AI and education. *Learning, Media and Technology*, *45*(3), 223–235. DOI: 10.1080/17439884.2020.1798995

Woolf, B. P. (2010). *Building intelligent interactive tutors: Student-centered strategies for revolutionizing e-learning*. Morgan Kaufmann.

Zawacki-Richter, O., & Jung, I. (2023). Systematic review of AI applications in higher education assessment. *Journal of Educational Technology & Society*, *26*(1), 1–15. https://www.j-ets.net/ETS/journals/26_1/1.pdf

Zawacki-Richter, O., Marín, V. I., Bond, M., & Gouverneur, F. (2019). Systematic review of research on artificial intelligence applications in higher education. *International Journal of Educational Technology in Higher Education*, *16*(1), 1–27. DOI: 10.1186/s41239-019-0171-0

Chapter 4

Ethical AI in Engineering Education:

A Case Study on Mindset, Behaviors, and AI Literacy

Christina Merl
https://orcid.org/0009-0000-4268-6336
TalkShop/2CG®, Austria

David Guralnick
Kaleidoscope Learning, USA

Dominik Dolezal
https://orcid.org/0000-0002-0125-4817
TGM Vienna, Austria

Alexandra Posekany
TGM Vienna, Austria

Gottfried Koppensteiner
TGM Vienna, Austria

ABSTRACT

This chapter presents a pilot case study exploring the ethical, cultural, and pedagogical implications of AI integration in technical education, conducted at the IT department of TGM, a leading secondary vocational school in Vienna. Recognizing that AI in education constitutes not merely a technological shift but a broader socio-cultural transformation, the study applied a mixed-methods diagnostic approach, which was designed to capture complex social and ethical dimensions beyond technical literacy. Seven thematic patterns emerged from the data, informing pedagogical responses

DOI: 10.4018/979-8-3373-2235-3.ch004

to promote ethical awareness and responsible AI use. Rigorous scientific oversight ensured a comprehensive and ethically grounded analysis. Conducted over a defined period in 2025, the project delivers the first comprehensive AI mindset and ethics diagnostic scan in Austrian vocational education and training (VET), offering a scalable framework for ethical AI integration in learning environments.

1. INTRODUCTION: REFRAMING ETHICS IN AI-ENHANCED TECHNICAL EDUCATION

As artificial intelligence (AI) rapidly evolves from novelty to norm in global education systems, a pressing set of ethical and pedagogical questions emerges: What does it mean to know, to learn, and to teach in a world where algorithmic agents co-create, co-decide, and co-assess? How can educators maintain academic integrity, inclusivity, and learner agency in the presence of powerful generative systems? And what literacies are needed to prepare engineering students not only for technical mastery but for ethical participation in socio-technical systems that are increasingly shaped by machine logic? Nowhere are these questions more urgent than in vocational education and training (VET), where the demands of rapid technological innovation intersect with the need for ethical responsibility. As Selwyn (2021) argues, AI in education is not simply a matter of technological change, but of social, cultural and ethical transformation. Engineering students today are entering professional landscapes in which AI is embedded almost everywhere – in infrastructure design, manufacturing, health technologies, environmental modeling, and national security systems.

Becoming fluent and savvy in these new technologies is no longer sufficient for these learners - the designers and decision-makers of the future who will determine how society lives with AI. The implications are substantial. As Floridi (2019) emphasizes in his work on *digital ethics by design*, the central challenge for education in the AI age is not only to foster technical proficiency, but to develop a generation of professionals capable of foreseeing and mitigating the societal consequences of algorithmic choices. This includes sensitivity to issues such as AI bias, lack of transparency, data ownership, and the unintended amplification of inequities. These concerns must be addressed through policy, guidelines, and compliance training, as well as through learning experiences that cultivate critical awareness, systems thinking, and ethical imagination – so called 21st century skills.

What is more, engineering education is no longer limited to full-time students at the start of their careers. Increasingly, it includes "working learners" — professionals who return to formal education to reskill, upskill, or adapt to the demands of new technologies (Merl, 2022). These learners frequently confront real-world applications of AI in their workplaces and must reconcile their evolving expertise with the practical ethical dilemmas they encounter. For them, the classroom is not a rehearsal for future action; it is a site of meaning-making (Wenger, 1998) and ethical negotiation.

1.1. Knowledge, Identity and AI as Co-Constructor

We begin by conceptualizing AI not just as a technological tool, but as an epistemic partner reshaping how students and educators think and act. Furthermore, we see a shift in how learners perceive knowledge, identity, and the role of AI in their development. Emerging research from behavioral and narrative inquiry shows that students now see AI not merely as a tool, but as a kind of second teacher — an advisor, explainer, or even a collaborator (Gruenhagen et al, 2023). In fact, AI-based approaches to learning have the potential to create educational systems that foster creativity and critical thinking skills, and can change the structure of both traditional education and workplace learning (Guralnick, 2024). However, overreliance on AI risks diminishing core skills and may undermine students' sense of capability, autonomy, and agency. Kumar et al. (2023) discuss in their systematic review the ethical implications of AI in education, emphasizing the need for robust policies to mitigate academic misconduct. All these questions and implications are particularly relevant in vocational education and training (VET), where hands-on expertise is traditionally valued and where the integration of emerging technologies must be balanced against human-centered skill development.

2. THEORETICAL AND CONCEPTUAL FOUNDATIONS

This book chapter, which features a first ethical AI use diagnostic study at the IT Department of the Technologisches Gewerbemuseum (TGM) vocational secondary school in Vienna, is suitable for an audience of educational leaders and experts for several key reasons: First, it addresses an urgent gap in evidence-based understanding of how Artificial Intelligence (AI) is actually being used — and perceived — by both teachers and students in secondary technical education. As AI tools such as ChatGPT, Claude, and DALL·E become increasingly integrated into the learning environment, educational institutions must move beyond abstract discussions of "AI in education" to concrete, context-sensitive insight into real behaviors, mindsets, ethical tensions, and pedagogical needs. This chapter delivers precisely that. It is one of the first empirical studies in a vocational secondary school context to explore the ethical dimensions of AI use through both quantitative data and qualitative narratives, providing a rare dual lens on both mindset and practice.

Second, the findings of the study speak directly to strategic priorities identified by education policy leaders across Europe and globally — namely, the need to foster digital integrity, AI literacy, inclusive learning cultures, and ethical preparedness in students and staff (European Commission & OECD, 2025). The seven cross-cutting behavioral patterns identified through the study (including moral dissonance, covert use of AI, teacher role tension, epistemic shifts, lack of guidance and diversity) offer a nuanced map of the cultural transformation currently underway in classrooms shaped by automation and generative tools. The data and findings give decision-makers a grounded basis for designing ethical guidelines, professional development pathways, and curricular reforms rooted in real needs rather than speculative fears. Third, the chapter does not stop at diagnosis. It proposes a reflective, and scalable pedagogical framework that helps educational institutions respond systemically. The multi-method approach supports educational institutions that need to move toward cultural leadership by offering dialogic tools for collaborative norm-setting, learner identity development, and critical engagement with AI. All this is crucial in vocational education and training (VET) where technical training must now be matched with ethical foresight, creativity, and collaborative sense-making.

2.1. Student-Centered and Motivational Pedagogy

Building on humanistic and constructivist insights, this section positions AI literacy within a blended framework, combining technical skills with ethical and reflexive capacity. The pedagogical foundation of this approach is grounded in the principles of student-centered learning, originally articulated by Carl Rogers in his humanistic psychology and later adapted to educational contexts. Drawing on his work in client-centered therapy (Rogers, 1959), Rogers extended his approach to education by advocating for environments that prioritize the learner's agency, emotional presence, and capacity for self-direction. In *Freedom to Learn* (1969), he famously argued that "the only person who is educated is the one who has learned how to learn", emphasizing the importance of adaptability, openness to change, and epistemic humility in a rapidly evolving world. In the context of AI-enhanced learning—where information is ubiquitous and knowledge is co-produced with algorithmic systems—this insight becomes increasingly salient. Rogers' call for "*changingness*" as a pedagogical goal resonates with current shifts toward dynamic, process-oriented approaches to knowledge and therefore is particularly relevant in engineering and vocational education where learners must constantly recalibrate their understanding in response to technological advancement.

Student-centered learning, as articulated by Rogers and elaborated in his later work (*Freedom to Learn for the 80s*, 1983), includes practical methodologies such as self- and peer-evaluation, problem-based learning, and learning contracts. These are not merely instructional techniques but reflect a deeper philosophical commitment to learner autonomy, empathy, and authentic teacher–student relationships. Teachers become facilitators and coaches rather than transmitters of fixed knowledge, creating spaces where students develop both technical and interpersonal competencies. This approach aligns strongly with Vygotsky's (1978) theory of social constructivism, which posits that learning is inherently social and dialogical. In this view, cognition is shaped through mediated interaction with both the environment and others, making peer collaboration, shared inquiry, and reflective dialogue essential pedagogical components—particularly when engaging with complex and ethically ambiguous technologies such as AI.

Complementing the Rogerian framework, the Self-Determination Theory (SDT) by Ryan and Deci (2000) offers a contemporary psychological model that underscores the conditions under which learners thrive. According to SDT, human motivation is optimally supported when three basic needs are met: competence (feeling effective), autonomy (experiencing volition and agency), and relatedness (feeling connected to others). These needs provide a compelling rationale for rethinking AI integration in education. When students experience AI as a co-agent that supports competence (e.g., by providing real-time feedback), reinforces autonomy (e.g., through personalized scaffolding), and sustains relatedness (e.g., by prompting peer collaboration or dialogic reflection), their engagement with both content and context deepens. Conversely, when AI is introduced in ways that undermine these dimensions—by replacing teacher-student relationships, prescribing rigid learning paths, or obscuring learners' agency—the motivational and ethical value of the technology is compromised. Taken together, student-centered learning, peer exchange learning and self-determination theory provide a robust pedagogical rationale for the AI-enhanced 2CG® content and context framework discussed later in this chapter. Both traditions emphasize the importance of empowering learners not only to acquire disciplinary knowledge, but to develop reflective, ethical, and socially embedded identities as they engage with complex technological systems.

Within the context of the IT Department at TGM, where learners are preparing to enter real-world environments shaped by algorithmic decision-making and automation, these approaches offer a necessary corrective to instrumentalist models of education. They help ensure that learning is not reduced to technical proficiency alone, but remains a process of human development, meaning-making, and ethical orientation in a digitally mediated world.

2.2 The 2CG® Framework: Content and Context Method

The 2CG® methodology, or Content- and Context-Specific Generic Competency Coaching, is a transformative, interdisciplinary educational framework developed, implemented and continually enhanced since 2008 (Merl, 2020). It aims to cultivate 21st century skills, such as communication skills, creativity, critical reflection, collaboration, ethical reasoning, and systemic thinking. The acronym "2CG" refers to the integration of domain skills (content) and real-world relevance, cultural identity, and emotional meaning (context) in the design and facilitation of learning experiences.

At its core, 2CG® builds on theories of constructivist and humanistic learning, including communities of practice (Wenger, 1998), a learner-centered approach (Rogers, 1959), social constructivism (Vygotsky, 1978), systems thinking (Senge, 1990), critical pedagogy (Freire, 1970), the concept of double loop learning (Argyris and Schön, 1991), and embodiment theory (Caracciolo and Kukkonen, 2021). The multi-method approach treats students as co-creators of knowledge and identity, not passive recipients of information. Teachers take the role of facilitator and coach; learning is dialogic, situated, and fundamentally social, unfolding through reflection, feedback, and collaboration (Merl, 2022). This aligns with the broader shift from instructionism to constructivist and experiential learning approaches advocated by educational thinkers like Donald Schön (1983).

In practice, 2CG® includes diverse pedagogical modalities, such as reflective writing and dialogue; storylistening and narrative inquiry; the use of poetry and metaphors as analytical tools; visual thinking and collaborative design; and artistic inquiry for emotional and ethical insight. These practices allow learners to externalize internal meaning-making processes, bridge disciplinary and emotional understanding, and negotiate values in ways that are difficult to access through conventional didactic methods. Greene (1995) emphasized the necessity of aesthetic experience in education to awaken consciousness and deepen ethical imagination—a premise echoed in 2CG®'s integration of the arts. The framework is especially effective in culturally diverse and technology-mediated settings because it centers human interaction, perspective-taking, and identity work. As Eisner (2002) observed, learning environments that include aesthetic and narrative forms of engagement foster deeper cognitive and emotional insight. In engineering education, this is critical: technical accuracy must be paired with ethical foresight and the capacity for dialogic learning.

Importantly, 2CG® encourages learners to understand the interdependencies and feedback loops that shape technological, social, and ecological systems. This systemic lens is key in helping students navigate complex problems, such as climate change, algorithmic bias, or digital exclusion – issues that require ethical deliberation as much as technical knowledge.

2.3 AI Literacy as a Pillar of 21st Century Competence

In an era of pervasive algorithmic mediation, the concept of AI literacy has emerged as a key educational priority. According to the draft *AI Literacy Frame-*

work developed by the European Commission and OECD (2025), it comprises "the technical knowledge, durable skills, and future-ready attitudes required to thrive in a world influenced by AI." Accordingly, AI literacy enables learners not only to engage with, manage, and co-create AI systems, but also to critically evaluate their benefits, limitations, and ethical implications. Crucially, this moves beyond operational proficiency to include reflective judgment, bias awareness, and agency in human–machine interaction. AI literacy not only covers the skills required to operate AI technologies, but also its critically-reflected and ethical use. If used properly, AI should enable humans to be creative, productive, and innovative, all while being aware of the limitations of AI such as bias and hallucinations. As articulated by Trilling and Fadel (2012), future-oriented education must integrate domains such as learning and innovation, digital literacy, and life skills.

While generative AI tools have led Meyer et al (2023) to AI-generated text inspiring students' writing process, recent empirical studies raise important concerns about the cognitive and ethical costs of uncritical AI reliance during learning phases. For example, a study at MIT conducted by Kosmyna et al. (2025) revealed that students relying on large language models (LLMs) to compose essays exhibited the lowest levels of brain activation and reported diminished authorship and memory of their output, compared to peers who worked unaided or used search engines. These findings suggest that overdependence on generative AI may impair both cognitive engagement and long-term learning processes. In education, such risks extend to reduced development of creativity, critical thinking, problem-solving, and interpersonal skills--all core capacities of what are now widely termed *21st century skills*.

AI literacy naturally aligns with this framework but also deepens its ethical dimension, given the epistemic and societal shifts introduced by AI. Educational facilities currently seem to miss a systematic integration of 21st century skills in educational practice (see, e.g., Voogt et al., 2013 and Dolezal et al., 2025). Effective AI literacy acquisition demands integration into real-world, content-rich learning contexts, self-directed and peer-based learning formats (van Laar et al., 2019 and Dolezal et al., 2025), and facilitation through student-centered pedagogies (Rotherham & Willingham, 2009) --all of which inform the case study presented in this chapter.

3. CASE STUDY CONTEXT: TGM VIENNA'S IT DEPARTMENT

3.1 Institutional Profile and Vocational Mission

The case study presented in this chapter draws from the IT Department of The *Technologisches Gewerbemuseum* (TGM) in Vienna, Austria's second-largest technical upper secondary school (*Höhere Technische Lehranstalt*, HTL), with approximately 2,500 students and 300 teachers. Founded in 1888 as a center for industrial education, TGM continues to be a flagship institution in Austria's vocational education and training (VET) sector, offering rigorous academic instruction in tandem with practice-oriented training across disciplines, including Mechanical Engineering, Electrical Engineering, Biomedical Engineering, and Information Technology (IT).

The IT Department at TGM, comprising over 550 students and more than 70 teachers, is particularly noted for its early and pragmatic adoption of digital tools in instruction and administration. Since 2016, the department has integrated future-oriented teaching strategies, including a distinctive student-centered model known as the *Learning Office (Lernbüro)*, which has shaped both curriculum and department culture. This model is aligned with Austria's educational goals for fostering 21st-century competencies such as creativity, problem-solving, communication, and systemic thinking.

3.2. The Learning Office Model

The *Learning Office* represents an alternative, self-directed approach to technical education, emphasizing autonomy, personalized learning, and emotional engagement. Students entering the IT department may choose between the conventional curriculum and the Learning Office track. In each of the five grades (K9–13), two cohorts are taught under each model, with 50% of the department's students enrolled in the Learning Office pathway. In this model, students select from a range of subjects during dedicated learning office periods and work at their own pace using curated, self-explanatory learning materials provided in specialized rooms. Each room is staffed by a subject-specific facilitator who assumes the role of coach, guiding students toward both academic and personal growth. The approach integrates the principles of student-centered learning (Rogers, 1959; 1983), social constructivism (Vygotsky, 1978), and self-determination theory (Ryan & Deci, 2000), fostering intrinsic motivation through autonomy, competence, and relatedness. Generative AI tools such as ChatGPT are already part of everyday academic practice. In this environment, students and teachers are actively negotiating the meaning and boundaries of ethical AI use, frequently without clear policy or guidelines.

The parallel offering of both instructional models across all grade levels has enabled the implementation of robust, longitudinal research studies evaluating the pedagogical efficacy and systemic implications of the student-centered Learning Office model. These studies, conducted between 2018 and 2022, provided some key findings:

- **Adjustment Period and Student Engagement:** Learning Office students typically exhibited a one- to two-semester adjustment phase before achieving performance parity with their peers in traditional classrooms. Despite this initial lag, these students reported significantly higher levels of peer collaboration and school satisfaction (Dolezal et al., 2018).
- **Dropout and Retention Rates:** After two years, students in the Learning Office track demonstrated a lower dropout rate compared to their peers in the conventional track, alongside improved perceptions of classroom comfort and teacher support (Dolezal et al., 2019).
- **Attendance and Motivation:** Attendance records revealed that students in the student-centered model were markedly less likely to be absent on laboratory days—an indicator of increased engagement with hands-on learning activities (Dolezal, 2020).
- **Development of Transversal Competencies:** Students in the Learning Office cohort self-reported higher gains in a range of transversal, 21st-century competencies, such as critical thinking, self-efficacy, personal responsibility, openness to experience, and reflective thinking (Dolezal et al., 2021).
- **Digital Proficiency and Coping Skills:** Furthermore, these students exhibited elevated levels of digital literacy, ICT fluency, and problem-solving confidence--skills that are increasingly critical in today's technology-saturated learning and working environments (Dolezal et al., 2022).

Taken together, these findings suggest that the Learning Office model fosters academic outcomes that are at least equivalent to those achieved in traditional settings, while concurrently promoting the development of key transversal competencies, known as 21st century skills. Given this alignment, it is plausible to infer that students engaged in the Learning Office model are particularly well-positioned to develop AI literacy, a complex and interdisciplinary construct that intersects with digital literacy, computational thinking, ethical reasoning, and problem-solving. As AI literacy becomes increasingly central to modern vocational education, the Learning Office may serve as an effective incubator for equipping learners not only with technical knowledge but also with the metacognitive and ethical frameworks necessary to engage critically and productively with AI technologies in both academic and workplace contexts.

Table 1. Student numbers by grade, approach, and gender at the IT department of the TGM.

Grade	Approach	Male	Female
9	LO	61	9
	TR	61	10
10	LO	48	11
	TR	50	5
11	LO	56	7
	TR	53	7
12	LO	37	10
	TR	46	5
13	LO	30	4
	TR	39	1
	total	481	69

Note. LO… Learning office approach, TR… Traditional teaching.

3.3 Why TGM? Rationale for the Pilot Ethical Scan

The choice of TGM's IT Department as the pilot site for the Diagnostic Study and analysis was guided by three main considerations:

A. **High AI Penetration and Spontaneous Adoption:**

As early as late 2022, students and teachers began independently using generative AI tools, particularly large language models (LLMs) like ChatGPT, for tasks such as code generation, debugging assistance, technical summaries, and even creative ideation. By 2024, these tools were widespread in use, but largely unregulated and often invisible in formal settings. The rapid and decentralized uptake of AI in this environment provided a fertile ground for studying emergent norms, ethical tensions, and pedagogical gaps.

B. **Vocational Specificity and Real-World Relevance:**

Unlike purely academic institutions, TGM prepares students for direct entry into industry. Students often undertake internships, participate in industry-sponsored projects, or work part-time in technical fields. As such, they encounter AI not only in the classroom but also in workplaces where automation, data analysis, and algorithmic tools are already in use. This dual exposure makes their engagement with

AI particularly reflective of real-world tensions between efficiency, transparency, and ethical responsibility.

C. **Cultural and Social Diversity**

The student body at TGM includes people from a wide range of socio-economic backgrounds, first-generation learners, and culturally diverse groups. The presence of female, non-binary, and religiously diverse students in a male-dominated technical environment makes inclusion and representation in AI-enhanced tools a critical dimension for study. Moreover, this diversity invites pedagogical models that go beyond technical skills to include social learning, participatory ethics, and identity formation.

3.4 A Culture Poised for Transformation

What is more, over the past five years, TGM's IT Department has actively invested in reflective, interdisciplinary pedagogy — including collaboration with external partners from research, design, and the arts. For example, 2CG® (content- and context-specific generic competency coaching)-facilitated workshops using poetic inquiry and visual mapping have been implemented with engineering students to explore future skills, including creativity, imagination, communication skills, empathy, systemic thinking, sustainability, and learner identity. These workshops formed part of the TGM Lernbuero program and were supported by the school's leadership team as essential "future literacy" experiences.

With all this theoretical framing and beginning practical implementations in place, the IT Department of TGM provided a digitally mature, learner-centered vocational setting with high relevance and readiness for ethical probing.

4. RESEARCH DESIGN AND METHODOLOGY

Artificial Intelligence (AI) is no longer a distant prospect in education--it is a present and powerful force reshaping classrooms, assessments, teacher roles, and student identity. As Selwyn (2019) cautions, "AI in education is not simply a matter of technological change, but of social, cultural and ethical transformation." The rapid uptake of tools such as ChatGPT or DALL-E in both formal and informal learning environments has created an urgent need for educational institutions to examine not just technical adoption, but also the cultural, ethical, and behavioral implications of AI integration. In response to this need, a diagnostic study on the ethical use of AI was piloted with the Telluz diagnostic tool in the IT Department of TGM, which reflects a digitally mature and diverse educational ecosystem, making it an ideal testbed for investigating emerging patterns of AI usage in learning and teaching. By early 2023, it was evident that both students and teachers at TGM had begun to spontaneously adopt AI tools across a wide range of activities - coding, problem-solving, feedback, ideation, and more. Yet this adoption occurred in the absence of consistent ethical guidance, policy frameworks, or shared understanding. The Scan was therefore introduced as both a diagnostic and developmental instrument that does not merely measure attitudes or behaviors, but reveals underlying tensions, unmet ethical needs, and systemic blind spots in AI integration. Unlike traditional assessment tools, such as dilemma-based surveys or AI readiness checklists, the mixed-method approach used has been designed to surface the emotional climate, cultural friction, and social learning behaviors surrounding AI use in real educational or organizational contexts. The integrated narrative prompts and storylistening techniques are aimed at revealing how participants relate to AI not just as users, but as members of learning communities shaped by norms, identities, and institutional dynamics.

4.1. Objectives of the Pilot Study

This pilot study aimed to explore how students and teachers in the context of technical secondary education perceive and engage with AI, with a particular focus on ethical, behavioral, and cultural dimensions. Rather than assessing AI literacy in terms of skills acquisition, the project investigated the deeper dynamics of mindset, value orientation, and social integrity within a real-world school setting. The study was exploratory in nature, designed to inform future educational interventions and policy frameworks for ethical AI adoption at the IT Department of TGM and beyond. Overall, it should provide a robust foundation for generating actionable insight into how students and teachers at the IT Department of TGM navigate the ethical and pedagogical complexities of AI in their learning environment, surfacing not only what participants think but how they think--eliciting assumptions, tensions, and unspoken norms.

4.2 Participant Demographics and Scope

The pilot study involved students and teachers from the IT department at TGM Vienna. A total of 432 participants participated in the scan, including 393 students and 39 teachers. 54% of respondents were enrolled in the Learning Office, 46% participated in the classical study program. Most teachers worked across Learning Office and classical teaching models. The largest student groups came from form one and form two (14-16 year old students), indicating strong early-grade input. Participation was voluntary and anonymous, and demographic information was collected in aggregate to protect identity while enabling cultural and contextual interpretation. A strong student representation (91%) gives high insight into learner perspectives. A high male ratio (79%) signals a potential gender imbalance in the response profile. However, it reflects the current system and conditions at the IT Department of TGM.

4.3 Research Design

A mixed-methods research design was employed to combine narrative depth with pattern-based analysis (Miles, Huberman and Saldana, 2014). The integrated diagnostic tool and analysis, which was developed for complex organisational, social as well as socio-technical settings, served as primary research tool, enabling the simultaneous capture of qualitative and quantitative data. The instrument was adapted for piloting conditions and administered over a defined period in spring 2025. The Scan included:

- Likert-scale items assessing general attitudes toward AI, ethical concerns, trust, and perceived risks.
- Open-response prompts, designed to elicit participants' reflections on AI's broader societal impact, ethical dilemmas, and personal experiences.
- Two central open questions ("AI is good for humankind" and "AI improves education"), which served as a diagnostic probe to explore the range of student reasoning, emotions, and value frameworks.

Unlike conventional surveys that focus on usage frequency or technical proficiency, the approach invited participants to engage with nuanced scenarios and value-laden dilemmas, providing for reflection, norm articulation, and meaning-making. By combining quantitative data with narrative reflection, the approach illuminates how participants experience AI not just cognitively, but relationally – shaping how they define fairness, authorship, trust, and their own roles within the AI-enhanced learning system.

A note on language: Themes refer to the seven pre-defined conceptual categories (e.g., language, inclusion); patterns refer to the empirically derived behavioral/ethical response types (e.g., moral dissonance).

Structure of the Survey: Seven Core Themes

Grounded in systemic constructivism, behavioral science, participatory ethics, and non-directional hypothesis framing, the research approach recognizes that ethical competence cannot be imposed but must be co-created through reflective dialogue, shared norm-setting, and culturally responsive pedagogy. The survey itself covered 32 items that were structured around seven core dimensions of ethical AI use in education: 1. Social Integrity; 2. AI in Teaching and Learning; 3. Personal Motivation, Meta Awareness and Responsibility; 4. AI Literacy and Conditions of Use; 5. Future Skills and Perspectives with AI; 6. Hopes and Fears for the Future; 7. Language, Diversity & Inclusion. These core themes were co-developed by an interdisciplinary team of TGM teachers, experts, and facilitators in a pre-scan scoping session. Specifically, the survey aimed to:

1. Analyze the ethical mindset of students and educators by exploring their values, concerns, and dissonances in AI use.
2. Assess AI literacy through a lens of responsible engagement—not just how well users navigate AI tools, but how critically and ethically they do so.
3. Identify current strengths and vulnerabilities in AI practice, including areas of trust erosion, covert usage, or superficial application.
4. Generate culturally grounded ethical guidelines, co-developed with students and teachers, that reflect lived realities and shared values.
5. Support strategic cultural transformation, ensuring that AI adoption enhances rather than undermines integrity, inclusion, and critical thinking.

What has emerged is not a static snapshot of AI deployment but a situated interpretation of cultural tensions and ethical reasoning as experienced by participants. It should be pointed out, though, that this pilot study did not attempt to measure compliance or identify individual misuse. Instead, the research frames AI behavior through a cultural and pedagogical lens, treating students and teachers as co-constructors of a digital learning culture.

4.4 Data Analysis: Mixed-Methods Strategy

The approach integrated quantitative survey data, qualitative open responses, and narrative insights derived from the scoping session, with the aim to triangulate behavioral evidence, emotional undercurrents, and institutional dynamics related to AI use in the classroom. The combination of methods ensures that the findings reflect current key patterns and lived experiences in the IT Department of TGM. More specifically, quantitative data were analyzed using descriptive statistics to identify patterns in AI perceptions, ethical stances, and risk awareness. Qualitative responses were coded thematically using an inductive approach, supported by elements of narrative inquiry and ethnographic interpretation (Miles, Huberman and Saldana, 2014) (Freire,1970). Recurring themes were grouped into seven dominant "patterns of ethical positioning", which form the basis of the findings section in this chapter. These patterns reflect the interplay of moral reasoning, emotional response, and contextual behaviors.

Quantitative and Narrative: The survey consisted of seven thematic clusters (see Core Themes). Each Theme included multiple Items (e.g., "AI replaces teachers?" or "AI is used for feedback"), where respondents indicated their ethical judgment, perceived frequency, personal involvement, and disapproval levels. Responses were collected through an anonymous online survey platform; analysis covered both aggregate trends and subgroup patterns (female, diverse, age groups).

Thematic Categories: To define the thematic categories, the research team conducted a scoping session based on the 2CG® storylistening framework, which invited a core group of six TGM teachers and experts into a shared reflective space where narratives, images, metaphors, and non-linear expressions could be used to surface ethical discomforts, hopes, and imaginative potentials for AI in their learning environment. The method draws on principles of participatory learning and dialogic sense-making, where the facilitator acts as listener and co-learner. The insights gained from the session provided the key language and concepts for designing the survey questionnaire.

Quantitative Analysis: The structured scan results were analyzed using descriptive statistics (e.g., percentage distribution, approval/disapproval rates, behavioral frequency). Comparative analysis between teachers and students enabled identification of normative gaps - discrepancies between what is considered appropriate, acceptable, or ideal behavior or norms, such as moral dissonance, hidden AI use, or diverging beliefs about transparency.

Qualitative Analysis: Open-ended responses were subjected to thematic coding, with patterns emerging around: ethical tensions (e.g., fairness, authorship, truth); learner identity and emotional shifts; role models and AI transparency; systemic gaps in rules, inclusion, and support.

Emerging patterns were then matched against the seven analytical themes, and cross-referenced with the storylistening narratives to ensure semantic validity and alignment with learner experience.

Given the sensitive nature of ethical reflection, especially regarding assessment or hidden AI use, self-report data had to be interpreted with caution. Questions often employed third-person formulations to reduce fear of judgment or disciplinary consequence. Accordingly, the triangulation with disapproval rates, frequency ratings, and qualitative responses was essential to interpret these patterns meaningfully.

Drawing from 432 responses—primarily student-generated—the process unfolded in four key steps:

1. Initial Familiarization: The research team conducted multiple readings of the full dataset, identifying frequently recurring terms, moral qualifiers, and tone

markers. Examples like *"kann gefährlich sein"* ("can be dangerous") and *"kommt drauf an, wie man es nutzt"* ("depends on how you use it") signaled early ethical ambivalence and conditional trust.

2. Open Coding (First-Cycle): Text segments were coded inductively without pre-set categories. For example, *"Es wird eh schon überall verwendet"* (everybody uses it), indicating normalized adoption. "*Wir sollten nicht alles der KI überlassen" (we should not delegate everything to AI), indicating* delegated agency concern.
3. Pattern Coding and Theme Consolidation

Similar codes were clustered into broader patterns of ethical positioning. For instance, comments combining trust and fear informed the Moral Dissonance pattern. Frequent statements like *"KI ist gut, solange man's richtig nutzt"* (AI is good as long as we use it appropriately) contributed to Conditional Ethics and Contextual Reasoning.

4. Validation and Semantic Triangulation

The emerging thematic structure was cross-checked against insights from the core team pre-scan storylistening session to ensure that categories reflected both student experience and institutional context. For example, student responses expressing discomfort with "hidden" use of AI echoed teacher concerns about unregulated practices and assessment integrity.

This process led to the definition of seven empirically grounded patterns (see Findings section), each representing a distinctive cluster of ethical-emotional reasoning.

4.5 Ethical Considerations

This study was conducted under piloting conditions with institutional support from TGM Vienna and the Austrian Ministry of Education. Participants were informed of the research aims, and all responses were collected anonymously. While formal ethical board approval was not required for this pilot, the research adhered to principles of informed consent, confidentiality, and respect for participant voice. Due to budgetary constraints, intercoding could not be fully implemented in this pilot study. To ensure interpretive rigor, coding outcomes were triangulated with storylistening data gathered during the pre-scan scoping session. This process confirmed semantic alignment between the extracted patterns and the lived experiences of the core team. The overall aim was to capture the diversity and depth of ethical stances emerging from the complex educational ecosystem under investigation.

5. SCAN FINDINGS: MINDSETS, BEHAVIORS, AND ETHICAL PATTERNS

Having outlined the methodological framework, this next section turns to the empirical findings derived from the pilot study. Drawing on both quantitative indicators and qualitative narratives, the analysis reveals seven distinct behavioral-ethical patterns that capture how students and teachers at TGM's IT Department engage with, reflect on, and ethically negotiate their use of AI in education. These patterns not only illustrate the current state of AI literacy and mindset within the institution but also shed light on the systemic gaps, cultural tensions, and pedagogical opportunities that emerge at the intersection of human learning and machine intelligence. It should be noted that the findings of this pilot study are shaped by contextual specificity and should be interpreted as exploratory. While narrative and emotional insights offer rich depth, they also reflect subjective self-reporting influenced by social desirability or institutional norms.

5.1. AI Optimism: "AI Is Good for Humankind"

The open-ended prompt *"AI improves humankind"* elicited overwhelmingly positive responses across the sample, with 87% of all participants affirming the statement. Among students, the approval rate was strikingly high and consistent across cohorts: 77% in Form 1, 83% in Form 5, and 87% in Form 3, suggesting a generational optimism that aligns with broader cultural narratives about technological progress. Notably, the highest levels of agreement emerged from Form 3 students, indicating a possible "mid-cycle" confidence point in their educational journey, where familiarity with AI may converge with peak usage before critical fatigue or disillusionment sets in.

Teacher responses, while still predominantly positive, were marked by more cautious endorsement, with agreement ranging from 67% to 71% across age brackets. The most optimistic group of educators were those aged 36–45 (71%), followed closely by the youngest cohort (69%). Teachers aged 46–65 exhibited slightly lower agreement (67%), suggesting a generational divide in how AI's role in societal advancement is perceived. This divergence may reflect different lived experiences with digitalization, degrees of trust in automation, or pedagogical values shaped before the ubiquity of AI tools.

These results illustrate a broad cultural acceptance of AI as a force for good, particularly among digital-native students who experience AI as a natural extension of their learning and social environments. Yet, they also reveal a subtle undercurrent of skepticism among educators. From an ethical and pedagogical standpoint, this discrepancy underscores the importance of meaningful dialogue across generations to understand and responsibly guide AI's impact on human development (Floridi, 2024). Overall, the results suggest that while belief in AI's potential to improve humanity is widespread, it is somewhat unevenly distributed and requires nuanced, participatory reflection in education to ensure alignment between hope, practice, and value formation.

5.2 Seven Ethical Behavior Patterns

In this section, we present the seven cross-cutting patterns derived from the thematic and narrative analysis of the Telluz scan results. Each pattern reflects a distinctive tension or transformation occurring at the intersection of AI use, educational culture, and ethical identity formation. Together, they offer a diagnostic lens through which educators, policymakers, and institutional leaders can understand the lived realities of AI-mediated learning and craft targeted, context-sensitive interventions for cultural change.

Pattern 1: Moral Dissonance - Knowing vs. Doing

Moral dissonance arises when individuals act contrary to their stated values, often due to systemic, cultural, or situational pressures. In the context of AI in education, this dissonance becomes especially revealing: students and teachers alike report high disapproval of certain AI uses—yet still engage in those very behaviors.

Evidence from the Survey

The data revealed a striking discrepancy between disapproval and practice. For instance, 78% of students disapproved of using AI to generate feedback on assignments, yet 83% admitted doing so. A similar tension exists around the use of AI in tests: 79% stated they disapproved while 21% openly acknowledged having done so. Teachers to some extent mirror this contradiction. While 95% of teachers disapproved of using AI in assessments, many reported using AI themselves for lesson planning without revealing it. It seems that the dissonance here is not rooted in ignorance, but in lack of systemic alignment and institutional support. Educators and learners are both navigating ethical grey zones without clear boundaries, norms, or mechanisms for ethical reflection.

Ethical Implications

Looking at the bigger picture, this dissonance presents a foundational ethical challenge. It weakens trust, erodes classroom integrity, and fosters a culture of silence. In moral philosophy, such a gap between belief and behavior has been framed as "akrasia"—the failure to act in accordance with one's own better judgment (Davidson, 1969). The ethical risk is not only the behavior itself, but the normalization of contradictory practices under institutional neglect. Remaining silent – or even rigid – bears the risk that current student behavior may become "normless experimentation", shaped by pragmatism rather than principle. Students, especially those under academic pressure, may turn to AI not because they believe it is ethical, but because it is available, efficient, and unregulated. In this sense, the system itself produces ethical dissonance by failing to acknowledge and structure these new realities.

Educational Leadership

For school leaders and policy makers, this pattern is a call to action. Ethical clarity cannot be legislated top-down but must be cultivated collaboratively. Students and teachers both need spaces to negotiate what constitutes "fair use" of AI in an academic context. Leaders must create a culture where ethical reflection is not an add-on, but a core design feature of learning. If no action is taken, this ethical dissonance may result in a deeper identity crisis where students begin to see themselves not as agents of knowledge but as "hackers" of the system and teachers feel torn between enforcement and experimentation. In such environments, even well-intentioned actors may default to silence or avoidance. Over time, this corrodes educational integrity and trust. Ultimately, addressing moral dissonance is not about controlling behavior—it is about aligning learning culture with emerging norms of AI use. Schools that avoid this dialogue risk cultivating a silent gap between values and actions. As the philosopher Charles Taylor (1989) observed, "We define our identity always in dialogue with, sometimes in struggle against, the things our significant others want to see in us." Today, AI is one of those "significant others." It is reshaping how students define competence, identity, and integrity.

Pattern 2: Hidden or Unacknowledged AI Use

Overview and Definition

One of the most striking findings from the Telluz Ethical AI Use Scan is the disconnect between actual AI use and its disclosure. This pattern — identified as Hidden or Unacknowledged AI Use — describes the widespread but covert use of AI technologies by students and, in some cases, teachers, without corresponding transparency. While AI is used for test preparation, feedback generation, homework assistance, or ideation, its role often remains concealed, either due to institutional ambiguity, fear of punishment, or lack of reflective norms.

From the dataset: 51% of students report observing AI use in tests despite explicit bans, and many openly admit using AI for homework while perceiving the practice as "not fully okay." At the same time, only 13% report having encountered openly AI-generated feedback, which points to a systemic underreporting or normalization of unacknowledged AI interaction.

Ethical Implications

The ethical implications may be profound. First, the need to hide the use of AI erodes trust in the learning community. When students feel compelled to hide their use of AI — even for tasks that could benefit from it — this fosters an environment of ambiguity, stress, and moral disengagement. As one student stated in the open-ended feedback: "It's not like I'm cheating. I just don't want my teacher to think I didn't try. So I ask ChatGPT for ideas and then change them." — Student, age 17 This reflects what Bandura (2011) describes as moral disengagement—a cognitive process by which individuals justify ethically ambiguous behavior due to unclear norms or systemic pressure.

Second, hidden AI use undermines educational integrity and distorts assessment outcomes. When students use generative tools like ChatGPT, CoPilot, or Grammarly without disclosure, teachers cannot accurately gauge what the student understands, where they need support, or what they have actually learned. Feedback loops collapse.

Third, it puts ethical pressure on teachers. While some – quietly – admit to using AI in preparation or content generation, they feel reluctant to model it transparently due to institutional uncertainty. This creates role conflict: teachers are asked to enforce AI rules while lacking the space or norms to experiment themselves.

Lack of shared language and responsibility

This pattern speaks to the moral architecture of AI in education. In the absence of trust-based, future-facing frameworks, AI becomes something to hide rather than harness. Moreover, students are already forming norms of behavior around AI. Hidden use teaches that success means knowing how to game the system or fly under the radar—not how to engage ethically, experiment responsibly, or articulate learning transparently. The educational risk here is not merely academic dishonesty but a loss of shared language and shared responsibility. When AI use is normalized in private but stigmatized in public, we erode the foundations of collective learning.

Pattern 2 is not just about student behavior – it reflects a system unprepared to align its ethical language with its technological reality. Left unaddressed, it risks entrenching mistrust and moral disengagement. But when met with participatory, dialogic responses, it becomes an entry point for ethical transformation. Through visibility, reflection, and co-ownership, students and teachers can move from concealment to collective responsibility—and from isolated use to informed co-creation.

Pattern 3: Teacher Role Tensions

From Knowledge Authority to Ethical Facilitator in the Age of AI

As artificial intelligence (AI) becomes more integrated into classrooms, the role of the teacher is undergoing significant transformation. Pattern 3 from the Telluz Ethical AI Use Scan reveals acute "Role Tensions Among Teachers", highlighting a paradox: teachers express high ethical concern about student use of AI, yet often engage with AI themselves — for preparation, assessment, or planning — without disclosure or systemic support.

From the dataset: 95% of teachers disapproved of student use of AI in tests, yet 58% admitted using AI in classroom preparation without disclosing it. This misalignment indicates institutional gaps in training, ethical frameworks, and cultural expectations, placing educators in ethically precarious positions.

Open responses indicated underlying tensions in authority, accountability, and the evolving norms around digital ethics: "*Teachers shouldn't use AI — YOU (yes, you) are being paid to teach*" or "*Teachers shouldn't use AI for their own tasks they are being paid for. But AI should be integrated into the classroom in a way that students learn how to use it ethically and correctly — and perhaps even to their advantage (ignorance is not an advantage).*" These statements signal a perceived asymmetry in expectations: students sense they are being held to strict standards about AI use, while teachers may be seen as bypassing their own responsibilities through automation. The emphasis on *"you are being paid"* reveals a contractual, possibly even adversarial, view of the teacher's role — as someone who must *do the work themselves*, not delegate it to machines.

Ethical Implications

This perception challenges the traditional authority of educators and highlights a growing need for transparency and ethical modeling (Bass et al, 2018). While we see recognition of AI's potential value in student learning, we also see discomfort with its use as a teacher shortcut. Students implicitly understand that a teacher who outsources core pedagogical responsibilities to AI undermines the authenticity of the learning experience. Overall, students want to be taught how to use AI properly, rather than being banned from it. The comment *"ignorance is not an advantage"* suggests that students value competence, not avoidance. Fundamentally, these statements reflect a critical shift in the pedagogical culture of schools. Instead of seeing AI as a threat to teaching, schools must reframe their role: from enforcing rigid control to enabling shared responsibility. This shift resonates with Freire's notion of "education as the practice of freedom" (Freire, 1970), where teachers and students engage in mutual inquiry.

Pattern 4: Epistemic Re-Definition

Education is facing a fundamental epistemological shift: the redefinition of what constitutes knowledge, how it is acquired, and how it is valued. This shift is particularly pronounced in technical and engineering education, where the automation of cognitive functions—from problem-solving to generating explanations—challenges long-standing paradigms of instruction, assessment, and professional practice.

Evidence from the Scan: Only 15% of students disapprove of using AI to support factual learning, yet 88% still choose to actively learn and memorize facts themselves. This apparent contradiction points to an emerging phenomenon: AI tools like ChatGPT are seen as powerful extensions of human memory and calculation, but not replacements for understanding. Students are beginning to differentiate between "knowing" as internalized, embodied understanding, and "knowing" as quickly accessible output from a machine. The redefinition of knowledge is thus not merely cognitive, but also existential.

Ethical Implications

If we reduce knowledge to content retrieval or efficiency, we risk producing engineers who are technically proficient but epistemologically shallow. This narrow perspective can lead to neglecting the nuanced ways in which knowledge facilitates innovation, learning, and collaborative problem-solving (Sutanto et al, 2018). Pedagogically, this pattern requires a shift from outcome-based instruction to process-based inquiry. If AI can deliver correct answers, what matters is how learners frame questions, interpret responses, and critique them. Culturally, it reframes knowledge from static content to dynamic process. This aligns with constructivist views of learning, where meaning is co-constructed rather than transmitted (Vygotsky, 1978). Last but not least, ethically, it pushes educational institutions to define what counts as "learning." If a student uses AI to solve a problem but does not reflect on it, is that still learning?

Pattern 5: Gaps in Diversity and Representation

Artificial Intelligence is increasingly present in educational systems, not only as a technical tool but also as a co-actor shaping how knowledge is accessed, evaluated, and contextualized (Chassignol et al, 2018). Yet, as the Telluz Scan revealed in the TGM case study, significant gaps remain in how AI systems represent cultural, gender, and religious diversity.

Evidence from the Scan: Only 8% of respondents reported seeing non-binary identities in AI-generated content, and more than half (55%) indicated that they did not believe it was appropriate to require such representation. Only 18% said the topic came up in school discussions; 31% were unsure whether it ever had. Qualitative responses reinforced this pattern: *"AI should remain objective and be based on scientifically grounded content — that is, on verifiable and transparent findings (...) The issue of gender-inclusive language also plays a role — primarily with regard to politeness and inclusion. (...) For most users, however, the result is more important than how the AI addresses them. Ultimately, people use AI primarily for its functionality — for its efficiency and the quality of its answers — not for linguistic nuances."* The speaker emphasizes a preference for *objectivity* and *functionality* over inclusive language or ideological framing, warning against the potential "manipulation" of scientific content by social or political agendas. From an ethical and educational standpoint, such statements reveal the tension between instrumentalist views of AI (as neutral, task-driven tools) and critical pedagogical perspectives.

Ethical Implications

Adolescence and early adulthood are key phases in identity development. If learners do not see themselves reflected in learning tools - or worse, if they are misrepresented - it may damage their sense of belonging, lower trust in educational systems, and limit engagement. Judith Butler's concept of "recognizability" (Ikäheimo, 2022) is relevant here. If AI tools fail to recognize non-normative identities, they delegitimize them, reinforcing societal hierarchies and contributing to epistemic injustice (Fricker, 2007). Justice in education, therefore, requires more than preventing harm—it demands the intentional recognition and inclusion of difference.

Pattern 6: Fragility of Integrity and Assessment Culture

As generative AI becomes increasingly normalized in educational settings, traditional frameworks for academic integrity and assessment face mounting pressures. The Telluz Scan data gathered at TGM Vienna revealed a growing normalization of AI use in tasks previously considered core to demonstrating individual learning — from problem-solving and creative writing to idea generation and grading, blurring the boundaries between support and substitution. We can say that the credibility of grades as indicators of effort, originality, and understanding is under strain.

Evidence from the Scan: Multiple survey items in the Telluz Scan pointed to widespread AI use in assessment-related tasks: 65% of respondents said they found it acceptable to let AI solve math problems. A majority admitted to using AI in preparing creative tasks or summaries. A mere 13% reported seeing AI being used explicitly by teachers to generate feedback or grades, suggesting that much AI use in accomplishing tasks and assessment is hidden or unacknowledged. As many as 51% of participants reported that AI was used in tests despite it being forbidden —

a clear integrity breach, but also a sign of shifting norms and unclear boundaries. Qualitative comments further underline this ambiguity.

Ethical Implications

This current erosion of assessment integrity must be understood within the broader philosophical debate on the nature of knowledge and authorship. Hannah Arendt, in her reflections on education, warned against the "*withdrawal from thinking*". For her, education is the means whereby we achieve personal autonomy through the exercise of independent judgement (Nixon, 2020). When AI tools provide ready-made outputs that bypass the cognitive struggle of learning, they risk undermining the very habits of mind — judgment, curiosity, responsibility — that education seeks to cultivate. Moreover, integrity practices such as proctoring, grading, and plagiarism detection, which are rooted in historical mechanisms of control, are disrupted by AI tools. Traditional notions of authorship and intention are complicated and educators and students are faced with grey zones of authorship. Traditional assessment models are ill-equipped to interpret these.

If students perceive that AI is routinely used without acknowledgment — or worse, that "*everyone is doing it*", as stated in the open reponses of the Telluz survey — trust in peer fairness and institutional standards begin to erode. This leads to what the philosopher Annette Baier (1986) termed "trust decay" in moral communities. Once integrity becomes a private negotiation rather than a shared norm, the collective meaning of assessment collapses. When traditional assessments that prioritize individual performance, factual recall, and static outputs risk of being substituted by AI tools, this raises a fundamental pedagogical question: what, exactly, are we assessing in the age of co-authorship, algorithmic support, and remix culture? Attempts to preserve academic integrity through surveillance technologies risk reinforcing "a culture of suspicion" rather than cultivating ethical reasoning (Trust & Watters, 2020). AI thus exposes a deeper crisis in educational assessment: a tension between control-based models of learning and trust-based, reflective pedagogies. When students use AI not to deceive but to cope, improve, or express themselves differently, their actions may fall outside existing evaluative frameworks. We may conclude that Pattern 6 signals not merely a technical disruption, but a deep challenge to the epistemological and ethical assumptions that underpin educational assessment.

Pattern 7: Reflective Potential - Cultivating Ethical Agency

Pattern 7 reveals a critical insight: students are not passive users of AI — they actively reflect on its influence on their learning, identity, and values. This finding offers a profound opportunity to shift AI use from unconscious automation toward ethical engagement and learner empowerment. Philosopher John Dewey famously said, *"We do not learn from experience... we learn from reflecting on experience."* (Dewey, 1933). The same principle applies to the integration of AI in education. As students begin to question how AI alters their thinking, creativity, and self-perception, educational systems are called to promote that reflection — turning internal dialogue into collective ethical literacy.

Evidence from the Scan: The survey uncovered widespread learner reflection across multiple contexts: 59% of students report reflecting on how AI changes their learning behavior or self-perception. 77% of teachers and 45% of students endorse the statement: "To understand AI, one must understand society, ethics, and one-self." In open-ended responses, students frequently note how AI is shaping their sense of authorship, agency, and fairness. Students' comments reveal emerging meta-cognition and ethical ambivalence: they sense that AI changes not just how they learn, but *who* they are becoming as learners. This dynamic sits at the heart of identity development in AI-mediated education.

At the core of this pattern lies a profound educational question: How do students develop agency in a system increasingly shaped by algorithmic scaffolding? As Ricoeur (1992) argues, individuals make sense of themselves through reflective interpretation — *emplotting* their experiences into meaningful narratives. If students are to retain authorship of their learning journey, they must be supported in making sense of their relationship with AI: not merely using it, but situating themselves in relation to it.

6. FROM PATTERNS TO PRACTICE: ETHICAL & PEDAGOGICAL IMPLICATIONS

The survey data shows that reflection is present but not systematized. Without structured opportunities, many students reflect in isolation, leading to confusion or guilt rather than ethical clarity. Reflection without dialogue can reinforce hidden practices rather than normalize ethical use. What is more, while students reflect on the use of AI, few have tools to assess its biases, limitations, or assumptions. Pattern 7 reveals a powerful opportunity: many students are aware, curious, and ready to engage. But they need pedagogical frameworks that transform their reflections into agency — helping them not only ask ethical questions, but act on them.

6.1. Pattern-Based Reframing

The preceding analysis of the seven cross-cutting patterns paints a picture of a learning ecosystem in transition. Teachers and students alike are navigating a rapidly shifting educational landscape, which is marked by growing dependence on generative AI, uneven ethical norms, emerging tensions around assessment and authorship, and deeply felt needs for inclusion, clarity, and reflection. While the patterns themselves reflect latent strengths, such as students' openness to AI, teachers' ethical concern, and an overall recognition of AI's potential, they also reveal critical pedagogical vulnerabilities. These include moral dissonance, hidden AI use, role confusion among teachers, and an urgent need to rethink how we define knowledge, assessment, and diversity in AI-mediated contexts. Leveraging each Pattern, the next section demonstrates how the 2CG® approach operationalizes ethical insights into concrete pedagogical strategies, fostering systemic culture shifts.

From Moral Dissonance to Co-Created Norms

The 1st pattern—*moral dissonance between AI use and ethical beliefs about the use of AI*—signals the need for schools to create spaces of ethical coherence. Students and teachers may privately question AI use in exams or feedback generation, yet lack forums for addressing these concerns. The pedagogical implication is clear: ethics cannot be taught solely through rules; it must be co-constructed through dialogue. Within the AI-enhanced 2CG® model, this is enacted through norm-shaping phases that invite learners to collaboratively author charters for AI use in class. These are not static codes of conduct but living documents, revised through peer feedback and ethical debate.

From Hidden Use to Rituals of Disclosure

Pattern 2—*hidden or unacknowledged use of AI*—identifies covert AI use in assignments and assessments, not due to misconduct, but to unclear norms and insufficient ethical scaffolding. In response, AI-enhanced 2CG® integrates disclosure rituals such as "AI was used to…" prompts and guided journaling on tool use, intent, and perceived impact. This makes ethical AI use visible without punitive framing, allowing it to be discussed, questioned, and improved.

From Role Tension to Teacher as Ethical Facilitator

Pattern 3 – *role tensions*- TGM teachers reported discomfort with the unclear expectations around AI. Some use AI in planning but hesitate to disclose that they have done so. Others enforce rules that lack communal legitimacy. This points to Pattern 3, a role identity crisis in the teacher's function. 2CG® supports teachers not as gatekeepers of AI but as co-learners and ethical facilitators, providing tools such as role reflection grids, scenario-based training, and teacher peer circles where AI dilemmas are explored collaboratively rather than hierarchically.

From Knowledge Redefinition to Epistemic Flexibility

Pattern 4 – *redefining knowledge and learning* - challenges the epistemological foundations of traditional pedagogy. Students are learning not just from teachers or textbooks but from dynamic, dialogic AI systems that challenge the notion of authoritative knowledge. The implication is that educators must reorient from knowledge transmission to knowledge curation and interpretation. AI-enhanced 2CG® meets this need by encouraging multimodal knowledge representation (e.g., mind maps, metaphor maps, speculative design), and by cultivating interpretive judgment as a key 21st-century skill. AI becomes a co-agent in these practices—not just providing content, but provoking epistemic inquiry.

From Representation Gaps to Participatory Pluralism

The 5th Pattern—*a lack of non-binary or religious representation in AI-generated materials*—has deep ethical implications. Pedagogically, this means teaching must design for inclusion, not just accommodate it. AI-enhanced 2CG® employs identity-expanding prompts, storylistening, and artistic modalities (e.g., poetry, visual storytelling) to enable underrepresented students to see themselves in the learning process as well as in the tools that mediate it. Teachers, in their role of facilitators, are supported in critically auditing AI outputs for cultural bias and initiating conversations about who AI speaks for—and who it silences.

From Assessment Fragility to Integrity via Process

Pattern 6—*Integrity and Assessment Culture Are Fragile*—reveals cracks in the logic of performance assessment. If AI can write a summary, solve a math problem, or generate a prototype, then what is left to assess? The implication is not to discard assessment but to rethink it around process, reflection, and self-authorship. AI-enhanced 2CG® embeds assessment into every phase of the learning journey—from ideation to dialogue to ethical critique. Rubrics are adapted to reward transparency, collaboration, and decision-making, not just outcomes.

From Reflective Potential to Cultivating Ethical Agency

Finally, Pattern 7—*Learners Actively Reflect on AI Use*— shows that both students and teachers are reflecting on AI use but lacking formal support to transform this reflection into ethical agency. The pedagogical opportunity is to harness reflection as a site of growth, not guilt. Within the 2CG® model, this includes metacognitive coaching, peer learning dialogues, and AI-supported provocations. In this way, reflection becomes not a side-effect but a central driver of personal and professional development.

Table 2. Summary of Pedagogical Shifts

Ethical Pattern	Pedagogical Shift
Moral dissonance	Co-create ethical norms
Hidden AI use	Ritualize ethical disclosure
Role tensions	Redefine teacher as ethical facilitator
Epistemic instability	Foster epistemic flexibility
Representation gaps	Promote pluralistic AI literacy
Assessment challenges	Emphasize process-based integrity
Underused reflection	Embed reflective ethical practice

7. CONCLUSION AND FUTURE DIRECTIONS: TOWARD A SCALABLE EDUCATIONAL RESPONSE

We close by articulating how vocational institutions can embed ethics into AI integration – not as external compliance or top-down regulations, but as an integral learning dimension. What makes AI-enhanced 2CG® a viable model for TGM and similar educational institutions is not only its theoretical robustness but its modular and adaptable implementation pathways. It can be embedded in workshops; in cross-curricular modules; in teacher development programs; and in tech-enabled or onsite norm-setting retreats and institutional charters. What is more, the approach works across stakeholder levels and hierarchies (student, teacher, leadership); invites co-design; and positions ethics not as an add-on but as an integrated aspect of learning in the age of AI.

This chapter has highlighted that integrating AI into engineering education is not merely a matter of technological adoption but a deep cultural and ethical transformation. The Telluz and 2CG® mixed-method approach, implemented in the TGM Vienna pilot case study, revealed complex patterns of perception, emotional response, and ethical awareness among students and educators—underscoring the importance of values-based AI literacy. The findings (P1-P7) suggest that learners are navigating AI in ways that reflect both aspirational potential and unresolved anxieties, particularly around fairness, identity, and the social impact of automation. Moving forward, educational systems must embed diagnostic and reflective frameworks to assess and cultivate ethical readiness across diverse learning contexts. Future research should explore longitudinal impacts of such interventions, comparative case studies across educational sectors, and the co-creation of policy grounded in lived classroom experiences.

ACKNOWLEDGEMENT

The authors acknowledge the support of Stefanie Hagmann-Schramm, Headmaster of TGM Vienna, whose openness to educational research and institutional collaboration enabled the implementation of this pilot study within the IT Department. We also thank Wolfgang Kern, Head of the Department for Vocational Education and Training at the Austrian Federal Ministry of Education, for facilitating the integration of this research initiative into the broader discourse on ethics and AI in technical and vocational education. Finally, thank you to Fred van der Zwaard for providing the Telluz diagnostic tool under pilot conditions.

REFERENCES

Baier, A. (1986), Trust and Antitrust. In Ethics, Vol. 96, No. 2 (Jan., 1986), pp. 231-260 (30 pages), Published By: The University of Chicago Press

Bandura, A. (2011): Moral Disengagement: , last accessed: 30 June 2025DOI: 10.1002/9780470672532.wbepp165

Bass, L., Frick, W. C., & Young, M. D. (2018). *Developing Ethical Principles for School Leadership* (1st ed.). ImprintRoutledge., DOI: 10.4324/9781315688237

Chassignol, M., Khoroshavin, A., Klimova, A., & Bilyatdinova, A. (2018): Artificial Intelligence trends in education: a narrative overview, Procedia Computer Science, Volume 136, 2018, Pages 16-24, ISSN 1877-0509, DOI: 10.1016/j.procs.2018.08.233

Davidson, D. (1969). How is weakness of the will possible?.

Dolezal, D. (2020, October). The learning office approach to modern 21st century education: third evaluation of a self-driven concept for student-centered engineering education. In 2020 IEEE Frontiers in Education Conference (FIE) (pp. 1-9). IEEE. DOI: 10.1109/FIE44824.2020.9274211

Dolezal, D., Motschnig, R., & Ambros, R. (2025). Pre-Service Teachers' Digital Competence: A Call for Action. *Education Sciences*. Advance online publication. DOI: 10.3390/educsci15020160

Dolezal, D., Posekany, A., Ambros, R., Koppensteiner, G., & Motschnig, R. (2022, October). Technology-enhanced and student-centered learning as a method to foster students' ICT competence and problem coping skills. In 2022 IEEE Frontiers in Education Conference (FIE) (pp. 1-8). IEEE.

Dolezal, D., Posekany, A., Koppensteiner, G., Vittori, L., & Motschnig, R. (2021). Learner-Centered Engineering Education as an Incubator of 21st Century Skills. *International Journal of Engineering Education*, *37*, 1605–1618.

Dolezal, D., Posekany, A., Vittori, L., Koppensteiner, G., & Motschnig, R. (2018, October). Student-centered classrooms in engineering education: concept and evaluation of a learning office for software development and applied mathematics. In 2018 IEEE Frontiers in Education Conference (FIE) (pp. 1-9). IEEE.

Dolezal, D., Posekany, A., Vittori, L., Koppensteiner, G., & Motschnig, R. (2019, October). Fostering 21st century skills in student-centered engineering education at the secondary school level: second evaluation of the learning office. In 2019 IEEE Frontiers in Education Conference (FIE) (pp. 1-9). IEEE.

EISNER. E. W. (2002). Front Matter. In *The Arts and the Creation of Mind* (pp. i–vi). Yale University Press. https://www.jstor.org/stable/j.ctt1np7vz.1

European Commission. (2025). OECD: Empowering Learners for the Age of AI - Review Draft (May 2025). An AI Literacy Framework for Primary and Secondary Education

European Commission & OECD. 2025 https://education.ec.europa.eu/focus-topics/digital-education/action-plan, last accessed 28 June 2025

Floridi, L. (2019). Translating Principles into Practices of Digital Ethics: Five Risks of Being Unethical. *Philosophy & Technology*, *32*, 185–193. DOI: 10.1007/s13347-019-00354-x

Freire, P. (1970a). *Pedagogy of the oppressed*. The Continuum Pushing Company.

Fricker, M. (2007). *Epistemic injustice: Power and the ethics of knowing*. Oxford university press.

Greene, M. (1995). *Releasing the imagination: Essays on education, the arts, and social change*. Jossey-Bass.

Gruenhagen, J. H., Sinclair, P., Carroll, J., Baker, P., Wilson, A., & Demant, D. (2023).The rapid rise of generative AI and its implications for academic integrity: Students' perceptions and use of chatbots for assistance with assessments, Computers and Education: Artificial Intelligence, Volume 7, 2024, 100273, ISSN 2666-920X, DOI: 10.1016/j.caeai.2024.100273

Guralnick, D. (2024): Reimagining Learning Experiences with the Use of AI, in *Artificial Intelligence in Education: The Intersection of Technology and Pedagogy*, edited by Peter Ilic, Imogen Casebourne, and Rupert Wegerif; November 2024, Springer Nature, Switzerland. DOI: 10.1016/j.ijinfomgt.2018.01.009

Ikäheimo, H. (2022). Recognizability and recognition as human—Learning from Butler and Manne. *Journal for the Theory of Social Behaviour*, *52*(4), 579–594. DOI: 10.1111/jtsb.12352

Kosmyna, N., Hauptmann, E., Yuan, Y. T., Situ, J., Liao, X. H., Beresnitzky, A. V., . . . Maes, P. (2025). Your brain on chatgpt: Accumulation of cognitive debt when using an ai assistant for essay writing task. arXiv preprint arXiv:2506.08872.

Kumar, R., Eaton, S. E., Mindzak, M., & Morrison, R. (2023). *Handbook of academic integrity*. Springer.

Merl, C. (2020). Fostering 21st Century Skills in Engineering and Business Management Students. In Auer, M., & Tsiatsos, T. (Eds.), *The Challenges of the Digital Transformation in Education. ICL 2018. Advances in Intelligent Systems and Computing* (Vol. 916). Springer., DOI: 10.1007/978-3-030-11932-4_15

Merl, C. (2022). Lab 21 – A Space for Learning, Sharing and Innovating. In Guralnick, D., Auer, M. E., & Poce, A. (Eds.), *Innovations in Learning and Technology for the Workplace and Higher Education. TLIC 2021. Lecture Notes in Networks and Systems* (Vol. 349). Springer., DOI: 10.1007/978-3-030-90677-1_20

Merl, C. (2022). Human intelligence cultivation with the 2CG® poetry machine: How to boost future skills development and idea generation with artistic impulses in Lab 21. [iJAC]. *Int. J. Adv. Corp. Learn.*, *15*, 61–74. DOI: 10.3991/ijac.v15i1.27079

Meyer, E., Wessels, D.: Natural Language Processing im akademischen Schreibprozess -- mehr Motivation durch Inspiration?. Künstliche Intelligenz in der Hochschulbildung. Chancen und Grenzen des KI-gestützten Lernens und Lehrens. 2023

Miles, M. B., Huberman, A. M., & Saldana, J. (2014). *Qualitative Data Analysis: A Methods Sourcebook*. Sage.

Nixon, J. (2020). Hannah Arendt: The Promise of Education. Hannah Arendt: The Promise of Education. DOI: 10.1007/978-3-030-37573-7

Ricoeur, P. (1992). *Oneself as Another*. University of Chicago Press.

Rogers, C. R. (1959): A Theory of Therapy, Personality and Interpersonal Relationships as Developed in the Client-centered Framework. In: Koch, S. (ed.) Psychology: A Study of a Science, vol. 3, pp. 184–256. McGraw-Hill, New York, NY Rotherham, A.J., Willingham, D.: 21st-century skills: The challenges ahead. Educational Leadership 67, 16–21 (2009)

Rogers, C. R. (1983). *Freedom to Learn for the 80s* (2nd ed.). Merrill Publishing.

Ryan, R. M., & Deci, E. L. (2000). Self-determination theory and the facilitation of intrinsic motivation, social development, and well-being. *The American Psychologist, 55*(1), 68–78. DOI: 10.1037/0003-066X.55.1.68 PMID: 11392867

Ryan, R. M., & Deci, E. L. (2000). Self-determination theory and the facilitation of intrinsic motivation, social development, and well-being. *The American Psychologist.* Advance online publication. DOI: 10.1037/0003-066X.55.1.68 PMID: 11392867

Schön, D. A. (1991). *The reflective practitioner.* Ashgate Publishing.

Selwyn, N. (2019). *Should robots replace teachers? AI and the Future of Education* (1st ed.). Polity Press.

Senge, P. M. (1990). *The fifth discipline: The art & practice of the learning organization.* Doubleday/Currency.

Sutanto, J., Liu, Y., Grigore, M., Lemmik, R. (2018): Does knowledge retrieval improve work efficiency? An investigation under multiple systems use; published in International Journal of Information Management, Volume 40, June 2018, Pages 42-53

Taylor, C. (1989). *Source of the Self: The Making of the Modern Identity.* Harvard University Press.

Trilling, B., & Fadel, C. (2012). *21st Century Skills. Learning for Life in our Times.* Jossey-Bass.

Trust, T., & Watters, A. (2020). The trouble with edtech: Persistent equity, surveillance, and control issues in educational technology. *Learning, Media and Technology, 45*(2), 105–110. DOI: 10.1080/17439884.2020.1761641

Valtonen, T., Hoang, N., Sointu, E., Näykki, P., Virtanen, A., Pöysä-Tarhonen, J., Häkkinen, P., Järvelä, S., Mäkitalo, K., & Kukkonen, J. (2021). How pre-service teachers perceive their 21st-century skills and dispositions: A longitudinal perspective. *Computers in Human Behavior.* Advance online publication. DOI: 10.1016/j.chb.2020.106643 van Laar, E., van Deursen, A. J., van Dijk, J. A., & de Haan, J. (2019). Determinants of 21st-century digital skills: A large-scale survey among working professionals. *Computers in Human Behavior*. Advance online publication. DOI: 10.1016/j.chb.2019.06.017

Voogt, J., Erstad, O., Dede, C., & Mishra, P. (2013). Challenges to learning and schooling in the digital networked world of the 21st century. *Journal of Computer Assisted Learning*. Advance online publication. DOI: 10.1111/jcal.12029

Vygotsky, L. S. (1978). *Mind in Society: The Development of Higher Psychological Processes*. Harvard University Press.

Wenger, E. (1998). *Communities of Practice: Learning, Meaning, and Identity*. Cambridge University Press.

Chapter 5
Ensuring Fair Representation of Neurodiverse Stakeholders Within the AI-Learning Ecosystem

Gerlinde Weger
https://orcid.org/0000-0002-5126-2938
In-Sight Consulting, Canada

ABSTRACT

As education is influenced by AI, learners are required to conform to their directive. For the majority of learners with normal automated nervous systems, this is a great advantage because these systems are trained predominately for them. But the learners who are outliners and are neurodiverse? Neurodiversity comprises up to 30% of the population. Individuals with ADHD, Autism, Dyslexia, hyper-mobility and PTSS are often challenged with prescriptive systems. The IEEE has two tools to ensure neural diverse learners are considered: CertifAIEd Algorithmic Bias Criteria and the standard Algorithmic Bias Consideration considers system bias to maximize productive bias, intentionally. By acknowledging AI systems require specific biases, they can be calibrated to consider neural diverse stakeholders thus AI Learning systems can maximize their benefits to both normal neural and diverse neural stakeholders. This chapter will review the CertifAIEd Algorithmic Bias Criteria and the standard Algorithmic Bias Consideration to demonstrate how neurodiverse learners can be considered.

DOI: 10.4018/979-8-3373-2235-3.ch005

INTRODUCTION

The COVID-19 pandemic significantly changed and reshaped how we engage and interact with each other. Most significantly, education and how we learn went remote and online classes became a necessity. As virtual education became the norm, it provided an opportunity for commercial AI Education (AIE) providers to step in and fill the void for online education.

AIE has grown exponentially with AI products encompassing the full learning ecosystem. AIE providers are claiming their AIE products offer improved learning experiences and that they cater to diverse learners (Rai, 2025). Yet research indicates that for neurodiverse learners, online education increases the amount of mental effort required to process information during learning tasks due to poorly designed digital environments, inaccessible content, and lack of structured support (Le Cunff, Giampietro & Dommett, 2024).

The concept of neurodiversity acknowledges that individuals have diverse neurological conditions as a result of normal variations in cognitive functioning (Murphy, 2022). Neurodiverse individuals, those not neurotypical, comprise up to 30% of the population. (Milliken) This concept of moving neurodiversity from a disability to a neurological variation has opened the possibility of creating education systems that acknowledge differing learning modes (Chapman, 2020).

It is critical that the needs of neurodiverse learners are included in the design and delivery of AIE products. Education is a basic human right as is non-discriminatory access to education. (United Nations). International organizations and national governmental committees concur on this. For example. European Union, in their creation of the EU AI Act, classified AI education as high risk (European Parliament, 2023).

AIE providers of online learning platforms collect vast amounts of data yet according to Le Cunff et al., there is a lack of data and research on how AIE products impact the unique needs of neurodivergent learners (Le Cunff et al., 2025). Without accessible data and research in how online education impacts neurodivergent learners, design, delivery and support of online learning for neurodiversity cannot be empirically grounded nor can AIE products be critically assessed. To close this gap and in support of international principles and regulation, a practical framework that AIE organizations can use to assess and prove fairness for neurodiverse learners is necessary.

IEEE CertifAIEd is a programme that certifies AI systems for their trustworthiness in upholding ethical principles. When an organization proves it has met specific ethical requirements for their AI system, IEEE grants the AI system a mark of AI Ethics. The requirements are based on a set of criteria that addresses the socio-technical ethical aspects of autonomous intelligent systems. (CertifAIEd)

The *IEEE 7003-2024 Consideration of Algorithmic Bias* standard acknowledges that bias in AI is a requirement for system outputs that recommend and predict. For example, a search engine positively biases its results by recommending links according to the request. It would have a negative bias if recommendations were based on criteria that had little to do with the request. The standard's goal is to optimize wanted and productive bias across the spectrum of stakeholders that are impacted by the AI system in use within a specific environment (IEEE, 2025).

IEEE CertifAIEd together with *IEEE-7003-2024 Consideration of Algorithmic Bias* standard can be applied to AIE products to establish appropriate indicators and data set requirements to validate and verify if the AIE products are inclusive for the range of learners on the neurodiverse spectrum.

This chapter will present the issues and challenges of fair representation for neurodiverse learners interacting with AIE products and then demonstrate how *IEEE CertifAIEd* together with *IEEE-7003-2024 Consideration of Algorithmic Bias* standard can be practically applied to assess AIE products for fair representation of neurodiverse learners by establishing appropriate indicators and data set requirements.

The use case that demonstrates the application of the *CertifAIEd* and *7003-2024* methods is a theoretical example that a university uses. Applying these frameworks to AIE products that come under regulation is recommended as the next phase.

AI IN EDUCATION

The COVID-19 pandemic caused an extremely rapid shift in education and how we learn. Remote access and online classes became a necessity.

It was not a strategic shift in education to provide improved and more equitable learning. Instead, it was a shift of protecting individuals and society from contacting the virus. The move from in-person to virtual was abrupt and instantaneous. Remote education and learning came with significant challenges. In a study by the US government National Center for Education Statistics, 84% of postsecondary students had some or all of their classes move online(Cameron, Lacy, Siegel, Wu, Wilson, Johnson, Burns & Wine, 2021). However, according to Walden University research from 2022, 32% of higher education faculty had no prior experience teaching online (Hebert, Wood, Jeon & Reena. 2022). Without prior experience, educators had no time for trial and testing for usability by the learners.

As virtual education became the norm, it provided an opportunity for AIE providers to step in and fill the void for online education. Harnessing the power of AI, AIE providers, specializing in digital learning environments, created support applications for educators to improve the quality of the curriculum and online courses that they hastily created during the pandemic. Digital environments could now move from a life-death necessity to an opportunity for more flexible and automated learning experiences. In a survey by the Cengage Group from 2025 of 3,000 higher education students and instructors and over 1,000 K12 teachers and administrators, 45% use generative AI to create course content and student-facing materials, 42% use AIE to support their lectures and curriculum planning (Cengage Group, 2025).

The AIE industry has exploded. The research firm Strait Research estimates that in 2024 the global AIE market size was valued at USD 4.43 billion and is expected to grow from USD 6.05 billion in 2025 to reach USD 72.45 billion by 2033, growing at a compounded annual growth rate(CAGR) of 36.4% during the forecast period 2025-2033 (Rai, 2025). This explosion of growth is characterized by the solutions segment leading with over 70% growth. This is due to the overwhelming adoption of AI-powered Learning Management Systems and their personalized learning paths, automated grading processes and real-time analytics. (Grand View Research).

According Grandview Research, 46% of AIE product development focus is using machine learning capabilities for content recommendation systems, virtual chatbot assistants, automated assessments and performance forecasting. Educators are integrating these virtual tutors and virtual teaching assistants into their classrooms, replacing real-time interaction with human teachers, teaching assistants and tutors with virtual assistants whose assistance is created by generative AI. (Grand View Research)

Governments are supporting the trend to AI in education. For example, in 2024, *Innovate UK* provided £1 million of funding to 16 AIE providers to build AI tools for education that will help with teacher workload. Under the *Contracts for Innovation* program, the UK government is investing an additional £1m of funding to accelerate the development of AI tools for teachers. And the Oak National Academy was granted £2 million for AI tools. A total of £7 million for AIE (Gov.UK, Department for Education, 2025). Yet is government investment into AIE supporting fair representation for all learners?

AIE providers are claiming their AIE products cater to diverse learners. Yet as noted by Le Cunff there is limited research on the impact of online education on neurodiverse learners and the research there shows AIE products increased the required mental efforts for neurodiverse learners (Le Cunff et al., 2024).

This exponential growth is unchecked for equity and fairness for all learners. A practical framework to assess AIE products is necessary to close the gap between claims of inclusion and reality, addressing the issues and challenges of neurodiverse learners.

NEURODIVERSITY

Traditionally, neurodiversity was seen as a disability and a deficit (Robb, Politis, & Boot, 2023). However, in 1999, Judy Singer, a sociologist published her doctoral thesis that proposed that "mental disability" may be a socially constructed oppression, a feature of being different, as opposed to ill or injured. She claimed that human minds are naturally diverse, with between-person variations being part of the rich tapestry of humanity (Corker, French, & Singer, 1999). The concept of neurodiversity that Singer proposed acknowledges that individuals generally experience and interact differently and there is no one correct way of perceiving, learning, thinking and acting. There is not one correct intelligence; individuals do not all think the same; we humans think differently, not based on cultural and experiential differences but because our neurological wiring is different (Murphy, 2022). Instead of being a mental disability, neurodiversity promotes individuals as having diverse neurological conditions as a result of normal variations in cognitive functioning. The majority of the human population are classified as neurotypical (Murphy, 2022). Yet neurodiverse individuals, those not neurotypical comprise between 15% to 20% of the human population. They are individuals with dyslexia, autism, ADHA, dyscalculia, dyspraxia, Tourette syndrome. When acquired syndromes and mental health issues are included that share similar neurological conditions, for example including long-covid, hyper mobility, post traumatic stress syndrome and schizophrenia, the percentage of the population that are neurodiverse rises to 30%. Almost 1 in 3 individuals are non-neurotypical. (Milliken) Additionally, neurodiversity is complex, with neurodiverse individuals often having more than one type of diagnosis. According to research by the Birkbeck University of London's *'Neurodiversity at Work 2023'* report of 1,117 individuals surveyed, only 370 reported one diagnosis, 328 reported two and 190 reported three (the remainder of respondents preferred not to say) (Milliken).

Milliken, a products company based in the UK produced a white paper in conjunction with the consulting group Henigan and the research agency Sapio Research that focused on neurodiversity in business. Their findings offer a comprehensive overview of the specific characteristics of non-neurotypical individuals that extend into the realm of education. They delved into neurodiversity because the company observed an increase of neurodiverse individuals in the workforce. They noted that in the US, 1 in 150 children were diagnosed with autism in 2000, but by 2020, this had increased to 1 in 36 (Milliken).

The Milliken paper considered the strengths and challenges of those with dyslexia, autism and ADHD, which comprises approximately 70% of neurodivergent diagnosis. When compared to neurotypical individuals, neurodivergent individuals' strengths include: hyperfocus, heightened creativity, greater innovative thinking, better detail processing and greater authenticity. Challenges though include they can be are more easily distracted and may need to be regularly or consistently mobile, can have sensory sensitivity, may have challenges understanding written information under time pressures and challenges to task schedules (Milliken).

Neurodiversity and AI Education

The progression of moving neurodiverse from a disability and a pathology to be cured has opened the possibility of creating education systems that acknowledge differing learning modes. And neurodevelopmental conditions are the largest category of qualifying disabilities in education (Hubble & Bolton, 2021).

As Lk Fung points out:

Education has a vital role in contributing to social constructs that encourage and enable individuals to develop their full potential. The neurodiversity movement provides a framework for how society, particularly educators, can view differences between individuals, transforming classrooms into equitable spaces for all students by rejecting cultural norms that are limiting. A respect for diversity is an essential part of education and requires the collaboration of teachers, parents, students, and the community to produce a working system seeking to optimize human potential for everyone. (Fung, 2021)

Chapman and Le Cunff et al. go further to stress that when a social model of disability is taken, neurodivergent challenges can arise from environmental and institutional barriers instead of inherent deficits of the learner. It is the existing educational systems that fail neurodivergent learners through the format taken, the environment for the learner, the delivery of educational materials and their instruction and support (Chapman, 2020; Le Cunff et al., 2025). Diamond has noted that:

Variations in working memory, cognitive flexibility, and inhibitory control can affect how students engage with multiple learning platforms, organize materials, and maintain attention during lectures. (Diamond, 2013)

Considering working memory and cognitive flexibility it is helpful to consider the cognitive load of learners. Cognitive load is the amount of mental effort required to process and retain new information. There are two types of cognitive load: intrinsic cognitive load is the actual difficulty of the material being taught. Extraneous cognitive load is how educational materials are delivered and how learners are supported. It *is the unnecessary mental effort imposed by poor instructional design or distracting elements in the learning environment* (Mayer & Moreno, 2003). For neurodivergent learners extraneous cognitive load is particularly important because they often have differences in working memory to neurotypical learners (Habib, Harris, Pollick, & Melville, 2019; Jeffries & Everatt, 2004; Kofler, Singh, Soto, Chan, Miller, Harmon, & Spiegel, 2020).

As noted, for neurotypical learners there is extensive research on the impact of online education and learning. Yet for neurodivergent learners this research is limited (Le Cunff et al., 2025).

Without research in how online education impacts cognitive load of neurodivergent learners, design, delivery and support of online learning for neurodiversity cannot be empirically grounded. According to Le Cunff et al,

This gap in research has significant implications for the design and delivery of inclusive online education, as it may lead not only to the development of online learning materials and strategies that do not adequately address the unique needs of neurodivergent students but might also hinder the identification of accessibility issues in software that is already widely used. (Le Cunff et al., 2025)

The claims made by AIE providers that their AIE products cater to the diverse needs of learners need to be validated. The AIE product requirements and specifications should include engineering features addressing extraneous cognitive load and testing of AIE products needs to verify that learners on the neurodiverse spectrum are included.

FAIRNESS FOR STUDENTS IN EDUCATION

Education is a basic human right. The right of every child to an education is proclaimed in the Universal Declaration of Human Rights (United Nations, 1994). If education is a basic human right, then fair, non-discriminatory access is necessarily a key criterion. And if fairness for all is a key criterion, then acknowledging the unique needs of all students is fundamental. International organizations and national governmental committees concur on this.

UNESCO Framework for Meeting Basic Learning Needs

In 1990 UNESCO held the *World Conference on Education for All* and published its *Framework for Action to Meet Basic Learning Needs*. The *Framework* noted that the conference was in response to the recognition that education is essential for human development and progress. At the same time there was widespread concern over inadequacies in education systems worldwide (UNESCO, 1990).

The *Framework* recognized fair and equitable basic education for every person.

Educational opportunities are to be designed to meet their basic learning needs... consistent measure must be taken to reduce disparities. learning needs of the disabled demand special attention. (UNESCO, 1990)

They recognized the scale and complexity of the challenge of an education for all and they recognized that technological literacy and capacity were essential. AIE products are providing the technology and capacity, yet fair and equitable education is lagging for those on the neurodiverse spectrum.

Salamanca Declaration

Shortly after the UNESCO Framework was declared, in 1994, the UN held a world conference on special needs education in Salamanca Spain and produced the *Salamanca Declaration* advocating for the fundamental right to access quality education regardless of diverse needs and abilities.

The Salamanca statement of principles and its policy renewed the pledge made by the world community that the right for all is enshrined in the 1948 Universal Declaration of Human Rights (United Nations, 1994).

Salamanca Statement the principles and policy includes these specific attributes of inclusivity:

- *education systems should be designed and educational programmes implemented to take into account the wide diversity of these characteristics and needs,*
- *those with special educational needs must have access to regular schools which should accommodate them within a child-centred pedagogy capable of meeting these needs*
- *give the highest policy and budgetary priority to improve . . . education systems to . . . include all children regardless of individual differences or difficulties,*
- *establish decentralized and participatory mechanisms for planning, monitoring and evaluating educational provision for children and adults with special education needs,* (United Nations, 1994)

Evaluating education for learners of special needs is essential in ensuring inclusivity. Already in 1994, there was an understanding and acknowledgement of the importance of data. Without facts as to what programmes are being designed and deployed and tested; without the exchange of research and pilot programme results, progress cannot be assessed. Salamanca principles called for collecting indicators which would/should include the unique attributes of neurodiverse learners, establishing a worldwide database on the effectiveness of neurodiverse-inclusive education programmes and sharing and exchanging of programmes and policies that are effective or that pose a risk (United Nations, 1994).

However, 30 years later, the data sets that include the attributes and features of neurodivergent learners is sparse and robust data on outcomes for neurodivergent students in higher education are not currently available (Hamilton & Petty, 2023).

EU AI Act and Education

In 2024 the EU AI Act formally went into effect with compliance and enforcement becoming effective by mid 2026. It is the first legal framework for regulating AI systems across the 27 EU member states, impacting a citizenship of approximately 450 million (2024 Eurostat data). Non-compliance with the EU AI Act will be met with a maximum financial penalty to the company in violation of up to EUR 35 million or 7 percent of worldwide annual turnover, whichever is higher (Hickman, Lorenz, Teetzmann, & Jha, 2024). The Act is a risk-based legislation that categorizes AI systems and products according to their risk to individuals and society.

Recognizing the importance of AI Education and its impact on individuals and society, the EU AI Act classifies education as high risk (European Parliament, 2023). The Act singles out AI Education products, specifically AI solutions used in education institutions, that may determine the access to education and development of someone's professional life. Discriminatory outcomes are unlawful. A provision, within the Act to mitigate this is:

- high-quality of the datasets feeding the system to minimise risks of discriminatory outcomes (European Commission)

Therefore, the EU AI Act is an extremely important legislation for a significant proportion of learners and has rippling effects across the globe as regional and national bodies enact similar legislation requiring datasets that ensure neurodivergent learners are considered.

Recognizing that effective compliance to the Act requires knowledge and competency of what they are developing and using, inscribed within the Act is that:

Providers and deployers of AI systems shall take measures to ensure, to their best extent, a sufficient level of AI literacy of their staff and other persons dealing with the operation and use of AI systems on their behalf, taking into account their technical knowledge, experience, education and training and the context the AI systems are to be used in, and considering the persons or groups of persons on whom the AI systems are to be used. (European Parliament, 2023)

In the EU, AIE products will require trusted assessments by accredited institutions to prove measures have been taken that they are fair for all learners on the neurodivergent spectrum.

National AIE Regulation

Internationally, Australia as of 2025 proposes mandatory guardrails for AIE, China has mandatory rules and Korea has guidance measures. Additional jurisdictions are in the process of creating and enacting protections for fair non-discriminatory AIE.

The *World Declaration on Education for All* along with the *Salamanca Statement* promoted the need for a learner-centred pedagogy. It called for flexible and adaptive systems that acknowledges the needs of all learners including those with particular needs (United Nations, 1994). An important aspect that was acknowledged for fair, non-discriminatory education for all learners, including those with special needs, is strengthening research and networking to establish centers of information and documentation (United Nations, 1994). Information and research centres are to integrate the particular attributes of special needs education into their research and their development of curriculum and programmes to promote innovative teaching and learning strategies (United Nations, 1994).

The drive by the international and national organizations was and is to promote fairness through inclusion of learners with special needs into education. The call was and is for a child-centred pedagogy where the needs of the learner are identified and acknowledged and requires the education community work together in cooperative programmes to strengthen collaboration in mobilizing support for the teaching profession (United Nations, 1994).

Given international, regional and national mandates for fair education for all and the extremely rapid proliferation of commercial AIE products within education, a practical and applicable framework to assess how cognitive load is impacted for all on the neurodiverse spectrum is required.

ETHICAL AIE FOR ALL ON THE NEURODIVERSE SPECTRUM

IEEE CertifAIEd Ethical Criteria Set and IEEE 7003-2024 Standard for the Consideration of Algorithmic Bias

Education is a right for all individuals. This was established by the UN in its universal declaration of human rights. Neurodivergence is a significant proportion of the human population, with estimates of up to 30% of individuals being non-neurotypical. How neurodivergent individuals learn is not the same as neurotypical individuals. Overlaying these facts, the AIE industry has become an integral component to education in general. This is substantiated by the revenue size of the industry, its exponential growth and the support it is receiving from national governments.

And regulation has and is coming into effect globally to govern AIE with specific criteria for non-discrimination and inclusion.

What are the comparable indicators for inclusion? What are the relevant data sets and models that will lead to online and automated education that is inclusive for those with neurodivergent features?

The Institute of Electrical and Electronics Engineers (IEEE) is the technical professional society dedicated to fostering technological innovation and excellence for the benefit of humanity. IEEE Standards' division focuses on creating consensus-based technical standards and solutions for ethical AI systems, data governance, fairness in data trade, digital intelligence and societal issues that transpire with technology. (IEEE)

IEEE members, volunteers and consultants have developed a solution that sets out a framework and a methodology that can evaluate AIE products for fairness and inclusivity: *IEEE CertifAIEd* and the *IEEE-7003-2024 Consideration of Algorithmic Bias.*

IEEE CertifAIEd is a programme that certifies AI systems for their trustworthiness in upholding ethical principles. When an organization proves it has met specific ethical requirements for their AI system, IEEE grants its AI system a mark of AI Ethics. The requirements are based on a set of criteria that addresses the socio-technical ethical aspects of the development deployment and use of autonomous intelligent systems. (IEEE CertifAIEd)

IEEE-7003-2024 Consideration of Algorithmic Bias acknowledges that bias in AI is a requirement for system outputs that recommend and predict. Its goal is to optimize the wanted and productive bias that recommend and predict fairly across the spectrum of stakeholders that are impacted by the AI system in use within a specific environment. The method of optimizing productive bias is through profiling the algorithmic bias of a system evaluated against how stakeholders are represented by the data that the AI system uses throughout its life-cycle (IEEE Standards Association, 2025).

IEEE CertifAIEd together with *IEEE-7003-2024 Consideration of Algorithmic Bias* standard can be applied to AIE to establish appropriate indicators and data set requirements to validate and verify that AIE products are inclusive for the range of learners on the neurodiverse spectrum.

IEEE-CertifAIEd

The *CertifAIEd* criteria are based on four human rights principles: respect for autonomy, harm prevention, fairness, and explicability. The framework includes positive factors (drivers) that promote human values and negative factors (inhibitors) that cause harm. These are organized into four criteria suites, each with a specific focus:

- Ethical Accountability: Organizations' answerability and liability for the ethical impact of their AI systems.
- Ethical Transparency: Disclosing essential information to enable self-determination and autonomy.
- Ethical Privacy: Allowing individuals to control their personal data.
- Ethical Algorithmic Bias: Establishing boundaries to promote productive bias and prevent harmful bias.

These criteria are supported by ethical foundations such as human oversight, technical robustness, data governance, transparency, diversity, well-being, and accountability.

The *CertifAIEd* framework is reward and risk-based, evaluating how AI impacts stakeholder well-being. Higher risks require more stringent prevention, mitigation, and monitoring measures. The assessment provides a framework to understand, quantify, and address potential benefits and probable risks throughout the AI system's lifecycle. To be deemed ethically trustworthy, organizations must provide documentation demonstrating compliance with these ethical foundational requirements.

CertifAIEd Method

G Weger, co-creator and educator of the *CertifAIEd* method explains the method as being divided into 3 phases:

Enquiry Phase

I) Define the AI System's Concept of Operations, illustrating how it interacts with all impacted stakeholders within its specific context. The Concept of Operations for AIE would be a diagram that shows interactions with the AIE product for every stakeholder.

II) Identify stakeholders by grouping users and impacted individuals based on their interaction with the AI. Separating neurodivergent learners from the neurotypical group is especially relevant. Features that vary between neurodiverse and neurotypical stakeholders would be separately classified. Protected characteristics would be recognized as relevant.

Profiling Phase

I) Values Elicitation assesses how the AI influences stakeholder well-being, considering that values vary by stakeholder and context. It identifies how interactions impact well-being, using the Concept of Operations as a reference. Neurodivergent groups will have different impacts on their well-being than of neurotypical groups.

II) Impact Assessment qualitatively evaluates the severity and likelihood of well-being changes, categorizing impacts as low, medium or high for each distinct neurodiverse and neurotypical group.

III) Value Classification links impacts to appropriate criteria sets as defined by the ethical values they protect.

IV) *CertifAIEd* criteria are selected based on the most impacted values. The magnitude of the value impact will also determine the extent of the requirements that the AI system must comply with. AIE product requirements would address the needs of neurodiverse learners, and the company whose product is being assessed must demonstrate compliance by submitting appropriate documentation to be deemed trustworthy by a licensed assessor.

Assessment Phase

I) The organization provides evidence showing that the requirements via documentation have been met. For AIE products, this would include testing scenarios to evaluate how cognitive load affects neurodiverse learners.

II) A licensed *CertifAIEd* reviewer assesses the evidence. When the requirements are satisfied, IEEE-ICAP issues the CertifAIEd Mark of AI Ethics.

CertifAIEd Method Applied to AI Education

Applying the *CertifAIEd* framework to an AIE product can move the theoretical debate of fair and inclusive education for all learners on the neurodiverse spectrum to a practical evaluation that yields actionable results.

Assessing AIE products with the *CertifAIEd* framework identifies distinct stakeholder groups, what ethical values are at risk and what requirements are necessary to mitigate the identified risks. Applying the framework will demonstrate its viable role in ensuring neurodiverse learners are considered within AIE product design, deployment use and maintenance.

Focusing on the largest segment – AIE solutions with 72% market share, (Market.us) and universities being the largest customer base (Grand View Research) a course created within an AI platform will be evaluated with the CertifAIEd method. The example is a theoretical use case that demonstrates the application of the *CertifAIEd* method. It is not a real AIE product that a university uses.

Concept of Operations

Figure 1. Concept of Operations of a University Course created within an AI Education Platform

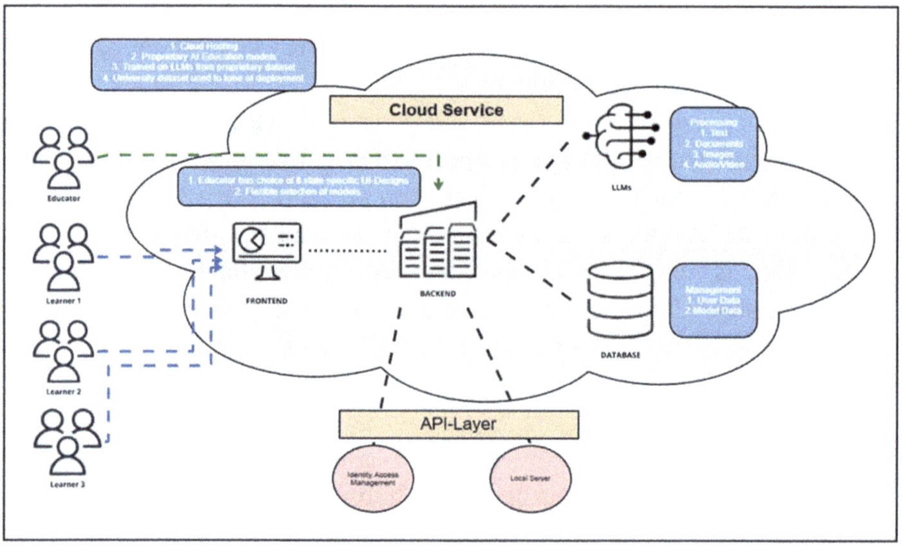

In this use case there is i) an AI platform wherein course materials are created and delivered; ii) 3 types of learners accessing the course created using the frontend of the AI platform iii) one educator accessing the backend of the AI platform to create their content.

In this use case, the AIE product was bought by the university from a private company specializing in AIE. The company's training dataset is proprietary and the classification of learners is not disclosed. University data is used at deployment to tune and to verify that the created course includes the required curriculum content. Its data does not classify learners along the neurodiverse spectrum. It is assumed that the course material was created for neurotypical learners because they comprise the majority of learners and hence the training dataset would be verified against this group. The educator has a choice of 8 format-designs to create their course material and they have flexibility to choose which modules for their courses.

Stakeholder Identification

Table 1. Stakeholder Persona Identification of 3 Learner Groups and 1 Educator

Feature	Learner 1	Learner 2	Learner 3	Educator
Role	Newly enrolled university student, their first higher education experience	Enrolled 2 years at the university;	Returning student, newly enrolled after 15-year hiatus	Tenured professor with 12 years' experience
Size of Group	30% of learner group	60% of learner group	10% of learner group	100% as educator group
Neurodiversity identifier	not included			
Gender Protected feature	Female	Male	Non-binary	Male
Age	19	28	44	55
Cognitive load challenges – potentially a protected feature	Dyslexic feature of slow reading and difficulty with multi-step instructions; need to move frequently to self-regulate	Typical learning pace; typical sensory processing	Autism feature of sensitivity to bright colours, lights and noise; need to move frequently to self-regulate	ADHD feature of difficulty sustaining attention and frequently making errors
Weighting of Persona	Not weighted	100% Typical learning	Not weighted	100% as educator
Learning Environment	Dormitory with shared room and university library	Shared student house and university library	Personal Apartment	University Office and home office

Source of features: International Dyslexia Association and American Psychiatric Association

For the purposes of highlighting how AIE s products have varied impacts on different types of learners on the neurodiverse spectrum, 3 distinct learners are identified: a newly enrolled 19-year-old woman with dyslexia, a neurotypical 22-year-old man with 2 years' experience and an autistic 44-year-old returning student who identifies as non-binary. In addition to being neurodiverse, a newly arrived student would have additional extraneous cognitive load brought on by the change from school to university. A learner with 2 years' experience would not have the extraneous load brought on by the change in academic institutions. An autistic returning learner would have an additional extraneous load brought on by the change to teaching over the last 15 years. The cognitive load challenges are important features that will have the greatest impact of how the AIE product impacts the learners as they interact with it. Their learning environment is another important feature that impacts their cognitive load.

The educator is another stakeholder group with a very different experience with the AIE product. They are identified as having ADHD. According to the American Psychiatric Association, ADHD symptoms include difficulty sustaining attention and frequently making errors. Their cognitive load is impacted not from the learning aspect but through creating their course materials.

Values Elicitation, Classification and Impact Assessment

For purposes of this example, value classifications were used to assess the impact on the well-being for each learner and the educator of the AI created course. The value classification are three overarching universal values: i) Agency is the capacity to make choices and act upon them. ii) Fairness in education is inclusion of all learners and the opposite is discrimination where the quality of learning for minority groups is inequitable and negatively biased. iii) Calm is the feeling of peacefulness, characterized by the prevention of harm. Distress is the opposite of calm and is characterized by a sense of being harmed.

When assessing how the neurodiverse learners learn, the format, design, pace and complexity of information presented in online content are sources of extraneous cognitive load. As Le Cunff et al have highlighted, the extraneous load of different formats and user interface designs vary significantly among learners (Le Cunff et al., 2024). Captions for dyslexic learners help with cognitive load but for learners with ADHD it may increase cognitive load. With respect to pace, neurodiverse learners require more time than neurotypical learners to process information therefore the pace in presenting the material is different between neurodiverse and neurotypical learners. Complexity of information is another factor where content packed too tightly for neurodiverse, compared to neurotypical can increase cognitive load (Le Cunff et al., 2024).

Based on the cognitive load impacts, neurodiverse learners feel disempowered and experience discrimination and distress in high degrees when required to learn based on content created for neurotypical learners. Opposite to the experience of the neurodiverse learner, the neurotypical learner is positively impacted across the dimensions of agency, fairness and calm/peace because the content has been optimized for their learning traits.

For the educator automated content creation can be a benefit because the material is delivered by the AI thereby reducing the time they are required to focus on content creation and their errors are mitigated by the AI.

Table 2. Value Impact Assessment of AI Education Product Use Case

CertifAIEd VALUE IMPACT ASSESSMENT					
ORGANIZATION: University					
CONCEPT OF OPERATIONS: AI Coarse Material for Undergraduate Introduction to Data Science					
Value	**Definition of Value**	**AIS Context**	**Benefit or Risk**	**Impact**	**Likelihood**
LEARNER GROUP 1					
Agency	self-determination and empowerment	the content format cannot be changed; the presentation of material is fixed	risk of violation and negative impact to well-being	high	high
Discrimination / opposite of fairness	Non-inclusivity; unfair representation	the content is not created for the best way the Learner learns; the tests do not make sense and are incomprehensible and results are poor	risk and negative impact to well-being	high	high
Distress / opposite of calm and well-being	feeling of heightened anxiety and apprehension; the parasympathetic nervous system is activated	inability to understand the content; fixed format online; the material advances before Learner is finished reading; confusing explanations and Learner does not understand what is being presented	risk and negative impact to well-being	high	high
LEARNER GROUP 2					
Agency	self-determination and empowerment	access to the content is flexible and open 24/7 giving choice of when, where and frequency	benefit and positive impact to well-being	low	low
Fairness	Fair representation	the content presented is clear and easy to understand	benefit and positive impact to well-being	low	low
Calm /Well-being	feeling of ease and safety	content is interesting and the minor quirks of the format is easy to ignore	benefit and positive impact to well-being	low	low
LEARNER GROUP 3					
Agency	self-determination and empowerment	the content format cannot be changed; the presentation of material is fixed	risk of violation and negative impact to well-being	high	high
Discrimination / opposite of fairness	Non-inclusivity; unfair representation	the content is not created for the best way the Learner learns; test format taxes cognitive load and results are poor	risk and negative impact to well-being	high	high

Distress / opposite of calm and well-being	restlessness with feelings of anger	the content design is distracting and taxes the cognitive load because it is colourful with chirping sounds when links are activated	risk and negative impact to well-being	high	high
EDUCATOR					
Agency	self-determination and feeling of empowerment	options in the AI programme allows Educator to prompt content outputs and to select style	benefit and positive impact to well-being	moderate	moderate
Fairness	Fair representation	the choices in curriculum and coarse creation presents fulsome choice	benefit and positive impact to well-being	moderate	moderate
Calm / Well-being	feeling of ease and safety	the AI programme significantly aids in correcting mistakes in their content creation (typos incorrect links +)	benefit and positive impact to well-being	high	high

Criteria Selection, Ethical Foundational Requirements and Accompanying Evidence to Foster Fair and Inclusive AI Education

When the values of the learners were evaluated against the AI created content, neurodiverse learners were negatively discriminated against because their learning needs were not included in the course design. The positive bias towards neurotypical learners produced one course design that did not allow for neurodiverse learners to adjust the material to better suit their needs. The negative impact on their agency, on being treated unfairly and feeling distressed was high.

The *CertifAIEd Ethical Algorithmic Bias* criteria addresses these risks because ethical algorithmic bias is the primary contributor to system fairness. Fairness is reliant on ethical bias where ethical bias as defined by IEEE within the Ethical Algorithmic Bias Criteria and its Ontological Specification is:

> *A contextual set of values pertaining to a framework of expectations that ensures algorithmic biases that negatively impact individuals, communities, and society have established boundaries of acceptance to protect autonomy and freedoms, where autonomy is defined by one's capacity to direct one's life. Ethical algorithmic bias may be an intentional bias that recognizes a bias requirement for there to be an AIS outcome that mitigates a harmful negative bias and preserves autonomy. (IEEE Standards Association, 2023).*

Ethical Algorithmic Bias specification consists of six drivers that foster AI benefits. The AIE product will need to provide evidence that their AIE platform meets the requirements of these goals

1. *Suitable and sufficient organization governance* The university is to have the capability, maturity, governance processes and good faith for ethical algorithmic bias assurance. It is responsible to ensure that the level of bias within the AIE product it purchased does not negatively bias neurodiverse learners. This requires that the university allocate sufficient resources to ensure the harmful bias towards neurodiverse learners does not add to their existing cognitive load. Evidence to support compliance is an organizational chart with appropriate levels of personnel with education and experience to sufficiently govern the AI product for optimum learner experience for all learners on the neurodiverse spectrum (IEEE Standards Association, 2023). Considering that online education instructors across the globe have been given little or no preparation in this mode, (Burns 2023) requiring proof of competency for those preparing and delivering AIE will mitigate the standing issue of a lack of professional development of educators using AIE products competently.
2. *Clarity of concept of operation* The university along with the AIE company needs to clearly define and communicate the concepts and results of operation of the AIE product, identifying all intended use scenarios and allow access to this information by the relevant stakeholders. For AIE products, neurodiverse learners and all their learning scenarios are to be identified. The systemic biases towards neurodiverse learners are to be identified throughout the system's operation. Technical specifications, test results and audits would prove compliance (IEEE Standards Association, 2023). With the explosion of commercial AIE products, there has not been a commensurate regulatory framework for transparency of the technology nor for the data that is used by the companies selling to education institutions and managing the AI platforms. (Livingston 2023). By requiring transparency of the technology and the data sets used, the issue of a lack of data sharing from commercial AIE providers and educational institutions can be improved if not mitigated.
3. *Context alignment* The AI course creation and delivery system must be tuned with university data and testing conducted to verify the system is aligned to its use and unjustified bias is addressed. The feedback by all learning types is to be acknowledged and appropriately incorporated. Evidence required are university tuning and test logs and documentation of which stakeholders were consulted and the extent of their feedback that was incorporated (IEEE Standards Association, 2023). Actively seeking and engaging with neurodiverse learners with the intent of embracing their particular learning attributes so as to improve

their educational experience can ameliorate the data sets used to improve AIE product design and implementation.

4. *Justified use of protected characteristics* This driver goal ensures that protected characteristics are considered within specific concepts of operation to achieve a fair outcome. Due to the sensitivity of these characteristics, their inclusion and evaluation must be clearly documented with appropriate justification. The Values Elicitation revealed that when the learning needs of neurodiverse learners are not incorporated into the feature and knowledge engineering of AI-created courses, it results in discrimination and undermines their right to education. The university and the AIE provider must provide documentation detailing the protected characteristics and justifying their use in delivering fair, non-discriminatory AI-created courses for learners in the registered programs. This documentation should also explain the potential consequences of not using these protected characteristics. It must be accessible to university oversight, regulatory bodies, and the affected learners (IEEE Standards Association, 2023).
5. *System behavior monitoring:* Recognizing that the discriminatory impact on neurodiverse learners is after the course has been created, some bias in system behavior may only become apparent after the AIE product is in operation and may arise due to operational factors beyond the initial development. Therefore, the AIE product is to be monitored throughout its life cycle in order to identify bias problems as early as possible. The AIE system bought and deployed by the university would be continually optimized and unexpected behaviours monitored. To mitigate discriminatory features entering the system during its use, the university is required to implement an assessment and monitoring methodology for the AIE system in use that validates and verifies its bias profile against the stakeholders that represent the current learners (IEEE Standards Association, 2023).
6. *Maintaining bias profile* The university is to have the capability to correct emerging or detected harmful bias during development, deployment, and operation through risk management, design changes and compensation mechanisms. Through the system behaviour monitoring, they are required to track and document that the bias profile is maintained for each application. Included is evidence there are sufficient and competent resources to maintain the bias profile (IEEE Standards Association, 2023). The university would have completed the creation of the AIE system's bias profile using the methodology within the *IEEE 7003-2024* standard.
7. *Lack of process transparency:* This inhibitory goal concerns the lack of an adequate degree of transparency in overall decision-making, including the selection of appropriate data sets and the sources from which data is drawn. This lack of

transparency will hinder the ability of stakeholders to assess the level of bias in the AIE product performance (IEEE Standards Association, 2023).

Commercial AIE providers will need to collaborate with the university to have accessible the appropriate documentation and audit reports to substantiate the AIE product is providing inclusive education to all learners required to use the system.

Using the *CertifAIEd* framework to assess an AIE product is an effective method to evaluate its course materials for neurodiverse inclusivity. When an AIE product is tuned only for neurotypical learners, the well-being of neurodiverse learners is impacted. Complying with the requirements to uphold ethical levels of algorithmic bias as outlined within the *CertifAIEd Ethical Algorithmic Bias* criteria, educational institutions that choose to deploy AIE products can set in place guardrails that supports inclusive education for neurodiverse learners.

IEEE-SA 7003-2024 Consideration of Algorithmic Bias Standard and Its Application to AI Education

The IEEE 7003-2024, *Consideration of Algorithmic Bias* standard provides a recommended methodology for creating and maintaining an ethical bias profile. Similar to the *CertifAIEd* definition, "ethical bias" refers to wanted bias – the type that ensures correct system functioning within its context of use. The bias profile framework helps optimize wanted bias while mitigating unwanted bias, which may arise from:

1. *Insufficient contextual understanding.* Inadequate recognition of stakeholders and their specific features prevents detection of unwanted bias. Effective mitigation requires incorporating perspectives from all relevant stakeholder groups.
2. *Poorly defined decision criteria.* Algorithmic decisions may appear objective, but are based on human choices in data, models and interpretation. Unwanted bias can emerge without clear mapping of data sources, provenance and representation.
3. *Inadequate life-cycle tracking.* Misalignment between training data, operational data, model outputs and intended outcomes can shift ethical and wanted bias into unethical and unwanted bias (IEEE Standards Association, 2025).

Bias Profile

Figure 2. Bias Profile Development

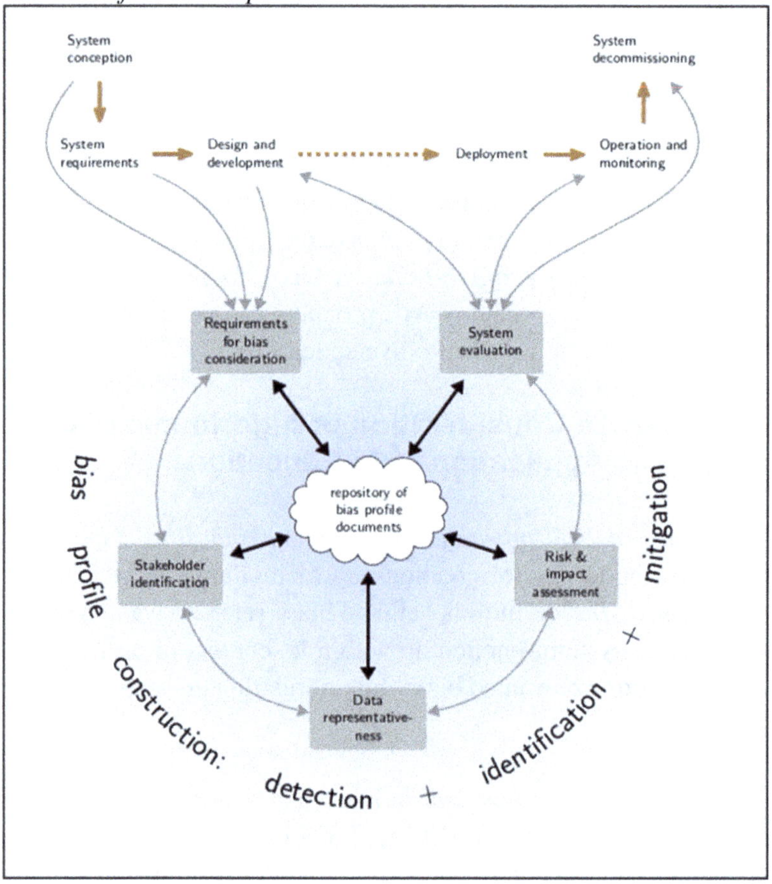

Reproduced with permission from Julian Padget ©2024

The *Consideration of Algorithmic Bias* standard complements and supports the *CertifAIEd Ethical Algorithmic Bias Criteria* by providing a detailed methodology to assess and optimize bias in AIE products throughout their life cycles. When a university chooses to implement an AIE product, conducting a requirements-setting process for bias consideration is essential. This process acknowledges bias as necessary and when used productively it ensures fairer learning outcomes for neurodiverse learners. Complimenting *CertifAIEd*, it necessitates establishing a bias profile and the creation of an appropriate governance structure and allocation of resources to manage the bias profile throughout the AI product's life cycle.

Applying the bias profile framework to AIE acknowledges learner diversity but also recognizes that productive bias insertion may be necessary to support inclusive learning environments. The clear identification of stakeholder roles enables accountability of those who influence the design and use of the AIE. Ultimately, ethical algorithmic bias can be harnessed to benefit neurodiverse learners by optimizing AI education systems to meet their distinct cognitive and educational needs.

Five-Stage Bias Profile Process

Requirements Setting

This initial stage defines assumptions about the desired biases aligned with the AI's objectives and identifies potential unwanted biases that could cause harm. It also clarifies the AI's purpose, design, governance and organizational context to establish clear boundaries for acceptable bias (IEEE Standards Association, 2025). For instance, requiring that all neurodivergent learners receive fair treatment and an equitable curriculum enables universities to implement policies facilitating fair representation.

Stakeholder Identification

AIE providers, university governance bodies, university IT departments and the educators all have roles in delivering AIE. By identifying their roles within the AI life-cycle, their influence in establishing and maintaining the ethical bias in their AIE products can be assessed and they can be held accountable towards upholding international human rights principles and regional and national regulations covering AIE (IEEE Standards Association, 2025)

The AIE provider, creating the AIE products, would be the stakeholder accountable for the algorithmic bias within their training data sets. When held accountable, they would need to include identified patterns in feature engineering and would need to favorably optimize bias to support neurodiverse learners while maintaining the quality of the AIE product for neurotypical learners. The university governance body as a stakeholder, would be held accountable for the impact of their AIE products on neurodiverse learners. The IT influencers who have authority to purchase and deploy the AIE system would be accountable that the provider has trained and tuned its AIE product with productive levels of algorithmic bias for the benefit of neurodiverse learners within the university student body. The educator, as a stakeholder, using the AIE product to create their curriculum and content, would be accountable for ensuring that they have created inclusive content for neurodiverse learners.

Educators would evaluate the existing bias profiles of the AIE product by using data on the types of learners in their programs and the effectiveness of the products they use. Those responsible for maintaining the AIE bias profiles at the university would keep governing bodies informed about evolving learner profiles and how well these learners are included in the AIE product. In turn, the governing bodies would support AIE providers by setting requirements for neurodiverse inclusivity as the AIE product expands within the university network. This allows AIE providers to incorporate informed product requirements into future updates.

Data Representation

Data used by the AI system is examined in terms of how it may affect all learners on the neurodivergent spectrum. Attributes of data are mapped against stakeholder characteristics, with thorough documentation of inclusions, exclusions, and potential disproportionate representation. Given the relative scarcity of data on neurodivergent learners compared to neurotypical groups, AIE providers must be transparent about strategies to balance datasets and incorporate neurophysiological and cognitive load data. This enables feature engineering that optimizes productive bias to reduce extraneous cognitive load particularly for neurodiverse learners (IEEE Standards Association, 2025).

Risk and Impact Assessment (RIA)

From commencement of the design through to the decommissioning of the AI, a risk and impact assessment (RIA), identifying and analysing bias-related risks and impacts is performed and mitigation activities outlined. As the AI progress through its life-cycle and as context of use changes, the RIA is reviewed, the mitigation activities assessed and updated. This is particularly important to counter when unwanted systemic bias creates AIE products that increase the cognitive load of learners (IEEE Standards Association, 2025).

Evaluation

Evaluation is an ongoing activity requiring dedicated resources at every stage of the AIE product's lifecycle. It can be segmented between AIE providers responsible for design, development, and updates, and university personnel, typically IT, responsible for product maintenance. A critical aspect of evaluation is assessing user interface and experience with respect to cognitive load and learning characteristics of neurodiverse learners. Test scenarios should reflect this diversity. Outcomes of university evaluations inform AIE providers' design updates, fostering a continuous feedback loop that optimizes productive bias (IEEE Standards Association, 2025).

Governance and Accountability

Specific accountability structures are established through this framework. The AIE provider is accountable for managing algorithmic bias within their training data sets, including incorporating emerging research findings on cognitive load and neurophysiological data patterns for neurodiverse learners. The governance body oversees the impact of AIE products on neurodiverse learners, while IT departments are responsible for verifying that AIE products have been appropriately tuned to maintain beneficial bias levels. Educators, as influential stakeholders, ensure curricula and content are inclusive of neurodiverse learners' needs.

Collaboration amongst influencing stakeholders facilitates evaluation of bias profiles against evolving student demographics and learning outcomes. University bias profile maintainers relay data on learner inclusivity metrics to governing bodies, which then communicate refined neurodiverse inclusivity requirements to AIE providers for ongoing product enhancement.

CONCLUSION

Acknowledging the ever-increasing role of AIE products within learning ecosystems, it is imperative that they are inclusive of all learners including those on the neurodiverse spectrum. Equitable education is a human right and increasingly protected by regulation. To ensure fair representation, AIE providers and institutions delivering AIE need to come together within the AI learning ecosystem to share data on how all learners within the neurodivergent spectrum are represented and cooperatively assess the ethical impact of the learning experience. Utilizing the complimentary frameworks of *IEEE CertifAIEd and IEEE 7003-2024* AIE research and product development can be directed to practically improving AI education products for all learners.

Viewing neurodiverse characteristics neutrally as engineering features creates space for collecting and integrating neurodiverse learning data into AIE product design and testing. Given the unique needs of neurodiverse learners and the limited data compared to neurotypical learners, ethical consideration of algorithmic bias allows for the intentional insertion of positive, productive bias toward neurodiverse attributes.

Including all influencing stakeholders within the life-cycle of an AIE product within the context of their environment supports the UN and Salamanca reports for collaborative sharing of data.

Inclusive AIE for neurodivergent learners can be achieved. Yet it needs also to be acknowledged that the frameworks demand requirements that AIE providers may not wish to comply with for market and commercial competitive reasons. Of particular concern is the transparency of data representation and testing outcomes. Livingston noted that current regulation puts responsibility on educational institutions without empowering them to have oversight in how the AIE providers collect and process student data. (Livingston 2022)

Universities and educational institutions will need to hold AIE providers accountable for their AIE product 'fairness'. Given it is the educational institutions that are purchasing and implementing the AIE products, it behoves the governing bodies of the educational institutions to mandate appropriate oversight of their AIE products.

The *CertifAIEd* and *IEEE-7003-2024* frameworks can be foundational towards ensuring fair representation of neurodiverse stakeholders within the AI-Learning ecosystem. AIE oversight regulation is coming into effect that can move the theoretical to reality.

REFERENCES

American Psychiatric Association. (2013). *Diagnostic and statistical manual of mental disorders* (5th ed.)., DOI: 10.1176/appi.books.9780890425596

Burns, M. (2023). *Distance Education for Teacher Training: Modes, Models and Methods* (2nd ed.). Education Development Center.

Cameron, M., Lacy, T. A., Siegel, P., Wu, J., Wilson, A., Johnson, R., Burns, R., & Wine, J. (2021). 2019–20 National Postsecondary Student Aid Study (NPSAS:20): *First Look at the Impact of the Coronavirus (COVID-19) Pandemic on Undergraduate Student Enrollment, Housing, and Finances (preliminary data)* (NCES 2021-456). U.S. Department of Education. Washington, DC: National Center for Education Statistics. Retrieved 2025-08-21 from https://nces.ed.gov/pubsearch/pubsinfo.asp?pubid=2021456

Cengage Group. 2025, AI in Education Report: New Cengage Group Data Shows Growing GenAI Adoption in K12 & Higher Education Retrieved 2025-08-21 from https://www.cengagegroup.com/news/press-releases/2025/ai-in-education-report-new-cengage-group-data-shows-growing-genai-adoption-in-k12--higher-education/

Chapman, R. (2020). The reality of autism: On the metaphysics of disorder and diversity. *Philosophical Psychology, 33*, 799–819. DOI: 10.1080/09515089.2020.1751103

Corker, M., French, S., & Singer, J. (1999). 'Why can't you be normal for once in your life?' from a 'problem with no name' to a new category of disability. In *Disability discourse* (pp. 57–59). essay, Open University Press

Diamond, A. (2013). Executive functions. *Annual Review of Psychology, 64*, 135–168. DOI: 10.1146/annurev-psych-113011-143750 PMID: 23020641

European Commission. (n.d.) *AI Act* https://digital-strategy.ec.europa.eu/en/policies/regulatory-framework-ai

European Parliament. (2023). EU AI Act: first regulation on artificial intelligence Retrieved 2025—-08-21 from https://www.europarl.europa.eu/topics/en/article/20230601STO93804/eu-ai-act-first-regulation-on-artificial-intelligence

Fung, L. K. (2021). *Neurodiversity: From phenomenology to neurobiology and enhancing technologies*. American Psychiatric Association Publishing.

Gov.UK, Department for Education. (2025) AI in schools and colleges: What you need to know Retrieved 2025-08-21 from https://educationhub.blog.gov.uk/2025/06/artificial-intelligence-in-schools-everything-you-need-to-know/

Grand View Research. (n.d.) AI in education market size & share, industry report. Report ID: GVR 4-68039-948-8 Retrieved 2025-08-21 from https://www.grandviewresearch.com/industry-analysis/artificial-intelligence-ai-education-market-report

Habib, A., Harris, L., Pollick, F., & Melville, C. (2019). A meta-analysis of working memory in individuals with autism spectrum disorders. *PLoS One*, *14*, e0216198. DOI: 10.1371/journal.pone.0216198 PMID: 31039192

Hamilton, L. G., & Petty, S. (2023). Compassionate pedagogy for neurodiversity in higher education: A conceptual analysis. *Frontiers in Psychology*, *14*, 1093290. DOI: 10.3389/fpsyg.2023.1093290 PMID: 36874864

Hebert, E., Wood, R., Jeon, K., & Reena, I. (2022). Faculty making the emergency online transition during the COVID-19 pandemic: Effects of prior online teaching experience and strategies used to learn to teach online (special edition 2022). *Higher Learning Research Communications, 12*(0). https://doi.org/DOI: 10.18870/hlrc.v12i0.1322

Hickman, T., Lorenz, S., Teetzmann, C., & Jha, A. (2024) Long awaited EU AI Act becomes law after publication in the EU's Official Journal, Retrieved 2025-08-21 from https://www.whitecase.com/insight-alert/long-awaited-eu-ai-act-becomes-law-after-publication-eus-official-journal

Hubble, S., & Bolton, P. (2021). *Support for disabled students in higher education in England* (Briefing Paper No. 8716). House of Commons Library. Retrieved 2025-08-21 from https://researchbriefings.files.parliament.uk/documents/CBP-8716/CBP-8716.pdf

IEEE. (n.d) IEEE Retrieved 2025-08-21 from https://www.ieee.org/about-ieee

IEEE CertifAIEd. (n.d) IEEE CertifAIEd product certification. Retrieved 2025-08-21 from https://standards.ieee.org/products-programs/icap/ieee-certifaied/product-certification

IEEE Standards Association. (2023). *IEEE CertifAIEd ontological specification for ethical accountability* IEEE. https://standards.ieee.org

IEEE Standards Association. (2023). *IEEE CertifAIEd ontological specification for ethical algorithmic bias*. IEEE. https://standards.ieee.org

IEEE Standards Association. (2023). *IEEE CertifAIEd ontological specification for ethical privacy*. IEEE. https://standards.ieee.org

IEEE Standards Association. (2023). *IEEE CertifAIEd ontological specification for ethical transparency*. IEEE. https://standards.ieee.org

IEEE Standards Association (2025). *IEEE Standard for Algorithmic Bias Considerations*. (IEEE Standard 7003-2024) doi:DOI: 10.1109/ieeestd.2025.10851955

International Dyslexia Association and American Psychiatric Association. (2013). Definition of Dyslexia Retrieved 2025-08-21 from https://dyslexiaida.org/definition-of-dyslexia/

Jeffries, S., & Everatt, J. (2004). Working memory: Its role in dyslexia and other specific learning difficulties. *Dyslexia (Chichester, England)*, *10*, 196–214. DOI: 10.1002/dys.278 PMID: 15341198

Kofler, M. J., Singh, L. J., Soto, E. F., Chan, E. S., Miller, C. E., Harmon, S. L., & Spiegel, J. A. (2020). Working memory and short-term memory deficits in ADHD: A bifactor modeling approach. *Neuropsychology*, *34*, 686–698. DOI: 10.1037/neu0000641 PMID: 32437194

Le Cunff, A.-L., Giampietro, V., & Dommett, E. (2024). Neurodiversity and cognitive load in online learning: A focus group study. *PLoS One*, *19*(4), e0301932. DOI: 10.1371/journal.pone.0301932 PMID: 38626101

Le Cunff, A.-L., Martis, B.-L., Glover, C., Ahmed, E., Ford, R., Giampietro, V., & Dommett, E. J. (2025). Cognitive load and neurodiversity in online education: A preliminary framework for educational research and policy. *Frontiers in Education*, *9*. Advance online publication. DOI: 10.1371/journal.pone.0301932 PMID: 38626101

Market.us. (2024). AI in higher education market. Report IE 121472. Retrieved 2025-08-21 from https://market.us/report/ai-in-higher-education-market/

Mayer, R. E., & Moreno, R. (2003). Nine ways to reduce cognitive load in multimedia learning. *Educational Psychologist*, *38*, 43–52. DOI: 10.1207/S15326985EP3801_6

Milliken & Company, Henigan Consulting Group, and Sapio Research. (2023). Designing a Neuro-Inclusive Workplace: A Practical Guide for Creating Neuro-Inclusive Workplaces. Milliken & Company. Retrieved 2025-08-21 from https://floorseurope.milliken.com

Murphy, K. (2022). Reflections on studying with a neurodiverse difference. Museum of Childhood Ireland. Retrieved 2025-08-21 from https://museumofchildhood.ie/reflections-on-studying-with-a-neurodiverse-difference/

Rai, R. 2025, Artificial intelligence in education market size. (Report Code: SRT-E61DR) Straits Research. Retrieved 2025-08-21 from https://straitsresearch.com/report/artificial-intelligence-in-education-market#:~:text=The%20global%20artificial%20intelligence%20in,period%20(2025%2D2033)

Robb, N., Politis, Y., & Boot, F. H. (2023). Editorial: Championing inclusion and diversity: inclusive design practices and approaches for education. *Frontiers in Education*, *8*. Advance online publication. DOI: 10.3389/feduc.2023.1234892

UNESCO. (1990). *World declaration on education for all and framework for action to meet basic learning needs*. Secretariat of the International Consultative Forum on Education for All. https://unesdoc.unesco.org/ark:/48223/pf0000086701

United Nations. (1994). *The Salamanca statement and framework for action on special needs education* (World Conference on Special Needs Education: Access and Quality, ED-94/WS/18) Retrieved 2025-08-21 from https://www.european-agency.org/sites/default/files/salamanca-statement-and-framework.pdf

Chapter 6

Personalizing Learning Pathways Through Standards-Based AI:

How AI Standards Support Personalized Learning Journeys

Frederic Andres
National Institute of Informatics, Japan

Jake Knoppers
Informan, Canada

Swarup Dhungana
https://orcid.org/0000-0002-3519-7574
Citytech Global Pvt. Ltd., Nepal

ABSTRACT

Artificial Intelligence (AI) is transforming education through adaptive platforms, intelligent tutoring, predictive analytics, and generative feedback, enabling personalization at scale. While these tools can enhance engagement, retention, and teaching efficiency, they also raise ethical, technical, and social concerns, including bias, privacy, and learner autonomy. This chapter explores how technical, ethical, and educational standards can guide responsible AI personalization. It examines frameworks for ensuring transparency, equity, and pedagogical alignment while balancing innovation with oversight. By integrating established and emerging standards, the chapter offers practical foundations for building trustworthy personalized learning ecosystems that expand educational opportunities while safeguarding fairness, accountability, and individual dignity.

DOI: 10.4018/979-8-3373-2235-3.ch006

1. INTRODUCTION

Artificial Intelligence (AI) is reshaping education in profound ways. From adaptive learning platforms, personalizing learning (Yang, 2025) and intelligent tutoring systems to predictive analytics and generative feedback tools, AI has begun to permeate both formal and informal learning environments. These technologies offer the potential to support more responsive and efficient teaching, automate routine administrative tasks, and generate real-time insights into learner progress. Most significantly, they enable the long-sought promise of personalizing education at scale—adapting content, pace, and pedagogical strategies to individual learners' needs, abilities, and aspirations.

The imperative for personalization is growing in contemporary education systems, which must serve increasingly diverse populations of learners across varied contexts. Traditional, standardized modes of instruction often fail to accommodate the full range of learner variability, contributing to disengagement, inequity, and suboptimal outcomes. AI-driven personalization holds the potential to address these challenges by dynamically adjusting learning pathways in response to evolving learner profiles, thereby enhancing engagement, retention, and long-term learning efficacy.

However, this technological promise is accompanied by serious ethical, technical, and social questions. Personalization through AI systems can introduce significant risks—ranging from algorithmic bias and opacity to threats to data privacy and learner autonomy. Without clear and enforceable guidelines, these systems may reproduce or exacerbate existing inequalities. In this context, standards—whether technical, ethical, or educational—are not merely procedural artifacts but foundational mechanisms for safeguarding the integrity, fairness, and accountability of AI-enhanced learning environments.

This chapter examines the critical role of standards in supporting responsible AI-driven personalization in education. It explores how emerging and established standards provide essential frameworks for designing, deploying, and evaluating AI systems that align with pedagogical goals, regulatory requirements, and ethical values. The discussion focuses on striking a balance between innovation and oversight: how to enable adaptive, personalized learning experiences while ensuring transparency, equity, and protection of learner rights (Berendt, 2020).

By investigating the intersection of AI, personalization, and standardization, this chapter aims to inform educators, researchers, developers, and policymakers about the practical and normative foundations needed to build trustworthy personalized learning ecosystems—ones that advance educational opportunities while upholding societal expectations and individual dignity.

The remainder of this chapter is organized as follows.Section 2 explores the promise and pedagogical foundations of AI-driven personalized learning, outlining key concepts, examples, and benefits across diverse learner profiles. Section 3 examines the challenges and risks associated with personalization, including bias, opacity, privacy, and trust. Section 4 discusses the emerging role of AI standards in education, highlighting major frameworks from IEEE, ISO, UNESCO, OECD, and the EU AI Act.

Section 5 presents a standards-based design approach for adaptive learning systems, introducing formal principles and predicate-based rules for fairness, transparency, privacy, interoperability, and accountability. Section 6 focuses on the integration of learning analytics, metadata, and competency frameworks to ensure alignment between personalization and educational benchmarks.

Sections 7 and 8 address privacy-preserving architectures and ethical–regulatory considerations essential for trustworthy AI in education. Section 9 provides best practices and implementation guidelines for developers, educators, and policymakers, while Section 10 outlines future directions and opportunities.

Finally, Section 11 concludes with reflections on the transformative yet responsible role of AI standards in shaping personalized learning ecosystems.

2. THE PROMISE OF PERSONALIZED LEARNING

Personalized learning refers to educational approaches that tailor instruction, content, and assessment to the individual needs, goals, preferences, and prior experiences of each learner. While educators have long pursued personalization through differentiated instruction, the emergence of Artificial Intelligence (AI) dramatically expands both the feasibility and the scale at which personalization can be achieved. In the AI era, personalization moves beyond manual instructional strategies and becomes increasingly automated, data-driven, and responsive to real-time changes in learner behavior and performance.

2.1 What Personalized Learning Means in the AI Era

In traditional settings, personalization often relied on teacher observation, static learner profiles, or predefined learning pathways. AI introduces the possibility of *dynamic* personalization, in which real-time learner data—such as click patterns, problem-solving sequences, facial expressions, and even tone of voice—can inform decision-making within milliseconds. These systems use machine learning algorithms, including reinforcement learning, collaborative filtering, and Bayesian knowledge tracing, to build evolving models of learners' cognitive states and affective engagement (Koedinger et al., 2012; Vanlehn, 2011).

AI-driven personalized learning environments can continuously monitor progress, predict likely misconceptions, and adapt resources, instructional strategies, and pacing to match learners' evolving needs. This continuous feedback loop allows for the real-time reconfiguration of the learning journey, creating an experience that feels increasingly responsive and individualized.

2.2 Examples of AI-Enabled Adaptive Learning Systems

Several cutting-edge platforms exemplify how AI enables adaptive learning across different contexts and subjects:

- **Carnegie Learning's MATHia** employs cognitive modeling and intelligent tutoring techniques to detect students' problem-solving strategies and misconceptions. The system provides personalized feedback and just-in-time scaffolding, enabling learners to build conceptual understanding at their own pace (Ritter et al., 2007).
- **Duolingo**, a language-learning platform, integrates reinforcement learning to adjust lesson content, difficulty, and timing based on learner error patterns and proficiency levels. Its user model tracks fluency and retention, ensuring that users review content just before forgetting occurs (Settles & Meeder, 2016).
- **DreamBox Learning** supports K–8 mathematics by combining real-time data analytics with curriculum mapping. The platform dynamically adjusts the sequence and complexity of tasks based on learner responses, thereby reinforcing conceptual understanding and problem-solving fluency.
- **Large language models (LLMs)**, such as GPT-4, further extend personalization through conversational interaction. These models can engage in real-time dialogue with learners, offering explanations, feedback, and scaffolding in natural language. They also support multilingual learning environments, enabling cross-linguistic tutoring and culturally responsive pedagogy (Liu et al., 2024).

These AI systems illustrate a shift from static curriculum delivery to learning environments that are inherently responsive, interactive, and attuned to learner variability.

2.3 Benefits for Diverse Learner Profiles

AI-powered personalization holds particular promise for populations often underserved by conventional education systems, including neurodiverse learners, multilingual students, and adult learners.

- **Neurodiverse learners** benefit from the application of Universal Design for Learning (UDL) principles, which advocate for multiple means of representation, engagement, and expression (Meyer et al., 2014). AI can tailor interface designs (e.g., adjustable font sizes, color contrasts), deliver multimodal content (e.g., text, audio, video), and scaffold executive functioning skills (e.g., breaking tasks into steps, providing reminders), thereby accommodating cognitive and sensory profiles more effectively.
- **Multilingual learners** are supported through real-time language translation, adaptive vocabulary scaffolding, and pronunciation modeling. AI systems can track lexical acquisition, identify language-specific challenges, and provide culturally relevant content, thus reducing linguistic barriers and supporting bilingual or multilingual development.
- **Adult learners**, who often balance learning with work, caregiving, or other responsibilities, benefit from the flexibility of AI-enhanced systems that offer asynchronous access, modular content, and self-paced progression. Personalization allows these learners to revisit foundational concepts or skip familiar material, creating an efficient and empowering learning experience.

Moreover, personalized systems can reduce stigma by offering private, adaptive support that does not single out learners publicly—an especially important consideration for marginalized or self-conscious populations.

2.4 Broader Educational Impacts

Beyond supporting individual learners, AI-driven personalization contributes to broader educational outcomes. Research has shown that adaptive learning technologies can improve engagement, reduce dropout rates, and enhance long-term knowledge retention (Ma et al., 2014; Walkington, 2013). By collecting granular data on learner interactions, these systems also generate insights that help educators identify gaps in curriculum coverage, address systemic inequities, and make data-informed instructional decisions.

In addition, personalization can foster a greater sense of agency and motivation among learners. When content aligns with personal interests and goals, and when progress is visibly tracked and rewarded, learners are more likely to persist and invest effort. This aligns well with self-determination theory, which emphasizes the importance of autonomy, competence, and relatedness in fostering intrinsic motivation (Deci & Ryan, 2000).

2.5 The Path Forward

While the potential of personalized learning is immense, its realization hinges on responsible design, ethical oversight, and alignment with educational values—a theme explored in the following sections. The promise of AI lies not merely in its capacity to automate or scale instruction, but in its ability to elevate human learning by meeting individuals where they are and helping them grow toward their full potential.

3. CHALLENGES AND RISKS IN AI-DRIVEN PERSONALIZATION

While AI-driven personalization holds significant promise for enhancing educational outcomes, it also presents a range of technical, ethical, and social risks that must be critically examined. These challenges—if unaddressed—may undermine trust in AI systems, exacerbate existing inequities, and compromise the very goals of inclusive and responsible education.

3.1 Risks of Bias, Overfitting, and Lack of Transparency

AI systems are only as unbiased as the data and algorithms on which they are built. If training datasets reflect historical inequities or systemic disparities, models may perpetuate or even amplify those biases (Binns, 2018; Holstein et al., 2019). In educational contexts, this can result in misclassification of student abilities, culturally unrepresentative content recommendations, or discriminatory performance predictions for marginalized groups.

Overfitting is another technical concern. When AI systems are optimized too closely to past learner data, they may fail to generalize to novel or evolving learning behaviors, limiting the adaptability that personalization purports to offer (Zliobaite, 2017). Compounding this is the issue of algorithmic opacity—many AI systems, especially those using deep learning or ensemble methods, function as "black boxes," making it difficult for educators, learners, or even developers to understand how decisions are made (Burrell, 2016).

3.2 Ethical Dilemmas and Unintended Consequences

Beyond bias and opacity, ethical dilemmas emerge when AI systems make consequential decisions without human oversight or contextual judgment. These include unintended tracking of students' cognitive and emotional states, or automated feedback that shapes learner identity and motivation in subtle yet profound ways (Williamson & Piattoeva, 2022). Without clear ethical guardrails, personalization may veer into behavioral manipulation, reinforcing fixed learning trajectories rather than nurturing growth and exploration (Knox et al., 2020).

Additionally, the delegation of pedagogical responsibility to algorithms raises philosophical questions about the role of human agency in learning. Overreliance on AI may diminish the relational and dialogic aspects of education—those essential for critical thinking, empathy, and democratic engagement (Selwyn, 2019).

3.3 Privacy, Surveillance, and Data Ownership Concerns

Personalized AI systems require vast amounts of data to function effectively. This dependency raises acute concerns about data privacy, surveillance, and ownership—particularly when systems collect granular data on learners' behaviors, locations, biometric signals, or emotional expressions (Regan & Jesse, 2019). Inadequate data governance frameworks risk exposing sensitive student data to misuse, breaches, or monetization by third parties.

The use of facial recognition, keystroke dynamics, and emotion AI for educational personalization has also drawn criticism for enabling forms of "surveillance pedagogy"—where monitoring takes precedence over learning (Zeide, 2017). Moreover, students and educators are often not fully informed about what data are collected, how they are used, or who ultimately controls them.

3.4 Trust and the Digital Divide

Trust is foundational for the adoption and effectiveness of AI systems in education. However, opaque algorithms, historical data misuse, and inconsistent regulatory protections contribute to public skepticism—especially among communities already marginalized in digital environments (Ahn et al., 2021). If learners or educators do not understand how AI works or do not feel it acts in their best interests, the benefits of personalization may go unrealized.

Equally concerning is the deepening digital divide. While AI-enabled tools promise democratization, they also risk entrenching inequality by disproportionately benefiting well-resourced schools and learners with stable internet access, modern devices, and digital literacy. Marginalized populations may be excluded from advanced

AI interventions or subjected to lower-quality automated systems—reproducing the very disparities education aims to eliminate (Eubanks, 2018).

4. THE ROLE OF AI STANDARDS IN EDUCATION

As Artificial Intelligence becomes increasingly embedded in education systems, the development and adoption of standards play a critical role in shaping how these technologies are deployed responsibly and equitably. AI standards—technical, ethical, and regulatory—serve as foundational instruments that ensure alignment between innovation and societal values. In the context of personalized learning, these standards help translate abstract principles such as fairness, transparency, and inclusivity into actionable frameworks.

4.1 Overview of Existing and Emerging AI Standards relevant in Education

A number of global organizations have initiated efforts to standardize the design, development, deployment, and evaluation of AI systems, with education identified as a critical domain.

The **Institute of Electrical and Electronics Engineers (IEEE)**, through its *Ethically Aligned Design* and *P7000-series* standards, addresses transparency, algorithmic bias, data governance, and human well-being in autonomous systems (IEEE, 2020).

The interesting standards P7006 focus on Personal Data Artificial Intelligence (AI) Agent, are directly relevant to Adaptive Learning Environments (ALEs).

P7006 enables to empower learners through personalized AI agents as it envisions Personal AI Agents (PAIAs) that act on behalf of individuals in machine-to-machine interactions, using human-readable, ethics-aligned inputs and preferences. There are new implication for ALEs: (1) students can deploy Personal Learning Agents that negotiate their learning pace, preferred styles, privacy boundaries, and as differentiatied from PAIAs. Or are these the same? This is not clear.cognitive/emotional needs with the learning system. (2) shifting from a one-size-fits-all personalization (algorithm-centered) to learner-centered personalization, where the student's agency is central to how AI adapts content.

In addressing Asymmetry in AI Decision-Making, P7006 aims to mitigate black-box decision-making by allowing individuals to understand and influence algorithmic logic. In education, many adaptive systems operate on hidden logic, offering little transparency into why a certain resource or pace is recommended. In addition, P7006 supports the inclusion of transparent models, enabling learners and educators to understand, contest, or refine how the learning system adapts—fostering trust and explainability.

As it is so important in term of Ethical Mediation of Data Processing in Education, P7006 emphasizes that AI systems should align with human rights, social norms, and individual ethical stances. Data in ALEs often includes behavioral, emotional, and cognitive analytics. These are highly sensitive. A P7006-compliant system would allow the learner (or guardian) to define the ethical boundaries of data use (e.g., refusing emotional tracking, limiting data retention, etc).

Finally, P7006 standard promotes value-sensitive design in educational AI, promoting ethical personalization rather than pure optimization.

In term of Shaping Systemic Fairness and Inclusion, P7006 facilitates negotiation between personal preferences and shared societal ethics. So adaptive systems often encode cultural and cognitive biases. A Personal AI Agent (PAIA) aligned with P7006 could act as a cultural translator or ethical advocate, ensuring learning content, pacing, and assessments are inclusive and context-aware. Please do not forget that this is especially important in multilingual, multicultural, or neurodiverse classrooms.

In term of enhancing Human-AI Teaming in education, P7006 standard enables a shift to co-agency between humans and AI, rather than top-down control. This facilitates that teachers and students could co-design AI behaviors, share responsibility, and adjust ethical rules as needed (e.g., when working with students who have disabilities, or during sensitive topics). Also this fosters distributed agency, aligning with pedagogical values like autonomy, critical thinking, and mutual respect.

The International Organization for Standardization (ISO), in collaboration with the International Electrotechnical Commission (IEC), has established the *ISO/IEC JTC 1/SC 42* subcommittee, which develops standards such as *ISO/IEC 22989:2022* (AI concepts and terminology) and *ISO/IEC 23894:2023* (risk management in AI). These provide comprehensive guidance on lifecycle risk assessments that can be tailored to educational applications.

Intergovernmental bodies have also advanced normative frameworks. The OECD's AI Principles, adopted by over 40 countries, emphasize human-centered values, transparency, robustness, and accountability (OECD, 2019). The UNESCO Recommendation on the Ethics of Artificial Intelligence (2021) extends this further by addressing cultural diversity, data sovereignty, and equitable access—principles vital for global education systems.

The European Union's AI Act was finalized with its entry into force on August 1, 2024, but it will be fully applicable in two years, on August 2, 2026. It introduces a tiered risk-based regulatory model. However, some provisions have staggered application dates, with prohibitions and AI literacy rules becoming applicable by

February 2, 2025, and rules for general-purpose AI (GPAI) models taking effect by August 2, 2025.

It classifies educational AI systems as "high-risk," thereby subjecting them to strict requirements on data quality, human oversight, and algorithmic transparency (European Commission, 2021). The Act explicitly mentions systems used for assessing students or determining access to education—placing personalization tools squarely under scrutiny.

4.2 Promoting Fairness, Transparency, Safety, and Interoperability

Standards function not only as compliance tools but as design enablers recommending design principles. When applied in educational contexts, standards help developers encode societal and pedagogical values into AI systems. Core guiding principles in the design of AI systems include fairness, transparency, safety, and interoperability which are defined in several standards.

Fairness is promoted through data representativeness benchmarks and algorithmic audit protocols, which can help reduce disparities in how different learner groups are treated (Binns, 2018).

Transparency is enabled through standards for explainability, such as IEEE P7001, which mandate intelligibility of algorithmic decisions for end users—especially important for educators and learners with limited technical expertise.

Safety and robustness are supported by ISO/IEC risk management frameworks that include adversarial testing, fault tolerance, and data integrity—ensuring learning systems behave predictably even under stress.

Interoperability standards ensure that personalized learning platforms can integrate with diverse educational technologies and data infrastructures, fostering scalability and innovation across regions and institutions (ISO/IEC, 2023).

By embedding these principles, AI standards help preempt harms and establish trust—turning personalization from a black-box promise into a participatory and accountable process.

4.3 Aligning Educational Goals with Technical Standards

For AI standards to meaningfully support personalized learning, alignment between educational objectives and technical specifications is crucial. This requires an ongoing dialogue between educators, policymakers, technologists, and standard-setting bodies.

For example, adaptive learning platforms designed to foster metacognition or creativity must align not only with learning sciences but also with technical standards on explainability and feedback loops (Luckin et al., 2016). Similarly, ethical norms about learner autonomy must be translated into machine-readable protocols that limit overpersonalization or surveillance (Williamson & Eynon, 2020).

Moreover, contextual factors—such as local curricula, cultural practices, and resource constraints—must inform the customization of global standards. This ensures that standards are not imposed as one-size-fits-all models but serve as scaffolds adaptable to diverse educational ecosystems.

Ultimately, aligning educational goals with AI standards fosters coherence between pedagogical intent and technical implementation, paving the way for responsible personalization that is both effective and just.

5. DESIGNING STANDARDS-BASED ADAPTIVE LEARNING SYSTEMS

As AI-enabled personalized learning systems [Kabudi et al., 2021] proliferate, ensuring their alignment with educational standards becomes both a technical and pedagogical imperative. While personalization emphasizes learner-centered pathways, it must remain grounded in shared learning goals, curricular coherence, and institutional accountability. Standards-based adaptive learning systems aim to balance individualization with alignment to recognized benchmarks—such as national curricula, competency frameworks, or global education priorities—ensuring that learners achieve both personal growth and societal-relevant competencies.

Each principle defines desired properties, behaviors, or requirements. First Order Predicate (noted FOP) rules formalize these as predicates over system entities, actors, processes, or datasets.

5.1 Integrating AI Standards into Personalized Learning Technologies

A foundational principle in designing such systems is the **interoperability of AI tools with curricular and assessment standards**. This involves embedding competencies, learning objectives, and performance indicators into the very architecture of adaptive algorithms and recommendation engines. For instance, an AI system should not only guide a learner through a math module but also be able to tag each exercise with relevant grade-level standards (e.g., Common Core Math 7.EE.B.4) and monitor mastery over time.

To operationalize this, system designers must adhere to the six (6) **AI development principles** (AIDPs) that promote:

- **Fairness and Inclusivity**
- **Transparency and explainability**, allowing learners and educators to understand how content recommendations are made and why a particular task or resource is suggested.
- **Privacy and DataProtection**
- **Interoperability and Standards Compliance**
- **Traceability**, ensuring each learning path can be mapped back to curricular standards.
- **Ethical compliance**, respecting learners' privacy, agency, and data rights throughout the process.
- **Unambiguity**

These six (6) AI development principles are increasingly supported by emerging **AI education guidelines**, such as those under development by IEEE Learning Technology Standards Committee and UNESCO's guidance on AI in education.

In the following, the 5 principles and the related rules are defined to be checked to respect each principle.

A) Principle of Fairness and Inclusivity

Definition: Ensure that personalized learning systems provide equitable access and unbiased experiences for all learners, regardless of background, identity, or ability.

Related Rules to Check:

- **Rule 01**

Narrative expression: AI models are required to be regularly audited for biases related to gender, ethnicity, disability, language, and socio-economic status.

First Order Predicate expression:

Table 1. Summary of Predicates Used

Predicate	Meaning
IsAIModel(m)	m is an AI model
RegularlyAuditedForBias(m, B)	AI model m is regularly audited for biases in dimensions B

- **Rule 02**

Narrative expression: Learning content and recommendations are required to be accessible to learners with diverse cognitive and sensory needs (e.g., following Universal Design for Learning guidelines).

Table 2. First Order Predicate expression: Summary of Predicates Used

Predicate	Meaning
IsLearningContent(c)	c is instructional content or recommendation
AccessibleToDiverseNeeds(c)	c is accessible to cognitive/sensory diverse learners

- **Rule 03**:

Narrative: System design is required to accommodate multilingual learners and culturally diverse populations.

First Order Predicate expression:

Table 3. Summary of Predicates Used

Predicate	Meaning
IsLearningSystem(s)	s is a learning system/platform
AccommodatesMultilingualCulturalDiversity(s)	s supports multilingual and culturally diverse learners

- **Rule 04**

Narrative expression: Data sets used for training AI are required to include representative samples across diverse learner groups.

First Order Predicate expression:

Table 4. Summary of Predicates Used

Predicate	Meaning
IsTrainingDataset(d)	D is a dataset intended for training purposes (e.g., for machine learning, AI model training, or educational evaluation).
IncludesRepresentativeDiversity(d,LearnerGroups)	d contains samples that reflect a wide range of learners, ensuring fairness and inclusivity in training.

B) Principles of Transparency and Explainability

Definition: Provide clear, understandable explanations of how AI algorithms personalize learning pathways and make decisions affecting learners.

Specific rules to check:

- **Rule 05**:

Narrative expression: Learners and educators are required to receive accessible descriptions of the AI system's decision-making processes.

First Order Predicate expression:

Table 5. Summary of Predicates Used

Predicate	**Meaning**
IsUser(x)	x is a learner or educator
ReceivesAccessibleExplanation(x, DecisionMakingProcess)	x receives an understandable explanation of the AI's decision-making logic

- **Rule 06**

Narrative expression: System interfaces are required to include explanations for recommendations, feedback, and content adaptations.

First Order Predicate expression:

Table 6. Summary of Predicates Used

Predicate	**Meaning**
IsSystemInterface(i)	i is a user interface of an AI system
IncludesExplanations(i, X)	interface I includes explanations for items in set X

- **Rule 07**

Narrative expression: The documentation of the AI models, training data, and updates is required to be publicly available at no cost.

First Order Predicate expression:

Table 7. Summary of Predicates Used

Predicate	Meaning
IsAIModel(m)	m is an AI model used in education
PublicDocumentationAvailable(m, X)	documentation for elements X of model mmm is available to stakeholders

- **Rule 08**

Narrative expression: Mechanisms are required to exist for learners to be able to query or challenge AI-driven decisions.

First Order Predicate expression:

Table 8. Summary of Predicates Used

Predicate	Meaning
IsLearningSystem(s)	s is an AI-enabled learning platform
HasQueryMechanism(s, AI_Decision)	system s allows querying or disputing AI decisions

C) Principle of Privacy and DataProtection

Definition: Safeguard learner data by minimizing collection, securing storage, and enforcing strict data governance aligned with legal and ethical standards.

Related Rules to Check:

- **Rule 09**

Narrative expression: Data collection is required to adhere to the principle of data minimization—only essential information is gathered.

Table 9. First Order Predicate expression: Summary of Predicates Used

Predicate	Meaning
IsLearningSystem(s)	system s is an AI-based educational system
AdheresToDataMinimization(s)	s collects only essential learner data

- **Rule 10**

Narrative expression: Data anonymization or differential privacy techniques are required to be able to be implemented.

First Order Predicate expression:

Table 10. Summary of Predicates Used

Predicate	Meaning
IsLearningSystem(s)	*s* is recognized as a learning system (e.g. an LMS, AI-based tutoring platform, adaptive learning environment).
ImplementsPrivacyPreservingTechniques(s, X)	system s implements at least one X technique from set {Anonymization, DifferentialPrivacy}

- **Rule 11**

Narrative expression: Learner consent is required to be obtained and can be withdrawn at any time, with clear opt-in/out options.

First Order Predicate expression:

Table 11. Summary of Predicates Used

Predicate	Meaning
IsLearner(u)	u is a learner
ConsentObtained(u)	learner u has provided informed consent
ConsentRevocable(u)	u can withdraw consent at any time
HasOptInOutOptions(u)	u has access to opt-in/opt-out features

- **Rule 12**

Narrative expression: Compliance with relevant regulations and standards (e.g., GDPR, FERPA, COPPA, ISO/IEC 29817-1) is verified regularly.

First Order Predicate expression:

Table 12. Summary of Predicates Used

Predicate	Meaning
IsLearningSystem(s)	s is a system designed for learning (e.g., an LMS, educational platform, or AI tutoring system).
RegularlyVerifiedCompliance(s,{GDPR,FERPA,COPPA, 29187-1})))	s is regularly checked to ensure it complies with these regulations. • **GDPR** → General Data Protection Regulation (EU) • **FERPA** → Family Educational Rights and Privacy Act (US) • **COPPA** → Children's Online Privacy Protection Act (US) • **29187-1** → ISO/IEC 29187-1 (example standard, possibly for privacy protection or educational systems)

- **Rule 13**

Narrative expression: Verifiable secure data transmission and storage protocols are required to be in place prior to the use or implementation of the system (e.g., encryption, access controls, quality of service (QoS)).

First Order Predicate expression:

Table 13. Summary of Predicates Used

Predicate	Meaning
IsSystem(s)	s is a system (software, platform, or network component).
HasSecureProtocols(s)	s has secure data transmission and storage protocols in place.
UsesEncryption(s)	s encrypts data to protect confidentiality during storage or transmission.
HasAccessControls(s)	s enforces restrictions on who can access or modify data.
EnsuresQoS(s)	s guarantees quality of service, ensuring reliability, performance, and integrity of data transmission/storage.

D) Principles of Interoperability and Standards Compliance

Definition: Design systems to align with widely accepted technical and educational standards to enable seamless integration, scalability, and sustainability.

Related Rules to Check:

- **Rule 14**

Narrative expression: Learning analytics and activity data are required to comply with metadata standards such as xAPI and IMS Global Learning Tools Interoperability (LTI).

First Order Predicate expression:

Table 14. Summary of Predicates Used

Predicate	Meaning
IsLearningAnalyticsData(d)	d is a dataset containing learning analytics or activity data collected from learners.
CompliesWithMetadataStandards(d, {xAPI, LTI})	d follows the required metadata standards for interoperability and consistency. {xAPI, LTI} → the set of metadata standards it must comply with

- **Rule 15**

Narrative expression: Competency frameworks and curriculum standards (e.g., Common Core, P21, SDGs) are required to be incorporated into AI models and learning pathways.

First Order Predicate expression:

Table 15. Summary of Predicates Used

Predicate	Meaning
IsAIModelOrLearningPathway(m)	m is either an AI-driven learning model or a structured learning pathway
IncorporatesStandards(m, {CommonCore, P21, SDGs})	m includes the listed frameworks and standards in its design or guidance {CommonCore, P21, SDGs} → the set of competency frameworks or curriculum standards

- **Rule 16**

Narrative expression: APIs and data formats are required to follow open standards to facilitate integration with other educational technologies.

Table 15. First Order Predicate expression: Summary of Predicates Used

Predicate	Meaning
IsAPIOrDataFormat(x)	x is either an API (Application Programming Interface) or a data format used in educational technologies.
FollowsOpenStandards(x)	x adheres to publicly available standards, ensuring compatibility and interoperability.

- **Rule 17**

Narrative expression: The system is required to be able to support standardized credentialing and reporting mechanisms.

First Order Predicate expression:

Table 16. Summary of Predicates Used

Predicate	Meaning
IsSystem(s)	s is a system (e.g., an educational platform, LMS, or credentialing system).
SupportsCredentialing(s)	s can issue or manage standardized credentials (e.g., certificates, badges, diplomas).
SupportsReporting(s)	s can generate standardized reports about learning outcomes, progress, or achievements.

E) Principles of Accountability and Ethical Governance

Definition: Establish clear accountability mechanisms and ethical oversight to monitor AI system impacts and mitigate risks.

Related Rules to Check:

- **Rule18**

Narrative expression: A governance framework is required to be in place defining roles and responsibilities for AI system design, deployment, and monitoring.

First Order Predicate expression:

Table 17. Summary of Predicates Used

Predicate	Meaning
IsAISystem(a)	a is an AI system.
GovernanceFramework(g)	g is a governance framework that defines rules, roles, and responsibilities
CoversRolesAndResponsibilities(g,a)	The governance framework g defines roles and responsibilities related to AI system a.
CoversDesignDeploymentMonitoring(g,a)	The framework g specifies how a should be designed, deployed, and monitored.

- **Rule 19**

Narrative expression: Regular impact assessments (e.g., ethical, social, educational) are required to be conducted and documented.

First Order Predicate expression:

Table 18. Summary of Predicates Used

Predicate	Meaning
IsAISystem(a)	a is an AI system that falls under governance.
ImpactAssessmentType(t)	t is a category of assessment (e.g., ethical, social, educational).
ConductsAssessmentRegularly(a,t)	AI system a undergoes regular assessments of type t.
DocumentsAssessment(a,t)	The results of the assessment of type t for system a are recorded/documented.

- **Rule 20**:

Narrative expression: Processes are required to exist for reporting and addressing harms, errors, or unintended consequences.

First Order Predicate expression:

Table 19. Summary of Predicates Used

Predicate	Meaning
IsAISystem(a)	a is an AI system under governance.
Process(p)	p is a defined organizational process/procedure.
ForReporting(p,a)	p provides a channel to report issues in a.

continued on following page

Table 19. Continued

Predicate	Meaning
ForAddressing(p,a)	p defines remediation/mitigation for issues in a.
Covers(p, {…})	p explicitly handles the listed issue categories. Constants: Harm, Error, Unintended Consequence denote issue types

- **Rule 21**:

Narrative expression: Human-in-the-loop mechanisms are required to ensure that educators can intervene and override AI decisions as needed.

First Order Predicate expression:

Table 20. Summary of Predicates Used

Predicate	Meaning
IsAISystem(s)	Predicate stating that *s* is an AI system.
HumanInLoopMechanism(m,s)	Mechanism *m* is implemented in AI system *s* to allow human participation.
CanIntervene(m,Educator,s)	The mechanism *m* enables an educator to intervene in the functioning of the AI system *s*.
CanOverride(m,Educator,Decision(s))	The mechanism *m* allows the educator to override the AI system's decision outputs.
Decision(s)	Represents the decision or action produced by the AI system *s*.

Rule 22:

Narrative expression: Stakeholder feedback loops (including learners) are required to be incorporated into system updates.

First Order Predicate expression:

Table 21. Summary of Predicates Used

Predicate	Meaning
IsAISystem(s)	s is an AI system.
FeedbackLoop(f,s)	f is a feedback loop associated with AI system s.
IncludesStakeholders(f,Stakeholders)	The feedback loop f collects input from stakeholders (e.g., learners, educators, administrators).

continued on following page

Table 21. Continued

Predicate	Meaning
IncorporatedIntoUpdates(f,s)	Feedback collected through f is used to inform and update the system s.
Stakeholders	The set of relevant participants providing feedback, explicitly including learners but potentially also educators or administrators.

F) Adaptability and Continuous Improvement

Definition: Enable ongoing system refinement based on real-world performance, learner outcomes, and emerging standards.

Related Rules to Check:

- **Rule 23:**

Narrative expression: AI models are required to be updated periodically with new data to maintain accuracy and relevance.

First Order Predicate expression:

Table 22. Summary of Predicates Used

Predicate	Meaning
Model(x)	x is an AI model
UpdatedPeriodically(x)	x receives regular updates (e.g., retraining with new data).
MaintainsAccuracyAndRelevance(x)	x continues to provide valid, precise, and up-to-date outputs after updates.

- **Rule 24:**

Narrative expression: Learning outcomes and user satisfaction metrics are required to be monitored to inform system enhancements.

First Order Predicate expression:

Table 23. Summary of Predicates Used

Predicate	Meaning
MonitorsLearningOutcomes(y)	system y measures and tracks learners' performance results (e.g., test scores, progress).
MonitorsUserSatisfaction(y)	system y collects feedback on learner/educator satisfaction (e.g., surveys, ratings).
InformsEnhancements(y)	system y uses those metrics to guide improvements (content adaptation, interface redesign, AI tuning).

- **Rule 25**:

Narrative expression: The system architecture is required to be able to support modular upgrades aligned with evolving AI and educational standards.

First Order Predicate expression:

Table 24. Summary of Predicates Used

Predicate	Meaning
SupportsModuleUpgrades(y)	system y is designed so components can be independently updated or replaced (e.g., plug-and-play AI modules).
AlignedWithStandards(y)	system y adheres to current AI standards and educational regulations/ frameworks.

- **Rule 26:** Research partnerships and collaborations are required to be maintained to integrate latest findings and practices.

First Order Predicate expression:

Table 25. Summary of Predicates Used

Predicate	Meaning
MaintainsResearchPartnerships(y)	system/organization y engages in collaborations with research institutions or communities.
IntegratesLatestFindings(y)	system y applies new knowledge, methods, and best practices from those partnerships.

6. LEVERAGING LEARNING ANALYTICS, METADATA STANDARDS, AND COMPETENCY FRAMEWORKS

A key enabler of standards-based adaptation is the structured use of learning analytics and metadata. Technologies such as xAPI 2.0 specification (IEEE 9274.1.1-2023) and IMS Global's Caliper Analytics (IMS Global Learning Consortium, 2020) have been allowing learning activities to be tracked and encoded in machine-readable formats, facilitating real-time assessment, cross-platform interoperability, and actionable insights into learner progress. These data streams can be aligned with multiple educational frameworks to enhance personalized learning (Dhupia et al., 2019) . For example, competency-based education (CBE) frameworks enable systems to recommend content that addresses specific skill gaps, ensuring learners receive targeted support.

Similarly, 21st-century learning frameworks, such as the P21 Partnership for 21st Century Skills (Gisore, 2023; Pecson et al., 2024), emphasize the development of critical thinking, collaboration, communication, and creativity, guiding AI-driven adaptations to reinforce these competencies. Alignment with global development goals, particularly the UN Sustainable Development Goals (SDG 4) on inclusive and equitable quality education, further ensures that adaptive learning systems promote lifelong learning while helping reduce educational disparities worldwide.

Several contemporary implementations showcase the integration of adaptive AI with educational standards (Tan, 2025). For example, Carnegie Learning's MATHia (Carnegie Learning, 2025) employs cognitive models to personalize learning experiences for individual students, aligning each activity with the Common Core State Standards. This approach has enabled educators to monitor class-wide progress relative to benchmarks. At Carnegie Mellon University, the Open Learning Initiative (OLI, 2025) utilizes structured analytics aligned with competency-based frameworks, offering modular courses where learner interactions are linked to measurable outcomes. Research indicates that students using OLI materials performed as well or better in half the time compared to traditional courses.

Smart Sparrow (SS 2025), part of Pearson since 2020, has been provided adaptive STEM courseware (Dritsas, 2025) that can be tagged to custom curriculum maps or global educational goals. This capability allows educators to author lessons with embedded learning objectives, which the system uses to adjust sequencing and feedback dynamically.

Adaptive AI is also advancing education in low-resource contexts. Platforms such as Kolibri (Learning Equality) (Kolibri, 2025) and Rumie implement open standards (Rumie, 2025) and lightweight AI to deliver SDG-aligned learning experiences (Glasser et al., 2018; Buerkle et al., 2023). These platforms has been adapting content delivery to user behavior while maintaining relevance to local curricula and community needs. By embedding metadata and tagging schemes directly into learning objects, these systems have tried to provide granular personalization without losing sight of broader educational objectives, demonstrating how standards-based AI can enhance equity, accessibility, and quality in diverse learning environments.

6.1 Takeaway

Designing standards-based adaptive learning systems requires a thoughtful integration of AI personalization with established educational benchmarks. By embedding interoperability through metadata and analytics, these systems ensure personalized learning pathways remain aligned with shared curricular goals. This approach transforms personalization from potential fragmentation into a scalable, transparent, and equitable bridge between individual learner needs and broader educational objectives.

7. BALANCING PERSONALIZATION AND PRIVACY

Personalized learning systems rely heavily on collecting and analyzing learner data to tailor educational experiences. However, this dependence on data raises critical concerns about privacy, data security, and learner autonomy. Balancing the benefits of AI-driven personalization with robust privacy protections is essential to foster trust and ensure ethical educational practices.

7.1 Data Minimization and Differential Privacy in AI Applications

A foundational strategy for protecting learner privacy is data minimization, which mandates collecting only the data strictly necessary to achieve personalization objectives. By restricting collection to essential information, this principle mitigates exposure to potential breaches and reduces the risk of misuse of sensitive learner data. Data minimization is a cornerstone concept across global privacy frameworks—including the GDPR—and remains pivotal in shaping privacy-by-design systems (Bu, 2020; Adapa, 2024).

Complementing this, differential privacy introduces carefully calibrated noise into datasets or query outputs, enabling AI systems to derive meaningful insights while limiting the identifiability of individual learners, a critical element for ethical and legally compliant deployment in educational analytic. Recent work by Pan and his team delivered a thorough survey of differentially private methods in centralized deep learning, exposing both their capabilities and limitations in balancing privacy and utility (Pan, 2024). Further, Alzoubi & Mishra (2025) have explored the synergy between differential privacy and AI—highlighting DP's role in promoting responsible AI, facilitating anonymized data exchange, and reducing bias, even as it underscores persistent challenges like accuracy degradation, computational demands, and scalability hurdles (Alzoubi, 2025).

7.2 Federated Learning and Secure Multi-Party Computation as Alternatives

Emerging architectural approaches in privacy-preserving AI, such as federated learning (Yang, 2019) and secure multi-party computation (SMPC) (Bhattacharya et al.,2023;Liu, 2024), have offered compelling alternatives to centralized data storage for safeguarding learner privacy. In federated learning (Banabilha, 2022), the model is trained locally on institutions' or learners' devices; only the encrypted model is updated. Raw data which are not updated, are shared and merged by a central server. This method significantly curtails data exposure while maintaining capabilities for continuous personalization and improvement. A foundational reference is the comprehensive monograph Advances and Open Problems in Federated Learning (2021), which articulates FL's capacity to reduce systemic risks tied to centralized data storage (Kairouz et al., 2021). More recently, Khalil, Shakya, and Liu (2025) experimentally demonstrated that, in educational contexts, federated learning attains predictive performance on par with traditional centralized methods—and exhibits enhanced resilience to adversarial attacks (Khalil et al., 2025)

Complementarily, Secure Multi-Party Computation (SMPC) enables multiple parties to collaboratively compute functions over their private inputs without revealing those inputs. This ensures learner data remains encrypted and private throughout collaborative training and evaluation, while still supporting effective data-driven educational interventions. SMPC is now well-established in cryptographic research for privacy-preserving computation (Zhou et al., 2024). Its practical viability is underscored in domains such as healthcare, where SMPC techniques like garbled circuits have been successfully applied to cross-institutional risk stratification without exposing individual-level data (Dong, 2021).

7.3 Consent, Explainability, and Learner Agency

Beyond technical safeguards, ethical personalization requires that one ensure that learners give informed consent and maintain ongoing control over their data. AI systems should deliver clear, accessible explanations about what data are being collected, how they're processed, and how decisions around personalization are made, empowering learners to make genuinely informed choices. Slade & Prinsloo

(2013) have underscored the ethical necessity of transparent data practices to preserve trust and respect learner autonomy (Slade et al., 2013). Promoting learner agency also means offering individuals the option to opt in or out of data sharing, customize their privacy settings, and understand the trade-offs between the benefits of personalization and potential privacy risks. Williamson & Eynon (2020) have highlighted the critical importance of transparency in algorithmic processes, data surveillance, and ethical logic in AI-driven education (Williamson et al., 2020; Williamson, 2024). Such transparency not only fosters trust but also aligns with established legal frameworks like the GDPR. Voigt & von dem Bussche's practical guide (2017) emphasizes data subject rights around informed consent, clear access to information, and control over automated decision-making (Voigt et al., 2017). Moreover, emerging AI-specific legislation—such as the forthcoming EU AI Act—places strong emphasis on accountability, transparency, and human oversight in AI systems, reinforcing the need for ethical personalization aligned with legal mandates (Ebers, 2021).

7.4 Takeaway

Balancing personalization and privacy demands a multi-layered strategy combining data minimization, advanced privacy-preserving AI techniques, and ethical principles centered on consent and transparency. Prioritizing learner agency and secure data practices ensures personalized learning can thrive without compromising privacy or trust.

8. ETHICAL AND REGULATORY CONSIDERATIONS

AI becomes increasingly embedded in educational environments, navigating ethical and regulatory landscapes is essential to safeguard learners and promote equitable outcomes. This section discusses ethical AI frameworks tailored for education, key legal compliance requirements, and the critical role of standardization bodies and cross-sector collaboration in shaping responsible AI deployment.

8.1 Ethical AI Frameworks for Education

Ethical AI in education is anchored in foundational values like fairness, transparency, accountability, and learner autonomy—concepts elaborated in global ethical AI discourse (Jobin et al., 2019). UNESCO's Recommendation on the Ethics of Artificial Intelligence (UNESCO, 2021) further stresses inclusive access, non-discrimination, and the protection of human dignity—urging educational institutions and AI developers to embed such ethical principles throughout the entire AI lifecycle, from design to deployment and ongoing assessment (Floridi et al., 2019).Within educational contexts, ethical AI efforts must particularly target equity by design, ensuring systems do not reinforce disparities but instead uplift marginalized learners. W. Holmes and K. Porayska-Pomsta have advocated for bias detection and mitigation, and emphasized the need for interpretability and explainability, so educators and learners alike can interact with and understand AI decisions transparently and meaningfully (Holmes et al., 2022).

To further support interpretability, Zhou and his team presented a thorough evaluation framework for machine learning explanations, detailing attributes like simplicity (parsimony) and fidelity, and highlighting the role of human-centered metrics such as trust and confidence in assessing explanation quality (Zhou et al., 2021).

8.2 Compliance with Legal and Policy Frameworks

Alongside ethical imperatives, compliance with legal and regulatory frameworks is a non-negotiable foundation of responsible AI in education. These laws define the standards for handling personal and educational data, shaping how AI systems must be designed, deployed, and governed. Let us list the major of them as follows:

- GDPR (General Data Protection Regulation, EU) establishes comprehensive rules for processing personal data, emphasizing lawful bases, explicit consent, data minimization, and enforceable rights to access, portability, rectification, and erasure. Its extraterritorial scope has influenced data governance practices globally (Voig et al., 2017).
- COPPA (Children's Online Privacy Protection Act, US) regulates online collection of personal information from children under 13, requiring verifiable parental consent and transparent data usage practices (Federal Trade Commission, 2020). This is particularly crucial for AI-powered platforms targeting younger learners.
- FERPA (Family Educational Rights and Privacy Act, US) safeguards the privacy of student education records, granting parents and eligible students rights over inspection, amendment, and disclosure, ensuring AI-driven learning analytics comply with student record protections (U.S. Department of Education, 2021).
- LGPD (Lei Geral de Proteção de Dados, Brazil) aligns closely with GDPR principles, regulating the collection and use of personal data across sectors, including education. It introduces rights to data access, correction, portability, and erasure, and mandates the designation of data protection officers in

educational institutions processing sensitive data (Brazilian Data Protection Law LGPD, 2020).

- APPI (Act on the Protection of Personal Information, Japan) requires organizations—including educational institutions—to specify the purpose of data use, obtain consent for sensitive data, and implement safeguards for cross-border transfers. Amendments in 2022 strengthened transparency and individual rights, bringing APPI closer to GDPR-level protections (Greenleaf et al., 2021).

Together, these frameworks highlight the global movement toward stronger learner data protections, reflecting common principles: lawfulness, transparency, accountability, and user rights.

To ensure compliance, AI systems in education must embed privacy-by-design (Cavoukian, 2010; Cavoukian et al., 2010), implement robust security measures, and empower learners and guardians with meaningful control over personal data. Beyond mitigating legal risks, such measures reinforce trust, legitimacy, and fairness, ensuring AI contributes positively to educational ecosystems.

8.3 Role of Standardization Bodies and Cross-Sector Collaboration

Standardization bodies such as IEEE, ISO, and OECD, along with regional initiatives like the EU AI Act, play a central role in shaping the ethical, safe, and interoperable use of AI in education. By developing guidelines and standards, they provide a foundation for technical design, assessment protocols, and governance frameworks. Equally important is cross-sector collaboration: educators, policymakers, technologists, ethicists, and civil society must work together to harmonize standards and ensure regulatory frameworks evolve in step with rapid technological change. Such multi-stakeholder partnerships enable knowledge sharing, coordinated oversight, and the co-creation of AI systems that are not only innovative but also firmly rooted in societal needs and values.

8.4 Takeaway

Ethical and regulatory considerations are foundational to trustworthy AI in education. By embedding ethical frameworks, ensuring compliance with legal protections, and fostering cross-sector collaboration through standardization bodies, stakeholders can collectively promote AI systems that are fair, transparent, and respectful of learner rights.

9. BEST PRACTICES AND IMPLEMENTATION GUIDELINES

The successful integration of AI-driven personalized learning systems depends on coordinated efforts across developers, educators, and policymakers. This section outlines actionable recommendations tailored to each stakeholder group, promoting ethical design, responsible use, and effective governance to maximize AI's educational benefits while minimizing risks.

9.1 Recommendations for Developers: Ethical Design and Model Auditing

Developers play a pivotal role in creating AI systems that are fair, transparent, and aligned with educational goals. Best practices include ethical design principles in order to integrate fairness, inclusivity, and privacy-by-design from the outset and to conduct regular bias audits to detect and mitigate disparities across demographic groups (Mehrabi et al., 2019; Floridi et al., 2019). Regarding explainability and transparency, it is important to develop interpretable models that allow educators and learners to understand decision-making processes, supporting trust and accountability (Czerwinska, 2022; Guidotti et al., 2018). In term of robustness testing and validation, it is important to use diverse, representative datasets for model training and testing to enhance generalizability and reduce overfitting. Employing continuous monitoring enables to detect performance degradation or emerging biases post-deployment (Mitchell et al., 2021). Finally, in term of model auditing, best practices focus on establishing formal auditing protocols to assess ethical compliance, privacy safeguards, and educational efficacy before and during deployment (Raji et al., 2020).

9.2 For Educators: Responsible Adoption and Human-in-the-Loop Practices

Educators act as intermediaries between AI systems and learners, ensuring that technology augments rather than replaces human judgment. Guidelines include (1) critical engagement in oder to develop an informed understanding of AI capabilities and limitations to interpret recommendations effectively and intervene where necessary (Holmes et al., 2021); (2) human-in-the-loop integration in order to retain active educator involvement in decision-making, especially in assessment and personalized interventions, to preserve human expertise and contextual sensitivity (Luckin, 2017); (3) continuous professional development to participate in training to build AI literacy, enabling critical evaluation and pedagogically sound adoption of AI tools (Zawacki-Richter et al., 2019); and (4) safeguarding learner agency to ensure that students are informed about AI use, can provide consent, and retain meaningful control over their learning choices (Williamson et al., 2020).

9.3 For Policymakers: Policy Alignment, Procurement Criteria, and Oversight

Policymakers shape the regulatory and institutional frameworks within which AI in education operates. Their responsibilities include policy alignment: (1) update education policies to embed ethical AI standards, ensuring technologies support equity, privacy, and high-quality learning outcomes (UNESCO, 2021); (2) procurement criteria to establish clear, enforceable guidelines for selecting AI vendors, emphasizing compliance with ethical, legal, and interoperability requirements (Shahriari et al., 2022); (3) oversight and accountability in order to create mechanisms for monitoring, reporting, and redress to mitigate unintended consequences, discriminatory impacts, or data breaches (Raji et al., 2020); and (4) cross-sector collaboration in order to facilitate dialogue among developers, educators, learners, and civil society to align AI implementation with broader societal values and priorities (Selwyn, 2019).

9.4 Takeaway

Effective AI personalization in education requires collaborative adherence to best practices across development, classroom integration, and governance. Ethical design, active human oversight, and robust policy frameworks collectively ensure AI enhances learning equitably and responsibly.

10. FUTURE DIRECTIONS AND OPPORTUNITIES

As AI continues to reshape education, evolving standards and innovative applications present significant opportunities to enhance personalized learning pathways. This section explores emerging trends and future prospects that can further integrate AI with educational goals, enabling lifelong learning, formative assessment, and trusted credentialing.

10.1 Evolving Standards for Lifelong and Skills-Based Learning Pathways

The trajectory of education is steadily shifting toward lifelong learning and the mastery of practical, real-world skills that extend beyond traditional academic content. For AI standards to genuinely support these dynamic and continuous learning journeys, educational systems have to ensure interoperability across diverse learning platforms, enabling seamless recognition of competencies acquired through formal, non-formal, and informal contexts—thus fostering a learner-centered ecosystem of credentials (Brown et al, 2021). Then the second key issue is to support modular and micro-credential frameworks aligned with real-world skills and workforce standards, empowering learners to construct personalized, evolving profiles over time and to stack competencies as needed for career adaptability (OECD, 2023; Gamage et al., 2025). Finally, educational systems should promote inclusivity and accessibility, ensuring that lifelong learning pathways accommodate diverse learners—regardless of background, needs, or career trajectory—by reducing barriers and enabling equitable participation in skills recognition (Zdunek et al., 2024). By advancing AI-enabled standards in this direction, educational systems will be better positioned to meet evolving learner goals and global workforce demands, fostering a more flexible, equitable, and responsive economy.

10.2 AI-Driven Formative Assessment Aligned with Curriculum Goals

Formative assessment plays a pivotal role in steering instruction and nurturing learner growth. AI brings transformative capabilities to real-time, adaptive formative assessment by enabling: (1) continuous analysis of learner interactions to deliver immediate, actionable feedback that aligns with curriculum standards and learning objectives (Shute et al., 2013); (2)identification of knowledge gaps, misconceptions, and learners' preferred learning styles, thereby informing personalized scaffolding and tailored instructional adjustments (Yesilyurt, 2023); (3) enhanced scalability and precision of assessment, empowering educators to efficiently monitor progress and proactively intervene (Mousa, 2025). The seamless integration of AI-driven formative assessments within established curriculum frameworks hinges on robust standards that uphold the validity, reliability, and transparency of AI-generated insights such as a foundation rooted in evidence-centered design and psychometric rigor (Rahimi et al., 2023).

10.3 Role of AI Standards in Credentialing and Recognition Systems

As digital credentials and recognition systems become more prevalent, AI standards are essential in ensuring the authenticity, security, and interoperability of certificates, badges, and micro-credentials across institutions and platforms (e.g., through blockchain-based frameworks offering immutable, portable credentials) (MacGreal,2023;Jirgensons etal., 2018). They also support transparent issuance criteria with AI-augmented verification, as seen in emerging models integrating AI and blockchain to validate competency claims and automate badge issuance (McGreal, 2024). Additionally, such systems enable learners to accumulate and share verifiable achievements across educational and professional contexts—enhancing mobility and lifelong career development via decentralized, blockchain-secured credential repositories (Awaji et al.,2020). Finally, standardization and AI oversight help build trust and promote equitable recognition of diverse learning pathways by ensuring transparency, authenticity, and learner control.

10.4 Takeaway

The future of AI in education hinges on adaptive, interoperable standards that support lifelong learning, dynamic assessment, and trustworthy credentialing. By advancing these frontiers, stakeholders can unlock AI's full potential to create flexible, learner-centered ecosystems that empower individuals throughout their educational and career journeys.

11. CONCLUSION

Artificial Intelligence holds unprecedented promise to revolutionize education by enabling truly personalized learning experiences that respond to the unique needs, preferences, and aspirations of individual learners. However, as this chapter has outlined, realizing this promise requires more than technological innovation alone. The integration of AI into education must be firmly grounded in rigorous standards that ensure fairness, transparency, privacy, and ethical responsibility.

Standards play a pivotal role in establishing the trustworthiness of AI-driven personalization, providing essential frameworks that align adaptive learning technologies with pedagogical objectives and societal values. They facilitate interoperability across diverse systems, safeguard learner data, and promote equitable access, thereby upholding the integrity of educational processes in an increasingly digital landscape. The collaborative development and widespread adoption of robust, standards-based approaches are critical. Policymakers, educators, developers, and standardization bodies must work in concert to shape adaptive learning ecosystems that are not only effective and scalable but also accountable and inclusive. This collective effort is imperative to unlock the full potential of AI in education—crafting personalized learning pathways that empower all learners while safeguarding their rights and dignity. Through shared commitment to responsible innovation, let us ensure that AI enhances education in ways that are both transformative and trustworthy.

REFERENCES

Adapa, V. R. K. (2024). Navigating the privacy paradox: Balancing AI advancement and data protection in the digital age. *International Journal of Scientific Research in Computer Science. Engineering and Information Technology*, *10*(6), 99–110. DOI: 10.32628/cseit24106158

Ahn, J., Beck, A., Rice, J., & Foster, M. (2021). Exploring people's thoughts about the future of education with artificial intelligence. *Computers and Education: Artificial Intelligence*, *2*, 100010. Advance online publication. DOI: 10.1016/j.caeai.2021.100010

Alzoubi, Y. I., & Mishra, A. (2025). Differential privacy and artificial intelligence: Potentials, challenges, and future avenues. *EURASIP Journal on Information Security*, *2025*(1), 2. Advance online publication. DOI: 10.1186/s13635-025-00203-9

Awaji, B., Solaiman, E., & Marshall, L. (2020). Blockchain-based trusted achievement record system design. In *Proceedings of the 5th International Conference on Information and Education Innovations* (pp. 47–52). Association for Computing Machinery. DOI: 10.1145/3411681.3411689

Berendt, B., Littlejohn, A., & Blakemore, M. (2020). AI in education: Learner choice and fundamental rights. *Learning, Media and Technology*, *45*(3), 312–324. DOI: 10.1080/17439884.2020.1786399

Bhattacharya, S., Vyas, P., Yarradoddi, S., & Dasari, B. Sumathy, Kaluri, R., & Gadekallu, T. R. (2023). Towards smart education in the industry 5.0 era: A mini review on the application of federated learning. In *2023 IEEE Intl Conf on Dependable, Autonomic and Secure Computing, Intl Conf on Pervasive Intelligence and Computing, Intl Conf on Cloud and Big Data Computing, Intl Conf on Cyber Science and Technology Congress (DASC/PiCom/CBDCom/CyberSciTech)* (pp. 0602–0608). IEEE. DOI: 10.1109/dasc/picom/cbdcom/cy59711.2023.10361510

Binns, R. (2018). Fairness in machine learning: Lessons from political philosophy. In *Proceedings of the 1st Conference on Fairness, Accountability and Transparency (FAT* 2018)* (pp. 149–159). PMLR.

Brazilian Data Protection Law (Lei Geral de Proteção de Dados Pessoais – LGPD). Lei No. 13.709, de 14 de Agosto de 2018 (2020). https://www.gov.br/anpd/pt-br/centrais-de-conteudo/outros-documentos-e-publicacoes-institucionais/lgpd-en-lei-no-13-709-capa.pdf

Brown, M., Nic Giolla Mhichíl, M., Beirne, E., & Mac Lochlainn, C. (2021). The global micro-credential landscape: Charting a new credential ecology for lifelong learning. *Journal of Learning for Development*, *8*(2), 228–254. DOI: 10.56059/jl4d.v8i2.525

Buerkle, A., O'Dell, A., Matharu, H., Buerkle, L., & Ferreira, P. (2023). Recommendations to align higher education teaching with the UN sustainability goals – A scoping survey. *International Journal of Educational Research Open*, *5*, 100280. Advance online publication. DOI: 10.1016/j.ijedro.2023.100280

Burrell, J. (2016). How the machine 'thinks': Understanding opacity in machine learning algorithms. *Big Data & Society*, *3*(1). Advance online publication. DOI: 10.1177/2053951715622512

Carnegie Learning. (2025). *MATHia®: The 1-to-1 math coach that makes your life easier*. https://www.carnegielearning.com/solutions/math/mathia/

Cavoukian, A. (2010). *Privacy by Design: The 7 foundational principles*. Information and Privacy Commissioner of Ontario, Canada. https://www.ipc.on.ca/wp-content/uploads/Resources/7foundationalprinciples.pdf

Cavoukian, A., Taylor, S., & Abrams, M. E. (2010). Privacy by Design: Essential for organizational accountability and strong business practices. *Identity in the Information Society*, *3*(2), 405–413. DOI: 10.1007/s12394-010-0053-z

Czerwinska, U. (2022). Interpretability of machine learning models. In *Applied data science in tourism* (pp. 275–303). Springer., DOI: 10.1007/978-3-030-88389-8_14

Deci, E. L., & Ryan, R. M. (2000). The "what" and "why" of goal pursuits: Human needs and the self-determination of behavior. *Psychological Inquiry*, *11*(4), 227–268. DOI: 10.1207/S15327965PLI1104_01

Dhupia, B., & Alameen, A. (2019). Adaptive eLearning system: Conceptual framework for personalized study environment. In *Communications in Computer and Information Science* (pp. 334–342). Springer., DOI: 10.1007/978-981-15-0108-1_31

Dong, X., Randolph, D. A., Weng, C., Kho, A. N., Rogers, J. M., & Wang, X. (2021). Developing high performance secure multi-party computation protocols in healthcare: A case study of patient risk stratification. *AMIA Joint Summits on Translational Science Proceedings AMIA Summit on Translational Science*, *2021*, 200–209. PMID: 34457134

Dritsas, E., & Trigka, M. (2025). Methodological and technological advancements in e-learning. *Information (Basel)*, *16*(1), 56. Advance online publication. DOI: 10.3390/info16010056

Ebers, M., Hoch, V. R. S., Rosenkranz, F., Ruschemeier, H., & Steinrötter, B. (2021). The European Commission's proposal for an Artificial Intelligence Act—A critical assessment by members of the Robotics and AI Law Society (RAILS). *J, 4*(4), 589–603. DOI: 10.3390/j4040043

Eubanks, V. (2018). *Automating inequality: How high-tech tools profile, police, and punish the poor*. St. Martin's Press.

European Commission. (2021). *Proposal for a regulation laying down harmonised rules on artificial intelligence (Artificial Intelligence Act) and amending certain Union legislative acts* (COM/2021/0206 final). https://eur-lex.europa.eu/legal-content/EN/TXT/?uri=CELEX:52021PC0206

Federal Trade Commission. (2020). *Children's Online Privacy Protection Rule ("COPPA")*. https://www.ftc.gov/legal-library/browse/rules/childrens-online-privacy-protection-rule-coppa

Floridi, L., & Cowls, J. (2019). A unified framework of five principles for AI in society. *Harvard Data Science Review, 1*(1). Advance online publication. DOI: 10.1162/99608f92.8cd550d1

Gamage, K. A. A., & Dehideniya, S. C. P. (2025). Unlocking career potential: How micro-credentials are revolutionising higher education and lifelong learning. *Education Sciences, 15*(5), 525. Advance online publication. DOI: 10.3390/educsci15050525

Gisore, B. N. (2023). Integration of 21st century skills into teacher education curriculum. In *Advances in higher education and professional development* (pp. 225–238). IGI Global. DOI: 10.4018/978-1-6684-6339-0.ch013

Glasser, H., Rea, A., & Green, I. (2018). Catch: A new, SDG-aligned learning for transformative change game. *Sustainability, 11*(3), 111–117. DOI: 10.1089/sus.2018.29134.hg

Greenleaf, G., & Makiyama, T. (2021). Japan's APPI amendments: Asia's first GDPR convergence? *Privacy Laws & Business International Report, 171*, 18–21. https://papers.ssrn.com/sol3/papers.cfm?abstract_id=3818994

Guidotti, R., Monreale, A., Ruggieri, S., Turini, F., Giannotti, F., & Pedreschi, D. (2019). A survey of methods for explaining black box models. *ACM Computing Surveys, 51*(5), 93. Advance online publication. DOI: 10.1145/3236009

Holmes, W., Bialik, M., & Fadel, C. (2021). *Artificial intelligence in education: Promises and implications for teaching and learning*. Center for Curriculum Redesign.

Holstein, K., Wortman Vaughan, J., Daumé, H., III, Dudík, M., & Wallach, H. (2019). Improving fairness in machine learning systems: What do industry practitioners need? In *Proceedings of the 2019 CHI Conference on Human Factors in Computing Systems* (Paper 600). Association for Computing Machinery. DOI: 10.1145/3290605.3300830

IEEE. (2020). *Ethically aligned design: A vision for prioritizing human well-being with autonomous and intelligent systems* (2nd ed.). IEEE Global Initiative on Ethics of Autonomous and Intelligent Systems. https://standards.ieee.org/content/dam/ieee-standards/standards/web/restricted/eadv2_2020.pdf

IEEE 9274.1.1-2023. *IEEE standard for learning technology—JavaScript Object Notation (JSON) data model format and Representational State Transfer (RESTful) web service for learner experience data tracking and access.* IEEE Standards Association. (2023).

IMS Global Learning Consortium. (2020). *Caliper Analytics 1.2 specification.* https://www.imsglobal.org/spec/caliper/v1p2

Jirgensons, M., & Kapenieks, J. (2018). Blockchain and the future of digital learning credential assessment and management. *Journal of Teacher Education for Sustainability, 20*(1), 145–156. DOI: 10.2478/jtes-2018-0009

Jobin, A., Ienca, M., & Vayena, E. (2019). The global landscape of AI ethics guidelines. *Nature Machine Intelligence, 1*(9), 389–399. DOI: 10.1038/s42256-019-0088-2

Kabudi, T., Pappas, I., & Olsen, D. H. (2021). AI-enabled adaptive learning systems: A systematic mapping of the literature. *Computers and Education: Artificial Intelligence, 2*, 100017. Advance online publication. DOI: 10.1016/j.caeai.2021.100017

Kairouz, P., McMahan, H. B., Avent, B., Bellet, A., Bennis, M., Nitin Bhagoji, A., … Zhao, S. (2021). Advances and open problems in federated learning. *Foundations and Trends® in Machine Learning, 14*(1–2), 1–210. DOI: 10.1561/2200000083

Khalil, M., Shakya, R., & Liu, Q. (2025). Towards privacy-preserving data-driven education: The potential of federated learning. In *2025 International Conference on New Trends in Computing Sciences (ICTCS)* (pp. 113–118). IEEE. DOI: 10.1109/ictcs65341.2025.10989403

Knox, J., Williamson, B., & Bayne, S. (2020). Machine behaviourism: Future visions of 'learnification' and 'datafication' across humans and digital technologies. *Learning, Media and Technology, 45*(1), 31–45. DOI: 10.1080/17439884.2019.1623251

Koedinger, K. R., Corbett, A. T., & Perfetti, C. (2012). The knowledge-learning-instruction framework: Bridging the science–practice chasm to enhance robust student learning. *Cognitive Science*, *36*(5), 757–798. DOI: 10.1111/j.1551-6709.2012.01245.x PMID: 22486653

Learning Equality. (2025). *Kolibri*. https://learningequality.org/kolibri/about-kolibri/

Liu, F., Zheng, Z., Shi, Y., Tong, Y., & Zhang, Y. (2024). A survey on federated learning: A perspective from multi-party computation. *Frontiers of Computer Science*, *18*(1), 181302. Advance online publication. DOI: 10.1007/s11704-023-3282-7

Liu, S., Guo, X., Hu, X., & Zhao, X. (2024). Advancing generative intelligent tutoring systems with GPT-4: Design, evaluation, and a modular framework for future learning platforms. *Electronics (Basel)*, *13*(24), 4876. Advance online publication. DOI: 10.3390/electronics13244876

Luckin, R. (2017). Towards artificial intelligence-based assessment systems. *Nature Human Behaviour*, *1*(3), 0028. Advance online publication. DOI: 10.1038/s41562-016-0028

Luckin, R., Holmes, W., Griffiths, M., & Forcier, L. B. (2016). *Intelligence unleashed: An argument for AI in education*. Pearson. https://www.pearson.com/content/dam/one-dot-com/one-dot-com/global/Files/efficacy-and-research/Intelligence-Unleashed-Publication.pdf

Ma, W., Adesope, O. O., Nesbit, J. C., & Liu, Q. (2014). Intelligent tutoring systems and learning outcomes: A meta-analysis. *Journal of Educational Psychology*, *106*(4), 901–918. DOI: 10.1037/a0037123

McGreal, R. (2023). Blockchain and micro-credentials in education. *Journal of Distance Education*, *38*(1). Advance online publication. DOI: 10.55667/ijede.2023.v38.i1.1250

McGreal, R. (2024). Empowering micro-credentials using blockchain and artificial intelligence. In *Global perspectives on micro-learning and micro-credentials in higher education* (pp. 75–90). IGI Global., DOI: 10.4018/979-8-3693-0343-6.ch006

Mehrabi, N., Morstatter, F., Saxena, N., Lerman, K., & Galstyan, A. (2022). A survey on bias and fairness in machine learning. *ACM Computing Surveys*, *54*(6), 115. Advance online publication. DOI: 10.1145/3457607

Meyer, A., Rose, D. H., & Gordon, D. (2014). *Universal design for learning: Theory and practice*. CAST Professional Publishing.

Mitchell, M., Wu, S., Zaldivar, A., Barnes, P., Vasserman, L., Hutchinson, B., & Gebru, T. (2019). Model cards for model reporting. In *Proceedings of the Conference on Fairness, Accountability, and Transparency* (pp. 220–229). Association for Computing Machinery. DOI: 10.1145/3287560.3287596

Mousa, M. (2025). AI-supported formative assessments: Enhancing student-centered learning and teacher perceptions. *Journal of Pedagogy and Education Science, 4*, 127–141. DOI: 10.56741/jpes.v4i02.857

OECD. (2019). *OECD recommendation of the Council on Artificial Intelligence*. https://legalinstruments.oecd.org/en/instruments/OECD-LEGAL-0449

OECD. (2023). *Micro-credentials for lifelong learning and employability: Uses and possibilities* (OECD Education Policy Perspectives, No. 66). OECD Publishing. DOI: 10.1787/9c4b7b68-en

Open Learning Initiative. (2025). https://oli.cmu.edu/

Pan, K., Ong, Y.-S., Gong, M., Li, H., Qin, A. K., & Gao, Y. (2024). Differential privacy in deep learning: A literature survey. *Neurocomputing, 589*, 127663. Advance online publication. DOI: 10.1016/j.neucom.2024.127663

Pecson, R., & Sarmiento, J. (2024). Integrating 21st-century skills into instructional materials for sustainable education. *Indonesian Journal of Instructional Media and Model, 6*(2), 89–99. DOI: 10.32585/ijimm.v6i2.5934

Rahimi, S., & Shute, V. J. (2023). Stealth assessment: A theoretically grounded and psychometrically sound method to assess, support, and investigate learning in technology-rich environments. *Educational Technology Research and Development*. Advance online publication. DOI: 10.1007/s11423-023-10232-1

Raji, I. D., Smart, A., White, R. N., Mitchell, M., Gebru, T., Hutchinson, B., & Barnes, P. (2020). Closing the AI accountability gap. In *Proceedings of the 2020 Conference on Fairness, Accountability, and Transparency* (pp. 33–44). Association for Computing Machinery. DOI: 10.1145/3351095.3372873

Regan, P. M., & Jesse, J. (2019). Ethical challenges of edtech, big data and personalized learning: Twenty-first century student sorting and tracking. *Ethics and Information Technology, 21*(3), 167–179. DOI: 10.1007/s10676-018-9492-2

Ritter, S., Anderson, J. R., Koedinger, K. R., & Corbett, A. (2007). Cognitive Tutor: Applied research in mathematics education. *Psychonomic Bulletin & Review, 14*(2), 249–255. DOI: 10.3758/bf03194060 PMID: 17694909

Rumie. (2025). *Welcome to Rumie.* https://learn.rumie.org/jR/bytes/welcome-to-rumie/

Selwyn, N. (2019). *Should robots replace teachers? AI and the future of education.* Polity Press.

Settles, B., & Meeder, B. (2016). A trainable spaced repetition model for language learning. In *Proceedings of the 54th Annual Meeting of the Association for Computational Linguistics (*Volume 1*: Long Papers)* (pp. 1848–1858). Association for Computational Linguistics. DOI: 10.18637/j.acl16.1175

Shahriari, K., & Shahriari, M. (2017). IEEE standard review — Ethically aligned design: A vision for prioritizing human wellbeing with artificial intelligence and autonomous systems. In *2017 IEEE Canada International Humanitarian Technology Conference (IHTC)*. IEEE. DOI: 10.1109/ihtc.2017.8058187

Shute, V., & Ventura, M. (2013). *Stealth assessment: Measuring and supporting learning in games.* MIT Press., DOI: 10.7551/mitpress/9589.001.0001

Slade, S., & Prinsloo, P. (2013). Learning analytics. *The American Behavioral Scientist, 57*(10), 1510–1529. DOI: 10.1177/0002764213479366

Tan, L. Y., Hu, S., Yeo, D. J., & Cheong, K. H. (2025). Artificial intelligence-enabled adaptive learning platforms: A review. *Computers and Education: Artificial Intelligence, 9*, 100429. Advance online publication. DOI: 10.1016/j.caeai.2025.100429

UNESCO. (2021). *Recommendation on the ethics of artificial intelligence.* https://unesdoc.unesco.org/ark:/48223/pf0000381137

U.S. Department of Education. (2021). *Family Educational Rights and Privacy Act (FERPA).* https://studentprivacy.ed.gov/resources/parent-guide-family-educational-rights-and-privacy-act-ferpa

VanLehn, K. (2011). The relative effectiveness of human tutoring, intelligent tutoring systems, and other tutoring systems. *Educational Psychologist, 46*(4), 197–221. DOI: 10.1080/00461520.2011.611369

Voigt, P., & von dem Bussche, A. (2017). *The EU General Data Protection Regulation (GDPR): A practical guide* (1st ed.). Springer., DOI: 10.1007/978-3-319-57959-7

Walkington, C. A. (2013). Using adaptive learning technologies to personalize instruction to student interests: The impact of relevant contexts on performance and learning outcomes. *Journal of Educational Psychology, 105*(4), 932–945. DOI: 10.1037/a0031882

Williamson, B. (2024). The social life of AI in education. *International Journal of Artificial Intelligence in Education, 34*(1), 97–104. DOI: 10.1007/s40593-023-00342-5

Williamson, B., & Eynon, R. (2020). Historical threads, missing links, and future directions in AI in education. *Learning, Media and Technology, 45*(3), 223–235. DOI: 10.1080/17439884.2020.1798995

Williamson, B., & Piattoeva, N. (2022). Objectivity and subjectivity in AI-driven education: From data infrastructures to psychosocial effects. In Macgilchrist, A., Williamson, B., & Potter, J. (Eds.), *Digital data, education and childhood* (pp. 95–112). Bloomsbury Academic.

Yang, L. (2025). The potential of AI in education: Personalizing learning. *International Journal of Artificial Intelligence for Science, 1*(2). Advance online publication. DOI: 10.63619/ijai4s.v1i2.003

Yang, Q., Liu, Y., Chen, T., & Tong, Y. (2019). Federated machine learning. *ACM Transactions on Intelligent Systems and Technology, 10*(2), 12. Advance online publication. DOI: 10.1145/3298981

Yesilyurt, Y. E. (2023). AI-enabled assessment and feedback mechanisms for language learning. In *Advances in educational technologies and instructional design* (pp. 25–43). IGI Global. DOI: 10.4018/978-1-6684-9893-4.ch002

Zawacki-Richter, O., Marín, V. I., Bond, M., & Gouverneur, F. (2019). Systematic review of research on artificial intelligence applications in higher education – where are the educators? *International Journal of Educational Technology in Higher Education, 16*(1), 39. Advance online publication. DOI: 10.1186/s41239-019-0171-0

Zdunek, K., Dobrowolska, B., Dziurka, M., Galazzi, A., Chiappinotto, S., Palese, A., & Wells, J. (2024). Challenges and opportunities of micro-credentials as a new form of certification in health science education—A discussion paper. *BMC Medical Education, 24*(1), 1169. Advance online publication. DOI: 10.1186/s12909-024-06174-8 PMID: 39425060

Zeide, E. (2017). The structural consequences of big data-driven education. *Big Data, 5*(2), 164–172. DOI: 10.1089/big.2016.0061 PMID: 28632444

Zhou, I., Tofigh, F., Piccardi, M., Abolhasan, M., Franklin, D., & Lipman, J. (2024). Secure multi-party computation for machine learning: A survey. *IEEE Access : Practical Innovations, Open Solutions, 12*, 53881–53899. DOI: 10.1109/access.2024.3388992

Zhou, J., Gandomi, A. H., Chen, F., & Holzinger, A. (2021). Evaluating the quality of machine learning explanations: A survey on methods and metrics. *Electronics (Basel)*, *10*(5), 593. Advance online publication. DOI: 10.3390/electronics10050593

Zliobaite, I. (2017). Measuring discrimination in algorithmic decision making. *Data Mining and Knowledge Discovery*, *31*(4), 1060–1089. DOI: 10.1007/s10618-017-0506-1

Chapter 7
AI Literacy in Code: Identifying and Explaining ChatGPT-Generated Programs in Educational Settings

Teeradaj Racharak
Tohoku University, Japan

Chaiyong Ragkhitwetsagul
https://orcid.org/0000-0002-6502-1107
Faculty of Information and Communication Technology, Mahidol University, Thailand

Pachanitha Saeheng
Faculty of Information and Communication Technology, Mahidol University, Thailand

Napat Boongaree
Faculty of Information and Communication Technology, Mahidol University, Thailand

Chutweeraya Sriwilailak
Faculty of Information and Communication Technology, Mahidol University, Thailand

Ekapol Chuangsuwanich
https://orcid.org/0000-0001-6104-4857
Faculty of Engineering, Chulalongkorn University, Thailand

ABSTRACT

The growing use of Generative Pre-trained Transformers (GPTs) or large language models (LLMs) in programming education has raised concerns about academic dishonesty and the trustworthiness of student submissions. To support educators in evaluating programming skills, it is crucial to identify whether code is written by students or generated by models like ChatGPT. This chapter introduces a framework consisting of two key components: (1) a supervised learning-based detector that distinguishes between human-written and ChatGPT-generated code, and (2) a novel post-hoc explanation mechanism that leverages GPT models to produce human-

DOI: 10.4018/979-8-3373-2235-3.ch007

readable justifications for each classification. By combining accurate detection with interpretable explanations, the framework enhances assessment transparency, fosters educator trust, and supports academic integrity in AI-assisted learning environments.

1 INTRODUCTION

In recent years, large language models (LLMs) like ChatGPT, Gemini, and Claude have significantly impacted the way programming is taught and learned. These tools provide valuable assistance to beginners by generating code, offering quick solutions, simplifying complex concepts, reducing cognitive load, and making programming more accessible (Yan, Chen, Hu, & Ye, 2025). However, while LLMs help students overcome initial hurdles, there is a risk that increased reliance on these tools may hinder the development of fundamental programming skills, particularly algorithmic thinking, i.e., students' ability to independently solve programming tasks (Joˇst, Taneski, & Karakatiˇc, 2024). As students begin to depend more on LLMs for solutions, they may miss out on the opportunity to engage with the problem-solving process and fully understand key concepts required for long-term success.

One of the main concerns is that students may rely too heavily on AI-generated code when completing programming assignments. While AI tools provide quick and advanced solutions, they may not reflect a student's true understanding or skill set. This easy access to AIgenerated solutions undermines the learning process by allowing students to skip crucial steps in problem-solving and code development, which are essential for acquiring a deep understanding of programming. The most pressing issue, however, is the potential for academic dishonesty. As AI-generated code becomes more prevalent, there is an increasing risk that students will pass off AI-generated code as their own, compromising the integrity of academic assessments (Hoq et al., 2024; Nguyen et al., 2024). This makes it difficult for educators to accurately evaluate student progress and knowledge. Being able to distinguish between human-written and AIgenerated code is crucial for maintaining fairness and validity in academic evaluations (Pirntke & Rindebrant, 2024).

Differentiating computer programs that are written by LLMs from those written by humans is not an easy task. Since the LLMs also learn from the human-written programs, the code they generate is mostly syntactically correct and somewhat reminiscent of human-written code. Moreover, depending on the number of student submissions, educators may not be able to manually and carefully review all student programs to ensure originality. To address this, some Learning Management Systems (LMSs) have begun integrating code similarity and AI-detection tools. For example, Moodle supports plagiarism plugins such as MOSS (Aiken, 1994) and JPlag (Prechelt, Malpohl, & Philippsen, 2002) for source code, while commercial platforms like CodeGrade (CodeGrade B.V., 2025) and Turnitin (Turnitin LLC, 2025) now provide integrated modules to flag potential AI-generated content. These systems can automatically highlight suspicious patterns and offer explanations or similarity reports to assist educators in understanding why a piece of code may be considered inauthentic. In parallel, several research studies have proposed machine-learning approaches to detect GenAI code (Wang, Z., et al., 2024); Hoq et al., 2024; Pirntke & Rindebrant, 2024; Nguyen et al., 2024). However, most of these methods still function as black-box classifiers, labeling programs as "GenAI" or "human-written" without providing transparent reasoning.

This research addresses the aforementioned gap by developing an automated method to detect code generated by large language models (LLMs) and introducing a novel post-hoc explanation approach to interpret the detection results. Unlike prior work that relies on traditional explainable AI techniques, our method leverages GPT models to generate humanreadable explanations. Specifically, we adopt a local neighborhood sampling strategy (Pawar, Beder, O'Reilly, & O'Shea, 2024), in which perturbed code samples are generated around the instance of interest. These neighborhood samples help identify key features and patterns that distinguish AI-generated code from human-written code, enabling the GPT-based explainer to articulate why a specific classification was made. This helps educators understand the reasoning behind each identification and highlights the specific patterns and anomalies typical of AI-generated content. By doing so, our method enhances the accuracy of academic assessments, ensuring that they more accurately reflect student learning and effort. This approach is critical for maintaining academic integrity while fostering an educational environment where genuine learning is prioritized (Hoq et al., 2024). Moreover, by identifying AI-generated code, educators can better understand where students may need more practice with critical skills, such as problem-solving and algorithm design.

2 BACKGROUND

2.1 Academic Dishonesty

Academic dishonesty encompasses unethical behaviors that compromise the integrity of academic work (Northern Illinois University, 2024). Plagiarism, one of the most common forms, involves using someone else's work, ideas, or words without proper acknowledgment, ranging from copying text verbatim to paraphrasing without citation. Cheating also plays a significant role, where students use unauthorized materials or assistance during exams or assignments, such as copying from peers or using notes during closed-book exams.

Other offenses include fabrication, which involves falsifying data, information, or citations, and facilitation, where a student aids another in committing dishonesty, like providing answers or writing papers. Deception, such as misrepresenting attendance or submitting false research study information, also falls under academic dishonesty. These actions undermine academic integrity and can lead to severe consequences for students.

2.2 Generative AI

Generative AI (GenAI) (IBM, 2023) is a transformative branch of artificial intelligence focused on creating original content, such as text, images, audio, and software code, in response to user prompts. Unlike traditional AI systems, generative AI uses deep learning models to simulate human-like decision-making by identifying patterns within vast datasets, allowing it to generate relevant and contextually appropriate content.

The rise of generative AI has led to significant advancements across various industries, boosting productivity, streamlining workflows, and enhancing products and services. Many organizations have already begun integrating generative AI into their operations, with studies indicating even broader adoption in the near future. However, several challenges persist, including concerns about bias, security, and the accuracy of generated content. Developing generative AI systems remains resource-intensive, often requiring the creation of foundational models trained on massive datasets, followed by fine-tuning for domain-specific applications. The field continues to evolve rapidly, with innovations such as Variational Autoencoders (VAEs), Generative Adversarial Networks (GANs), and Transformer-based architectures driving the creation of high-quality content and solidifying generative AI's central role in modern technologies.

Generative AI is advancing at an unprecedented pace, with several flagship models driving innovation across natural language processing, content creation, and a wide range of applications. The following highlights some of the most influential models as of 2024:

1. **ChatGPT** (Charan, 2022): ChatGPT, developed by OpenAI, is one of the most widely adopted conversational AI systems. It is highly effective in managing open-domain dialogues, addressing complex queries, and supporting creative writing as well as language translation. Offered in both free and premium versions, ChatGPT is extensively used for interactive communication, content generation, and educational support.

2. **Gemini** (Google, 2024): Gemini, introduced by Google and built on the LaMDA architecture, is tailored for tasks such as code generation, content creation, and natural dialogue. The model emphasizes flexibility and ethical AI design, positioning it as a strong competitor to GPT-4, especially in domains like programming and software development.
3. **LLaMA** (Meta AI, 2023): Meta's LLaMA (Large Language Model Meta AI) is an adaptable and resource-efficient model optimized for scalability. It supports diverse applications including code automation, academic research, and content production, while prioritizing computational efficiency without sacrificing performance.
4. **Claude** (Anthropic, 2024): Claude, created by Anthropic, is an AI assistant designed with a strong emphasis on ethical alignment. It excels at processing large volumes of text, providing structured and transparent responses, and assisting with automation, programming, and casual dialogue. Its focus on responsible AI practices makes it particularly well-suited for sensitive domains such as healthcare and finance.

2.3 Adoption of Generative AI in Education

Generative AI is improving education by enhancing learning tools such as chatbots, content creators, and adaptive learning platforms. AI-powered tutoring programs, for example, offer personalized, real-time feedback, simulating one-on-one tutoring sessions. Tools like OpenAI's Codex and Khan Academy's AI assistant are also automating assignments, tests, and essays, while offering specialized resources like simplified explanations and language assistance.

In higher education, universities are experimenting with generative AI for research, helping researchers analyze large datasets and write academic papers more efficiently. However, the reliance on AI-generated content raises concerns about academic integrity, assessment, and evaluation. In programming courses, AI tools like OpenAI's Codex (OpenAI, 2024) assist students in writing, debugging, and understanding code. University College London (UCL) has integrated generative AI into their assessments, allowing students to use AI to solve coding problems while also emphasizing their ability to explain and interpret AI-generated solutions (University College London, 2024).

The case study by Hamamra et al. (Hamamra, Mayaleh, & Khlaif, 2024) explores how ChatGPT is integrated into educational practices. According to the study, student participation has been reduced, absences have increased, and there is a decrease in excitement for traditional methods of evaluation. Maintaining academic integrity is difficult since students frequently simply copy and paste texts generated by AI without making modifications, and dealing with sensitive subjects like governance, sexuality, and religion poses challenges. The authors suggest an effective approach that emphasizes critical thinking, creativity, and engagement while establishing specific requirements for the use of AI and providing training for educators and students. To evaluate students' comprehension and minimize their dependency on work produced by artificial intelligence, they recommend converting from product-based to process-based evaluation techniques. The report highlights how critical it is to foster AI literacy among students and educators to promote responsible AI use.

2.4 Generative AI for Computer Science Education

Currently, there is a wide adoption of GenAI in computer science education because of the good performance on coding from the latest GenAI models such as ChatGPT, Gemini, and Claude. There are a few studies regarding the adoption of GenAI in computer science education, discussing the opportunities and challenges.

Schefer-Wenzl et al. (Schefer-Wenzl, Vogl, Peiris, & Miladinovic, 2025) performed a survey about the adoption and utilization of generative AI tools among computer science students at the University of Applied Sciences Campus Vienna in Austria. They reported that 90% of surveyed students use GenAI tools for their studies. ChatGPT is the most frequently used tool. Students primarily use GenAI for generating simplified explanations, programming, and exam preparation. A study of integration of a suite of AI-based software tools into Harvard University's introductory computer science course (CS50) (Liu et al., 2024), found that the students were overwhelmingly positive of the integration, likening the tools to having a personal tutor and appreciating the non-judgmental assistance.

On the other hand, a few studies also raise concerns regarding the usage of GenAI in computer science courses. The concerns include superficial learning, over-reliance on AI, and academic integrity issues due to students potentially taking shortcuts or presenting AI-generated work as their own (Beale, 2025). It highlights the difficulty in verifying originality as AIgenerated code can be syntactically correct and functionally viable. Similarly, a review study by Reihanian et al. (Reihanian, Hou, Chen, & Zheng, 2025) shows that AI blurs the lines between student-authored and AI-generated work, raising concerns about authorship and academic integrity. Over-reliance on AI can diminish students' ability to produce original work and hinder critical thinking.

Thus, it is important for computer science educators to be aware of the students' usage of GenAI for their submissions. However, there is currently limited understanding of how well educators can differentiate GenAI code from student-written code.

2.5 Adoption of Generative AI in Software Development

Generative AI is transforming software development by generating code, creating functions, and automating repetitive tasks. Tools such as GitHub Copilot (GitHub, 2024), powered by OpenAI's Codex (OpenAI, 2024), enhance developer productivity by suggesting relevant code snippets and reducing manual effort. Beyond code generation, generative AI contributes to software engineering by improving documentation, accelerating prototyping, and facilitating automated problem detection. AI-driven approaches also support automated testing, thereby enhancing code quality and reliability. While organizations increasingly adopt these technologies for documentation and issue resolution, challenges persist in mitigating security risks and ensuring the correctness of generated code. Despite these concerns, the potential of generative AI to shorten development cycles and improve product quality is rapidly accelerating its integration into the modern software development lifecycle.

2.6 Manual Detection of GenAI Content

A study by Russell et al. (Russell, Karpinska, & Iyyer, 2025) demonstrates that individuals who frequently use Large Language Models (LLMs) for writing tasks, identified as expert annotators, are remarkably accurate and robust at detecting AI-generated text, even without any specialized training or feedback. The study found that a majority vote among five such experts misclassified only 1 out of 300 non-fiction English articles, achieving near-perfect accuracy, in stark contrast to non-expert annotators who performed near random chance and overestimated their abilities. These human experts proved highly robust against articles generated by different LLMs (GPT-4o, Claude-3.5-Sonnet, o1-pro) and evasion tactics such as paraphrasing and humanization, consistently maintaining high detection rates. Their success stems from relying on a combination of clues, including the overuse of specific AI vocabulary, formulaic sentence and document structures, and a general lack of creativity or originality often found in AI-generated content. Critically, this expert human performance significantly outperformed most commercial and open-source automatic detectors, with only the commercial Pangram model matching their near-perfect accuracy, underscoring the value of human detection for high-stakes settings where explainability and nuanced judgment are crucial, although manual review remains unscalable for high-volume tasks.

2.7 Automated Detection of GenAI Code

The widespread use of AI tools in programming courses, particularly in CS1, has made maintaining academic integrity more challenging. (Hoq et al., 2024) examined a dataset from a CS1 course to differentiate between GenAI-generated and student-written code. Traditional machine learning techniques, such as SVM and XGBoost, as well as advanced models like code2Vec and ASTNN, were used to classify the code. The study found that code2Vec outperformed other models, achieving the highest accuracy of 95%. Overall, AI-generated code was found to be more sophisticated than human-written code, often using structures like ternary operators, which aided in classification. This research highlights the potential for detecting AIgenerated code and provides educators with tools to maintain academic honesty. The findings also suggest that educators should incorporate ethical guidelines on AI use into their teaching to ensure students understand how to use AI tools responsibly, reducing the risk of over-reliance on AI in assignments.

The research study by (Wang et al., 2024) presents an efficient and scalable method for detecting AI-generated text without requiring access to model logits or heavy likelihood computations. Building upon DetectGPT, which measures local curvature of log probabilities under small perturbations, Fast-DetectGPT introduces a fast approximation that estimates this curvature using lightweight sampling strategies. The authors show that Fast-DetectGPT retains comparable or even superior detection accuracy to DetectGPT across various large language models while reducing computational costs by more than an order of magnitude. Extensive experiments on both open-source and commercial LLMs demonstrate that the method generalizes well across domains, effectively distinguishing between human-written and machine-generated text. The proposed approach provides a practical foundation for real-time or large-scale deployment of AI-text detection systems in scenarios where efficiency and accessibility are crucial.

The study by (Nguyen et al., 2024) addresses the challenge of distinguishing AI-generated code from human-written code. With AI tools like ChatGPT generating high-quality code, academic institutions face difficulties in ensuring students' submissions are authentic. GPTSniffer, a CodeBERT-based classifier, helps educators reliably detect AI-generated code and uphold academic integrity.

The methodology involved collecting diverse human-written and GPT-generated code snippets across various languages. Preprocessing steps included standardizing formats, removing comments, normalizing variables, and harmonizing indentation. CodeBERT, optimized for programming language syntax, extracted syntactic and semantic features from the code, which were then used to train the classifier. GPTSniffer outperformed base classifiers like OpenAI's Text Classifier and GPTZero, achieving higher accuracy, precision, recall, and F1 scores. It identified distinguishing features in AI-generated code, such as consistent indentation and uniform variable naming. The tool demonstrated robustness across multiple programming languages, making it a valuable resource for educational institutions. Beyond code detection, GPTSniffer promotes academic integrity and responsible AI use by alerting educators to potential misuse. It also encourages students to develop their coding skills, helping maintain ethical standards in education.

(Pirntke & Rindebrant, 2024) address the challenge of detecting AI-generated content in programming courses, particularly from large language models like GPT, which complicates educators' ability to assess student independence. To tackle this, the study introduced a prototype system integrating Copyleaks, an AI detection tool, within GitLab CI pipelines to automatically identify potentially AI-generated code. Developed in collaboration with Linnaeus University instructors, the system supports popular languages like Python and Java, preprocesses code, and presents detection results directly on GitLab. Testing in a mock course environment showed the system met practical needs, though challenges like false positives and scalability in larger classes remain.

2.8 Prompt Engineering

Prompt engineering is an essential discipline centered on crafting and refining prompts to fully harness the capabilities of large language models (LLMs) such as ChatGPT-3.5 and ChatGPT4. By optimizing how prompts are constructed, researchers and developers can significantly enhance model performance across a wide range of tasks—from answering straightforward questions (Racharak, Jearanaiwongkul, Pooksook, & Takashima, 2025) to tackling complex challenges involving reasoning (Yu, Quartey, & Schilder, 2023) and natural language understanding (Racharak, Ragkhitwetsagul, Sontesadisai, & Sunetnanta, 2025). Effective prompt engineering not only improves the quality, accuracy, and relevance of responses but also provides valuable insights into the strengths and limitations of these models. Key techniques in prompt engineering include:

- **Zero-Shot Prompting** (Wei et al., 2022): Instructs the model to perform a task without examples. This method leverages pre-trained knowledge for tasks like sentiment analysis but may fall short for complex problems.
- **Few-Shot Prompting** (Touvron et al., 2023): Provides a few examples in the prompt, allowing the model to generalize and improve response accuracy, especially for tasks that require understanding context or nuances.
- **Chain-of-Thought Prompting** (Yin et al., 2022): Breaks problems into smaller steps, guiding the model through logical sequences. This is particularly useful for tasks that require complex reasoning, such as mathematical problems or understanding intricate relationships.

These techniques aim to improve model performance, leading to more intelligent and contextaware AI systems.

2.9 Explainable AI (XAI)

Explainable AI (XAI) (IBM, 2023) is a rapidly growing field aimed at making the decisionmaking processes of complex machine learning models more transparent and interpretable. It seeks to address the "black-box" nature of many AI systems by clarifying how specific inputs influence outputs, thereby fostering trust, accountability, and responsible AI use. Prominent state-of-the-art techniques include LIME (Local Interpretable Model-agnostic Explanations) (Ribeiro, Singh, & Guestrin, 2016) and SHAP (SHapley Additive exPlanations) (Lundberg & Lee, 2017)

& Lee, 2017), which approximate a model's local behavior through neighborhood sampling (Pawar et al., 2024). These methods generate perturbed data points around a given input to explain individual predictions. Other approaches, such as counterfactual explanations and saliency maps, highlight critical features or potential changes that affect outcomes (Parajuli & Racharak, 2025). For large language models (LLMs), emerging techniques like natural language justifications (Balog, Radlinski, & Petrov, 2023) produce intuitive, human-readable rationales that make outputs easier to interpret.

Despite their promise, current XAI methods face notable limitations. Neighborhood sampling can yield unstable or inconsistent explanations depending on sampling strategies and parameters. Visualizations such as saliency maps may be inaccessible to non-experts, while natural language justifications risk oversimplifying or misrepresenting the model's reasoning. Moreover, most tools remain focused on explaining individual predictions rather than offering systemic or pedagogical insights into model behavior.

In education, XAI holds significant potential to enhance the transparency and effectiveness of AI-driven systems such as intelligent tutoring, automated grading, and predictive analytics. By clarifying how models assess student work, identify learning gaps, and recommend interventions, XAI enables educators to make more informed, ethical, and student-centered decisions. Although challenges remain, the adoption of XAI techniques represents an important step toward building trustworthy, responsible, and equitable AI for learning environments.

3 HOW DO COMPUTER SCIENCE EDUCATORS DETECT GENERATIVE AI'S CODE?: AN EDUCATOR STUDY

We perform an empirical study of human detection of GenAI-generated code to gain insights into how well computer science educators can manually detect GenAI code. The findings from this preliminary study will motivate our design of an automated technique and tool for detecting and explaining GenAI code.

3.1 Research Questions

In this preliminary study, we aim to answer the following research questions.

1. RQ1: *To what extent can the educators identify GenAI code manually?* We aim to understand how accurately the educators can differentiate GenAI code from human-written code. The answer to this research question will shed light on whether we need an automated tool to help them with the task.
2. RQ2: *What are the clues that the educators used for identifying GenAI code?* For this RQ, we want to know the clues that the educators use to spot GenAI code. The answer to this question may lead to the development of new automated techniques to detect GenAI code.
3. RQ3: *To what extent does familiarity with GenAIs help in identifying GenAI code?* We are interested in whether having familiarity with using GPT models for generating code helps educators recognize GenAI code more easily.

3.2 Methodology

The methodology for this preliminary study is described below.

3.2.1 Experimental Setup

We set up an experiment to answer the research questions as shown in Figure 1, where we divide the experiment into two phases. First, we create a dataset of Java programs, both written by humans and generated by ChatGPT. Second, we hired educators to manually identify GPT programs. We explain the two phases in detail below.

Figure 1. The experimental setup

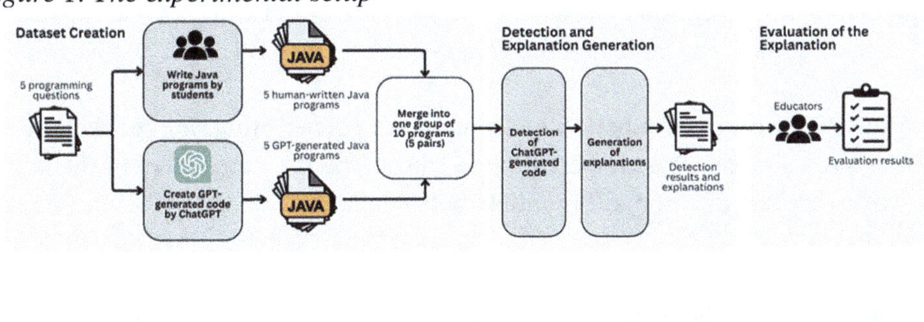

1. **Phase 1 – Dataset Creation:** To represent the actual code written by students, we hired undergraduate students to create Java programs for our study. First, we contacted an educator of the Object-oriented Programming course at the Faculty of Information and Communication Technology, Mahidol University, Thailand, to get 5 programming questions supposed to be written in Java, ranging from easy to hard, from their class. Next, we recruited five undergraduate students who had completed the Object-Oriented Programming class to participate, ensuring that the students possess adequate knowledge for the task.

Five undergraduate students in their third year participated in the code-writing activity. Every participant had already finished the object-oriented programming class and had basic experience in Java development.

The demographics of the students are displayed in Table 2, containing their perceived rating of their Java programming skills on the scale of 1 to 10 and the assigned programming problems

Every student received a distinct programming task and was directed to independently develop a complete solution, without utilizing online resources.

The session took place in a monitored setting on Wednesday, March 19, 2025, between 13:00 and 14:00.

Before participating, all students will be required to sign a consent form. To ensure the authenticity of the submissions, participants will write their code onsite, thereby confirming that the work is entirely their own. Then, we used ChatGPT-4o to generate another version of the code as follows. First, we gave the same programming question that was given to the students to ChatGPT-4o by uploading the PDF of the question and simply instructed the LLM to "*Solve the given problem*". Second, in the case that the question contains part of the code template given with a comment // TO DO, we then instructed the LLM to *"Fill in the TO DO section"*. We refrained from performing any prompt engineering because we tried to represent the actual student usage of LLMs for solving programming problems. It was very unlikely that the undergraduate students who needed help from LLMs would do so.

Lastly, we manually collected the generated code by the LLM[1].

2. **Phase 2 – Manual Detection of GenAI code:** After preparing the dataset, we recruited ten educators to perform the study. The main objective of this phase was to let the educators differentiate between GenAI code and human-written code.

Table 9 displays the background of the ten academic educators who took part in the code evaluation procedure. Every instructor possesses teaching experience in essential computer science topics, including software engineering, database systems, programming fundamentals, computer architecture, and algorithm analysis. The educators were chosen for their knowledge of undergraduate programming courses and their background in code assessment and critique[2].

Each educator was asked to review and compare 5 pairs of code. Each pair consists of one program written by a student and the other generated by ChatGPT. The authors sat with the educators and showed each code pair one at a time. For each pair, we allowed the educators to look at the code pair and make their selection of GenAI code. Lastly, we interviewed the educators on the clues and reasons they used to make such a judgment. The answers were noted for later analysis.

The aim of this step was to determine whether educators could accurately identify which code was human-written and which was generated by an LLM, as well as to understand the structural elements or clues they used to make their judgments.

3.3 Results

3.3.1 RQ1: To what extent can the educators identify GPT code manually?

Table 1 displays the accuracy of each instructor in the five programming questions (Q1–Q5).

Each row represents an educator participating in this study (E1 to E10), where a value of 1 represents a correct identification of GenAI or student code and 0 represents an incorrect one. From the total of 50 guesses (i.e., 5 questions x 10 educators), the educators were able to correctly identify the GenAI code 86% of the time. The question with the highest accuracy of detection is Q5, where the ten educators correctly selected the GenAI code. On the contrary, Q1 has the lowest accuracy, with 7 out of 10 educators correctly guessing the GenAI code. We discuss some of the interesting cases below. For the other questions (Q2, Q3, and Q4), 8, 8, and 9 educators could correctly select the GenAI code, respectively.

Looking at Q5, where all the educators correctly guessed the GenAI code, we made an observation as follows. The code created by ChatGPT is over-engineered. It includes additional helper methods and the use of TreeMap, which may not be selected by students. For Q1, which has the lowest accuracy of 70%, three educators were taken in by ChatGPT's simple structure, which makes the code look like student-written code. Figure 9 shows the code pair of Q1. The left side shows the code written by ChatGPT, and the right side shows the code written by a student. The student who wrote this code evaluated himself/herself as proficient in programming 6 out of 10 (see Table 2). The students wrote nicely formatted and well-organized code with a few code comments and calculation logic in the middle. On the other hand, the GenAI version has more comments and mainly focuses on the input and output of the program. However, the simplicity of the code may confuse the educators as student-written code.

The majority of misunderstandings regarding other questions resulted from instances in which ChatGPT produced less formal or simpler output, simulating actual student submissions and lowering the educators' confidence in GenAI code detection.

Looking at the educator angle, six educators (P2–P7, P10) accurately recognized all five codes generated by the LLM. One educator (P8) faced considerable difficulty, achieving just one accurate identification. Interestingly, this educator mainly teaches mathematics and theoretical computer science classes (e.g., linear algebra and calculus, algorithms, and probability and statistics). So he or she may not be very familiar with Java programming and student code compared to other educators who teach subjects mainly related to programming, such as fundamentals of programming, object-oriented programming, and web development. This finding shows that although the general human accuracy in detecting GenAI code is quite high (86%), some outputs generated by GenAIs can still pose challenges to individual educators based on their interpretation methods or knowledge of AI behaviors.

Table 1. Correct identification results per participant across five questions

Participant	Q1	Q2	Q3	Q4	Q5	Total	Percentage
E1	0	1	1	0	1	3	60%
E2	1	1	1	1	1	5	100%
E3	1	1	1	1	1	5	100%
E4	1	1	1	1	1	5	100%
E5	1	1	1	1	1	5	100%
E6	1	1	1	1	1	5	100%
E7	1	1	1	1	1	5	100%
E8	0	0	0	0	1	1	20%
E9	0	1	1	1	1	4	80%
E10	1	1	1	1	1	5	100%
Total	7	9	9	8	10	43	86%

Table 2. Demographics of students and the assigned programming questions

Student	Programming Skill	Assigned Question
S1	6/10	Q1 Room rental system
S2	8.5/10	Q2 Coffee shop billing system
S3	7.5/10	Q3 Theater System
S4	6.5/10	Q4 GroceryStore System
S5	7/10	Q5 Sorting

Overall, these results indicate that educators can identify GenAI-generated code with high accuracy, especially when the GenAI follows well-defined or structured guidelines.

Answer to RQ1: The ten educators correctly identified the GenAI code with 86% accuracy. Six out of ten educators perfectly identified all the GenAI code.

3.3.2 RQ2: What are the clues that the educators used for identifying GenAI code?

Table 4 outlines the main indicators that educators noted using to differentiate between code generated by GenAIs and code written by students. The clue most commonly cited was Structured and Consistent Formatting, highlighted by 8 educators, which is usually found in GenAI code. The next clue is Detailed and Formal Comments (mentioned by 7 educators), where ChatGPT frequently offered lengthy explanations for straightforward reasoning. The third clue is Patterned and Formal Print Output (6 mentions), which refers to the refined and repetitive character of printing outputs, resembling documentation rather than student code. Other significant clues comprise the use of Descriptive Variable Names (5 mentions), Over-Engineered or Modularized Logic, e.g., superfluous helper methods (4 mentions), and the impression that the code was too perfect for student work (3 mentions). This set of clues indicates that educators depend not just on the logical accuracy of the code but also on stylistic and structural elements when forming their classification of GenAI code. Our findings are corroborated by the study of detecting GenAI-written text by Russell et al. (Russell et al., 2025), that the annotators who excelled at detecting GenAI text rely on both specific lexical clues and more complex writing styles. Moreover, they understood that human writing often contains minor grammatical errors, while GenAI usually creates too-perfect writing output.

Table 3. The demographics of the educators in this study

Educator	Courses Taught	GenAI for Code Familiarity
E1	Computer Organization and Architecture, Principles of Operating Systems	3 (Moderately familiar)
E2	Software Engineering, Information Systems, Entrepreneurship	4 (Very familiar)
E3	Object-Oriented Programming, Computer Graphics	5 (Extremely familiar)
E4	Information Systems, Software Engineering, Entrepreneurship	4 (Very familiar)
E5	Database Systems, Data Visualization, Web Development	4 (Very familiar)
E6	Object-Oriented Programming	4 (Very familiar)
E7	Object-Oriented Programming, Data Structures, Algorithm Analysis	4 (Very familiar)
E8	Linear Algebra and Calculus, Algorithms, Probability and Statistics	1 (Not familiar)
E9	Database Management Systems, Data Visualization	4 (Very familiar)
E10	Fundamentals of Programming	3 (Moderately familiar)

Table 5 presents a detailed analysis of the identification outcomes for each question, showing the number of educators who answered each question incorrectly, along with the rationale behind their choices. This in-depth analysis helps shed light on the challenges and uncertainty of particular programming questions. For instance, Q1 had the greatest number of wrong identifications (3 educators), primarily because ChatGPT's straightforward flat structure was similar to student work, while the student employed object-oriented programming with getters and setters, which tends to appear more formal or organized. In comparison, Q5 achieved a 100% accuracy rate because the ChatGPT version excessively complicated the solution by utilizing TreeMap, sorting, and additional methods such as readFile() and removeDuplicate(), distinguishing it from the simpler student version.

Additionally, Q2 to Q4 displayed some ambiguity, frequently attributed to ChatGPT's neat formatting or structured logic that resembled the work of advanced learners. This table emphasizes that the accuracy of detection relies not just on the validity of logic but also on the resemblance of the structure and style to either humans or AI.

Table 4. Summary of the clues used for spotting GenAI code

clues	Description	Frequency
C1: Structured and Consistent Formatting	LLM code is well-organized, with consistent indentation, logic blocks, and formatting.	8
C2: Detailed and Formal Comments	LLM includes abundant comments that are structured, verbose, and often over-explain.	7
C3: Patterned & Formal Print Output	Output messages have a formal style, which is often too polished.	6
C4: Descriptive Variable Names	LLM uses clear, long, and selfexplanatory names; students often abbreviate or mix cases.	5
C5: Over-engineered or Modularized Logic	GenAI code often uses helper methods or generalized patterns, even when not required.	4
C6: Too Perfect Code	Some educators mentioned it felt too correct to be from a student.	3

Answer to RQ2: The 6 clues that educators used for differentiating GenAI code from student code include structured and consistent formatting, detailed and formal comments, patterned and formal print outputs, descriptive variable names, over-engineered or modularized logic, and too perfect code.

3.3.3 RQ3: To what extent does familiarity with GenAIs help in identifying GenAI code?

Based on the results in Table 9 and Table 1, we can observe some interesting relationships between the familiarity of educators with GenAI and their GenAI code detection performance. As the familiarity level increases, the detection performance tends to increase (0.64 Spearman correlation coefficient). In particular, E8, who is unfamiliar with GenAI for code, significantly underperforms his peers ($p < 0.05$ using the Mann-Whitney U test). On the other hand, experience teaching the Object-Oriented Programming class does not exhibit clear differences against those without ($p > 0.05$). Interestingly, E8 can identify GenAI code with the lowest accuracy (20%), which is lower than random guessing (50%), compared to other participants who are more familiar with GenAI. Future work should aim to disentangle different variables and their effect on detection performance.

Our finding is similar to a study by Russel et al (Russell et al., 2025). They found that people who often use LLMs like ChatGPT-4o and Claude-3.5-Sonnet are better at detecting AIgenerated content. In a study of 300 nonfiction essays, expert readers almost always guessed correctly, which did better than most AI detection tools, even when the text was changed. This shows that people with GenAI experience can be very good at identifying GenAI-created content. Our result shows that their findings may also be applied to source code as well.

Table 5. Per-question confusion analysis during manual identification of GenAI code

Question	Wrong Guesses	Summary of Reasons
Q1	3	GenAI code used simple String variables, while the student version used a class structure (RoomRentCalculator object with getters/setters). Moreover, the GPT version felt more studentlike due to its lack of class encapsulation, i.e., it was less formal and less structured.
Q2	1	GenAI code used a switch-case with .toLowerCase(), which is easy and logical. Some participants thought this was student code. In contrast, the student code used if-else chains and declared static variables globally, which looked more like GenAI logic to one educator.
Q3	1	The student code used a 2D array (int[][] seat) even though it was not needed, which seemed like something a GenAI might do.
Q4	2	ChatGPT used Arrays.toString() and had clear formatting — some evaluators thought a student might copy that from online. Moreover, the student manually printed arrays, reused the same grade variable (g), and had a longer loop, yet some educators believed this looked more like GenAI code due to repetition.
Q5	0	There is no wrong guess for this question, potentially due to the following reasons. First, the code from GenAI has an obviously over-engineered code pattern, such as Insertion sort, a TreeMap for deduplication, and Helper methods (readFile(), removeDuplicate()). Moreover, ChatGPT went beyond the requirement by adding more functionalities, making it easy to identify. The student stuck with just what was asked.

Answer to RQ3: All educators who are extremely or very familiar with using GenAI for code can differentiate GenAI code with high accuracy (80%–100%) while an educator with no familiarity with GenAI shows poorer performance (20%).

The results from this preliminary study show that computer science educators who are familiar with GenAI for code could accurately detect GenAI code submitted by students. Nonetheless, considering the number of submissions that the educators need to go through, it is a tedious and mundane task. We aim to alleviate this issue by introducing the automated detection and explanation of GenAI source code motivated by the clues and the reasons found from this preliminary study. We discuss our proposed approach in the next section.

4 AUTOMATED EXPLAINABLE DETECTION FRAMEWORK FOR GENAI SOURCE CODE

While our empirical study demonstrates that educators can identify GenAI-generated code with reasonably high accuracy, manual detection is neither scalable nor consistently reliable across different contexts and levels of familiarity. The variability in educators' performance, coupled with the increasing volume of student submissions, underscores the necessity of automated approaches. To complement human judgment, research has begun to explore computational methods that not only detect AI-generated code but also provide transparent explanations to support fair and trustworthy academic evaluation. This section introduces our approach to automated detection and explanation of GenAI source code.

4.1 Research Questions

In this section, we frame the research questions for the automated detection and explanation of GenAI source code as follows.

1. RQ1: *How well do the code BERT models perform on detecting GenAI code?* We aim to understand how accurately the state-of-the-art code BERT models can differentiate GenAI code from human-written code. The answer to this research question will lead to the selection of the model for GenAI code detection.
2. RQ2: *To what extent do the generated explanations correlate with the code?* This RQ aims to perform a sanity check of the generated explanations, whether they correlate with the code that they explain or not.
3. RQ3: *How do computer science educators perceive the quality and the usefulness of the explanation?* We aim to evaluate the quality and the usefulness of the explanations by employing several computer science educators to read and give feedback on the explanations.

4.2 Methodology

By leveraging cutting-edge machine learning models and explainability techniques, our approach ensures both robust performance and interoperability. For the detection of GPTgenerated code, we improved upon the work by (Nguyen et al., 2024) by evaluating four advanced models, including CodeBERT, UniXCoder, GraphCodeBERT, and LongCoder, which are highly effective in analyzing code structure and semantics, and selected the best one for the detection tasks. To ensure transparency and understability of the detection, we introduce a novel post-hoc explanation technique inspired by local neighborhood sampling (Pawar et al., 2024). Our core idea is to develop strategies for selecting the neighborhood samples that guide large language models (LLMs) with prompt engineering to generate explanations that satisfy sufficiency and necessity criteria.

4.2.1 Overview of the Proposed Approach

Figure 2 illustrates the proposed technique for detecting and explaining GenAI code, divided into two main phases: **Training** (Section 4.2.2) and **Deployment** (Section 4.2.3). Each stage incorporates specialized modules to ensure accurate classification and provide explainable insights into the model's decisions.

4.2.2 Training

Figure 2. Overview of the proposed approach

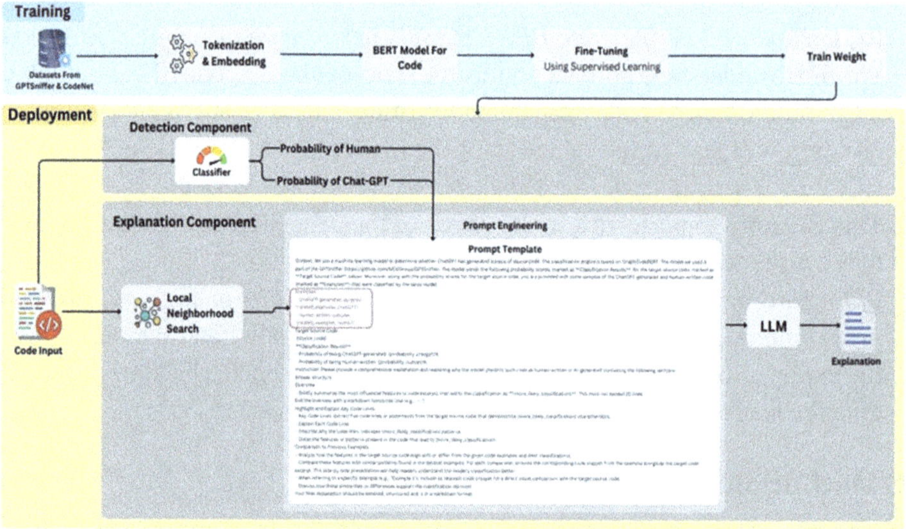

The training phase starts with the data preparation. The process begins with datasets sourced from the previous study (Nguyen et al., 2024; et al., 2024) and CodeNet (Puri et al., 2021), comprising human-written and GPT-generated code. These datasets are carefully curated and tokenized for compatibility with the model. The tokenized data is embedded using the BERT model for code, a pre-trained language model designed for programming languages. The model is then fine-tuned using supervised learning to identify distinguishing features between humanwritten and GPT-generated code. The outcome of this phase is a trained classifier capable of predicting the probability of a code sample being human-written or GenAI-generated.

4.2.3 Deployment

The deployment phase is divided into two interconnected modules: the detection module and the explanation module.

In the detection module, a trained classifier processes the input code and outputs two probabilities: one indicating the likelihood that the code is human-written, and the other representing the likelihood that it is generated by ChatGPT. These probabilistic outputs are then passed to the explanation module, which performs further analysis to interpret and justify the classification decision.

The explanation module receives the detection output, including the probabilities indicating whether a code sample is generated by ChatGPT, and proceeds to generate an interpretable explanation for the classification. The first step involves performing a local neighborhood search, which aims to identify a set of code samples that are semantically similar to the input instance. This process begins by encoding the input code using UniXcoder, a pretrained model for code representation, to obtain a dense embedding that captures the structural and semantic features of the code. These embeddings are then used with FAISS, a high-performance similarity search library, to efficiently retrieve the top-k nearest neighbors from a repository of test samples.

The purpose of this local neighborhood search is to explore how the classifier might behave in the immediate vicinity of the input, which is a common approach in post-hoc explanation for understanding model sensitivity and decision boundaries. The retrieved samples—representing both human-written and GenAI-generated code—are categorized based on their similarity scores and class labels. This local context serves as a foundation for constructing more faithful and contrastive explanations by highlighting how the input differs from or resembles nearby examples. Next, a structured prompt is built using both the classifier's probabilistic outputs and the retrieved neighborhood samples. This prompt includes exemplars and targeted cues to guide the LLM in reasoning about the classification decision. It provides contextual information for why the input code was predicted as either human-written or AI-generated. Finally, the prompt is passed to an LLM, which generates a natural language explanation that reflects both the classifier's prediction and the surrounding neighborhood evidence. The resulting output highlights the most salient code features that influenced the decision (e.g., code patterns, syntax features, or structures influencing the classifier's decision).

This systematic framework ensures accurate detection while maintaining transparency and interpretability, enabling users to understand the rationale behind classification decisions.

4.3 GenAI Code Detection Component

The detection of GenAI code poses significant challenges due to the advanced capabilities of language models such as ChatGPT, which can generate code that is highly similar to humanwritten code. To address these challenges, a specialized detection component is required. This component analyzes code snippets, extracts meaningful features, and applies machine-learning steps to distinguish between human-written and GPT-generated code. The detection process involves several key steps: the models, dataset preparation, model training, and evaluation. The models that are evaluated for GenAI code detection are as follows.

4.3.1 CodeBERT

CodeBERT (Feng et al., 2020) is a transformer-based model designed to learn code representations by training on natural language (NL) and programming language (PL) pairs. This allows CodeBERT to understand the relationship between human-readable text and code functionality, enabling tasks like code summarization, search, and generation. It is particularly useful for detecting GPT-generated code, as its embeddings capture syntax and stylistic markers typical of automated outputs, making it effective in identifying GPT-generated code with less fine-tuning compared to models trained on code data alone.

4.3.2 UniXCoder

UniXcoder (Guo et al., 2022) is a transformer-based model for cross-linguistic code understanding, trained on large datasets from multiple programming languages. It captures semantic and syntactic patterns in both human and GPT-generated code, making it highly effective for code classification and anomaly detection. UniXcoder is multilingual, handling multiple programming languages without requiring separate models, and excels in detecting stylistic patterns typical of machine-generated code, making it valuable for AI code detection and academic integrity applications.

4.3.3 GraphCodeBERT

GraphCodeBERT (Guo et al., 2021) extends the BERT model by integrating code-specific graph structures, such as data flow and syntax graphs, to better understand code logic and execution flow. This graph-based approach allows GraphCodeBERT to distinguish between human-written code and AI-generated patterns, particularly in identifying subtle automation cues like simplified data flows or unusual function dependencies. It is effective for tasks like code translation, summarization, and classification, making it useful for code verification in academic and secure software development.

4.3.4 LongCoder

LongCoder (Guo, Xu, Duan, Yin, & McAuley, 2023) is a transformer-based model optimized for handling long code sequences. Unlike standard transformers that truncate inputs due to fixed-length limitations, LongCoder employs enhanced attention mechanisms to capture long-range dependencies without loss of context. This allows it to model full-file structures, variable relationships, and stylistic patterns more effectively. It is particularly useful for code quality assessment, automated code review, and plagiarism detection in large codebases, where preserving the complete context is crucial.

4.4 Explanation Component

The explanation module provides transparent insights into the classification of source code as either human-written or GenAI (e.g., ChatGPT). It ensures that explanations are accurate, understandable, and meaningful, enabling users to comprehend the reasoning behind each classification. In particular, the module highlights the features that contribute to distinguishing GenAI-generated code from human-written code. To enhance interpretability, our methodology introduces a local neighborhood sampling strategy, which retrieves semantically similar code examples to create contextual contrast around the input. These examples are then integrated through in-context learning, where structured prompts guide an LLM to produce coherent, human-readable explanations. While other studies have explored alternative strategies (Pawar et al., 2024), our local neighborhood sampling approach provides a novel and effective means of generating natural language explanations for predictions, thereby fostering both trust and interpretability.

4.4.1 Local Neighborhood Sampling

Local neighborhood sampling is a foundational technique often used to support post-hoc explanation methods in explainable AI. In post-hoc explanation, the goal is to interpret a model's prediction after it has been made, without altering the internal structure of the model. Local neighborhood sampling contributes to this process by generating or retrieving data points that are similar—but not identical—to the instance being explained. These neighboring instances help approximate the local decision boundary of the model, allowing explanation methods such as LIME, SHAP, or custom strategies to analyze how small input variations affect the output.

By examining model behavior within this localized region, the explanation can highlight which features are most influential and provide insights into the robustness and consistency of the prediction. Thus, local neighborhood sampling plays a critical role in ensuring that post-hoc explanations are both context-aware and locally faithful to the model's actual behavior. The following describes our implementation strategy, centered on using semantic embeddings to represent code meaningfully and facilitate local neighborhood sampling.

The t-SNE visualization (Figure 3) illustrates the semantic relationships between the target source code (highlighted in red) and its neighborhood samples, categorized as human-written (green) and GPT-generated (purple). The projection is constructed using Euclidean distances in the embedding space, where shorter distances correspond to higher semantic similarity. The visualization shows that the retrieved samples cluster closely around the target instance, demonstrating that the neighborhood sampling strategy effectively captures semantically relevant examples. This clustering provides a meaningful contextual foundation for analyzing distinguishing features between GPT-generated and human-written code.

Figure 3. A t-SNE graph between source code and neighborhood samples

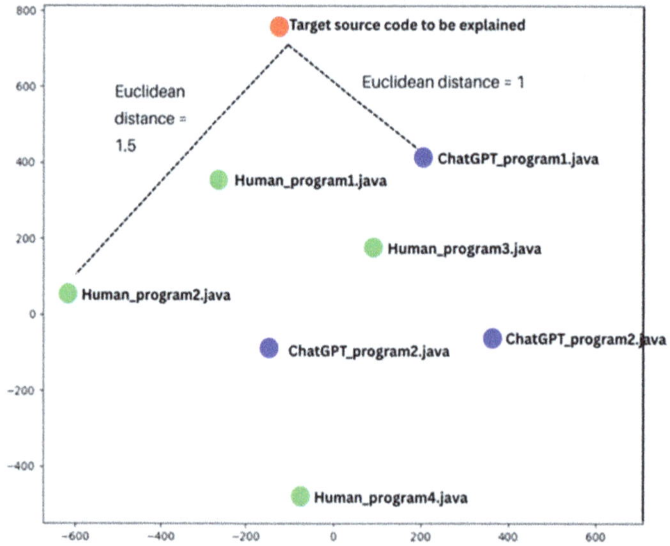

Figure 4. A process of neighborhood sampling module

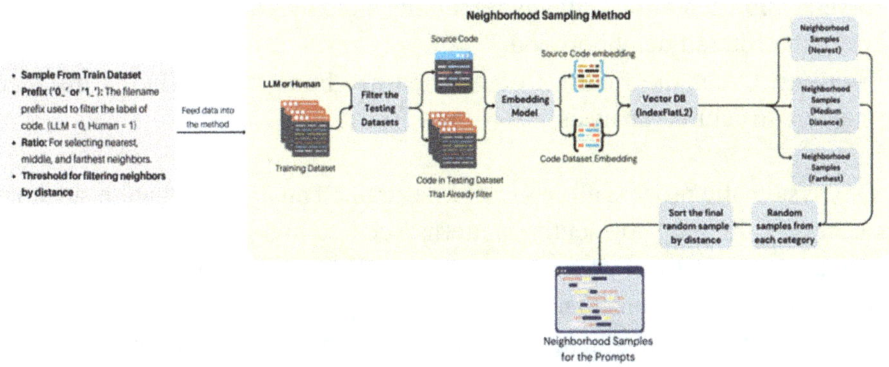

In our research, local neighborhood sampling serves as a core component of the posthoc explanation module. As shown in Figure 4, the strategy identifies semantically similar code samples, which are then incorporated into contextual prompts. These prompts guide a GPT-based explainer to generate coherent, human-readable justifications for the classifier's decisions, thereby clarifying why a given instance is classified as either GenAI-generated or human-written. The process can be outlined in the following steps:

1. **Embedding the target source code:** Generate an embedding of the target source code using UniXcoder, capturing both its structural and contextual properties.
2. **Dataset Filtering:** Filter the dataset for samples with filenames matching a specific category, i.e., GenAI-generated or human-written, to ensure contextually relevant comparisons. Avoid duplicate entries using a set of previously processed filenames.
3. **Embedding the filtered dataset:** Compute embeddings for the filtered samples with UniXcoder and store them in a structured array for efficient indexing.
4. **Indexing with a vector database:** Index all computed embeddings using a vector database, such as FAISS (Facebook AI Similarity Search), enabling efficient nearestneighbor retrieval based on Euclidean distance. Persist the FAISS index on disk to accelerate subsequent queries.
5. **Neighbor Retrieval:** Query the vector database with the target code's embedding to retrieve semantically similar neighbors, applying a similarity threshold to filter out overly dissimilar samples.
6. **Neighbor Categorization:** Partition the retrieved neighbors into three groups according to distance: Nearest ($\approx 70\%$), Middle ($\approx 20\%$), and Farthest ($\approx 10\%$), adjusting proportions as needed to meet the desired sample count.

7. **Random Sampling:** Randomly select instances from each group to ensure diverse representation. Fill any remaining slots by drawing additional samples from the filtered neighborhood.
8. **Sorting:** Order the final set of selected neighbors by ascending distance to support structured analysis.

This systematic process allows for a fine-grained analysis of feature sufficiency and necessity, helping to identify patterns such as syntax structures or variable naming conventions that influence model classification. By providing interpretable and transparent insights, local neighborhood sampling builds user confidence in the model's predictions and adheres to ethical standards for AI transparency.

4.4.2 In-context Learning

In-Context Learning (ICL) is a key capability of large language models (LLMs), enabling them to adapt to new tasks solely based on the contextual information provided in the prompt—without requiring retraining or model fine-tuning. By embedding a few relevant examples or taskspecific instructions directly into the prompt, ICL allows LLMs to generate accurate and context-aware outputs tailored to the immediate task. This makes ICL particularly advantageous in scenarios requiring rapid adaptability, as it eliminates the need for additional data collection or architectural modifications. As a result, LLMs leveraging ICL have been successfully applied across a broad range of domains.

ICL has been extensively investigated in the work of (Tanneru, Agarwal, and Lakkaraju, 2024), which introduced two complementary metrics — Verbalized Uncertainty, which asks LLMs to express confidence in their own explanations, and Probing Uncertainty, which measures stability under input and model perturbations. Through experiments on mathematical word problems and commonsense reasoning datasets using InstructGPT, GPT-3.5, and GPT-4, they find that LLMs' self-reported confidence is often overconfident and unreliable, while probing-based metrics correlate strongly with both faithfulness and answer correctness. The study highlights that explanations with lower uncertainty tend to more accurately reflect the model's reasoning, offering a new pathway for evaluating the trustworthiness of LLM-generated explanations.

In our approach, we apply ICL not for classification directly, but as a component of a "post-hoc explanation framework" aimed at distinguishing GenAI-generated code from humanwritten code. While the classification task itself is performed by a fine-tuned GraphCodeBERT model—similar in architecture to the GPTSniffer system—we leverage ICL to guide a GPTbased explainer in interpreting these classification results. Indeed, the explainer is prompted with the target source code alongside semantically similar code examples, previously labeled as either human-written or GenAI-generated. These neighborhood samples are selected using local neighborhood sampling in the embedding space, based on UniXcoder and FAISS.

The GPT-based explainer uses these in-context examples to generate human-readable justifications. It draws attention to distinguishing characteristics such as coding style, function, and control flow structure, naming conventions, and syntax patterns. By explicitly highlighting these features within the prompt, the model produces clear, interpretable explanations that help educators and users understand the rationale behind the classification—thereby supporting academic integrity through increased transparency in detecting AI-generated code.

4.4.3 Prompt Template

We employ prompt engineering in this study by designing a dedicated prompt template for generating explanations in the detection of GenAI-generated code. To implement this, we adopt LangChain (Repo, 2024), a framework that provides flexible prompt templates and modular components for interacting with large language models (LLMs). LangChain allows structured input with dynamic variables, streamlining tasks such as question answering, chatbot interactions, and multi-turn prompts.

A central feature of LangChain is the **PromptTemplate**, which enables the creation of reusable prompts with dynamic variables, thereby simplifying query construction. In addition, LangChain supports **Few-Shot Prompting**, a technique that incorporates contextual examples into prompts to improve model performance. This is particularly useful for **Chain-ofThought (CoT)** reasoning, where the model decomposes complex problems into intermediate steps to enhance interpretability and accuracy. The FewShotPromptTemplate in LangChain automates this process by embedding curated example interactions, enabling dynamic selection of relevant demonstrations and optimizing reasoning efficiency.

LangChain is compatible with both OpenAI and Hugging Face models and supports advanced prompt workflows through operators and Runnable objects for modular chaining. This functionality allows for efficient execution of workflows such as parallel tasks, dynamic example selection, and reasoning optimization within context constraints.

The final prompt template used to generate explanations in our study is presented below.

Context: We use a machine learning model to determine whether ChatGPT has generated a piece of source code. The classification engine is based on GraphCodeBERT. The model we used is part of the GPTSniffer (https://github.com/MDEGroup/GPTSniffer). The model yields the following probability scores, marked as **Clas-**

sification Results, for the target source code, marked as **Target Source Code**, below. Moreover, along with the probability scores for the target source code, you are provided with some samples of the GenAIgenerated and human-written code (marked as **Examples**) that were classified by the same model.

Examples:

```
GenAI-generated samples:
{related exampleschatGPT}
Human-written samples:
{related exampleshuman}
Target Source Code: {source code} Classification Results:
Probability of being GenAI-generated: {probability
chatgpt}%.
Probability of being Human-written: {probability human}%.
```

Instruction: Please provide a comprehensive explanation and reasoning as to why the model predicts such code as human-written or AI-generated containing the following sections:

Answer structure:

Overview: Briefly summarize the most influential features or code excerpts that led to the classification as {**more likely classification**}. This must not exceed 20 lines.

End the overview with a markdown horizontal line (e.g., ---). **Highlight and Explain Key Code Lines**:

Key Code Lines: Extract five code lines or statements from the target source code that demonstrate {more likely classification} characteristics.

Explain Each Code Line:

Describe why the code lines indicate {more likely classification} patterns.

Detail the features or patterns present in the code that lead to {more likely classification}.

Comparison to Previous Examples:

Analyze how the features in the target source code align with or differ from the given code examples and their classifications. • Compare these features with similar patterns found in the dataset examples. For each comparison, provide the corresponding code snippet from the example alongside the target code excerpt. This side-by-side presentation will help readers understand the model's classification better.

When referring to a specific example (e.g., ¨Example 1¨), include its relevant code snippet for a direct visual comparison with the target source code.

Discuss how these similarities or differences support the classification decision.

Your final explanation should be detailed, structured, and in markdown format.

Explanation

This template divides the explanation process into several key sections:

- **Context Section:** Introduces the classification task and specifies the use of the GraphCodeBERT model. It clarifies that decisions are based on probability scores derived from both the target source code and its neighborhood samples.
- **Neighborhood Samples Section:** Provides representative code snippets, labeled as either GenAI-generated or human-written, along with their similarity distances to the target. This contextual information supports comparative reasoning.
- **Target Source Code Section:** Presents the source code under evaluation together with its computed probability scores, indicating the likelihood of AI or human authorship.
- **Question Section:** Directs the LLM to explain its classification decision, with an emphasis on identifying the critical code features that suggest human or AI authorship.
- **Instruction Section:** Guides the model through a structured analytical framework by requiring it to highlight five key coding patterns that influenced the decision and to identify five specific lines of code indicative of AI authorship.

Leveraging LangChain's FewShotPromptTemplate, dynamic variables such as *source code* and *related examples chatGPT* are incorporated in a way that maintains clarity, adaptability, and consistency across different inputs, thereby ensuring that the explanation process is both interpretable and systematically aligned with user expectations.

5 EXPERIMENTAL FRAMEWORK FOR CODE DETECTION AND EXPLANATION

We designed an experiment to evaluate our technique's effectiveness in distinguishing humanwritten code from GenAI-generated code, while also assessing its ability to produce clear and meaningful explanations for educators.

5.1 Evaluation of GenAI-generated Code Detection

First, we start by evaluating the detection of GenAI-generated code. We explain our evaluation method below.

5.1.1 Experimental Setup: Comparative Evaluation of Detection Models

We employ the approach by Nguyen et al. (Nguyen et al., 2024) for detecting GenAI-generated code and expand it to cover more models. The study evaluates four transformer-based models, **CodeBERT**, **UniXcoder**, **GraphCodeBERT**, and **LongCoder**, on the task of GPTgenerated code detection. We explain the datasets that we use for evaluating and selecting the model and the configuration of the experiment as follows.

5.1.2 Dataset Construction and Composition

The dataset used in this experiment is primarily obtained from the existing GPTSniffer study (Nguyen et al., 2024; et al., 2024). This dataset contains Java programming samples consisting of 737 human-written programs and 650 GenAI-generated programs.

To enhance dataset diversity, we additionally incorporated human-written Java code samples from the CodeNet dataset (Puri et al., 2021), specifically selecting programs submitted to the AIZU Online Judge platform. For each of the 50 problems chosen, we randomly selected five human-written Java submissions. Correspondingly, we generated five AI-written Java programs per problem using ChatGPT, thereby ensuring consistency in coding style and complexity between human-written and GenAI-generated code. This process resulted in an additional 250 human-written and 250 GenAI-generated Java programs.

Combining both sources, the final compiled dataset consists of 1,887 Java programs, balanced between human-written and GenAI-generated code. This dataset was subsequently divided into an 80:20 ratio for training and testing purposes. Specifically, the training set comprises 1,509 Java programs, including 789 human-written and 720 GenAI-generated samples, whereas the testing set contains 378 programs with 198 human-written and 180 GenAIgenerated samples.

This balanced and carefully structured dataset enables effective training and robust evaluation of machine learning models designed to detect AI-generated source code. Maintaining consistent experimental conditions from the original GPTSniffer research further ensures reliable and comparable results.

5.1.3 Experimental Configuration and Model Training

We rely on the existing framework of GPTSniffer (Nguyen et al., 2024). The GPTSniffer's architecture is based on three major components: an **Extractor** that prepares code data, a **Tokenizer** that encodes this code into numerical form, and a Classifier that uses these representations to detect patterns characteristic of code generated by AI. We used unmodified code samples and the Configuration C1 of GPTSniffer, so each model could learn AI-specific patterns from the original structure of the code.

Each model was selected for its specific strengths: CodeBERT is more biased toward the natural language-code pattern, UniXcoder helps in multilingual analysis for diverse code languages, GraphCodeBERT uses graph-based insights on structural code patterns, and LongCoder is very effective in handling long sequences with context-maintenance across larger-sized code blocks. Fine-tuning was done for all models using CrossEntropyLoss and the AdamW optimizer. The performance metrics applied were precision, recall, F1-score, and accuracy to ensure that any differences due to the models would be comparable, standard, and consistent in finding GPT-generated code.

To generate the explanation, we employ 2 generative AI models in this project: ChatGPT4o and Gemini 1.5 Pro. Both models are called via their APIs, given the predefined prompt template with the information of the code snippet to be explained and the classification result from GraphCodeBERT.

5.2 Evaluation of Explanation Quality

To complement the detection experiments, we conducted a user study to evaluate the quality and usefulness of the explanations generated by our approach. The study was designed to assess how effectively the system provides clear, interpretable justifications that can support educators in distinguishing between human-written and GenAI-generated code.

Table 6. Questions the explanation evaluation

No.	Question
1	Please rate this explanation overall.
2	Is the explanation efficient and avoids unnecessary information, presenting only essential details to effectively understand whether the code is written by humans or LLMs effectively?
3	Is the explanation presented in a clear and understandable manner, enabling you to understand the origin of this code better?
4	Does the explanation help you to make a judgment about this student's coding submission better?
5	Are the selected lines from the target source code useful?
6	Is the additional provided code example useful?
7	Do you have any additional feedback?

5.2.1 Experimental Setup: User Study

The experimental setup of the user study consists of two main steps.

1. The first step is the preparation of the dataset. We reuse the dataset of student-written code and GenAI code from the preliminary study. These pairs of student code and GenAI code are analyzed using our approach. The detection results and the explanations are collected.
2. The second step is the evaluation of the explanation. After preparing the dataset and performing the analysis, we recruited ten educators to assist in evaluating the usability of our tool. The main objective of this evaluation was to assess how clearly and effectively the tool provides explanations for code-similarity detection. In this step, the participants are presented with the code files, the detection results, and the generated corresponding explanations. This step was conducted in two rounds: in the first round, explanations were generated by ChatGPT, and in the second round, by Gemini. This structure allowed participants to compare the two explanation styles and determine which was more helpful and suitable for real-world educational applications.

Lastly, the participants evaluated the quality of the explanations using a five-point Likert scale rating system. Each question addressed a specific aspect, as shown in Table 6. Participants were also encouraged to provide open-ended feedback to justify their ratings or suggest possible improvements.

6 RESULTS

In this section, we discuss the results of the experiment, including the comparison of models for detecting GenAI-generated code and the evaluation of the explanations using correlation analysis and the user study.

Table 7. The performance of the four code BERT models on detecting GenAI code

Model	Category	Precision	Recall	F1-score
CodeBERT	GenAI-generated	96.72%	98.33%	97.52%
	Human-written	98.46%	96.97%	97.71%
	Accuracy		97.62%	
	Macro avg	97.59%	97.65%	97.62%

continued on following page

Table 7. Continued

Model	Category	Precision	Recall	F1-score
	Weighted avg	97.63%	97.62%	97.62%
GraphCodeBERT	**GenAI-generated**	98.33%	98.33%	98.33%
	Human-written	98.48%	98.48%	98.48%
	Accuracy		98.41%	
	Macro avg	98.41%	98.41%	98.41%
	Weighted avg	98.41%	98.41%	98.41%
UnixCoder	**GenAI-generated**	97.79%	98.33%	98.06%
	Human-written	98.48%	97.98%	98.23%
	Accuracy		98.15%	
	Macro avg	98.13%	98.16%	98.14%
	Weighted avg	98.15%	98.15%	98.15%
LongCoder	**GenAI-generated**	49.28%	57.22%	52.96%
	Human-written	54.44%	46.46%	50.14%
	Accuracy		51.59%	
	Macro avg	51.86%	51.84%	51.55%
	Weighted avg	51.98%	51.59%	51.48%

6.1 RQ1: Comparison of Models for Detecting GPT-generated Code

Table 7 presents the performance metrics for four code BERT models in detecting GenAIgenerated code. Overall, the evaluation shows that GraphCodeBERT, UnixCoder, and CodeBERT consistently achieve high accuracy, precision, recall, and F1-scores, while LongCoder demonstrates markedly inferior performance.

1. **CodeBERT:** Achieves 97.62% accuracy, with strong precision (96.72%) and recall (98.33%) for GenAI-generated code. It also performs well for human-written code, with a precision of 98.46% and recall of 96.97%, demonstrating balanced performance across both categories.
2. **GraphCodeBERT:** Leads with 98.41% accuracy, and maintains consistent performance with precision, recall, and F1-scores of 98.33% for GenAI-generated code and slightly higher for human-written code (98.48%).
3. **UniXCoder:** Achieves 98.15% accuracy, with 97.79% precision and 98.33% recall for GenAI-generated code. It is highly competitive, showing similar results to GraphCodeBERT.

4. **LongCoder:** Performs poorly with 51.59% accuracy, and low precision (49.28%) and recall (57.22%) for GenAI-generated code, indicating it is unsuitable for this task.

Figure 5. Correlation analysis of the code and the explanations

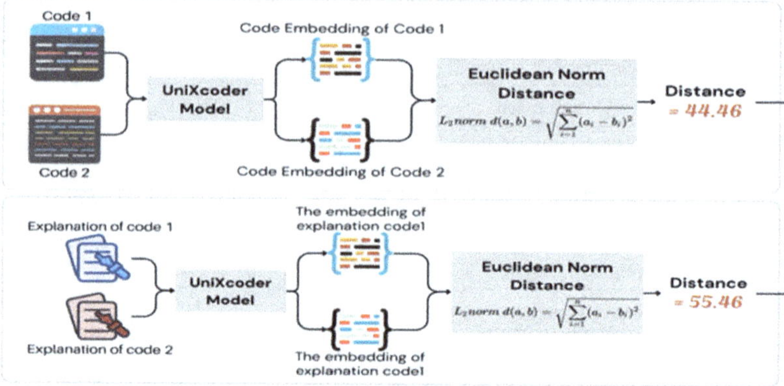

To answer RQ1, in summary, GraphCodeBERT emerges as the most effective model for detecting GPT-generated code, followed by UnixCoder and CodeBERT, which also show strong, consistent performance. In contrast, LongCoder's poor performance indicates that it is not suitable for this task. These findings underscore the advantages of transformer-based architectures—particularly GraphCodeBERT—in distinguishing between human-written and GPT-generated code.

6.2 RQ2: Correlation between the code and the explanations

The evaluation of the explanation focuses on assessing the alignment between the code to be explained and the generated explanations. We use the dataset from the GPTSniifer's study (Nguyen et al., 2024). The dataset comprises multiple exercises with each exercise containing several .java files representing chapters. For this analysis, only these three exercises (Exercises 5 to 7) are chosen to evaluate the relationship between the code and their explanations.

Table 8. The performance of explanation

Exercise	Correlation	P-value
Same Exercise	0.2038	0.0000
Across Exercise	0.1699	0.0000

The evaluation methodology, depicted in Figure 5, involves computing the absolute Euclidean norm distance between the two code embeddings, $|x_1 - x_2|$, derived from a code pair (C_1, C_2) and comparing them with the Euclidean norm distance of the embeddings of the corresponding explanations, $|e_1 - e_2|$. After retrieving the distances of the code and the explanations, we perform a correlation analysis using Pearson correlation. This process is applied across three contexts:

- **Within the same exercise**: Comparing chapters within Exercises 5, 6, and 7 individually.
- **Across different exercises**: Comparing chapters between different exercises (e.g., Exercise 5 vs. Exercise 6).
- **All combined**: Aggregating comparisons across both same and cross-exercise contexts.

The results, presented in Table 8, show the calculated correlation and p-values for each comparison type. It can be observed that the Pearson correlation coefficient for comparisons within the same exercise is **0.2038**, indicating some alignment between the structural differences and generated embeddings. For comparisons across exercises, the Pearson correlation coefficient is **0.1699**, reflecting a weaker relationship. The two p-values are **0.0000**, suggesting these correlations—though moderate—are statistically significant. This evaluation highlights that while in-context learning can generate embeddings that partially capture structural relationships within individual exercises, generalizing these explanations across different exercises remains a challenge and represents an area for potential improvement.

To answer RQ2, we found a weak correlation between the similarity of the code pair and its respective explanation pair generated by the LLM. This shows that the explanations tend to follow the semantics of the code being explained.

6.3 RQ3: User Study Result

This part of the evaluation included two participant groups: undergraduate students and educators, i.e., professors, from the Faculty of Information and Communication Technology, Mahidol University, Thailand.

Five undergraduate students in their third year participated in the code-writing activity. Every participant had already finished ITCS 123 object-oriented programming and had basic experience in Java development. Every student received a distinct programming task and was directed to independently develop a complete solution, without utilizing online resources. The session took place in a monitored setting on Wednesday, March 19, 2025, between 13:00 and 14:00 in room IT212.

The educators were chosen for their knowledge of undergraduate programming courses and their background in code assessment and critique. They are the same group of educators in the preliminary study. Their demographics are display in Table 3.

6.3.1 Evaluation of the Explanation

After generating and examining the three stacked bar charts (Figure 6, Figure 7, and Figure 8) corresponding to the overall feedback, the ChatGPT only feedback, and the Gemini only feedback, we observe the following.

Figure 6. Overall Survey Responses Distribution

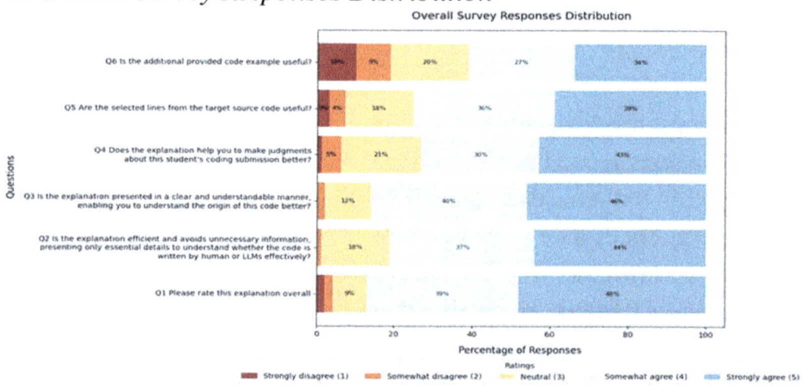

Overall Observations:

- Across all dimensions (*Overall*, *Conciseness*, *Clarity*, *Actionability*, *Selected Lines*, *Additional Code*), most participants selected *"Somewhat Agree (4)"* or *"Strongly Agree (5)"*.
- Fewer responses indicated *Neutral (3)* or negative ratings (*Somewhat Disagree (2)* or *Strongly Disagree (1)*). This suggests that, on the whole, participants found both ChatGPT and Gemini explanations beneficial.
- Nonetheless, a handful of responses revealed specific shortcomings such as contradictory statements, unclear references to which code segments were being discussed, and suggestions for simpler language or fewer examples.

Figure 7. Survey Responses Distribution for ChatGPT

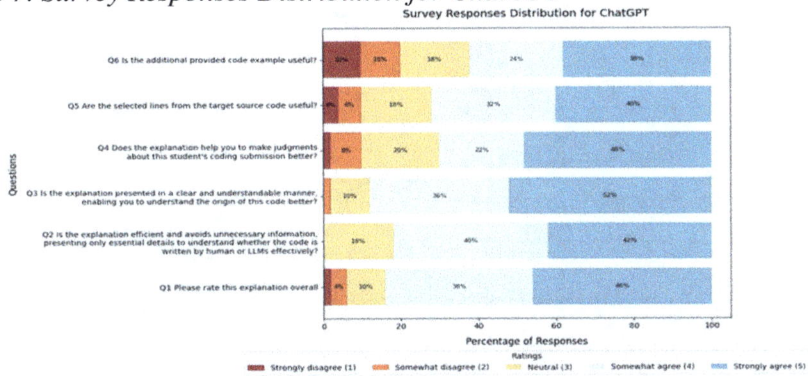

ChatGPT Specific Feedback:

- **Strengths:** ChatGPT's explanations typically received high marks for clarity, overall usefulness, and the relevance of the lines highlighted. Many respondents appreciated the detailed approach, especially when code snippets were directly linked to explanations.
- **Weaknesses and Suggestions:**
  - Some feedback mentioned that ChatGPT sometimes did not clearly indicate which parts of the code were the student's own versus provided examples.
  - A few respondents felt certain explanations were "unconvincing" or "contradictory" compared to prior statements, calling for more consistency.
  - Others recommended fewer but more focused examples, with simpler or more direct language to reduce confusion.

Figure 8. Survey Responses Distribution for Gemini

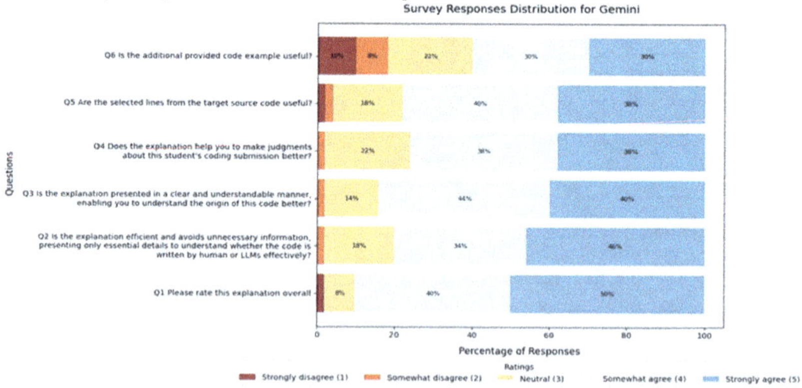

Gemini Specific Feedback:

- **Strengths:** Gemini also received many positive ratings, particularly regarding *actionability* (helpfulness in judging the code) and the usefulness of *selected lines* and *additional code*. Several users commented that the explanations were "thorough" and "detailed", providing a comprehensive overview.
- **Weaknesses and Suggestions:**
  - Some participants described Gemini's word choice as "more academic", occasionally making it harder to understand.
  - Certain comments noted confusion when lines from a code template were referenced without a clear context, or inconsistent references to the student's code.
  - Similar to ChatGPT, a few users suggested condensing the number of examples or simplifying the explanation style for better clarity.

Additional Feedback from Participants Beyond the main points already discussed, several participants offered more nuanced remarks about their experiences and preferences:

- **Code line explanation:** Some users appreciated it when the LLM (either ChatGPT or Gemini) provided explicit comments for each line of code, explaining its purpose or function. This was particularly helpful when the student's code included extra elements, such as unique package names.
- **Better structure:** A number of participants noted that they liked Gemini's use of bullet points, describing this format as "easy to read". In contrast,

ChatGPT often presents feedback in paragraph form, which some found slightly less scannable—though still clear.

- **Unclear human code explanations:** Participants found that the explanations of human-written code are worse than the explanations of GenAI code.
- **Level of details:** Some participants admitted they primarily read only the summary section (e.g., the short explanation) and rarely opened or read the longer "read more" or expanded content. Consequently, they tended to rate more neutrally (often selecting *"3"*) on detailed questions, as they had not fully explored the extended explanation.
- **Language style:** While Gemini's explanations were praised for being thorough, a few users felt the language could be "too fancy" or academic in the detailed sections. Conversely, ChatGPT's language was described as "better and easier to understand".
- **Usefulness of selected code Lines and examples:** Participants found the selected code lines and code examples are not clearly useful.

In summary, the quantitative data (Figure 6, Figure 7, and Figure 8) and qualitative feedback shows that participants generally find these GenAI explanations **useful, clear, and actionable**. However, the feedback suggests:

- Ensuring the explanations consistently match the code context (i.e., which lines belong to the student's code).
- Avoiding contradictory or repetitive statements by providing concise, cohesive examples.
- Offering simpler language and fewer examples when the audience is less technical or prefers brevity.
- Employing more accessible formatting (e.g., markdown with a dark theme) to improve readability.

These refinements would likely further enhance the clarity and utility of both ChatGPT and Gemini explanations.

To answer RQ3, the evaluation of the explanations by the computer science educators shows that the explanations generated by our approach are useful, easy to understand, and help them make a better differentiation of the GenAI code from the human-written code.

6.4 Estimated Cost of Generating Explanations

Our explanation generation process leverages two models: Gemini1.5Pro (Google, 2025) and ChatGPT4o (OpenAI, 2025). The Gemini1.5Pro API is accessed through a free tier, meaning that it does not contribute to the overall cost. In contrast, ChatGPT4o is a paid service, and its cost is determined by the number of tokens processed in both the input prompt and the generated output. For our experiments, each file, representing one detection result, triggersrs a single prompt. Based on our current testing data, an average file (approximately 797 lines of text) requires a prompt that consumes a certain number of tokens, translating to a cost of roughly $0.04 per explanation when processed through ChatGPT4o. When scaling the operation, for instance, processing 10 files results in a cumulative cost of about $0.22, which averages to approximately $0.022 per file. The estimation process involves the following.

- **Token Analysis**: We first evaluate the average token count per file, both for the input (the file content) and the output (the explanation generated). Variations in file size and content complexity cause fluctuations in token usage, which is why the cost per file ranges between $0.02 and $0.04.
- **Cost Aggregation**: By aggregating the cost over multiple test instances, we normalize the expense to derive a reliable average cost per explanation. For example, if the total cost for processing a batch of files is $M, and there are N files, then the average cost per file is $M/N.
- **Scalability Consideration**: The low per-prompt cost provided by ChatGPT4o allows us to scale our testing efficiently. Since Gemini 1.5 Pro does not add any additional cost, our overall expenditure is predominantly driven by ChatGPT4o's pricing model.

This detailed cost analysis is instrumental for budgeting and strategic planning, ensuring that our explanation generation remains cost-effective as we increase the number of test files or adjust the complexity of the input data.

7 DISCUSSION

7.1 Limitations

The study has some limitations as follows. First, the preliminary and the proposed approach are limited to only the Java language due to the constraint of the selected dataset from the GPTSniffer study (Nguyen et al., 2024). Thus, the findings may not be generalized to other programming languages. Moreover, the LLMs chosen for the study include only ChatGPT4o and Gemini 1.5 Pro. The explanations generated by other generative AI models may be different from what is reported in this study.

The preliminary study includes only 10 educators from the Faculty of Information and Communication Technology, Mahidol University, Thailand. The sample size is relatively small and may not be representative of all computer science educators. Moreover, the selected five questions in the study were selected from a single course and may not represent all the potential Java programming questions.

7.2 Implications for Software Engineering Researchers

Our study shows that computer science educators can manually detect GenAI code with high accuracy. However, manually checking the students' submissions can be tedious and cumbersome, given that there may be a large number of submissions to check, which may lead to human biases and errors. An automated tool is needed to aid the educators by filtering the student-written submissions from the potential GenAI ones. Currently, there are a few automated tools and techniques for detecting GenAI code (Hoq et al., 2024; Wang et al., 2023; Nguyen et al., 2024; Pirntke & Rindebrant, 2024). However, a proper study to evaluate their performance in the education setting is still needed across several programming question types and programming languages.

7.3 Implications for Computer Science Educators

The findings from RQ2 show that the educators who participated in our study relied on six clues to detect GenAI code. These clues can be used as guidelines for spotting GenAI code. Moreover, the finding from RQ3 shows that the educators who are familiar with using GenAI for code could detect GenAI code with high accuracy. Thus, it is recommended that the educators also familiarize themselves with the GenAI tools, such as using them to generate code for programming questions and reviewing the code that is generated by such models. Lastly, although there are automated tools for detecting GenAI code available, human educators, who are well-equipped, are still needed to make the final decisions in high-stakes settings where explainability is critical, such as exams.

8 CONCLUSION

The increasing reliance on large language models (LLMs) such as ChatGPT in programming education presents both opportunities and challenges. While these tools can accelerate learning and provide valuable support, they also risk undermining the development of core programming skills and threatening academic integrity when students present AI-generated code as their own. This chapter has introduced a comprehensive study and framework that addresses these concerns by combining accurate detection with a transparent explanation of GenAI code.

Our preliminary study of manual detection of GenAI code demonstrates that human educators can be quite effective at distinguishing between student-written code and code generated by Generative AI. We found that, on average, the ten educators who participated in our study correctly identified the GenAI-generated programs with 86% accuracy. Six of the ten educators achieved perfect scores, correctly identifying all the GPT-generated programs. This suggests that while some educators are highly proficient at this task, others may require more support. Based on our educators' feedback, we identified six key clues they used to differentiate the code. These clues ranged from specific programming patterns to more subtle stylistic and structural elements. Interestingly, we observed that educators' familiarity with using GenAI for programming may relate to their detection performance; educators with less experience using GenAI were less effective at identifying it. Our findings pave the way for building an automated technique for supporting computer science educators as they navigate the increasing presence of GenAI in their classrooms.

Our evaluation of our proposed automated framework for detecting GenAI code demonstrates that transformer-based models—particularly GraphCodeBERT, UniXcoder, and CodeBERT—are highly effective in distinguishing between human-written and AI-generated code, with GraphCodeBERT achieving the best overall performance. Beyond detection, we proposed a novel post-hoc explanation module built on local neighborhood sampling and in-context learning. This module not only clarifies why a classification decision was made but also provides educators with interpretable, structured justifications that highlight salient coding patterns. Feedback from user studies indicates that such explanations improve clarity, support actionable decision-making, and enhance trust in automated detection systems.

Importantly, the findings underscore that explanation is as critical as detection. While many existing approaches operate as black-box classifiers, our framework emphasizes interpretability, enabling educators to understand the reasoning behind classifications and to provide more informed guidance to students. We believe that generating these explanations is financially feasible at scale, particularly with hybrid use of open-source and commercial models. Future directions include refining detection accuracy, expanding scalability, and adapting the tool for broader use across universities. The system represents an important step toward automating AI detection and addressing academic integrity concerns in programming courses.

REFERENCES

Aiken, A. (1994). *MOSS (Measure of Software Similarity).* Stanford University. https://theory.stanford.edu/~aiken/moss/

Anthropic. (2024). *Claude AI by Anthropic.* https://www.anthropic.com/claude

Balog, K., Radlinski, F., & Petrov, A. (2023). Measuring the impact of explanation bias: A study of natural language justifications for recommender systems. In *Extended Abstracts of the 2023 CHI Conference on Human Factors in Computing Systems* (pp. 1–8).

Beale, R. (2025). *Computer science education in the age of generative AI.* University of Birmingham, https://pure-oai.bham.ac.uk/ws/portalfiles/portal/279998930/2507.02183v1.pdf

Charan, N. D. (2022). *A beginner's guide to using the ChatGPT API.* Medium. https://medium.com/@niteshdancharan2022/a-beginners-guide-to-using-the-chatgpt-api-047f275b65a0

CodeGrade B.V. (2025). *CodeGrade: Code grading and plagiarism detection for education.* https://www.codegrade.com/

Feng, Z., Guo, D., Tang, D., Duan, N., Feng, X., Gong, M., Shou, L., Qin, B., Liu, T., Jiang, D., & Zhou, M. (2020, November). *CodeBERT: A pre-trained model for programming and natural languages.* In T. Cohn, Y. He, & Y. Liu (Eds.), *Findings of the Association for Computational Linguistics: EMNLP 2020* (pp. 1536–1547). Online: Association for Computational Linguistics. https://doi.org/DOI: 10.18653/v1/2020.findings-emnlp.139

GitHub. (2024). *GitHub Copilot.* https://github.com/features/copilot

Google. (2024). *Google Gemini AI.* https://blog.google/technology/ai/google-gemini-ai/#availability

Google. (2025). *Gemini developer API pricing.* https://ai.google.dev/gemini-api/docs/pricing

Guo, D., Lu, S., Duan, N., Wang, Y., Zhou, M., & Yin, J. (2022, May). UniXcoder: Unified cross-modal pre-training for code representation. In Muresan, S., Nakov, P., & Villavicencio, A. (Eds.), *Proceedings of the 60th Annual Meeting of the Association for Computational Linguistics (*Volume 1*: Long Papers)* (pp. 7212–7225). Dublin, Ireland: Association for Computational Linguistics. https://doi.org/DOI: 10.18653/v1/2022.acl-long.499

Guo, D., Ren, S., Lu, S., Feng, Z., Tang, D., Liu, S., & Zhou, M. (2021). *GraphCodeBERT: Pre-training code representations with data flow.* In *International Conference on Learning Representations (ICLR 2021).* Retrieved from https://openreview.net/forum?id=jLoC4ez43PZ

Guo, D., Xu, C., Duan, N., Yin, J., & McAuley, J. (2023). LongCoder: A long-range pre-trained language model for code completion. In *Proceedings of the 40th International Conference on Machine Learning (ICML 2023)* (pp. 12098–12107).

Hamamra, B., Mayaleh, A., & Khlaif, Z. N. (2024). Between tech and text: The use of generative AI in Palestinian universities—a ChatGPT case study. *Cogent Education, 11*(1), 2380622.

Hoq, M., Shi, Y., Leinonen, J., Babalola, D., Lynch, C., Price, T., & Akram, B. (2024). Detecting ChatGPT-generated code submissions in a CS1 course using machine learning models. In *Proceedings of the 55th ACM Technical Symposium on Computer Science Education* (Vol. 1, pp. 526–532). Association for Computing Machinery. https://doi.org/DOI: 10.1145/3626252.3630826

IBM. (2023). *What is generative AI?* https://www.ibm.com/topics/generative-ai

Liu, R., Zenke, C., Liu, C., Holmes, A., Thornton, P., & Malan, D. J. (2024). Teaching CS50 with AI: Leveraging generative artificial intelligence in computer science education. In *Proceedings of the 55th ACM Technical Symposium on Computer Science Education* (Vol. 1, pp. 750–756). Association for Computing Machinery. https://doi.org/DOI: 10.1145/3626252.3630938

Lundberg, S. M., & Lee, S.-I. (2017). A unified approach to interpreting model predictions. In *Advances in Neural Information Processing Systems* (pp. 4765–4774). https://papers.nips.cc/paper/7062-a-unified-approach-to-interpreting-model-predictions.pdf

Meta, A. I., Touvron, H., Lavril, T., Izacard, G., Martinet, X., Lachaux, M. A., Lacroix, T., . . . Lample, G. (2023). *LLaMA: Open and efficient foundation language models* (Version 1) [Large language model]. Meta AI. https://ai.meta.com/llama/

Nguyen, P. T., ... (2024). *Dataset of GPTSniffer.* GitHub. https://github.com/MDEGroup/GPTSniffer/tree/master/DATASETS

Nguyen, P. T., Di Rocco, J., Di Sipio, C., Rubei, R., Di Ruscio, D., & Di Penta, M. (2024, July). GPTSniffer: A CodeBERT-based classifier to detect source code written by ChatGPT. *Journal of Systems and Software, 214*, 112059. DOI: 10.1016/j.jss.2024.112059

Northern Illinois University. (2024). *Types of academic dishonesty.* https://www.niu.edu/academic-integrity/faculty/types/index.shtml

Open, A. I. (2024). *OpenAI Codex.* https://openai.com/blog/openai-codex

Open, A. I. (2025). *OpenAI API pricing.* https://platform.openai.com/docs/pricing

Parajuli, P., & Racharak, T. (2025). A framework for identifying underspecification in image classification pipeline using post-hoc analyzer. In Santana, M. C., Marsico, M. D., & Fred, A. (Eds.), *Proceedings of the 14th International Conference on Pattern Recognition Applications and Methods (ICPRAM 2025)* (pp. 426–436). SCITEPRESS.

Pawar, U., Beder, C., O'Reilly, R., & O'Shea, D. (2024). On the impact of neighbourhood sampling to satisfy sufficiency and necessity criteria in explainable AI. In *CLEAR 2024.* https://api.semanticscholar.org/CorpusID:269648514

Pirntke, E., & Rindebrant, W. (2024). *Automatic detection of AI-generated source code in programming courses.*

Prechelt, L., Malpohl, G., & Philippsen, M. (2002). Finding plagiarisms among a set of programs with JPlag. *Journal of Universal Computer Science, 8*(11), 1016–1038. https://github.com/jplag/JPlag

Puri, R., Kung, D., Janssen, G., Zhang, W., Domeniconi, G., Zolotov, V., ... Reiss, F. (2021). *CodeNet: A large-scale AI for code dataset for learning a diversity of coding tasks.*

Racharak, T., Jearanaiwongkul, W., Pooksook, J., & Takashima, K. (2025). Towards assumption-based argumentation mining in hotel reviews. In T. Ågotnes & D. Doder (Eds.), *Logic and Argumentation: 6th International Conference (CLAR 2025)* (Vol. 15712, pp. 272–290). Springer.

Racharak, T., Ragkhitwetsagul, C., Sontesadisai, C., & Sunetnanta, T. (2025). Test it before you trust it: Applying software testing for trustworthy in-context learning. In R. Ichise (Ed.), *Natural Language Processing and Information Systems – 30th International Conference on Applications of Natural Language to Information Systems (NLDB 2025)* (Vol. 15836, pp. 243–258). Springer.

Reihanian, I., Hou, Y., Chen, Y., & Zheng, Y. (2025). A Review of Generative AI in Computer Science Education: Challenges and Opportunities in Accuracy, Authenticity, and Assessment. In *Computational science and computational intelligence* (pp. 144–158). Springer Nature Switzerland.

Repo, L. H. (2024). *Prompt engineering and LLMs with LangChain.* Pinecone. https://www.pinecone.io/learn/series/langchain/langchain-prompt-templates/

Ribeiro, M. T., Singh, S., & Guestrin, C. (2016). "Why should I trust you?" Explaining the predictions of any classifier. In *Proceedings of the 22nd ACM SIGKDD International Conference on Knowledge Discovery and Data Mining* (pp. 1135–1144).

Russell, J., Karpinska, M., & Iyyer, M. (2025, July). People who frequently use ChatGPT for writing tasks are accurate and robust detectors of AI-generated text. In *Proceedings of the 63rd Annual Meeting of the Association for Computational Linguistics* (Volume 1*: Long Papers)* (pp. 5342–5373). Association for Computational Linguistics. https://doi.org/DOI: 10.18653/v1/2025.acl-long.267

Schefer-Wenzl, S., Vogl, C., Peiris, S., & Miladinovic, I. (2025). Exploring the adoption of generative AI tools in computer science education: A student survey. In *Proceedings of the 2024 16th International Conference on Education Technology and Computers* (pp. 173–178). Association for Computing Machinery. https://doi.org/DOI: 10.1145/3702163.3702188

Studio, L. (n.d.). *LM Studio docs*. https://lmstudio.ai/docs

Tanneru, S. H., Agarwal, C., & Lakkaraju, H. (2024). *Quantifying uncertainty in natural language explanations of large language models*. In *Proceedings of the 27th International Conference on Artificial Intelligence and Statistics (AISTATS 2024)*. PMLR. arXiv:2311.03533. https://arxiv.org/abs/2311.03533

Turnitin, L. L. C. (2025). *Turnitin: Plagiarism and AI writing detection service*. https://www.turnitin.com/

University College London. (2024). *GenAI and academic integrity in assessment*. https://www.ucl.ac.uk/teaching-learning/generative-ai-hub/genai-and-academic-integrity-assessment

Wang, Z., Xie, C., & Yu, Z. (2024). *Fast-DetectGPT: Efficient zero-shot detection of machine-generated text via probability curvature*. In *Proceedings of the International Conference on Learning Representations (ICLR 2024)*.

Wei, J., Bosma, M., Zhao, V. Y., Guu, K., Yu, A. W., Lester, B., & Le, Q. V. (2022). Fine tuned language models are zero-shot learners. In *The Tenth International Conference on Learning Representations (ICLR'22)*.

Wei, J., Wang, X., Schuurmans, D., Bosma, M., Ichter, B., Xia, F., & Zhou, D. (2022). Chain-of-thought prompting elicits reasoning in large language models. In *Proceedings of the 36th International Conference on Neural Information Processing Systems (NIPS'22)*.

Yan, Y.-M., Chen, C.-Q., Hu, Y.-B., & Ye, X.-D. (2025). LLM-based collaborative programming: Impact on students' computational thinking and self-efficacy. *Humanities & Social Sciences Communications*, *12*(1), 149. DOI: 10.1057/s41599-025-04471-1

Yu, F., Quartey, L., & Schilder, F. (2023). Exploring the effectiveness of prompt engineering for legal reasoning tasks. In *Findings of the Association for Computational Linguistics* (pp. 13582–13596). ACL.

ENDNOTES

1 The programming questions and the generated code can be found on our study website (https://github.com/MUICT-SERU/CodeDetectives)

2 The study was approved by the university's ethics board (No. MU-CIRB 2025/078.0503)

APPENDIX

Q1 (Room Rental System) With the Lowest Accuracy of Detection by the Educators

GenAI Code

```
import java.util.Scanner;
public class RoomRentCalculator {   public static void main(String[] args) {
    // CODE HERE      String guestName;       double roomPricePerNight =
900.50;    String checkInDate, checkOutDate;
   // Create scanner object to capture user input
   Scanner scanner = new Scanner(System.in);
  // Input guest's name, check-in, and check-out dates   System.out.print("Enter
guest's name: ");    guestName = scanner.nextLine();
    System.out.print("Enter check-in date (yyyy-mm-dd): ");    checkInDate
= scanner.nextLine();
   System.out.print("Enter check-out date (yyyy-mm-dd): ");   checkOutDate
= scanner.nextLine();
   // Parse the check-in and check-out dates into
   // individual components
   String[] checkInDateParts = checkInDate.split("-");
    String[] checkOutDateParts = checkOutDate.split("-");     // Convert to
integers for calculations    int checkInYear = Integer.parseInt(checkInDate-
Parts[0]);   int checkInMonth = Integer.parseInt(checkInDateParts[1]);   int
checkInDay = Integer.parseInt(checkInDateParts[2]);      int checkOutYear
= Integer.parseInt(checkOutDateParts[0]);     int checkOutMonth = Integer.
parseInt(checkOutDateParts[1]);   int checkOutDay = Integer.parseInt(check-
OutDateParts[2]);    // Calculate the number of nights stayed using the helper
method   int numberOfNights = calculateDaysBetweenDates  (checkInYear,
checkInMonth, checkInDay,  checkOutYear, checkOutMonth, checkOutDay);
// Calculate the total rent
  double totalRent = roomPricePerNight * numberOfNights;    // Display the
output in the required format
   System.out.println("\n** No STAR Hotel **");
   System.out.println("== Hotel Invoice ==");
   System.out.println("Guest Name: " + guestName);
   System.out.println("Check-in Date: " + checkInDate);
   System.out.println("Check-out Date: " + checkOutDate);
```

```
System.out.println("Number of Nights: " + numberOfNights);
System.out.println("Total Rent: "
 + String.format("%.2f", totalRent)); //Close scanner scanner.close(); }
// Helper method to calculate the number of days between two dates
...

// Helper method to check if a year is a leap year
...
}
package test; import java.util.Scanner;
```

Student Code

```
public class RoomRentCalculator { private String guest_name; private final
double price = 900.5; private String check_in; private String check_out;
 public static void main(String[] args) {
  //CODE HERE
  RoomRentCalculator n = new RoomRentCalculator();
   Scanner in = new Scanner(System.in);     System.out.print("Enter your
name: ");
 n.setGuest_name(in.nextLine()); System.out.print("Enter check-in date: ");
  n.setCheck_in(in.nextLine()); System.out.print("Enter check-out date: ");
  n.setCheck_out(in.nextLine());
  System.out.println();
  System.out.println(n.toString());

  String[] in_date = n.getCheck_in().split("-");   String[] out_date = n.get-
Check_out().split("-");  int[] int_in = new int[3];  int[] int_out = new int[3];
  for(int i = 0; i < in_date.length; i++) {    int_in[i] = Integer.parseInt(in_
date[i]);     int_out[i] = Integer.parseInt(out_date[i]);
  }
  int night = calculateDaysBetweenDates(int_in[0], int_in[1],        int_
in[2], int_out[0], int_out[1], int_out[2]);   System.out.println("Number of
Nights: " + night);  double total = night * n.getPrice();  System.out.print-
ln("Total Rent: " + String.format("%.2f", total));
 }   public String getGuest_name() {   return guest_name; }
 public void setGuest_name(String guest_name) {    this.guest_name =
guest_name; }
 // other getters and setters ...
 public String toString() {
```

```
  String str = "** No STAR Hotel **\n== Hotel Invoice ==\n";     str +=
"Guest Name: " + guest_name +     "\nCheck-in Date: " + check_in +     "\
nCheck-out Date: " + check_out;     return str;   }
 // Helper method to calculate the number of days between two dates
 ...

 // Helper method to check if a year is a leap year
 ...
}
```

Chapter 8
Toward a Responsible and Inclusive AI–Learning Ecosystem

Frederic Andres
https://orcid.org/0000-0002-5003-7579
National Institute of Informatics, Tokyo, Japan

Teeradaj Racharak
https://orcid.org/0000-0002-8823-2361
Tohoku University, Japan

Gerlinde Weger
https://orcid.org/0000-0002-5126-2938
In-Sight Consulting, Canada

Andreas Pester
https://orcid.org/0000-0001-7278-7349
The British University in Egypt, Egypt

Chandrasekhar Anantaram
Bureau of Indian Standards, India

ABSTRACT

This concluding chapter synthesizes insights from the volume, highlighting the transformative potential of AI in education alongside the ethical, cultural, and pedagogical challenges it raises. Common themes include balancing standardization with innovation, ensuring fairness for neurodiverse and culturally diverse learners, and fostering responsible AI mindsets. Looking ahead, the chapter outlines priorities for future research on ethical benchmarks, inclusive design, and human–AI collab-

DOI: 10.4018/979-8-3373-2235-3.ch008

oration. Policy implications center on aligning global standards and safeguarding learners' rights. International collaboration is emphasized as essential to building a responsible and inclusive AI-learning ecosystem grounded in shared values and collective innovation.

1. INTRODUCTION

In a multipolar world with technologies and platforms that enable distance learning, self learning, online teaching, guidance, and virtual classrooms, education has truly reached the crossroads for next generation evolution. The widespread availability and use of AI technology has become a great leveler between the less-informed and the more well-founded students. The skill of using AI effectively to meet one's educational goals has suddenly become more prominent and a fundamental ability. Those who are average in concepts can now use AI effectively to outperform those with well-grounded knowledge but lesser AI skills (Jiao, 2024). At the same time those with learning disabilities and physically challenged situations (Toyokawa et al., 2025) can hope to achieve a level of education that can help them overcome some of their inabilities and achieve an acceptable level for possible job opportunities. This kind of power from AI technology can be usefully repurposed to deliver effective education across a large spectrum of the population. We now have the platforms for explaining concepts in a subject area using concepts from varied subject areas that can connect with the student's prior knowledge. Teachers do not always have the ability to cross-correlate concepts across fields, but using AI technology this is possible both for the teachers as well as the student.

The integration of Artificial Intelligence into education has brought unprecedented opportunities for personalization (Naayini, 2025; Kashyap et al., 2024) efficiency, and global knowledge sharing (Panwale et al., 2024). At the same time, it has raised deep concerns about equity, ethics (Hamidon et al., 2025), bias (Farheen, 2025; Boateng et al., 2025), and the societal consequences of human-AI interactions (Jia, 2025). The preceding chapters have illuminated multiple perspectives on how AI reshapes teaching, learning, and educational institutions. This final chapter consolidates those insights, identifies cross-cutting themes, and maps pathways for responsible and inclusive AI-driven learning ecosystems.

2. CROSS-CUTTING INSIGHTS FROM THE CHAPTERS

Several recurring themes emerge across the diverse contributions:

- **Human-AI Partnerships**: Effective AI in education must augment but not replace human agency (Atchley et al., 2024). Educators (Kottur, 2024) remain central as mentors, facilitators, and ethical guides (Hamidon et al, 2025).
- **Equity and Inclusion**: Access gaps risk widening if AI tools are unevenly distributed or culturally insensitive. Inclusive design (Melo-López et al., 2025) and multilingual support are essential.
- **Bias and Fairness**: GenAI systems (Memon et al., 2025) can inadvertently reproduce stereotypes and discrimination. Continuous auditing, transparent data practices, and participatory design help mitigate these risks.
- **Authenticity and Trust**: Students and educators alike are concerned about AI-generated outputs, hallucinations, and assessment integrity. Trustworthy AI requires explainability, reliability, and safeguards against misuse. AI Education companies must be accountable for the outcomes of their products.
- **Well-being and Human Development**: Beyond cognitive outcomes, AI impacts learners' stress, motivation, and psychological resilience. Responsible integration must account for well-being (Hadar Shoval, 2025).

3. FUTURE RESEARCH DIRECTIONS

The next phase of research should address gaps identified across the chapters:

- **AI Literacy for All**: Developing curricula that empower students, teachers, and citizens to critically understand and engage with AI systems (Walter,2024; Öner,2025).
- **Inclusive Learning Models**: Research on culturally adaptive AI, multilingual systems, and approaches that support underrepresented communities and how AI literacy is integrated across diverse cultural and educational contexts (Casal-Otero et al., 2023).
- **Evaluation and Standards**: Creating reliable benchmarks and international standards and frameworks for assessing AI's educational impact (Al-Abdullatif, 2025).
- **Longitudinal Studies**: Understanding the long-term effects of AI on learning trajectories, identity formation, and workforce readiness as the meta-review in (Mustafa et al., 2024) points out gap areas in the research agenda including a dearth of long-term, and longitudinal studies of AI in education.
- **Human–AI Co-learning**: Exploring how learners and intelligent systems evolve together, particularly in collaborative or creative domains (Yim et al., 2025).

4. POLICY IMPLICATIONS

Policy frameworks must keep pace with technological advancements to ensure that AI in education serves the public good:

- **Governance and Regulation**: Establishing clear rules for data privacy, algorithmic transparency and accountability in educational AI systems (Nguyen et al., 2022).
- **Funding Equity**: Investing in infrastructure and capacity building to reduce digital divides across regions and communities.
- **Ethical Guidelines**: Promoting shared principles for responsible AI design and deployment in education (Nguyen et al., 2023; Peddi et al., 2026).
- **Accreditation and Assessment**: Updating standards for credentialing and evaluation to reflect AI-enabled learning (Bulut, 2024).
- **Teacher Support**: Providing professional development, resources, and safeguards so educators can confidently work with AI (Küçükuncular, 2025).

5. INTERNATIONAL COLLABORATION OPPORTUNITIES

Given AI's global impact, no single nation or institution can address the challenges in isolation. Collaboration across borders is vital for:

- **Global Standards Development**: Collaborating with UNESCO, OECD, IEEE, ISO, and other bodies to harmonize ethical frameworks and technical standards (UNESCO, 2021; Ghimire et al., 2024; Thomas, 2024).
- **Knowledge Sharing Platforms**: Creating international networks for educators, researchers, and policymakers to exchange practices.
- **Joint Research Initiatives**: Funding and coordinating multinational projects that test AI models across cultural and institutional contexts.
- **Capacity Building in the Global South**: Supporting developing countries with resources, infrastructure, and open educational AI tools.
- **Cross-disciplinary Partnerships**: Fostering collaboration between computer scientists, educators, psychologists, ethicists, and policymakers.

6. CONCLUSION

Building a responsible and inclusive AI-learning ecosystem requires a shared commitment to human-centered values, gender equity (Bearman et al., 2025), and sustainability. The cross-cutting insights of this volume underline the importance of designing AI tools that empower learners, respect cultural diversity, and strengthen the role of educators. Looking ahead, the convergence of future research, thoughtful policy, and international collaboration will determine whether AI becomes a force of equitable learning—or one that deepens existing inequalities. The path forward lies in collective responsibility, inclusive innovation, and global solidarity.

7. REFERENCES

Al-Abdullatif, A. M. (2025). Auditing AI Literacy Competency in K–12 Education: The Role of Awareness, Ethics, Evaluation, and Use in Human–Machine Cooperation. *Systems, 13*(6), 490. DOI: 10.3390/systems13060490

Atchley, P., Pannell, H., Wofford, K., Hopkins, M., & Atchley, R. A. (2024). Human and AI collaboration in the higher education environment: Opportunities and concerns. *Cognitive Research: Principles and Implications, 9*(1), 20. DOI: 10.1186/s41235-024-00547-9 PMID: 38589710

Bearman, M., & Ajjawi, R. (2025). Artificial intelligence and gender equity: An integrated approach for health professional education. *Medical Education, 59*(10), 1049–1057. DOI: 10.1111/medu.15657 PMID: 40064176

Boateng, O., & Boateng, B. (2025). Algorithmic bias in educational systems: Examining the impact of AI-driven decision making in modern education. *World Journal of Advanced Research and Reviews, 25*(1), 2012–2017. DOI: 10.30574/wjarr.2025.25.1.0253

Bulut, O., & Beiting-Parrish, M. (2024). The rise of artificial intelligence in educational measurement: Opportunities and ethical challenges. *Chinese/English Journal of Educational Measurement and Evaluation, 5*(3). Advance online publication. DOI: 10.59863/miql7785

Casal-Otero, L., Catala, A., Fernández-Morante, C., Taboada, M., Cebreiro, B., & Barro, S. (2023). AI literacy in K-12: A systematic literature review. *International Journal of STEM Education, 10*(1). Advance online publication. DOI: 10.1186/s40594-023-00418-7

Farheen, S., Cheema, A. A., Ullah, R. S., & Bandeali, D. M. M. (2025). Equity and bias in AI educational tools: A critical examination of algorithmic decision-making in classrooms. *The Critical Review of Social Sciences Studies, 3*(3), 67–85. DOI: 10.59075/zqmnpa62

Ghimire, A., & Edwards, J. (2024). From guidelines to governance: A study of AI policies in education. In *Communications in Computer and Information Science* (pp. 299–307). Communications in Computer and Information Science., DOI: 10.1007/978-3-031-64312-5_36

Hadar Shoval, D. (2025). Artificial intelligence in higher education: Bridging or widening the gap for diverse student populations? *Education Sciences, 15*(5), 637. DOI: 10.3390/educsci15050637

Hamidon, Z., Abdullah, M. L., Yussof, Y., & Ismail, M. N. (2025). Exploring AI-driven personalization in open and distance learning: Learner engagement, inclusivity, and ethical implementation. *International Journal of Academic Research in Business & Social Sciences, 15*(6). Advance online publication. DOI: 10.6007/ijarbss/v15-i6/25791

Jia, C. (2025). The impact of curriculum design and educational equity in the age of artificial intelligence - A literature review. *Lecture Notes in Education Psychology and Public Media, 89*(1), 55–61. DOI: 10.54254/2753-7048/2025.22633

Jiao, D. (2024). AI-Driven Personalization in Higher Education: Enhancing Learning Outcomes through Adaptive Technologies. *Adult and Higher Education, 6*, 42–46. DOI: 10.23977/aduhe.2024.060607

Kashyap, R., Samuel, Y., Friedman, L. W., & Samuel, J. (2024). Editorial: Artificial intelligence education & governance -human enhancive, culturally sensitive and personally adaptive HAI. *Frontiers in Artificial Intelligence, 7*, 1443386. DOI: 10.3389/frai.2024.1443386 PMID: 39011026

Kottur, R. (2024). The Transformative Impact of AI-Driven Personalization in Educational Settings: From Administrative Efficiency to Enhanced Learning Outcomes. [IJCET]. *International Journal of Computer Engineering and Technology, 15*(6), 1349–1360. DOI: 10.5281/zenodo.14444522

Küçükuncular, A., & Ertugan, A. (2025). Teaching in the AI era: Sustainable digital education through ethical integration and teacher empowerment. *Sustainability, 17*(16), 7405. DOI: 10.3390/su17167405

Melo-López, V.-A., Basantes-Andrade, A., Gudiño-Mejía, C.-B., & Hernández-Martínez, E. (2025). The impact of artificial intelligence on inclusive education: A systematic review. *Education Sciences, 15*(5), 539. DOI: 10.3390/educsci15050539

Memon, T. D., & Kwan, P. (2025). A collaborative model for integrating teacher and GenAI into future education. *TechTrends : For Leaders in Education & Training*. doi:DOI: 10.1007/s11528-025-01105-w

Mustafa, M. Y., Tlili, A., Lampropoulos, G., Huang, R., Jandrić, P., Zhao, J., & Saqr, M. (2024). A systematic review of literature reviews on artificial intelligence in education (AIED): A roadmap to a future research agenda. *Smart Learning Environments, 11*(1). Advance online publication. DOI: 10.1186/s40561-024-00350-5

Naayini, P. (2025). AI and the Future of Education: Advancing Personalized Learning and Intelligent Tutoring Systems. *Frontiers in Educational Innovation and Research, 1*(1), 29–39. DOI: 10.62762/FEIR.2025.332098

Nguyen, A., Ngo, H. N., Hong, Y., Dang, B., & Nguyen, B.-P. T. (2023). Ethical principles for artificial intelligence in education. *Education and Information Technologies*, *28*(4), 4221–4241. DOI: 10.1007/s10639-022-11316-w PMID: 36254344

Öner, D. (2025). Building Artificial Intelligence Literacy for Research: Technical Understanding as the Foundation for Critical Evaluation. *IAFOR Journal of Education*, *13*(2). Advance online publication. DOI: 10.22492/ije.13.2.02

Panwale, S. B., & Vijayakumar, S. (2025). Evaluating AI-personalized learning interventions in distance education. *International Review of Research in Open and Distance Learning*, *26*(1), 157–174. DOI: 10.19173/irrodl.v26i1.7813

Peddi, S., & Manoharan, G. (2026). Ethical Guidelines for the thoughtful Implementation of AI in Higher Education. *EthAIca*, *5*, 409. DOI: 10.56294/ai2026409

Thomas, C., & Ostmann, F. (2024, March 15). *Enabling AI governance and innovation through standards*. UNESCO. https://www.unesco.org/en/articles/enabling-ai-governance-and-innovation-through-standards

UNESCO. (2021). Artificial Intelligence and Education: Guidance for Policy-Makers. Paris: United Nations Educational, Scientific and Cultural Organization (UNESCO). ISBN: 978-92-3-100447-6 [Available on Nov 5 2025 at: https://unesdoc.unesco.org/ark:/48223/pf0000376709]

Walter, Y. (2024). Embracing the future of Artificial Intelligence in the classroom: The relevance of AI literacy, prompt engineering, and critical thinking in modern education. *International Journal of Educational Technology in Higher Education*, *21*(1). Advance online publication. DOI: 10.1186/s41239-024-00448-3

Yim, I. H. Y., & Su, J. (2025). Artificial intelligence literacy education in primary schools: A review. *International Journal of Technology and Design Education*, *35*, 2175–2204. DOI: 10.1007/s10798-025-09979-w

Compilation of References

Adapa, V. R. K. (2024). Navigating the privacy paradox: Balancing AI advancement and data protection in the digital age. *International Journal of Scientific Research in Computer Science. Engineering and Information Technology*, *10*(6), 99–110. DOI: 10.32628/cseit24106158

Agell, N., & Prat-i-Pubill, Q. (2024, February). AI: Technological Revolution or Existential Threat? Retrieved from https://dobetter.esade.edu/en/artificial-intelligence-technological-revolution-existential-threat-AI

Ahn, J., Beck, A., Rice, J., & Foster, M. (2021). Exploring people's thoughts about the future of education with artificial intelligence. *Computers and Education: Artificial Intelligence*, *2*, 100010. Advance online publication. DOI: 10.1016/j.caeai.2021.100010

Aiken, A. (1994). *MOSS (Measure of Software Similarity).* Stanford University. https://theory.stanford.edu/~aiken/moss/

Al-Abdullatif, A. M. (2025). Auditing AI Literacy Competency in K–12 Education: The Role of Awareness, Ethics, Evaluation, and Use in Human–Machine Cooperation. *Systems*, *13*(6), 490. DOI: 10.3390/systems13060490

Alzen, J. L., Langdon, L. S., & Otero, V. K. (2018). A logistic regression investigation of the relationship between the Learning Assistant model and failure rates in introductory STEM courses. *International Journal of STEM Education*, *5*(1), 56. DOI: 10.1186/s40594-018-0152-1 PMID: 30631745

Alzoubi, Y. I., & Mishra, A. (2025). Differential privacy and artificial intelligence: Potentials, challenges, and future avenues. *EURASIP Journal on Information Security*, *2025*(1), 2. Advance online publication. DOI: 10.1186/s13635-025-00203-9

American Psychiatric Association. (2013). *Diagnostic and statistical manual of mental disorders* (5th ed.)., DOI: 10.1176/appi.books.9780890425596

Anthropic. (2024). *Claude AI by Anthropic.* https://www.anthropic.com/claude

Appleton, J. J., Christenson, S. L., & Furlong, M. J. (2008). Student engagement with school: Critical conceptual and methodological issues of the construct. *Psychology in the Schools*, *45*, 369–386. DOI: 10.1002/pits.20303

Arnold, A., Cafer, A., Green, J., Haines, S., Mann, G., & Rosenthal, M. (2021). Perspective: Promoting and fostering multidisciplinary research in universities. *Research Policy*, *50*(9), 104334. DOI: 10.1016/j.respol.2021.104334

Atchley, P., Pannell, H., Wofford, K., Hopkins, M., & Atchley, R. A. (2024). Human and AI collaboration in the higher education environment: Opportunities and concerns. *Cognitive Research: Principles and Implications*, *9*(1), 20. DOI: 10.1186/s41235-024-00547-9 PMID: 38589710

Awaji, B., Solaiman, E., & Marshall, L. (2020). Blockchain-based trusted achievement record system design. In *Proceedings of the 5th International Conference on Information and Education Innovations* (pp. 47–52). Association for Computing Machinery. DOI: 10.1145/3411681.3411689

Baier, A. (1986), Trust and Antitrust. In Ethics, Vol. 96, No. 2 (Jan., 1986), pp. 231-260 (30 pages), Published By: The University of Chicago Press

Baker, R., & Hawn, A. (2021). Algorithmic bias in education: Challenges and solutions. *Educational Technology Research and Development*, *69*(3), 123–138. DOI: 10.1007/s11423-021-09993-7

Balog, K., Radlinski, F., & Petrov, A. (2023). Measuring the impact of explanation bias: A study of natural language justifications for recommender systems. In *Extended Abstracts of the 2023 CHI Conference on Human Factors in Computing Systems* (pp. 1–8).

Bandura, A. (2011): Moral Disengagement: , last accessed: 30 June 2025DOI: 10.1002/9780470672532.wbepp165

Barnard, J. (1997). The World Wide Web and Higher Education: The Promise of Virtual Universities and Online Libraries. 37(3), 30–35. DOI:https://dl.acm.org/doi/10.5555/282065.282072

Bass, L., Frick, W. C., & Young, M. D. (2018). *Developing Ethical Principles for School Leadership* (1st ed.). ImprintRoutledge., DOI: 10.4324/9781315688237

Beale, R. (2025). *Computer science education in the age of generative AI.* University of Birmingham, https://pure-oai.bham.ac.uk/ws/portalfiles/portal/279998930/2507.02183v1.pdf

Bearman, M., & Ajjawi, R. (2025). Artificial intelligence and gender equity: An integrated approach for health professional education. *Medical Education, 59*(10), 1049–1057. DOI: 10.1111/medu.15657 PMID: 40064176

Berendt, B., Littlejohn, A., & Blakemore, M. (2020). AI in education: Learner choice and fundamental rights. *Learning, Media and Technology, 45*(3), 312–324. DOI: 10.1080/17439884.2020.1786399

Bernard, R. M., Abrami, P. C., Borokhovski, E., Wade, C. A., Tamim, R. M., Surkes, M. A., & Bethel, E. C. (2009). A Meta-Analysis of Three Types of Interaction Treatments in Distance Education. *Review of Educational Research, 79*(3), 1243–1289.

Bernard, R. M., Abrami, P. C., Lou, Y., Borokhovski, E., Wade, A., Wozney, L., Wallet, P. A., Fiset, M., & Huang, B. (2004). How Does Distance Education Compare With Classroom Instruction? A Meta-Analysis of the Empirical Literature. *Review of Educational Research, 74*(3), 379–439. DOI: 10.3102/00346543074003379

Bhagat, S., & Kim, D. J. (2020). Higher Education Amidst COVID-19: Challenges and Silver Lining. *Information Systems Management, 37*(4), 366–371. DOI: 10.1080/10580530.2020.1824040

Bhattacharya, S., Vyas, P., Yarradoddi, S., & Dasari, B. Sumathy, Kaluri, R., & Gadekallu, T. R. (2023). Towards smart education in the industry 5.0 era: A mini review on the application of federated learning. In *2023 IEEE Intl Conf on Dependable, Autonomic and Secure Computing, Intl Conf on Pervasive Intelligence and Computing, Intl Conf on Cloud and Big Data Computing, Intl Conf on Cyber Science and Technology Congress (DASC/PiCom/CBDCom/CyberSciTech)* (pp. 0602–0608). IEEE. DOI: 10.1109/dasc/picom/cbdcom/cy59711.2023.10361510

Binns, R. (2018). Fairness in machine learning: Lessons from political philosophy. In *Proceedings of the 1st Conference on Fairness, Accountability and Transparency (FAT* 2018)* (pp. 149–159). PMLR.

Bluemink, J., & Järvelä, S. (2004). Face-to-face encounters as contextual support for Web-based discussions in a teacher education course. *The Internet and Higher Education, 7*(3), 199–215.

Boateng, O., & Boateng, B. (2025). Algorithmic bias in educational systems: Examining the impact of AI-driven decision making in modern education. *World Journal of Advanced Research and Reviews, 25*(1), 2012–2017. DOI: 10.30574/wjarr.2025.25.1.0253

Bosch, N., D'Mello, S., & Baker, R. (2021). Detecting student affect from multimodal data. *IEEE Transactions on Affective Computing*, *12*(2), 280–293. DOI: 10.1109/TAFFC.2018.2878658

Bowen, R. S., & Cooper, M. M. (2022). Grading on a Curve as a Systemic Issue of Equity in Chemistry Education. *Journal of Chemical Education*, *99*(1), 185–194.

Brazilian Data Protection Law (Lei Geral de Proteção de Dados Pessoais – LGPD). Lei No. 13.709, de 14 de Agosto de 2018 (2020). https://www.gov.br/anpd/pt-br/centrais-de-conteudo/outros-documentos-e-publicacoes-institucionais/lgpd-en-lei-no-13-709-capa.pdf

Brinck, I. (2024). Craft thinking: A relational approach to making and design. In *Craft and Design Practice from an Embodied Perspective*. Routledge.

Brown, M., Nic Giolla Mhichíl, M., Beirne, E., & Mac Lochlainn, C. (2021). The global micro-credential landscape: Charting a new credential ecology for lifelong learning. *Journal of Learning for Development*, *8*(2), 228–254. DOI: 10.56059/jl4d.v8i2.525

Buerkle, A., O'Dell, A., Matharu, H., Buerkle, L., & Ferreira, P. (2023). Recommendations to align higher education teaching with the UN sustainability goals – A scoping survey. *International Journal of Educational Research Open*, *5*, 100280. Advance online publication. DOI: 10.1016/j.ijedro.2023.100280

Bulut, O., & Beiting-Parrish, M. (2024). The rise of artificial intelligence in educational measurement: Opportunities and ethical challenges. *Chinese/English Journal of Educational Measurement and Evaluation*, *5*(3). Advance online publication. DOI: 10.59863/miql7785

Burns, M. (2023). *Distance Education for Teacher Training: Modes, Models and Methods* (2nd ed.). Education Development Center.

Burrell, J. (2016). How the machine 'thinks': Understanding opacity in machine learning algorithms. *Big Data & Society*, *3*(1). Advance online publication. DOI: 10.1177/2053951715622512

Cameron, M., Lacy, T. A., Siegel, P., Wu, J., Wilson, A., Johnson, R., Burns, R., & Wine, J. (2021). 2019–20 National Postsecondary Student Aid Study (NPSAS:20): *First Look at the Impact of the Coronavirus (COVID-19) Pandemic on Undergraduate Student Enrollment, Housing, and Finances (preliminary data)* (NCES 2021-456). U.S. Department of Education. Washington, DC: National Center for Education Statistics. Retrieved 2025-08-21 from https://nces.ed.gov/pubsearch/pubsinfo.asp?pubid=2021456

Camilo, M. G. (2021). The Elkonin-Davidov System: A Grove of Developmental Teaching Theory. *Revista Científica Multidisciplinar Núcleo Do Conhecimento, 06*(06), 142–158.

Canning, E. A., Muenks, K., Green, D. J., & Murphy, M. C. (2019). STEM faculty who believe ability is fixed have larger racial achievement gaps and inspire less student motivation in their classes. *Science Advances, 5*(2), eaau4734. Advance online publication. DOI: 10.1126/sciadv.aau4734 PMID: 30793027

Carnegie Learning. (2025). *MATHia®: The 1-to-1 math coach that makes your life easier*. https://www.carnegielearning.com/solutions/math/mathia/

Casal-Otero, L., Catala, A., Fernández-Morante, C., Taboada, M., Cebreiro, B., & Barro, S. (2023). AI literacy in K-12: A systematic literature review. *International Journal of STEM Education, 10*(1). Advance online publication. DOI: 10.1186/s40594-023-00418-7

Casey, J. R., Russell, A., & Courey, A. J. (2023). Participation in high-structure general chemistry course increases student sense of belonging and persistence to organic chemistry. *Journal of Chemical Education, 100*(8), 2860–2872. DOI: 10.1021/acs.jchemed.2c01253 PMID: 37577453

Castelli, F. R., & Sarvary, M. A. (2021). Why students do not turn on their video cameras during online classes and an equitable and inclusive plan to encourage them to do so. *Ecology and Evolution, 11*(8), 3565–3576. DOI: 10.1002/ece3.7123 PMID: 33898009

Cavoukian, A. (2010). *Privacy by Design: The 7 foundational principles*. Information and Privacy Commissioner of Ontario, Canada. https://www.ipc.on.ca/wp-content/uploads/Resources/7foundationalprinciples.pdf

Cavoukian, A., Taylor, S., & Abrams, M. E. (2010). Privacy by Design: Essential for organizational accountability and strong business practices. *Identity in the Information Society, 3*(2), 405–413. DOI: 10.1007/s12394-010-0053-z

Cengage Group. 2025, AI in Education Report: New Cengage Group Data Shows Growing GenAI Adoption in K12 & Higher Education Retrieved 2025-08-21 from https://www.cengagegroup.com/news/press-releases/2025/ai-in-education-report-new-cengage-group-data-shows-growing-genai-adoption-in-k12--higher-education/

Chandler, K. (2016). Using Breakout Rooms in Synchronous Online Tutorials. *Journal of Perspectives in Applied Academic Practice, 4*(3). Advance online publication. DOI: 10.14297/jpaap.v4i3.216

Chapman, R. (2020). The reality of autism: On the metaphysics of disorder and diversity. *Philosophical Psychology, 33*, 799–819. DOI: 10.1080/09515089.2020.1751103

Charan, N. D. (2022). *A beginner's guide to using the ChatGPT API.* Medium. https://medium.com/@niteshdancharan2022/a-beginners-guide-to-using-the-chatgpt-api-047f275b65a0

Chassignol, M., Khoroshavin, A., Klimova, A., & Bilyatdinova, A. (2018): Artificial Intelligence trends in education: a narrative overview, Procedia Computer Science, Volume 136, 2018, Pages 16-24, ISSN 1877-0509, DOI: 10.1016/j.procs.2018.08.233

Chen, L., Chen, P., & Lin, Z. (2020). Artificial intelligence in education: A review. *IEEE Access : Practical Innovations, Open Solutions, 8*, 75264–75278. DOI: 10.1109/ACCESS.2020.2988510

Clarindo, C. B. da S., Miller, S., & Kohle, É. C. (2020). Learning Activity as a Means of Developing Theoretical Thinking Capacities. *Frontiers in Psychology, 11*. Advance online publication. DOI: 10.3389/fpsyg.2020.603753 PMID: 33381070

CodeGrade B.V. (2025). *CodeGrade: Code grading and plagiarism detection for education.* https://www.codegrade.com/

Corker, M., French, S., & Singer, J. (1999). 'Why can't you be normal for once in your life?' from a 'problem with no name' to a new category of disability. In *Disability discourse* (pp. 57–59). essay, Open University Press

Czerwinska, U. (2022). Interpretability of machine learning models. In *Applied data science in tourism* (pp. 275–303). Springer., DOI: 10.1007/978-3-030-88389-8_14

D'Mello, S. K., Bosch, N., & Baker, R. S. (2020). Affective computing in education: From detection to adaptation. *User Modeling and User-Adapted Interaction, 30*(1), 1–34. DOI: 10.1007/s11257-019-09222-0

Davidson, D. (1969). How is weakness of the will possible?.

Deci, E. L., & Ryan, R. M. (2000). The "what" and "why" of goal pursuits: Human needs and the self-determination of behavior. *Psychological Inquiry, 11*(4), 227–268. DOI: 10.1207/S15327965PLI1104_01

DeMonbrun, M., Finelli, C. J., Prince, M., Shekhar, P., Henderon, C., & Waters, C. (2017). Creating an Instrument to Measure Student Response to Instructional Practices. *Journal of Engineering Education, 106*, 273–298. DOI: 10.1002/jee.20162

Dhupia, B., & Alameen, A. (2019). Adaptive eLearning system: Conceptual framework for personalized study environment. In *Communications in Computer and Information Science* (pp. 334–342). Springer., DOI: 10.1007/978-981-15-0108-1_31

Diamond, A. (2013). Executive functions. *Annual Review of Psychology*, *64*, 135–168. DOI: 10.1146/annurev-psych-113011-143750 PMID: 23020641

Dixson, M. D. (2015). Measuring Student Engagement in the Online Course: The Online Student Engagement Scale (OSE). *Online Learning : the Official Journal of the Online Learning Consortium*, *19*(4). Advance online publication. DOI: 10.24059/olj.v19i4.561

Dolezal, D. (2020, October). The learning office approach to modern 21st century education: third evaluation of a self-driven concept for student-centered engineering education. In 2020 IEEE Frontiers in Education Conference (FIE) (pp. 1-9). IEEE. DOI: 10.1109/FIE44824.2020.9274211

Dolezal, D., Posekany, A., Ambros, R., Koppensteiner, G., & Motschnig, R. (2022, October). Technology-enhanced and student-centered learning as a method to foster students' ICT competence and problem coping skills. In 2022 IEEE Frontiers in Education Conference (FIE) (pp. 1-8). IEEE.

Dolezal, D., Posekany, A., Vittori, L., Koppensteiner, G., & Motschnig, R. (2018, October). Student-centered classrooms in engineering education: concept and evaluation of a learning office for software development and applied mathematics. In 2018 IEEE Frontiers in Education Conference (FIE) (pp. 1-9). IEEE.

Dolezal, D., Posekany, A., Vittori, L., Koppensteiner, G., & Motschnig, R. (2019, October). Fostering 21st century skills in student-centered engineering education at the secondary school level: second evaluation of the learning office. In 2019 IEEE Frontiers in Education Conference (FIE) (pp. 1-9). IEEE.

Dolezal, D., Motschnig, R., & Ambros, R. (2025). Pre-Service Teachers' Digital Competence: A Call for Action. *Education Sciences*. Advance online publication. DOI: 10.3390/educsci15020160

Dolezal, D., Posekany, A., Koppensteiner, G., Vittori, L., & Motschnig, R. (2021). Learner-Centered Engineering Education as an Incubator of 21st Century Skills. *International Journal of Engineering Education*, *37*, 1605–1618.

Dong, X., Randolph, D. A., Weng, C., Kho, A. N., Rogers, J. M., & Wang, X. (2021). Developing high performance secure multi-party computation protocols in healthcare: A case study of patient risk stratification. *AMIA Joint Summits on Translational Science Proceedings AMIA Summit on Translational Science*, *2021*, 200–209. PMID: 34457134

Dritsas, E., & Trigka, M. (2025). Methodological and technological advancements in e-learning. *Information (Basel)*, *16*(1), 56. Advance online publication. DOI: 10.3390/info16010056

Dutton, J., Dutton, M., & Perry, J. (2019). How do online students differ from lecture students? *Online Learning : the Official Journal of the Online Learning Consortium*, *6*(1). Advance online publication. DOI: 10.24059/olj.v6i1.1869

Eberlein, T., Kampmeier, J., Minderhout, V., Moog, R. S., Platt, T., Varma-Nelson, P., & White, H. B. (2008). Pedagogies of engagement in science: A comparison of PBL, POGIL, and PLTL. *Biochemistry and Molecular Biology Education*, *36*(4), 262–273. DOI: 10.1002/bmb.20204 PMID: 19381266

Ebers, M., Hoch, V. R. S., Rosenkranz, F., Ruschemeier, H., & Steinrötter, B. (2021). The European Commission's proposal for an Artificial Intelligence Act—A critical assessment by members of the Robotics and AI Law Society (RAILS). *J*, *4*(4), 589–603. DOI: 10.3390/j4040043

EISNER. E. W. (2002). Front Matter. In *The Arts and the Creation of Mind* (pp. i–vi). Yale University Press. https://www.jstor.org/stable/j.ctt1np7vz.1

Epstein, D. (2021). *Range: Why Generalists Triumph in a Specialized World*. Riverhead Books.

Ertl, B., Fischer, F., & Mandl, H. (2006). Conceptual and socio-cognitive support for collaborative learning in videoconferencing environments. *Computers & Education*, *47*(3), 298–315. DOI: 10.1016/j.compedu.2004.11.001

Eubanks, V. (2018). *Automating inequality: How high-tech tools profile, police, and punish the poor*. St. Martin's Press.

European Commission & OECD. 2025 https://education.ec.europa.eu/focus-topics/digital-education/action-plan, last accessed 28 June 2025

European Commission. (2021). *Proposal for a regulation laying down harmonised rules on artificial intelligence (Artificial Intelligence Act) and amending certain Union legislative acts* (COM/2021/0206 final). https://eur-lex.europa.eu/legal-content/EN/TXT/?uri=CELEX:52021PC0206

European Commission. (2025). OECD: Empowering Learners for the Age of AI - Review Draft (May 2025). An AI Literacy Framework for Primary and Secondary Education

European Commission. (n.d.) *AI Act* https://digital-strategy.ec.europa.eu/en/policies/regulatory-framework-ai

European Parliament. (2023). EU AI Act: first regulation on artificial intelligence Retrieved 2025—-08-21 from https://www.europarl.europa.eu/topics/en/article/20230601STO93804/eu-ai-act-first-regulation-on-artificial-intelligence

Farheen, S., Cheema, A. A., Ullah, R. S., & Bandeali, D. M. M. (2025). Equity and bias in AI educational tools: A critical examination of algorithmic decision-making in classrooms. *The Critical Review of Social Sciences Studies*, *3*(3), 67–85. DOI: 10.59075/zqmnpa62

Federal Trade Commission. (2020). *Children's Online Privacy Protection Rule ("COPPA").* https://www.ftc.gov/legal-library/browse/rules/childrens-online-privacy-protection-rule-coppa

Feng, Z., Guo, D., Tang, D., Duan, N., Feng, X., Gong, M., Shou, L., Qin, B., Liu, T., Jiang, D., & Zhou, M. (2020, November). *CodeBERT: A pre-trained model for programming and natural languages.* In T. Cohn, Y. He, & Y. Liu (Eds.), *Findings of the Association for Computational Linguistics: EMNLP 2020* (pp. 1536–1547). Online: Association for Computational Linguistics. https://doi.org/DOI: 10.18653/v1/2020.findings-emnlp.139

Fiock, H. (2020). Designing a Community of Inquiry in Online Courses. *International Review of Research in Open and Distance Learning*, *21*(1), 134–152. DOI: 10.19173/irrodl.v20i5.3985

Fischer, C., Xu, D., Rodriguez, F., Denaro, K., & Warschauer, M. (2020). Effects of course modality in summer session: Enrollment patterns and student performance in face-to-face and online classes. *The Internet and Higher Education*, *45*, 100710. DOI: 10.1016/j.iheduc.2019.100710

Flener-Lovitt, C., Bailey, K., & Han, R. (2020). Using Structured Teams to Develop Social Presence in Asynchronous Chemistry Courses. *Journal of Chemical Education*, *97*(9), 2519–2525. DOI: 10.1021/acs.jchemed.0c00765

Floridi, L. (2019). Translating Principles into Practices of Digital Ethics: Five Risks of Being Unethical. *Philosophy & Technology*, *32*, 185–193. DOI: 10.1007/s13347-019-00354-x

Floridi, L., & Cowls, J. (2019). A unified framework of five principles for AI in society. *Harvard Data Science Review*, *1*(1). Advance online publication. DOI: 10.1162/99608f92.8cd550d1

Fredricks, J. A., Blumenfeld, P. C., & Paris, A. H. (2004). School Engagement: Potential of the Concept, State of the Evidence. *Review of Educational Research*, *74*(1), 59–109. DOI: 10.3102/00346543074001059

Freire, P. (1970a). *Pedagogy of the oppressed.* The Continuum Pushing Company.

Freitas, D., & Damazio, A. (2022). Conceptual thinking of fractions: the Davydovian mode of teaching organization. *Educ. Pesqui., São Paulo,* 48, e236913. Retrieved from https://www.scielo.br/j/ep/a/dGVVjR4FMSxRVKzZWXHhJnf/?format=pdf &lang=en

Fricker, M. (2007). *Epistemic injustice: Power and the ethics of knowing*. Oxford university press.

Fulfer, K. D., Wachter, E., Muzyka, J. L., Demoranville, L. T., Fieberg, J. E., Haile, J. D., Scott, D., Song, Y., Workman, J. M., & Young, K. J. (2020). #StayCentred: Maintaining Personal Education at Centre College During COVID-19. *Journal of Chemical Education*, *97*(9), 2783–2787. DOI: 10.1021/acs.jchemed.0c00726

Fung, F. M., & Lam, Y. (2020). How COVID-19 Disrupted Our "Flipped" Freshman Organic Chemistry Course: Insights Gained from Singapore. *Journal of Chemical Education*, *97*(9), 2573–2580. DOI: 10.1021/acs.jchemed.0c00590

Fung, L. K. (2021). *Neurodiversity: From phenomenology to neurobiology and enhancing technologies*. American Psychiatric Association Publishing.

Furlong, M. J., & Christenson, S. L. (2008). Engaging students with school and academics: A relevant construct for all students. *Psychology in the Schools*, *45*, 365–368. DOI: 10.1002/pits.20302

Gamage, K. A. A., & Dehideniya, S. C. P. (2025). Unlocking career potential: How micro-credentials are revolutionising higher education and lifelong learning. *Education Sciences*, *15*(5), 525. Advance online publication. DOI: 10.3390/educsci15050525

Garrison, D. R., Anderson, T., & Archer, W. (1999). Critical Inquiry in a Text-Based Environment: Computer Conferencing in Higher Education. *The Internet and Higher Education*, *2*(2–3), 87–105. DOI: 10.1016/S1096-7516(00)00016-6

GDPR.eu. (n.d.). General Data Protection Regulation (GDPR) compliance guidelines. Retrieved from https://gdpr.eu

Gemmel, P. M., Goetz, M. K., James, N. M., Jesse, K. A., & Ratliff, B. J. (2020). Collaborative Learning in Chemistry: Impact of COVID-19. *Journal of Chemical Education*, *97*(9), 2899–2904. DOI: 10.1021/acs.jchemed.0c00713

Gherhe , V., imon, S., & Para, I. (2021). Analysing Students' Reasons for Keeping Their Webcams on or off during Online Classes. *Sustainability*, *13*(6), 3203. DOI: 10.3390/su13063203

Gherhe , V., Stoian, C. E., Fărca iu, M. A., & Stanici, M. (2021). E-Learning vs. Face-To-Face Learning: Analyzing Students' Preferences and Behaviors. *Sustainability, 13*(88), 4381. DOI: 10.3390/su13084381

Giesbers, B., Rienties, B., Tempelaar, D., & Gijselaers, W. (2013). Investigating the relations between motivation, tool use, participation, and performance in an e-learning course using web-videoconferencing. *Computers in Human Behavior, 29*(1), 285–292. DOI: 10.1016/j.chb.2012.09.005

Gillies, D. (2008). Student perspectives on videoconferencing in teacher education at a distance. *Distance Education, 29*(1), 107–118. DOI: 10.1080/01587910802004878

Gisore, B. N. (2023). Integration of 21st century skills into teacher education curriculum. In *Advances in higher education and professional development* (pp. 225–238). IGI Global. DOI: 10.4018/978-1-6684-6339-0.ch013

GitHub. (2024). *GitHub Copilot.* https://github.com/features/copilot

Glasser, H., Rea, A., & Green, I. (2018). Catch: A new, SDG-aligned learning for transformative change game. *Sustainability, 11*(3), 111–117. DOI: 10.1089/sus.2018.29134.hg

Google. (2024). *Google Gemini AI.* https://blog.google/technology/ai/google-gemini-ai/#availability

Google. (2025). *Gemini developer API pricing.* https://ai.google.dev/gemini-api/docs/pricing

Gotesman, R. (2018, May). Learning Backpropagation from Geoffrey Hinton. *TDS Archive.* Retrieved from https://medium.com/data-science/learning-backpropagation-from-geoffrey-hinton-619027613f0

Gov.UK, Department for Education. (2025) AI in schools and colleges: What you need to know Retrieved 2025-08-21 from https://educationhub.blog.gov.uk/2025/06/artificial-intelligence-in-schools-everything-you-need-to-know/

Grand View Research. (n.d.) AI in education market size & share, industry report. Report ID: GVR 4-68039-948-8 Retrieved 2025-08-21 from https://www.grandviewresearch.com/industry-analysis/artificial-intelligence-ai-education-market-report

Greene, M. (1995). *Releasing the imagination: Essays on education, the arts, and social change*. Jossey-Bass.

Greenleaf, G., & Makiyama, T. (2021). Japan's APPI amendments: Asia's first GDPR convergence? *Privacy Laws & Business International Report, 171*, 18–21. https://papers.ssrn.com/sol3/papers.cfm?abstract_id=3818994

Gromyko, Y. V. (2020). Vasiliy Davydov: The Founder of Activity Practice in Education. *Psychological Science and Education*, *25*(5), 5–18. DOI: 10.17759/pse.2020250501

Gruenhagen, J. H., Sinclair, P., Carroll, J., Baker, P., Wilson, A., & Demant, D. (2023).The rapid rise of generative AI and its implications for academic integrity: Students' perceptions and use of chatbots for assistance with assessments, Computers and Education: Artificial Intelligence, Volume 7, 2024, 100273, ISSN 2666-920X, DOI: 10.1016/j.caeai.2024.100273

Guidotti, R., Monreale, A., Ruggieri, S., Turini, F., Giannotti, F., & Pedreschi, D. (2019). A survey of methods for explaining black box models. *ACM Computing Surveys*, *51*(5), 93. Advance online publication. DOI: 10.1145/3236009

Gunning, D., Stefik, M., & Choi, J.. (2023). XAI: Explainable artificial intelligence for education. *AI Magazine*, *44*(1), 15–28. DOI: 10.1007/s43684-023-00039-9

Guo, D., Ren, S., Lu, S., Feng, Z., Tang, D., Liu, S., & Zhou, M. (2021). *GraphCodeBERT: Pre-training code representations with data flow.* In *International Conference on Learning Representations (ICLR 2021).* Retrieved from https://openreview.net/forum?id=jLoC4ez43PZ

Guo, D., Lu, S., Duan, N., Wang, Y., Zhou, M., & Yin, J. (2022, May). UniXcoder: Unified cross-modal pre-training for code representation. In Muresan, S., Nakov, P., & Villavicencio, A. (Eds.), *Proceedings of the 60th Annual Meeting of the Association for Computational Linguistics (*Volume 1*: Long Papers)* (pp. 7212–7225). Dublin, Ireland: Association for Computational Linguistics. https://doi.org/DOI: 10.18653/v1/2022.acl-long.499

Guo, D., Xu, C., Duan, N., Yin, J., & McAuley, J. (2023). LongCoder: A long-range pre-trained language model for code completion. In *Proceedings of the 40th International Conference on Machine Learning (ICML 2023)* (pp. 12098–12107).

Guralnick, D. (2024): Reimagining Learning Experiences with the Use of AI, in *Artificial Intelligence in Education: The Intersection of Technology and Pedagogy*, edited by Peter Ilic, Imogen Casebourne, and Rupert Wegerif; November 2024, Springer Nature, Switzerland. DOI: 10.1016/j.ijinfomgt.2018.01.009

Habib, A., Harris, L., Pollick, F., & Melville, C. (2019). A meta-analysis of working memory in individuals with autism spectrum disorders. *PLoS One*, *14*, e0216198. DOI: 10.1371/journal.pone.0216198 PMID: 31039192

Hadar Shoval, D. (2025). Artificial intelligence in higher education: Bridging or widening the gap for diverse student populations? *Education Sciences*, *15*(5), 637. DOI: 10.3390/educsci15050637

Hamamra, B., Mayaleh, A., & Khlaif, Z. N. (2024). Between tech and text: The use of generative AI in Palestinian universities—a ChatGPT case study. *Cogent Education*, *11*(1), 2380622.

Hamidon, Z., Abdullah, M. L., Yussof, Y., & Ismail, M. N. (2025). Exploring AI-driven personalization in open and distance learning: Learner engagement, inclusivity, and ethical implementation. *International Journal of Academic Research in Business & Social Sciences*, *15*(6). Advance online publication. DOI: 10.6007/ijarbss/v15-i6/25791

Hamilton, L. G., & Petty, S. (2023). Compassionate pedagogy for neurodiversity in higher education: A conceptual analysis. *Frontiers in Psychology*, *14*, 1093290. DOI: 10.3389/fpsyg.2023.1093290 PMID: 36874864

Hashemi-Pour, C. (2024, October). What Is a Learning Management System (LMS)? *Search CIO*. Retrieved from https://www.techtarget.com/searchcio/definition/learning-management-system

Hebert, E., Wood, R., Jeon, K., & Reena, I. (2022). Faculty making the emergency online transition during the COVID-19 pandemic: Effects of prior online teaching experience and strategies used to learn to teach online (special edition 2022). *Higher Learning Research Communications, 12*(0). https://doi.org/DOI: 10.18870/hlrc.v12i0.1322

Henrie, C. R., Halverson, L. R., & Graham, C. R. (2015). Measuring student engagement in technology-mediated learning: A review. *Computers & Education*, *90*, 36–53. DOI: 10.1016/j.compedu.2015.09.005

Herlo, S. (2024, March). What Is Structured Content and How Do You Create It? Retrieved from https://www.rws.com/content-management/blog/what-is-structured-content/

Hickman, T., Lorenz, S., Teetzmann, C., & Jha, A. (2024) Long awaited EU AI Act becomes law after publication in the EU's Official Journal, Retrieved 2025-08-21 from https://www.whitecase.com/insight-alert/long-awaited-eu-ai-act-becomes-law-after-publication-eus-official-journal

Holmes, W., Bialik, M., & Fadel, C. (2022). *Artificial intelligence in education: Promises and implications for teaching and learning*. Center for Curriculum Redesign.

Holstein, K., Wortman Vaughan, J., Daumé, H., III, Dudík, M., & Wallach, H. (2019). Improving fairness in machine learning systems: What do industry practitioners need? In *Proceedings of the 2019 CHI Conference on Human Factors in Computing Systems* (Paper 600). Association for Computing Machinery. DOI: 10.1145/3290605.3300830

Holstein, K., McLaren, B. M., & Aleven, V. (2020). Designing for complementarity: Teacher and AI support for student learning. *International Journal of Artificial Intelligence in Education, 30*(1), 1–28. DOI: 10.1007/s40593-019-00186-0

Hoq, M., Shi, Y., Leinonen, J., Babalola, D., Lynch, C., Price, T., & Akram, B. (2024). Detecting ChatGPT-generated code submissions in a CS1 course using machine learning models. In *Proceedings of the 55th ACM Technical Symposium on Computer Science Education* (Vol. 1, pp. 526–532). Association for Computing Machinery. https://doi.org/DOI: 10.1145/3626252.3630826

Hornby, G., & Greaves, D. (2022). Metacognitive Strategies. In Hornby, G., & Greaves, D. (Eds.), *Essential Evidence-Based Teaching Strategies: Ensuring Optimal Academic Achievement for Students* (pp. 95–104)., DOI: 10.1007/978-3-030-96229-6_7

Hubble, S., & Bolton, P. (2021). *Support for disabled students in higher education in England* (Briefing Paper No. 8716). House of Commons Library. Retrieved 2025-08-21 from https://researchbriefings.files.parliament.uk/documents/CBP-8716/CBP-8716.pdf

IBM. (2023). *What is generative AI?* https://www.ibm.com/topics/generative-ai

IEEE 9274.1.1-2023. *IEEE standard for learning technology—JavaScript Object Notation (JSON) data model format and Representational State Transfer (RESTful) web service for learner experience data tracking and access*. IEEE Standards Association. (2023).

IEEE CertifAIEd. (n.d) IEEE CertifAIEd product certification. Retrieved 2025-08-21 from https://standards.ieee.org/products-programs/icap/ieee-certifaied/product-certification

IEEE Standards Association (2025). *IEEE Standard for Algorithmic Bias Considerations*. (IEEE Standard 7003-2024) doi:DOI: 10.1109/ieeestd.2025.10851955

IEEE Standards Association. (2023). *IEEE CertifAIEd ontological specification for ethical accountability* IEEE. https://standards.ieee.org

IEEE Standards Association. (2023). *IEEE CertifAIEd ontological specification for ethical algorithmic bias*. IEEE. https://standards.ieee.org

IEEE Standards Association. (2023). *IEEE CertifAIEd ontological specification for ethical privacy*. IEEE. https://standards.ieee.org

IEEE Standards Association. (2023). *IEEE CertifAIEd ontological specification for ethical transparency*. IEEE. https://standards.ieee.org

IEEE. (2020). *Ethically aligned design: A vision for prioritizing human well-being with autonomous and intelligent systems* (2nd ed.). IEEE Global Initiative on Ethics of Autonomous and Intelligent Systems. https://standards.ieee.org/content/dam/ieee-standards/standards/web/restricted/eadv2_2020.pdf

IEEE. (2020). *Ethically aligned design: A vision for prioritizing human well-being with autonomous and intelligent systems*. IEEE Standards Association.

IEEE. (n.d) IEEE Retrieved 2025-08-21 from https://www.ieee.org/about-ieee

Ifenthaler, D., & Yau, J. Y.-K. (2020). Utilising learning analytics for study success: Reflections on current empirical findings. *Technology. Knowledge and Learning*, *25*(3), 545–559. DOI: 10.1007/s10758-019-09416-3

Ikäheimo, H. (2022). Recognizability and recognition as human—Learning from Butler and Manne. *Journal for the Theory of Social Behaviour*, *52*(4), 579–594. DOI: 10.1111/jtsb.12352

IMS Global Learning Consortium. (2020). *Caliper Analytics 1.2 specification*. https://www.imsglobal.org/spec/caliper/v1p2

International Dyslexia Association and American Psychiatric Association. (2013). Definition of Dyslexia Retrieved 2025-08-21 from https://dyslexiaida.org/definition-of-dyslexia/

ISO. (2022). ISO/IEC 23053:2022(en) Framework for Artificial Intelligence (AI) Systems Using Machine Learning (ML). Retrieved from https://www.iso.org/obp/ui/en/#iso:std:iso-iec:23053:ed-1:v1:en

ISO. (2022). *ISO/IEC JTC 1/SC 42 Artificial Intelligence – Overview and Standards*. International Organization for Standardization.

Jacobson, M. J., & Xue, Y. (2024). *Integrating Symbolic Reasoning into Neural Generative Models for Design Generation*. (arXiv:2310.09383). doi:/arXiv.2310.09383DOI: 10.48550

Jamieson, M. V. (2020). Keeping a Learning Community and Academic Integrity Intact after a Mid-Term Shift to Online Learning in Chemical Engineering Design During the COVID-19 Pandemic. *Journal of Chemical Education*, *97*(9), 2768–2772. DOI: 10.1021/acs.jchemed.0c00785

Jayasundara, J. M. P. V. K., Gilbert, T., Kersten, S., & Meng, L. (2022). How UK HE STEM Students Were Motivated to Switch Their Cameras on: A Study of the Development of Compassionate Communications in Task-focused Online Group Meetings. *Education Sciences*, *12*(5), 317. DOI: 10.3390/educsci12050317

Jean, P. (pj). (2024, June). When To Use Symbolic And Generative AI. *Forbes*. Retrieved from https://www.forbes.com/councils/forbestechcouncil/2024/06/05/when-to-use-symbolic-and-generative-ai/

Jeffries, S., & Everatt, J. (2004). Working memory: Its role in dyslexia and other specific learning difficulties. *Dyslexia (Chichester, England)*, *10*, 196–214. DOI: 10.1002/dys.278 PMID: 15341198

Jia, C. (2025). The impact of curriculum design and educational equity in the age of artificial intelligence - A literature review. *Lecture Notes in Education Psychology and Public Media*, *89*(1), 55–61. DOI: 10.54254/2753-7048/2025.22633

Jiao, D. (2024). AI-Driven Personalization in Higher Education: Enhancing Learning Outcomes through Adaptive Technologies. *Adult and Higher Education*, *6*, 42–46. DOI: 10.23977/aduhe.2024.060607

Jirgensons, M., & Kapenieks, J. (2018). Blockchain and the future of digital learning credential assessment and management. *Journal of Teacher Education for Sustainability*, *20*(1), 145–156. DOI: 10.2478/jtes-2018-0009

Jobin, A., Ienca, M., & Vayena, E. (2019). The global landscape of AI ethics guidelines. *Nature Machine Intelligence*, *1*(9), 389–399. DOI: 10.1038/s42256-019-0088-2

Kabudi, T., Pappas, I., & Olsen, D. H. (2021). AI-enabled adaptive learning systems: A systematic mapping of the literature. *Computers and Education: Artificial Intelligence*, *2*, 100017. Advance online publication. DOI: 10.1016/j.caeai.2021.100017

Kairouz, P., McMahan, H. B., Avent, B., Bellet, A., Bennis, M., Nitin Bhagoji, A., … Zhao, S. (2021). Advances and open problems in federated learning. *Foundations and Trends® in Machine Learning, 14*(1–2), 1–210. DOI: 10.1561/2200000083

Kashyap, R., Samuel, Y., Friedman, L. W., & Samuel, J. (2024). Editorial: Artificial intelligence education & governance -human enhancive, culturally sensitive and personally adaptive HAI. *Frontiers in Artificial Intelligence*, *7*, 1443386. DOI: 10.3389/frai.2024.1443386 PMID: 39011026

Khalil, M., Shakya, R., & Liu, Q. (2025). Towards privacy-preserving data-driven education: The potential of federated learning. In *2025 International Conference on New Trends in Computing Sciences (ICTCS)* (pp. 113–118). IEEE. DOI: 10.1109/ictcs65341.2025.10989403

Khosravi, H., Kitto, K., & Knight, S. (2022). Adaptive learning analytics: A review of AI-driven personalization in education. *British Journal of Educational Technology, 53*(4), 1012–1030. DOI: 10.1111/bjet.13294

Kizilcec, R. F., Lee, H., & Reich, J. (2021). Participatory design for equitable AI in education. *Computers & Education, 170*, 104225. DOI: 10.1016/j.compedu.2021.104225

Knox, J., Williamson, B., & Bayne, S. (2020). Machine behaviourism: Future visions of 'learnification' and 'datafication' across humans and digital technologies. *Learning, Media and Technology, 45*(1), 31–45. DOI: 10.1080/17439884.2019.1623251

Koedinger, K. R., Corbett, A. T., & Perfetti, C. (2012). The knowledge-learning-instruction framework: Bridging the science–practice chasm to enhance robust student learning. *Cognitive Science, 36*(5), 757–798. DOI: 10.1111/j.1551-6709.2012.01245.x PMID: 22486653

Kofler, M. J., Singh, L. J., Soto, E. F., Chan, E. S., Miller, C. E., Harmon, S. L., & Spiegel, J. A. (2020). Working memory and short-term memory deficits in ADHD: A bifactor modeling approach. *Neuropsychology, 34*, 686–698. DOI: 10.1037/neu0000641 PMID: 32437194

Kosmyna, N., Hauptmann, E., Yuan, Y. T., Situ, J., Liao, X. H., Beresnitzky, A. V., . . . Maes, P. (2025). Your brain on chatgpt: Accumulation of cognitive debt when using an ai assistant for essay writing task. arXiv preprint arXiv:2506.08872.

Kottur, R. (2024). The Transformative Impact of AI-Driven Personalization in Educational Settings: From Administrative Efficiency to Enhanced Learning Outcomes. [IJCET]. *International Journal of Computer Engineering and Technology, 15*(6), 1349–1360. DOI: 10.5281/zenodo.14444522

Küçükuncular, A., & Ertugan, A. (2025). Teaching in the AI era: Sustainable digital education through ethical integration and teacher empowerment. *Sustainability, 17*(16), 7405. DOI: 10.3390/su17167405

Kuh, G. D. (2001). Assessing What Really Matters to Student Learning Inside The National Survey of Student Engagement. *Change: The Magazine of Higher Learning, 33*(3), 10–17. DOI: 10.1080/00091380109601795

Kumar, P., Saxena, C., & Baber, H. (2021). Learner-content interaction in e-learning- the moderating role of perceived harm of COVID-19 in assessing the satisfaction of learners. *Smart Learning Environments, 8*. Advance online publication. DOI: 10.1186/s40561-021- 00149-8 PMID: 40477398

Kumar, R., Eaton, S. E., Mindzak, M., & Morrison, R. (2023). *Handbook of academic integrity*. Springer.

Le Cunff, A.-L., Giampietro, V., & Dommett, E. (2024). Neurodiversity and cognitive load in online learning: A focus group study. *PLoS One, 19*(4), e0301932. DOI: 10.1371/journal.pone.0301932 PMID: 38626101

Learning Equality. (2025). *Kolibri*. https://learningequality.org/kolibri/about-kolibri/

Li, N., Romera Rodriguez, G., Xu, Y., Bhatt, P., Nguyen, H. A., Serpi, A., Tsai, C., & Carroll, J. M. (2022). *Picturing One's Self: Camera Use in Zoom Classes during the COVID-19 Pandemic*. Proceedings of the Ninth ACM Conference on Learning @ Scale, 151–162. DOI:https://doi.org/DOI: 10.1145/3491140.3528284

Liu, F., Zheng, Z., Shi, Y., Tong, Y., & Zhang, Y. (2024). A survey on federated learning: A perspective from multi-party computation. *Frontiers of Computer Science, 18*(1), 181302. Advance online publication. DOI: 10.1007/s11704-023-3282-7

Liu, R., Zenke, C., Liu, C., Holmes, A., Thornton, P., & Malan, D. J. (2024). Teaching CS50 with AI: Leveraging generative artificial intelligence in computer science education. In *Proceedings of the 55th ACM Technical Symposium on Computer Science Education* (Vol. 1, pp. 750–756). Association for Computing Machinery. https://doi.org/DOI: 10.1145/3626252.3630938

Liu, S., Guo, X., Hu, X., & Zhao, X. (2024). Advancing generative intelligent tutoring systems with GPT-4: Design, evaluation, and a modular framework for future learning platforms. *Electronics (Basel), 13*(24), 4876. Advance online publication. DOI: 10.3390/electronics13244876

Luckin, R., Holmes, W., Griffiths, M., & Forcier, L. B. (2016). *Intelligence unleashed: An argument for AI in education*. Pearson. https://www.pearson.com/content/dam/one-dot-com/one-dot-com/global/Files/efficacy-and-research/Intelligence-Unleashed-Publication.pdf

Luckin, R. (2017). Towards artificial intelligence-based assessment systems. *Nature Human Behaviour, 1*(3), 0028. Advance online publication. DOI: 10.1038/s41562-016-0028

Luckin, R. (2020). *Machine learning and human intelligence: The future of education for the 21st century*. UCL Press., DOI: 10.14324/111.9781787358760

Lundberg, S. M., & Lee, S.-I. (2017). A unified approach to interpreting model predictions. In *Advances in Neural Information Processing Systems* (pp. 4765–4774). https://papers.nips.cc/paper/7062-a-unified-approach-to-interpreting-model-predictions.pdf

Market.us. (2024). AI in higher education market. Report IE 121472. Retrieved 2025-08-21 from https://market.us/report/ai-in-higher-education-market/

Martin, F., & Bolliger, D. U. (2018). Engagement Matters: Student Perceptions on the Importance of Engagement Strategies in the Online Learning Environment. *Online Learning : the Official Journal of the Online Learning Consortium, 22*(1). Advance online publication. DOI: 10.24059/olj.v22i1.1092

Ma, W., Adesope, O. O., Nesbit, J. C., & Liu, Q. (2014). Intelligent tutoring systems and learning outcomes: A meta-analysis. *Journal of Educational Psychology, 106*(4), 901–918. DOI: 10.1037/a0037123

Mayer, R. E., & Moreno, R. (2003). Nine ways to reduce cognitive load in multimedia learning. *Educational Psychologist, 38*, 43–52. DOI: 10.1207/S15326985EP3801_6

McGreal, R. (2023). Blockchain and micro-credentials in education. *Journal of Distance Education, 38*(1). Advance online publication. DOI: 10.55667/ijede.2023.v38.i1.1250

McGreal, R. (2024). Empowering micro-credentials using blockchain and artificial intelligence. In *Global perspectives on micro-learning and micro-credentials in higher education* (pp. 75–90). IGI Global., DOI: 10.4018/979-8-3693-0343-6.ch006

Mehrabi, N., Morstatter, F., Saxena, N., Lerman, K., & Galstyan, A. (2022). A survey on bias and fairness in machine learning. *ACM Computing Surveys, 54*(6), 115. Advance online publication. DOI: 10.1145/3457607

Melo-López, V.-A., Basantes-Andrade, A., Gudiño-Mejía, C.-B., & Hernández-Martínez, E. (2025). The impact of artificial intelligence on inclusive education: A systematic review. *Education Sciences, 15*(5), 539. DOI: 10.3390/educsci15050539

Memon, T. D., & Kwan, P. (2025). A collaborative model for integrating teacher and GenAI into future education. *TechTrends : For Leaders in Education & Training*. doi:DOI: 10.1007/s11528-025-01105-w

Merl, C. (2020). Fostering 21st Century Skills in Engineering and Business Management Students. In Auer, M., & Tsiatsos, T. (Eds.), *The Challenges of the Digital Transformation in Education. ICL 2018. Advances in Intelligent Systems and Computing* (Vol. 916). Springer., DOI: 10.1007/978-3-030-11932-4_15

Merl, C. (2022). Human intelligence cultivation with the 2CG® poetry machine: How to boost future skills development and idea generation with artistic impulses in Lab 21. [iJAC]. *Int. J. Adv. Corp. Learn.*, *15*, 61–74. DOI: 10.3991/ijac.v15i1.27079

Merl, C. (2022). Lab 21 – A Space for Learning, Sharing and Innovating. In Guralnick, D., Auer, M. E., & Poce, A. (Eds.), *Innovations in Learning and Technology for the Workplace and Higher Education. TLIC 2021. Lecture Notes in Networks and Systems* (Vol. 349). Springer., DOI: 10.1007/978-3-030-90677-1_20

Meta, A. I., Touvron, H., Lavril, T., Izacard, G., Martinet, X., Lachaux, M. A., Lacroix, T., . . . Lample, G. (2023). *LLaMA: Open and efficient foundation language models* (Version 1) [Large language model]. Meta AI. https://ai.meta.com/llama/

Meyer, E., Wessels, D.: Natural Language Processing im akademischen Schreibprozess -- mehr Motivation durch Inspiration?. Künstliche Intelligenz in der Hochschulbildung. Chancen und Grenzen des KI-gestützten Lernens und Lehrens. 2023

Miles, M. B., Huberman, A. M., & Saldana, J. (2014). *Qualitative Data Analysis: A Methods Sourcebook*. Sage.

Milliken & Company, Henigan Consulting Group, and Sapio Research. (2023). Designing a Neuro-Inclusive Workplace: A Practical Guide for Creating Neuro-Inclusive Workplaces. Milliken & Company. Retrieved 2025-08-21 from https://floorseurope.milliken.com

Mitchell, M., Wu, S., Zaldivar, A., Barnes, P., Vasserman, L., Hutchinson, B., & Gebru, T. (2019). Model cards for model reporting. In *Proceedings of the Conference on Fairness, Accountability, and Transparency* (pp. 220–229). Association for Computing Machinery. DOI: 10.1145/3287560.3287596

Moore, M. G. (1989). Editorial: Three types of interaction. *American Journal of Distance Education*, *3*(2), 1–7. DOI: 10.1080/08923648909526659

Mousa, M. (2025). AI-supported formative assessments: Enhancing student-centered learning and teacher perceptions. *Journal of Pedagogy and Education Science*, *4*, 127–141. DOI: 10.56741/jpes.v4i02.857

Murphy, K. (2022). Reflections on studying with a neurodiverse difference. Museum of Childhood Ireland. Retrieved 2025-08-21 from https://museumofchildhood.ie/reflections-on-studying-with-a-neurodiverse-difference/

Mustafa, M. Y., Tlili, A., Lampropoulos, G., Huang, R., Jandrić, P., Zhao, J., & Saqr, M. (2024). A systematic review of literature reviews on artificial intelligence in education (AIED): A roadmap to a future research agenda. *Smart Learning Environments*, *11*(1). Advance online publication. DOI: 10.1186/s40561-024-00350-5

Myers, T., Monypenny, R., & Trevathan, J. (2012). Overcoming the glassy-eyed nod: An application of process-oriented guided inquiry learning techniques in information technology. *Journal of Learning Design*, *5*(1), 12–22. DOI: 10.5204/jld.v5i1.97

Naayini, P. (2025). AI and the Future of Education: Advancing Personalized Learning and Intelligent Tutoring Systems. *Frontiers in Educational Innovation and Research*, *1*(1), 29–39. DOI: 10.62762/FEIR.2025.332098

Nguyen, P. T., ... (2024). *Dataset of GPTSniffer.* GitHub. https://github.com/MDEGroup/GPTSniffer/tree/master/DATASETS

Nguyen, A., Ngo, H. N., Hong, Y., Dang, B., & Nguyen, B.-P. T. (2023). Ethical principles for artificial intelligence in education. *Education and Information Technologies*, *28*(4), 4221–4241. DOI: 10.1007/s10639-022-11316-w PMID: 36254344

Nguyen, K. A., Borrego, M., Finelli, C. J., DeMonbrun, M., Crockett, C., Tharayil, S., Shekhar, P., Waters, C., & Rosenberg, R. (2021). Instructor strategies to aid implementation of active learning: A systematic literature review. *International Journal of STEM Education*, *8*, 9. DOI: 10.1186/s40594-021-00270-7

Nguyen, P. T., Di Rocco, J., Di Sipio, C., Rubei, R., Di Ruscio, D., & Di Penta, M. (2024, July). GPTSniffer: A CodeBERT-based classifier to detect source code written by ChatGPT. *Journal of Systems and Software*, *214*, 112059. DOI: 10.1016/j.jss.2024.112059

Nixon, J. (2020). Hannah Arendt: The Promise of Education. Hannah Arendt: The Promise of Education. DOI: 10.1007/978-3-030-37573-7

Northern Illinois University. (2024). *Types of academic dishonesty.* https://www.niu.edu/academic-integrity/faculty/types/index.shtml

Nugent, A., Carroll, A., Lodge, J. M., Matthews, K. E., MacMahon, S., & Sah, P. (2023). A qualitative exploration of expert perspectives on applying the science of learning to higher education. *Frontiers in Education*, *8*. Advance online publication. DOI: 10.3389/feduc.2023.1233651

OECD. (2019). *OECD recommendation of the Council on Artificial Intelligence.* https://legalinstruments.oecd.org/en/instruments/OECD-LEGAL-0449

OECD. (2023). *Micro-credentials for lifelong learning and employability: Uses and possibilities* (OECD Education Policy Perspectives, No. 66). OECD Publishing. DOI: 10.1787/9c4b7b68-en

Öner, D. (2025). Building Artificial Intelligence Literacy for Research: Technical Understanding as the Foundation for Critical Evaluation. *IAFOR Journal of Education, 13*(2). Advance online publication. DOI: 10.22492/ije.13.2.02

Open Learning Initiative. (2025). https://oli.cmu.edu/

Open, A. I. (2024). *OpenAI Codex.* https://openai.com/blog/openai-codex

Open, A. I. (2025). *OpenAI API pricing.* https://platform.openai.com/docs/pricing

Pan, K., Ong, Y.-S., Gong, M., Li, H., Qin, A. K., & Gao, Y. (2024). Differential privacy in deep learning: A literature survey. *Neurocomputing*, *589*, 127663. Advance online publication. DOI: 10.1016/j.neucom.2024.127663

Panwale, S. B., & Vijayakumar, S. (2025). Evaluating AI-personalized learning interventions in distance education. *International Review of Research in Open and Distance Learning*, *26*(1), 157–174. DOI: 10.19173/irrodl.v26i1.7813

Parajuli, P., & Racharak, T. (2025). A framework for identifying underspecification in image classification pipeline using post-hoc analyzer. In Santana, M. C., Marsico, M. D., & Fred, A. (Eds.), *Proceedings of the 14th International Conference on Pattern Recognition Applications and Methods (ICPRAM 2025)* (pp. 426–436). SCITEPRESS.

Pawar, U., Beder, C., O'Reilly, R., & O'Shea, D. (2024). On the impact of neighbourhood sampling to satisfy sufficiency and necessity criteria in explainable AI. In *CLEAR 2024.* https://api.semanticscholar.org/CorpusID:269648514

Pecson, R., & Sarmiento, J. (2024). Integrating 21st-century skills into instructional materials for sustainable education. *Indonesian Journal of Instructional Media and Model*, *6*(2), 89–99. DOI: 10.32585/ijimm.v6i2.5934

Peddi, S., & Manoharan, G. (2026). Ethical Guidelines for the thoughtful Implementation of AI in Higher Education. *EthAIca*, *5*, 409. DOI: 10.56294/ai2026409

Perets, E. A., Chabeda, D., Gong, A. Z., Huang, X., Fung, T. S., Ng, K. Y., Bathgate, M., & Yan, E. C. Y. (2020). Impact of the Emergency Transition to Remote Teaching on Student Engagement in a Non-STEM Undergraduate Chemistry Course in the Time of COVID-19. *Journal of Chemical Education*, *97*(9), 2439–2447. DOI: 10.1021/acs.jchemed.0c00879

Pirntke, E., & Rindebrant, W. (2024). *Automatic detection of AI-generated source code in programming courses.*

Podolskiy, A. (2012). Activity Theories of Learning. In Seel, N. M. (Ed.), *Encyclopedia of the Sciences of Learning* (pp. 83–85)., DOI: 10.1007/978-1-4419-1428-6_310

Prechelt, L., Malpohl, G., & Philippsen, M. (2002). Finding plagiarisms among a set of programs with JPlag. *Journal of Universal Computer Science*, *8*(11), 1016–1038. https://github.com/jplag/JPlag

Puri, R., Kung, D., Janssen, G., Zhang, W., Domeniconi, G., Zolotov, V., ... Reiss, F. (2021). *CodeNet: A large-scale AI for code dataset for learning a diversity of coding tasks.*

Racharak, T., Jearanaiwongkul, W., Pooksook, J., & Takashima, K. (2025). Towards assumption-based argumentation mining in hotel reviews. In T. Ågotnes & D. Doder (Eds.), *Logic and Argumentation: 6th International Conference (CLAR 2025)* (Vol. 15712, pp. 272–290). Springer.

Racharak, T., Ragkhitwetsagul, C., Sontesadisai, C., & Sunetnanta, T. (2025). Test it before you trust it: Applying software testing for trustworthy in-context learning. In R. Ichise (Ed.), *Natural Language Processing and Information Systems – 30th International Conference on Applications of Natural Language to Information Systems (NLDB 2025)* (Vol. 15836, pp. 243–258). Springer.

Rahimi, S., & Shute, V. J. (2023). Stealth assessment: A theoretically grounded and psychometrically sound method to assess, support, and investigate learning in technology-rich environments. *Educational Technology Research and Development*. Advance online publication. DOI: 10.1007/s11423-023-10232-1

Rai, R. 2025, Artificial intelligence in education market size. (Report Code: SRT-E61DR) Straits Research. Retrieved 2025-08-21 from https://straitsresearch.com/report/artificial-intelligence-in-education-market#:~:text=The%20global%20artificial%20intelligence%20in,period%20(2025%2D2033)

Raji, I. D., Smart, A., White, R. N., Mitchell, M., Gebru, T., Hutchinson, B., & Barnes, P. (2020). Closing the AI accountability gap. In *Proceedings of the 2020 Conference on Fairness, Accountability, and Transparency* (pp. 33–44). Association for Computing Machinery. DOI: 10.1145/3351095.3372873

Raker, J. R., Dood, A. J., Srinivasan, S., & Murphy, K. L. (2021). Pedagogies of engagement use in postsecondary chemistry education in the United States: Results from a national survey. *Chemistry Education Research and Practice*, *22*(1), 30–42. DOI: 10.1039/D0RP00125B

Regan, P. M., & Jesse, J. (2019). Ethical challenges of edtech, big data and personalized learning: Twenty-first century student sorting and tracking. *Ethics and Information Technology*, *21*(3), 167–179. DOI: 10.1007/s10676-018-9492-2

Reihanian, I., Hou, Y., Chen, Y., & Zheng, Y. (2025). A Review of Generative AI in Computer Science Education: Challenges and Opportunities in Accuracy, Authenticity, and Assessment. In *Computational science and computational intelligence* (pp. 144–158). Springer Nature Switzerland.

Reiserer, M., Ertl, B., & Mandl, H. (2023). Fostering Collaborative Knowledge Construction in Desktop Video-conferencing. Effects of Content Schemes and Cooperation Scripts in Peer Teaching Settings. In G. Stahl, Computer Support for Collaborative Learning (1st ed., pp. 379–388). *Routledge*. DOI:https://doi.org/DOI: 10.4324/9781315045467-55

Repo, L. H. (2024). *Prompt engineering and LLMs with LangChain.* Pinecone. https://www.pinecone.io/learn/series/langchain/langchain-prompt-templates/

Reschly, A. L., & Christenson, S. L. (Eds.). (2022). *Handbook of Research on Student Engagement*. Springer International Publishing., DOI: 10.1007/978-3-031-07853-8

Ribeiro, M. T., Singh, S., & Guestrin, C. (2016). "Why should I trust you?" Explaining the predictions of any classifier. In *Proceedings of the 22nd ACM SIGKDD International Conference on Knowledge Discovery and Data Mining* (pp. 1135–1144).

Richardson, J. C., Arbaugh, J. B., Cleveland-Innes, M., Ice, P., Swan, K. P., & Garrison, D. R. (2012). Using the Community of Inquiry Framework to Inform Effective Instructional Design. In Moller, L., & Huett, J. (Eds.), *The Next Generation of Distance Education* (pp. 97–125)., DOI: 10.1007/978-1-4614-1785-9_7

Ricoeur, P. (1992). *Oneself as Another*. University of Chicago Press.

Ritter, S., Anderson, J. R., Koedinger, K. R., & Corbett, A. (2007). Cognitive Tutor: Applied research in mathematics education. *Psychonomic Bulletin & Review*, *14*(2), 249–255. DOI: 10.3758/bf03194060 PMID: 17694909

Robb, N., Politis, Y., & Boot, F. H. (2023). Editorial: Championing inclusion and diversity: inclusive design practices and approaches for education. *Frontiers in Education*, *8*. Advance online publication. DOI: 10.3389/feduc.2023.1234892

Rodriguez, J.-M. G., Hunter, K. H., Scharlott, L. J., & Becker, N. M. (2020). A Review of Research on Process Oriented Guided Inquiry Learning: Implications for Research and Practice. *Journal of Chemical Education*, *97*(10), 3506–3520. DOI: 10.1021/acs.jchemed.0c00355

Rogers, C. R. (1959): A Theory of Therapy, Personality and Interpersonal Relationships as Developed in the Client-centered Framework. In: Koch, S. (ed.) Psychology: A Study of a Science, vol. 3, pp. 184–256. McGraw-Hill, New York, NY Rotherham, A.J., Willingham, D.: 21st-century skills: The challenges ahead. Educational Leadership 67, 16–21 (2009)

Rogers, C. R. (1983). *Freedom to Learn for the 80s* (2nd ed.). Merrill Publishing.

Rose, D. H., Gravel, J. W., & Domings, Y. (2020). *Universal design for learning: Theory and practice.* CAST Publishing.

Rumie. (2025). *Welcome to Rumie.* https://learn.rumie.org/jR/bytes/welcome-to-rumie/

Russell, J., Karpinska, M., & Iyyer, M. (2025, July). People who frequently use ChatGPT for writing tasks are accurate and robust detectors of AI-generated text. In *Proceedings of the 63rd Annual Meeting of the Association for Computational Linguistics (*Volume 1*: Long Papers)* (pp. 5342–5373). Association for Computational Linguistics. https://doi.org/DOI: 10.18653/v1/2025.acl-long.267

Ryan, R. M., & Deci, E. L. (2000). Self-determination theory and the facilitation of intrinsic motivation, social development, and well-being. *The American Psychologist, 55*(1), 68–78. DOI: 10.1037/0003-066X.55.1.68 PMID: 11392867

Schefer-Wenzl, S., Vogl, C., Peiris, S., & Miladinovic, I. (2025). Exploring the adoption of generative AI tools in computer science education: A student survey. In *Proceedings of the 2024 16th International Conference on Education Technology and Computers* (pp. 173–178). Association for Computing Machinery. https://doi.org/DOI: 10.1145/3702163.3702188

Schön, D. A. (1991). *The reflective practitioner.* Ashgate Publishing.

Schwartz, H. (2020). *Remote Learning Is Here to Stay: Results from the First American School District Panel Survey.* RAND Corporation., DOI: 10.7249/RRA956-1

Schwenck, C. M., & Pryor, J. D. (2021). Student perspectives on camera usage to engage and connect in foundational education classes: It's time to turn your cameras on. *International Journal of Educational Research Open, 2*, 100079. DOI: 10.1016/j.ijedro.2021.100079

Selco, J. I., & Habbak, M. (2021). STEM Students' Perceptions on Emergency Online Learning during the COVID-19 Pandemic: Challenges and Successes. *Education Sciences, 11*(12), 799. DOI: 10.3390/educsci11120799

Selwyn, N. (2019). *Should robots replace teachers? AI and the Future of Education* (1st ed.). Polity Press.

Selwyn, N. (2019). *Should robots replace teachers? AI and the future of education*. Polity Press.

Senge, P. M. (1990). *The fifth discipline: The art & practice of the learning organization*. Doubleday/Currency.

Sergeyeva, T. (2009). *Eco-Humanistic Self-Development: Monograph.* Kh. Blok., ISBN 966-961188-2-7.

Sergeyeva, T. (2014). Training course 'Eco-Humanistic Technology of Self-Development'. Retrieved from https://old.karazin.ua/docs/work/slavic_summer_2014_2_2.pdf

Sergeyeva, T., Bronin, S., & Glazar, T. (2023, November). Technology for Synergistic Solutions Co-Creation Based on Multi-Agents' Diversities Interaction. In Anisimov, A., Snytyuk, V., Chris, A., Pester, A., Mallet, F., Tanaka, H., Krak, I., Henke, K., Nikitchenko, M., Chertov, O., Marchenko, O., Bozóki, S., Tsyganok, V., & Vovk, V. (Eds.), *Selected Papers of the X International Scientific Conference "Information Technology and Implementation" (IT&I-2023)* (pp. 462–470). Conference Proceedings., Retrieved from https://ceur-ws.org/Vol-3624/#Short_7.pdf

Sergeyeva, T., Bronin, S., Glazar, T., & Degleria, V. (2023, May). Creating Digitized Tools for Supporting Multidisciplinary and Multi-Actor Solutions Based on Eco-Humanistic Model. *2023 IEEE International Conference on Smart Information Systems and Technologies (SIST)*, 251–256. doi:DOI: 10.1109/SIST58284.2023.10223539

Sergeyeva, T., Bronin, S., Glazar, T., & Njoo, J. (2022, December). E-learning Research within New European Paradigm. In Anisimov, A., Snytyuk, V., Chris, A., Pester, A., Mallet, F., Tanaka, H., Krak, I., Henke, K., Nikitchenko, M., Chertov, O., Marchenko, O., Bozóki, S., Tsyganok, V., & Vovk, V. (Eds.), *Selected Papers of the IX International Scientific Conference "Information Technology and Implementation" (IT&I-2022)* (pp. 137–147). Conference Proceedings., Retrieved from https://ceur-ws.org/Vol-3347/#Paper_12.pdf

Sergeyeva, T., Bronin, S., & Turlakova, N. (2022, April). Multidisciplinary Dimension of E-Learning in the Innovative Eco-System of a Modern University. *2022 International Conference on Smart Information Systems and Technologies (SIST)*, 1–8. doi:DOI: 10.1109/SIST54437.2022.9945768

Sergeyeva, T., Bronin, S., Turlakova, N., & Iamnytskyi, S. (2023). Integrating Educational Components into the Metaverse. In Guralnick, D., Auer, M. E., & Poce, A. (Eds.), *Innovative Approaches to Technology-Enhanced Learning for the Workplace and Higher Education* (pp. 412–425)., DOI: 10.1007/978-3-031-21569-8_39

Sergeyeva, T., Festeu, D., Bronin, S., & Turlakova, N. (2021, December). Student – Training Environment Interaction: Soft Skills Development within E-learning. In Anisimov, A., Snytyuk, V., Chris, A., Pester, A., Mallet, F., Tanaka, H., Krak, I., Henke, K., Nikitchenko, M., Chertov, O., Marchenko, O., Bozóki, S., Tsyganok, V., & Vovk, V. (Eds.), *Selected Papers of the VIII International Scientific Conference "Information Technology and Implementation" (IT&I-2021)* (pp. 290–298). Conference Proceedings., Retrieved from https://ceur-ws.org/Vol-3132/#Short_10.pdf

Settles, B., & Meeder, B. (2016). A trainable spaced repetition model for language learning. In *Proceedings of the 54th Annual Meeting of the Association for Computational Linguistics (*Volume 1*: Long Papers)* (pp. 1848–1858). Association for Computational Linguistics. DOI: 10.18637/j.acl16.1175

Shahriari, K., & Shahriari, M. (2017). IEEE standard review — Ethically aligned design: A vision for prioritizing human wellbeing with artificial intelligence and autonomous systems. In *2017 IEEE Canada International Humanitarian Technology Conference (IHTC)*. IEEE. DOI: 10.1109/ihtc.2017.8058187

Shah, W. (2022). *Hybrid AI Models: Combining Symbolic Reasoning and Deep Learning for Enhanced Decision-Making*. doi:DOI: 10.13140/RG.2.2.11493.61920

Shockley, K. M., Gabriel, A. S., Robertson, D., Rosen, C. C., Chawla, N., Ganster, M. L., & Ezerins, M. E. (2021). The fatiguing effects of camera use in virtual meetings: A within-person field experiment. *The Journal of Applied Psychology, 106*(8), 1137–1155. DOI: 10.1037/apl0000948 PMID: 34423999

Shute, V., & Ventura, M. (2013). *Stealth assessment: Measuring and supporting learning in games*. MIT Press., DOI: 10.7551/mitpress/9589.001.0001

Singhal, M. K. (2020). Facilitating Virtual Medicinal Chemistry Active Learning Assignments Using Advanced Zoom Features during COVID-19 Campus Closure. *Journal of Chemical Education, 97*(9), 2711–2714. DOI: 10.1021/acs.jchemed.0c00675

Slade, S., & Prinsloo, P. (2013). Learning analytics. *The American Behavioral Scientist, 57*(10), 1510–1529. DOI: 10.1177/0002764213479366

Slade, S., & Prinsloo, P. (2022). Educational data ethics in the age of AI. *British Journal of Educational Technology, 53*(2), 234–248. DOI: 10.1111/bjet.13191

Slavin, R. E. (2022). AI and equity in education: Opportunities and risks. *Journal of Educational Change*, *23*(1), 1–15. DOI: 10.1007/s10833-021-09424-1

Srinivas, N. (2023). ISSUES AND CHALLENGES OF E-LEANING TOWARDS HIGHER EDUCATION. *IJCRT - International Journal of Creative Research Thoughts (IJCRT)*. Retrieved from https://ijcrt.org/viewfull.php?&p_id=IJCRT2311300

Studio, L. (n.d.). *LM Studio docs*. https://lmstudio.ai/docs

Sutanto, J., Liu, Y., Grigore, M., Lemmik, R. (2018): Does knowledge retrieval improve work efficiency? An investigation under multiple systems use; published in International Journal of Information Management, Volume 40, June 2018, Pages 42-53

Swan, K., & Ice, P. (2010). The community of inquiry framework ten years later: Introduction to the special issue. *The Internet and Higher Education*, *13*(1–2), 1–4. DOI: 10.1016/j.iheduc.2009.11.003

Tank, A. (n.d.). Why the world needs deep generalists, not specialists | The Jotform Blog. *Jotform*. Retrieved from https://www.jotform.com/blog/the-world-needs -polymaths/

Tan, L. Y., Hu, S., Yeo, D. J., & Cheong, K. H. (2025). Artificial intelligence-enabled adaptive learning platforms: A review. *Computers and Education: Artificial Intelligence*, *9*, 100429. Advance online publication. DOI: 10.1016/j.caeai.2025.100429

Tanner, K. D. (2013). Structure Matters: Twenty-One Teaching Strategies to Promote Student Engagement and Cultivate Classroom Equity. *CBE Life Sciences Education*, *12*(3), 322–331. DOI: 10.1187/cbe.13-06-0115 PMID: 24006379

Tanneru, S. H., Agarwal, C., & Lakkaraju, H. (2024). *Quantifying uncertainty in natural language explanations of large language models*. In *Proceedings of the 27th International Conference on Artificial Intelligence and Statistics (AISTATS 2024)*. PMLR. arXiv:2311.03533. https://arxiv.org/abs/2311.03533

Taylor, C. (1989). *Source of the Self: The Making of the Modern Identity*. Harvard University Press.

Tharayil, S., Borrego, M., Prince, M., Nguyen, K. A., Shekhar, P., Finelli, C. J., & Waters, C. (2018). Strategies to mitigate student resistance to active learning. *International Journal of STEM Education*, *5*, 7. DOI: 10.1186/s40594-018-0102-y PMID: 30631697

Thomas, C., & Ostmann, F. (2024, March 15). *Enabling AI governance and innovation through standards*. UNESCO. https://www.unesco.org/en/articles/enabling-ai-governance-and-innovation-through-standards

Trilling, B., & Fadel, C. (2012). *21st Century Skills. Learning for Life in our Times*. Jossey-Bass.

Trust, T., & Watters, A. (2020). The trouble with edtech: Persistent equity, surveillance, and control issues in educational technology. *Learning, Media and Technology*, *45*(2), 105–110. DOI: 10.1080/17439884.2020.1761641

Turnitin, L. L. C. (2025). *Turnitin: Plagiarism and AI writing detection service*. https://www.turnitin.com/

U.S. Department of Education. (2021). *Family Educational Rights and Privacy Act (FERPA)*. https://studentprivacy.ed.gov/resources/parent-guide-family-educational-rights-and-privacy-act-ferpa

U.S. Department of Education. (n.d.). FERPA: Family Educational Rights and Privacy Act. Retrieved from https://studentprivacy.ed.gov/ferpa

UNESCO, Fengchun, M., Holmes, W., Ronghuai, H., & Zhang, H. (2021). AI and education: Guidance for policy-makers(45 p.). https://doi.org/DOI: 10.54675/PCSP7350

UNESCO. (1990). *World declaration on education for all and framework for action to meet basic learning needs*. Secretariat of the International Consultative Forum on Education for All. https://unesdoc.unesco.org/ark:/48223/pf0000086701

UNESCO. (2021). Artificial Intelligence and Education: Guidance for Policy-Makers. Paris: United Nations Educational, Scientific and Cultural Organization (UNESCO). ISBN: 978-92-3-100447-6 [Available on Nov 5 2025 at: https://unesdoc.unesco.org/ark:/48223/pf0000376709]

UNESCO. (2021). *Recommendation on the ethics of artificial intelligence*. https://unesdoc.unesco.org/ark:/48223/pf0000381137

UNESCO. (2021). *Recommendation on the ethics of artificial intelligence*. United Nations Educational, Scientific and Cultural Organization. https://unesdoc.unesco.org/ark:/48223/pf0000381137

UNESCO. (2023). AI competency framework for students. https://www.unesco.org/en/articles/ai-competency-framework-students?hub=32618

UNESCO. (2023). Guidance for generative AI in education and research. https://www.unesco.org/en/articles/guidance-generative-ai-education-and-research

UNESCO. (2025). AI competency framework for teachers. https://www.unesco.org/en/articles/ai-competency-framework-teachers?hub=32618

United Nations. (1994). *The Salamanca statement and framework for action on special needs education* (World Conference on Special Needs Education: Access and Quality, ED-94/WS/18) Retrieved 2025-08-21 from https://www.european-agency.org/sites/default/files/salamanca-statement-and-framework.pdf

University College London. (2024). *GenAI and academic integrity in assessment.* https://www.ucl.ac.uk/teaching-learning/generative-ai-hub/genai-and-academic-integrity-assessment

Valtonen, T., Hoang, N., Sointu, E., Näykki, P., Virtanen, A., Pöysä-Tarhonen, J., Häkkinen, P., Järvelä, S., Mäkitalo, K., & Kukkonen, J. (2021). How pre-service teachers perceive their 21st-century skills and dispositions: A longitudinal perspective. *Computers in Human Behavior*. Advance online publication. DOI: 10.1016/j.chb.2020.106643

Van Dusen, B., & Nissen, J. (2020). Associations between learning assistants, passing introductory physics, and equity: A quantitative critical race theory investigation. *Physical Review. Physics Education Research*, *16*(1), 010117. DOI: 10.1103/PhysRevPhysEducRes.16.010117

Van Heuvelen, K. M., Daub, G. W., & Ryswyk, H. V. (2020). Emergency Remote Instruction during the COVID-19 Pandemic Reshapes Collaborative Learning in General Chemistry. *Journal of Chemical Education*, *97*(9), 2884–2888. DOI: 10.1021/acs.jchemed.0c00691

van Laar, E., van Deursen, A. J., van Dijk, J. A., & de Haan, J. (2019). Determinants of 21st-century digital skills: A large-scale survey among working professionals. *Computers in Human Behavior*. Advance online publication. DOI: 10.1016/j.chb.2019.06.017

VanLehn, K. (2011). The relative effectiveness of human tutoring, intelligent tutoring systems, and other tutoring systems. *Educational Psychologist*, *46*(4), 197–221. DOI: 10.1080/00461520.2011.611369

Voigt, P., & von dem Bussche, A. (2017). *The EU General Data Protection Regulation (GDPR): A practical guide* (1st ed.). Springer., DOI: 10.1007/978-3-319-57959-7

Vonderwell, S., & Zachariah, S. (2005). Factors that Influence Participation In Online Learning. *Journal of Research on Technology in Education*, *38*(2), 213–230. DOI: 10.1080/15391523.2005.10782457

Voogt, J., Erstad, O., Dede, C., & Mishra, P. (2013). Challenges to learning and schooling in the digital networked world of the 21st century. *Journal of Computer Assisted Learning*. Advance online publication. DOI: 10.1111/jcal.12029

Vygotsky, L. S. (1978). *Mind in Society: The Development of Higher Psychological Processes*. Harvard University Press.

Walkington, C. A. (2013). Using adaptive learning technologies to personalize instruction to student interests: The impact of relevant contexts on performance and learning outcomes. *Journal of Educational Psychology, 105*(4), 932–945. DOI: 10.1037/a0031882

Walter, Y. (2024). Embracing the future of Artificial Intelligence in the classroom: The relevance of AI literacy, prompt engineering, and critical thinking in modern education. *International Journal of Educational Technology in Higher Education, 21*(1). Advance online publication. DOI: 10.1186/s41239-024-00448-3

Wang, M., & Tsai, C.-C. (2021). Students' trust in AI tutors: A study of perceptions and engagement. *Journal of Educational Technology & Society, 24*(3), 45–58. https://www.j-ets.net/ETS/journals/24_3/4.pdf

Wang, Y., Liu, S., & Zhang, H. (2023). Real-time feedback in AI-supported learning environments: A meta-analysis. *Computers & Education, 193*, 104663. DOI: 10.1016/j.compedu.2023.104663

Wang, Z., Xie, C., & Yu, Z. (2024). *Fast-DetectGPT: Efficient zero-shot detection of machine-generated text via probability curvature*. In *Proceedings of the International Conference on Learning Representations (ICLR 2024)*.

Wei, J., Bosma, M., Zhao, V. Y., Guu, K., Yu, A. W., Lester, B., & Le, Q. V. (2022). Fine tuned language models are zero-shot learners. In *The Tenth International Conference on Learning Representations (ICLR'22)*.

Wei, J., Wang, X., Schuurmans, D., Bosma, M., Ichter, B., Xia, F., & Zhou, D. (2022). Chain-of-thought prompting elicits reasoning in large language models. In *Proceedings of the 36th International Conference on Neural Information Processing Systems (NIPS'22)*.

Wenger, E. (1998). *Communities of Practice: Learning, Meaning, and Identity*. Cambridge University Press.

Wenzel, T. (2020). Collaborative Group Learning in Remotely Taught Analytical Chemistry Courses. *Journal of Chemical Education, 97*(9), 2715–2718. DOI: 10.1021/acs.jchemed.0c00520

Williamson, B. (2024). The social life of AI in education. *International Journal of Artificial Intelligence in Education, 34*(1), 97–104. DOI: 10.1007/s40593-023-00342-5

Williamson, B., & Eynon, R. (2020). Historical threads, missing links, and future directions in AI and education. *Learning, Media and Technology, 45*(3), 223–235. DOI: 10.1080/17439884.2020.1798995

Williamson, B., & Piattoeva, N. (2022). Objectivity and subjectivity in AI-driven education: From data infrastructures to psychosocial effects. In Macgilchrist, A., Williamson, B., & Potter, J. (Eds.), *Digital data, education and childhood* (pp. 95–112). Bloomsbury Academic.

Wise, A. F., Saghafian, M., & Padmanabhan, P. (2012). Towards more precise design guidance: Specifying and testing the functions of assigned student roles in online discussions. *Educational Technology Research and Development, 60*(1), 55–82. DOI: 10.1007/s11423-011-9212-7

Woodbury, J., Arneson, J. B., & Offerdahl, E. G. (2022). Adapting Team-Based Learning for an Online Biochemistry Course. *Journal of Chemical Education, 99*(8), 2964–2971. DOI: 10.1021/acs.jchemed.2c00259

Woolf, B. P. (2010). *Building intelligent interactive tutors: Student-centered strategies for revolutionizing e-learning*. Morgan Kaufmann.

Yang, L. (2025). The potential of AI in education: Personalizing learning. *International Journal of Artificial Intelligence for Science, 1*(2). Advance online publication. DOI: 10.63619/ijai4s.v1i2.003

Yang, Q., Liu, Y., Chen, T., & Tong, Y. (2019). Federated machine learning. *ACM Transactions on Intelligent Systems and Technology, 10*(2), 12. Advance online publication. DOI: 10.1145/3298981

Yan, Y.-M., Chen, C.-Q., Hu, Y.-B., & Ye, X.-D. (2025). LLM-based collaborative programming: Impact on students' computational thinking and self-efficacy. *Humanities & Social Sciences Communications, 12*(1), 149. DOI: 10.1057/s41599-025-04471-1

Yesilyurt, Y. E. (2023). AI-enabled assessment and feedback mechanisms for language learning. In *Advances in educational technologies and instructional design* (pp. 25–43). IGI Global. DOI: 10.4018/978-1-6684-9893-4.ch002

Yim, I. H. Y., & Su, J. (2025). Artificial intelligence literacy education in primary schools: A review. *International Journal of Technology and Design Education, 35*, 2175–2204. DOI: 10.1007/s10798-025-09979-w

Yu, F., Quartey, L., & Schilder, F. (2023). Exploring the effectiveness of prompt engineering for legal reasoning tasks. In *Findings of the Association for Computational Linguistics* (pp. 13582–13596). ACL.

Zawacki-Richter, O., & Jung, I. (2023). Systematic review of AI applications in higher education assessment. *Journal of Educational Technology & Society*, *26*(1), 1–15. https://www.j-ets.net/ETS/journals/26_1/1.pdf

Zawacki-Richter, O., Marín, V. I., Bond, M., & Gouverneur, F. (2019). Systematic review of research on artificial intelligence applications in higher education. *International Journal of Educational Technology in Higher Education*, *16*(1), 1–27. DOI: 10.1186/s41239-019-0171-0

Zdunek, K., Dobrowolska, B., Dziurka, M., Galazzi, A., Chiappinotto, S., Palese, A., & Wells, J. (2024). Challenges and opportunities of micro-credentials as a new form of certification in health science education—A discussion paper. *BMC Medical Education*, *24*(1), 1169. Advance online publication. DOI: 10.1186/s12909-024-06174-8 PMID: 39425060

Zeide, E. (2017). The structural consequences of big data-driven education. *Big Data*, *5*(2), 164–172. DOI: 10.1089/big.2016.0061 PMID: 28632444

Zhou, I., Tofigh, F., Piccardi, M., Abolhasan, M., Franklin, D., & Lipman, J. (2024). Secure multi-party computation for machine learning: A survey. *IEEE Access : Practical Innovations, Open Solutions*, *12*, 53881–53899. DOI: 10.1109/access.2024.3388992

Zhou, J., Gandomi, A. H., Chen, F., & Holzinger, A. (2021). Evaluating the quality of machine learning explanations: A survey on methods and metrics. *Electronics (Basel)*, *10*(5), 593. Advance online publication. DOI: 10.3390/electronics10050593

Zinchenko, P. I., & Sereda, G. K. (2011). Involuntary Memory and Classroom Instruction. *Journal of Russian & East European Psychology*, *49*(1), 17–30. DOI: 10.2753/RPO1061-0405490101

Zliobaite, I. (2017). Measuring discrimination in algorithmic decision making. *Data Mining and Knowledge Discovery*, *31*(4), 1060–1089. DOI: 10.1007/s10618-017-0506-1

About the Contributors

Frederic Andres received his Ph.D. in Information Systems from the University of Paris VI "Pierre et Marie Curie" in 1993 and his Dr. Habilitation in Informatics from the University of Nantes in 2000. Dr. Frederic Andres has been associate professor in the Digital Content and Media Sciences Research Division of the National Institute of Informatics (NII) in Tokyo, Japan since 2000. He is author of more than 150 papers on international journals, books and conferences. His main research areas of interest include several topics such as collective intelligence-based knowledge, AI ethics, data science, supply chain and pedagogy and didactical web-based science education for all. He has been co-organising the International DECOR workshop since 2018 in conjunction with IEEE ICDE. His team won the 1st prize in IEEE Brain Data Bank Challenges and Competitions at COMPSAC 2018, July 2018. Dr. Frederic Andres received the IEEE CertifAIEd Authorized Lead Assessor recognition from IEEE SA on September 15, 2023. In addition, he was named "R10 Ethics Champion" by IEEE Region 10 on 22 Oct 2023.

Teeradaj Racharak is a Senior Lecturer in the School of Information Science at the Japan Advanced Institute of Science and Technology (JAIST). He specializes in artificial intelligence (AI), particularly in neuro-symbolic AI, explainable AI, and knowledge representation. Racharak has a strong academic background, holding two Ph.D. degrees: one in Engineering and Technology from Thammasat University (majoring in formal argumentation) and another in Information Science from JAIST (majoring in description logic). Both of his PhD theses won the National Research Awards from National Research Council of Thailand. His research centers on enhancing AI transparency, fairness, and trustworthiness, working on topics such as argument mining, knowledge graphs, ontologies, and machine learning integration with reasoning systems. His work also includes developing AI systems that support fair and interpretable decision-making, aiming to address both technical and ethical AI challenges. In addition to his academic contributions, he is affiliated as

IEEE CertifAIEd Authorized Assessor from September 2023 and involved in the international standardization efforts in AI (ISO on Artificial Intelligence) from March 2024.

Gerlinde Weger is instrumental in establishing certification standards for the ethical use of advanced technologies and developing methodologies for enhancing human capacity and optimizing ethical technology deployment. Understanding that frameworks and processes are only as good as their implementation, Gerlinde focuses on education and communication for individuals and teams, enabling the power of technology to be harnessed responsibly. Her extensive international experience in governance, marketing/communications, and behavioral change positions her uniquely to anticipate the transformative demands necessitated by advanced technologies. Gerlinde is the Technical Lead for IEEE-SA CertifAIEd and is the chair of IEEE-SA P7003 The Standard for Algorithmic Bias Considerations.

Andreas Pester graduated in mathematics from Odessa State University in 1976, he got his PhD from Kiev State University in 1979 and he habilitated at the University of Technology Dresden in 1984. 2020 he retired from the University of Applied Sciences in Carinthia in Austria. Currently he is a professor for natural language processing and deep learning at the British University in Egypt in Sherouk. He is the author and co-author of more than 75 publications. He was a guest professor at the UPC Barcelona, Technical University Porto, Technical Universities of Kharkov, Technical University Kiev, Polytechnic University St. Petersburg, State University of Petrozavodsk, BTH Karlskrona, University Maribor, UNESP Bauru (Brazil), AUA Erivan and others. He was and is involved in more than 20 EU- and national projects (as project leader or as collaborator), including Erasmus +, TEMPUS, MINERVA etc. His research interests are in deep learning, especially Graph Neural Network architectures and Large Language Models. Actually, he is the co-chair of the IEEE Global Engineering Conference (EDUCON'26), and he chaired also EDUCON'21, Interactive Collaborative and Blended Learning (ICBL) conferences from 2008 – 2019, and is member of the PC of several other conferences etc. He holds the IEEE Education Society Distinguished Chapter Leader Award 2023. He also holds the EDUCON Meritorious Service Award for outstanding contributions to the administrative and management efforts for the IEEE EDUCON conference.

C. Anantaram specializes in application of Artificial Intelligence techniques to real- world systems and his areas of work include trustworthy AI systems, explainability, knowledge representation, reasoning, and integrating AI techniques in business applications. He has 38 years of experience in AI and has published over 45 papers and holds 8 patents. He is an active member of ISO/IEC JTC1/

SC42 Artificial intelligence committee, that is formulating international standards in the field of AI, and also an active member of the Indian standards committee, BIS LITD30, that focuses on both international and national standards in AI. He was a Visiting Faculty at the Department of Computer Science and Engineering, IIIT Delhi from 2019 to 2023. Prior to that he was a Principal Scientist in the R&D division of Tata Consultancy Services Limited. He was also an associate editor of the Acadlore Transactions on AI and Machine Learning journal for many years. He did his PhD in Computer Science from IIT Bombay.

***

Ekapol Chuangsuwanich received the B.S. and M.S. degrees in electrical and computer engineering from Carnegie Mellon University, in 2008 and 2009, respectively, and the Ph.D. degree from MIT, in 2016. He then joined the Spoken Language Systems Group, MIT Computer Science and Artificial Intelligence Laboratory. He is currently a Faculty Member of the Department of Computer Engineering with Chulalongkorn University. His research interests include speech processing, assistive technology, and health applications.

Swarup Raj Dhungana is a technology and product leader with a unique blend of research expertise and industry experience. As a Product Manager and member of the Senior Leadership Team at Citytech Global, he drives innovation in fintech products, working closely with banks, regulators, and financial institutions. Complementing his industry role, Swarup's research spans data privacy, applied ontology, and semantic web technologies, including contributions to the ISO/IEC JTC 1 SC-36 committee and the development of an ontology framework for privacy protection in learning, education, and training. He has published multiple papers in IEEE and other academic platforms, bridging theoretical research with real-world applications. A recipient of the Royal Thai His Majesty King's Scholarship and a Valedictorian of his undergraduate class, Swarup holds dual master's degrees in Information Management and Information Technology. Passionate about leveraging technology for impact, his work lies at the intersection of fintech, research, and innovation.

Dominik Dolezal holds a PhD from the University of Vienna and works as a postdoctoral researcher at the Faculty of Computer Science, University of Vienna. His research primarily focuses on the sustainable integration of digital competence into teacher education, and he teaches project management at the undergraduate level. In addition to his work at the University of Vienna, Dominik also teaches media technology and IT project management at the IT department of TGM, a higher vocational secondary school, where he leads the media technology group for upper grades and serves as the department's e-learning coordinator.

Oindrilla Ghosh is a Research Scholar hailing from the School of Law at Christ (Deemed to be University) Bangalore, India, focuses her research on health of tribal communities. Her work includes publications on Environmental Disasters of which 5 publications that are indexed in SCOPUS and Web of Sciences conference proceedings. She completed her early education at Loreto Day School, Bowbazar and went on to achieve distinction in her undergraduate (B.A/LL.B) and postgraduate (LL.M) studies at Calcutta University. Having served as an Assistant Professor of Law at Kingston Law College,Barasat, Kolkata, Ghosh has actively participated in numerous National Conferences, International Conferences, UN Global Summits, webinars, and seminars organized by prestigious academic institutions. Her expertise lies in health perspectives, environmental studies, human behavior, and related areas. Additionally, she has conducted various workshops, lectures in educational institutions, and is engaged with NGO's to help the needy.

David Guralnick holds a Ph.D. in computer science/artificial intelligence from Northwestern University, where his work integrated research and practice in cognitive science and education. He is President and CEO of Kaleidoscope Learning and also serves as an Adjunct Full Professor at Columbia University, focusing on the intersection of technology, learning, and human behavior. David has extensive expertise in AI-driven learning systems and ethical design. Among other roles, he is the current President of the International E-Learning Association and the founder and chair of The Learning Ideas Conference. His scientific guidance guarantees the academic rigor of the project, ensuring outcomes that align with both international standards and local policy relevance.

Jake Knoppers is currently president of Canaglobe International Inc and Senior Vice-President of Information Management. Services (INFOMAN) Inc. Dr. Knoppers received his Ph.D. (cum laude) from McGill University in the field of quantitative maritime economic history He was the awarded a (prestigious) Killam Post-doctoral Fellowship for advanced studies in quantitative history and economics, computer science and data analytics. He has served as senior advisor to key federal public sector Ministries and private corporations. This included working on Access to Information and Privacy (ATIP), as well as archives and records management legislation, copyright, changes to the Canadian Criminal Code on "data abuse" and the Evidence Act re admissibility of "electronic records" as evidence. Since the early 1990's, Dr. Knoppers became actively involved in national and international standards development work. He is a member of the Technical

Committee on Information Technology (TCIT) of the Standards Council of Canada (SCC) which coordinates and positions in international stand ament Canadian contributions and positions and international standards development in the area of information and telecommunications technologies (ITC). Here his initial focus was that of "data management and interchange" via ISO/IEC JTC1/SC32 for which he has served many years as the Chair of its Canadian mirror committee and Head of Delegation(HoD) to its international Plenary meetings (focussing on and leading the development of key international multipart ISO/IEC 15944-1 eBusiness standards (which are publicly available). In 2002, Dr. Knoppers served as a founding member of the establishment of the Canadian mirror committee to then recently established international ISO/IEC JTC1/SC36 committee titled "Information technology – Learning, Education & Training (ITLET)". Here he not only served as Canadian Chair and HoD for its first 10 years but also as lead ISO/IEC Project Editor for several of its standards including for the 1 st edition of ISO/IEC 291871- which serves as the touchstone basis for the development not only of this chapter but also the development of a new part of ISO/IEC 29187-2 (for which this article serves as a significant contribution to the development of this new standard). Dr. Knoppers has well over 100 published articles, reports, presentations to international academic and professional organizations, contributions to international standards development, etc.

Gottfried Koppensteiner did his Ph.D. in Electrical Engineering at the Automation and Control Institute at the Technical University of Vienna, Austria. The focus was on autonomous intelligent software agents in virtual enterprises as well as in the field of educational robotics. He is founder of the Practical Robotics Institute Austria (PRIA) as well as head of the department for Information Technology at the TGM, a higher vocational secondary school in Vienna. Currently, his research focus is about self-guided learning (learning office) as well as AI in education.

Binod Kumar is an undergraduate student known for his academic excellence, and his scholarly works are indexed in the Scopus database. Hailing from Ranchi, Jharkhand, in India, Binod is pursuing a Bachelor of Law at the prestigious Radha Govind University. His passion for technology, innovation, and climate change is evident through his high academic performance and numerous projects. Binod has a keen interest in artificial intelligence, machine learning, neuropsychology, climate change, and disaster management, where he has undertaken several research projects. He is particularly fascinated by the potential of AI to solve real-world problems and is dedicated to learning and applying new techniques in these areas. He volunteers at local NGOs, teaching underprivileged children basic computer skills. With a strong foundation in law and a commitment to making a positive impact, Binod Kumar is poised to become a future leader in the legal industry

Christina Merl holds a Ph.D. in Translation Studies from the University of Vienna and works as social learning strategist, ethnographic researcher, and university lecturer. She specializes in the design and facilitation of collaborative, hybrid, and interdisciplinary learning communities—particularly in multilingual and cross-hierarchical settings. Christina developed the 2CG® content & context methodology to foster 21st-century skills, including communication, collaboration, creativity, and critical thinking, through storylistening and arts-informed learning. Founder of TalkShop/2CG® and Poetry in Business, she blends research with practice to advance ethical, reflective education.

Alexandra Posekany holds a PhD in Statistical Modelling Approaches for Bioinformatics from the Vienna University of Technology. She first studied Applied Mathematics. For 16 years, she has worked in different fields at various Austrian universities. In addition, she started to work in a vocational high school focused on IT education and established Data Science and AI as an elective subject which has since then been established in the Austrian curriculum for informatics.

Bhuvaneswari working as an Assistant Professor of English at Dr.Mahalingam College of Engineering and Technology, Pollachi. To her credit she completed 10 NPTEL / SWAYAM and published few articles in Scopus indexed journals.

R. Velmurugan presently working as Professor, Department of Commerce, Karpagam Academy of Higher Education, Coimbatore. He started his career as a Project Fellow under UGC Sponsored Major Research Project at NGM College, Pollachi. He has 19 years of teaching experience has 15 years of research experience. To his credit he produced 22 Ph.D. Scholars and 5 M.Phil. Scholars. At present 1 scholar submitter his thesis, 6 Ph.D. Scholars are under his guidance. Moreover, to his credit he published 168 articles in various International Journals, of which 94 articles are published in Scopus Indexed Journals and 15 articles in Web of Science and 76 articles in edited volumes. He also participates and presented 27 papers in various International Seminar / Conference and 54 National Seminar / Conference. He acted as an external examiner for various M.Phil. and Ph.D. Viva voce examinations. He acted as a Vice Chancellor nominee for Doctoral Committee Expert at Bharathiar University, Coimbatore and Periyar University, Salem. He acted as a Chairperson at various National Level Conferences. He also acted as an Expert for Syllabus Scrutiny Committee, Question Paper Scrutiny Committee and Expert members for Board of Studies at various reputed Colleges. Considering his meritorious contribution, he received awards like Best Paper Presenter, Best Research Supervisor and Best Faculty Awards from various research foundations and councils. He too acted as a resource person for 27 Guest Lectures, 30 Workshops and 10 faculty development programmes.

Chaiyong Ragkhitwetsagul is an assistant professor at the Faculty of Information and Communication Technology (ICT), Mahidol University, Thailand. He received a Ph.D. degree in Computer Science (Software Engineering) from University College London. His research interests include software dependencies, software visualization, code search, code clone detection, and mining software repositories.

J. Sudarvel working as an Assistant Professor of Management at Karpagam Academy of Higher Education. He produced five Ph.D. Scholars and four Ph.D. Scholars are under his guidance. Further, to his credit he published 36 articles in Scopus indexed journals and published more than 50 articles in international journals. He is acting as a Subject Experts in Board of studies of various autonomous colleges.

Ravi Thirumalaisamy working as an Assistant Professor, Department of Business and Economics, Modern College of Business and Science. To his credit, he published more than 16 articles in Scopus indexed journals.

Index

Symbols

A

C

D

E

F

H

I

L

N

R

www.ingramcontent.com/pod-product-compliance
Lightning Source LLC
LaVergne TN
LVHW060002031026
849161LV00025B/1328
* 9 7 9 8 3 3 7 3 2 2 3 5 3 *